HENRY VIII AND HIS AFTERLIVES

Henry VIII remains one of the most fascinating, notorious, and recognizable monarchs in English history. In the five centuries since his accession to the throne, his iconic status has been shaped by different media. From Shakespeare to *The Tudors*, this book reassesses treatments of Henry VIII in literature, politics, and culture during the period spanned by the king's own reign (1509–47) and the twenty-first century. Historians and literary scholars investigate how representations of the king provoked varied responses from influential writers, artists, and political figures in the decades and centuries following his death. Individual chapters consider interrelated responses to Henry's character and policies during his lifetime; his literary and political afterlife; the king's impact on art and popular culture; and his debated place in historiography, from the Tudor period to the present.

MARK RANKIN is Assistant Professor of English at James Madison University.

CHRISTOPHER HIGHLEY is Professor of English at The Ohio State University.

JOHN N. KING is Distinguished University Professor and Humanities Distinguished Professor of English and of Religious Studies at The Ohio State University.

Hans Holbein the Younger, cartoon for the Privy Chamber wall-painting, ink and watercolour on paper, 1537. National Portrait Gallery, London.

HENRY VIII AND HIS AFTERLIVES

Literature, Politics, and Art

EDITED BY

MARK RANKIN

CHRISTOPHER HIGHLEY

JOHN N. KING

CAMBRIDGE UNIVERSITY PRESS

Cambridge, New York, Melbourne, Madrid, Cape Town, Singapore, São Paulo, Delhi

Cambridge University Press
The Edinburgh Building, Cambridge CB2 8RU, UK

Published in the United States of America by Cambridge University Press, New York

www.cambridge.org
Information on this title: www.cambridge.org/9780521514644

First published 2009

Printed in the United Kingdom at the University Press, Cambridge

A catalogue record for this publication is available from the British Library

ISBN 978-0-521-51464-4 hardback

Contents

Illustrations

Contributors

TOM BETTERIDGE is Professor of Early Modern English Literature and Drama at Oxford Brookes University.

ANDREW FLECK is Associate Professor in the Department of English at San José State University.

PETER HAPPÉ is Visiting Fellow in the Department of English at the University of Southampton.

CHRISTOPHER HIGHLEY is Professor in the Department of English at The Ohio State University.

DALE HOAK is Chancellor Professor of History at the College of William & Mary.

JOHN N. KING is Distinguished University Professor and Humanities Distinguished Professor of English and of Religious Studies at The Ohio State University.

PETER MARSHALL is Professor of History at the University of Warwick.

RONALD PAULSON is Professor Emeritus of English at The Johns Hopkins University.

MARK RANKIN is Assistant Professor in the Department of English at James Madison University.

ALEC RYRIE is Professor of the History of Christianity at the University of Durham.

MATTHEW SPRING is Senior Lecturer in Music at Bath Spa University.

TATIANA C. STRING is Senior Lecturer in the History of Art at the University of Bristol.

Acknowledgements

We are grateful to each of our contributors, whose collaboration has made the editing of this collection much easier than it might have been. For their hospitality and support, we would also like to thank librarians and archivists at the Bodleian Library, the British Library, the British and Foreign Bible Society Library (on deposit at Cambridge University Library), the Libraries of St. John's and Trinity College, Cambridge, the Folger Shakespeare Library, Lambeth Palace Library, the Rare Books and Manuscripts Library at The Ohio State University, and the Royal Armouries Library. Linda Bree at Cambridge University Press has enthusiastically supported this project from an early stage. We also thank two anonymous readers for the Press for their helpful commentary. The Departments of English at James Madison University and The Ohio State University have provided essential subvention. Colleagues at these institutions, especially Dabney Bankert, Marina Favila, Robert Hoskins, Bruce Johnson, and Mark Parker, have given generous support to this endeavor. Elizabeth Hillgrove and Stephanie Walker assisted in the assembly of the final edited typescript. Kathleen Rankin provided needed assistance at a crucial stage. However, the work would not have progressed in the first place without the generous support of our wives, Pauline G. King, Susie Kneedler, and Katie Rankin. We dedicate this volume to them.

Abbreviations

BL	The British Library
Bodl.	The Bodleian Library
CUL	Cambridge University Library
HL	The Henry E. Huntington Library
Madan	Falconer Madan, et al., *A Summary Catalogue of Western Manuscripts in the Bodleian Library at Oxford which have not hitherto been Catalogued in the Quarto Series*, 7 vols. in 8 [vol. 2 in 2 parts] (Oxford: Clarendon Press, 1895–1953; reprinted with corrections in vols. 1 and 7, Munich, 1980).
ODNB	H. C. G. Matthew and Brian Harrison (eds.), *The Oxford Dictionary of National Biography: In Association with the British Academy: from the Earliest Times to the Year 2000*, 60 vols. (Oxford: Oxford University Press, 2004) (print and online at http://www.oxforddnb.com).
OED	*The Oxford English Dictionary*
RSTC	*A Short-Title Catalogue of Books Printed in England, Scotland, and Ireland, and of English Books Printed Abroad, 1475–1640*, compiled by A. W. Pollard and G. R. Redgrave; 2nd edn. revised and enlarged by W. A. Jackson, F. S. Ferguson, and Katharine F. Pantzer, 3 vols. (London: The Bibliographical Society, 1976–91).
TNA	The National Archives

Introduction

Mark Rankin, Christopher Highley, and John N. King

The publication of this volume marks the five-hundredth anniversary of Henry VIII's accession to the throne of England. Along with his daughter Elizabeth I Henry remains one of England's most identifiable monarchs. Unlike the case of Elizabeth's posthumous reputation, however, the reason for Henry's enduring fascination is both notorious and controversial. This notoriety is not difficult to explain. Henry VIII divorced two of his wives, beheaded two more, and sanctioned the banishment or execution of numerous secretaries and ministers, whose names – Cromwell, Fisher, More, Pole, Wolsey, to name only a few – comprise a veritable pantheon of luminaries. At the same time, and in spite of this evidence, it is difficult to describe Henry VIII wholly as a "tyrant," in part because the king insisted so forcefully that he always acted on some nobler motivation, whether it be his "conscience," his ideal of Renaissance kingship, or his interpretation of the "divine" sanction of his royal office. He was undeniably egotistical and obsessively megalomaniacal, but many had a stake in the royal image – both in terms of how the king represented himself and how others represented him. The figure of Henry VIII is a study in contrasts between the prerogatives of his own lived life and his life as scripted by people who stood to gain – or lose – from the outcome of a collective national response to the iconic king.[1]

Essays in this volume grapple with the dichotomy of how Henry saw himself versus how others saw him. Struggle to reconcile these separate impulses began during the reign itself, particularly in terms of Henry's self-fashioning along the lines of an enlightened Renaissance prince. Henry VIII was accomplished by most any measure. He demonstrated skill in theological disputation in his tract against Luther, the *Assertio septem sacramentorum adversus Martinum Lutherum* (1521), even if that work was the product of collaboration with a team of scholars. When Henry determined to wrestle the papacy over control of his marital status to Catherine of Aragon, evangelicals in and around the court seized the opportunity to weld their devotional aims to the royal prerogative. As a number of scholars have realized, the promulgation of the royal supremacy in 1534 only increased the stakes for those who attempted to influence the king. Following the passage of the Act of Six Articles (1539), as is well known, the climate at court became more hostile toward evangelical Protestantism. The king himself is responsible for laying down competing signals for those who sought an indication on the direction of royal policy. Henry's death in 1547 initiated efforts to manipulate the royal afterlife – and define its significance in terms of ongoing cultural, political, and religious activities. It hardly needs saying that royal advisers, theologians, poets, fiction writers, artists, playwrights, musicians, and many others responded to this opportunity with alacrity.[2]

Henry VIII and Elizabeth I have both enjoyed a lively historical, cultural, and literary afterlife. The recent quatercentenary of Elizabeth's death (2003) witnessed an outpouring of studies and exhibits which chronicled the queen's enduring presence. Comparable investigation of Henry, however, has been absent.[3] Traditional disciplinary distinctions are partly to blame for this. Findings gleaned from debate among historians concerning the religious and political climate of the reign, including but not limited to controversies surrounding Henry's personal responsibility for the Reformation, have not influenced early modern literary scholars until relatively recently. Owing to pressures of canonicity, however, these scholars have tended not to investigate Henry's complex literary afterlife apart from its treatment in selected texts, including Shakespeare's *Henry VIII* (1613). Definition – and redefinition – of the Henrician legacy during the Shakespearean age has gone unnoticed. Henry's reign has shaped numerous fields of inquiry as diverse as literature, art history, theology, musicology, popular cultural studies, antiquarian studies, and more. One of the goals of this volume is to bring together scholars working in all of these disciplines and allow their voices to speak to a shared set of concerns. To a greater or lesser degree each contributor seeks to determine exactly how Henry acquired iconic status.

It is instructive to ponder the intellectual conditions that have given rise to this project. Of England's several dozen monarchs to rule since William the Conqueror, select few have come to dominate the national imagination. One struggles to imagine, for example, a modern edited collection on the posthumous afterlife of, say, the twelfth-century King Stephen. Such a project may be viable, but it would be a fundamentally different enterprise than the one undertaken here. Only Henry VIII and perhaps Elizabeth I and Victoria embody contrarieties so effectively as to generate a compelling, enigmatic presentation. Why was Henry VIII England's last great medieval prince? Did he revolutionize the monarchy and bring centralization to the government? Did Parliament grow bolder as a result of his actions, or was its growth independent? What is the precise relationship between the Henrician English Church and the later, Protestant religious settlement? What motivated his mercurial tendencies? These questions, of course, may remain unanswerable. The point is that many have attempted answers to them over the course of five centuries since Henry took the throne. In assessing their efforts, the essays contained within this volume contribute to an ongoing conversation on Henry VIII that began no later than 1547.

It is difficult to deny that Henry VIII has attained mythic status. As a larger-than-life cultural presence, he is a figment of collective imagination, and attempts to describe him as otherwise risk anachronism by applying to his life scenarios that are invariably foreign to conditions during which he actually lived. The question becomes merely how to delineate the contours of this myth and elaborate its trajectory up to the present moment. Numerous primary sources exist to support this undertaking, and one goal of the present volume is to assess what these materials tell us about Henry VIII's reign, particularly in terms of its reception over time and the uses to which it has been put. Analysis of books that Henry acquired, confiscated, and read is instructive. Recent research has reconstructed Henry's known library and suggested ways to investigate the reign's effect on reading and the book trade.[4] Henry scorned William Tyndale's 1526 English vernacular New Testament but ironically went on to authorize the Great Bible (1539), which relies heavily on Tyndale; this move opened the floodgates of Bible publication, and many thousands of copies of different translations were sold. William Thynne dedicated his folio edition of Chaucer's works (1532) to Henry VIII, in a move that added further prestige to Chaucer's status as England's premier poet. This edition helped to shape the market for printed editions of medieval authors by declaring implicitly what was most acceptable.[5] Much can also be gleaned concerning widespread perceptions of Henry's royal ethos, particularly following the advent of the royal supremacy, by scrutinizing manuscripts presented to him or acquired by him.[6] Despite their richness, though, such materials tell only part of the story. Beginning in the second half of the sixteenth century, treatises, propaganda, libel, and polemic concerning Henry VIII circulated both publicly, in the literary marketplace, and surreptitiously, depending on the political stance of both authors and readers. Roman Catholics disaffected with the Elizabethan settlement, as well as others (e.g., "puritans"), who opposed the policies of the regime, remade Henry VIII in their own images. It is to be expected that a monarch whose policies had such far-reaching effects would reappear in – and blend into – diverse genres and agendas over time.

Contributors to this collection seek to categorize these evolving and sometimes paradoxical textual remains. Their effort to grapple with nearly five centuries of evidence will inevitably leave gaps. These essays are far from exhaustive. Readers will look in vain, for example, for sustained treatment of Henry VIII among English Catholics. This omission is compensated for by highly specialized assessments which investigate Henry's long-term cultural influence from other perspectives. Contrary to what may at first appear, the Protestant Henry VIII does not descend to us through unambiguous channels of representation. Protestantism itself has given rise to its own history of dissent, and the legacy of Henry VIII has evolved along with it. If Catholic readers had reason to revile this king for divorcing Catherine of Aragon, Protestant readers – captured most memorably, perhaps, through the conflicting voices preserved in Foxe's *Book of Martyrs* (1563) – did not embrace him with jubilant unanimity. It is to be hoped that, by surveying selected responses to the king, the studies presented here will give rise to additional analyses and lead to other fruitful inquiry.

Beginning with texts produced during Henry's lifetime and continuing forward to the twenty-first century, this collection assesses the evolution of Henry VIII as a political and cultural icon. Its contributors investigate representations of Henry's marital adventures, his enduring egotism, and his entry into schism from the Church of Rome, both as these elements emerged during the reign itself and as they evolved posthumously. Henry remains an influential figure in popular culture, as a number of films, songs, and even a recent television miniseries indicate. He exerts a satirical force in modern British politics as well. In November 2006 the conservative MP Sir Peter Tapsell sardonically demanded that Prime Minister Blair apologize to the nation for Henry VIII's "disgraceful treatment" of his wives after Blair had expressed regret over the British slave trade.[7] This remark is as wry as it is poignant. Henry's achievement established the institutional foundation upon which English nationalists would build. This collection reconsiders the literary, political, and artistic texts through which writers debated Henry's ongoing importance. The essays collected here show how he moved from being a powerful living monarch to become an even more powerful force in the decades and centuries following his death.

Although Henry VIII continues to capture the attention of scholars, no collection or monograph of this kind has yet appeared. Controversy surrounding the king's responsibility for the upheavals of his reign thrives following the publication of G. W. Bernard's *The King's Reformation* (2005), and it rests on important studies and collections put forward by Alistair Fox (1989), Diarmaid MacCulloch (ed.) (1995), and many others. Recent studies of the cultural afterlife of Elizabeth I, mentioned above, suggest the viability of such an approach to England's most influential of monarchs. The plethora of extant literary, historical, artistic, and cultural artifacts concerning Henry VIII indicates its potential to stimulate interdisciplinary enquiry into the afterlife of this particular king. Literary scholars have broken new ground in studies of Henry VIII's influence on the literary culture of his reign, especially in works by Greg Walker (1991 and 2005), Peter Herman, ed. (1994), and Seth Lerer (1997). Important studies of Hans Holbein's memorable Privy Chamber mural have appeared in Roy Strong's classic account (1967) and in more recent work by Susan Foister (2004) and others. Nevertheless, we still lack an account of Henry VIII that takes the findings from these studies and investigates their applicability to the evolving uses of and debates surrounding Henry's posthumous reputation. This collection seeks to provide such an account.

Within a broadly chronological framework spanning Henry VIII's own reign and the present day, individual chapters cluster around the interrelated themes of (1) contemporary response to Henry's character and policies during his lifetime; (2) Henry's posthumous literary and political afterlife; (3) Henry's effect in shaping art and popular culture; and (4) Henry's debated place in historiography, from the Tudor period to the present moment.

Peter Happé opens the section on contemporary responses by revisiting Henry VIII's debated influence on the literary culture of his own reign, specifically the dramatic interlude. He argues that the dramatists John Skelton, John Heywood, and John Bale crafted a recognizable portrait of Henry for their own purposes in order to shape court opinion on controversial political issues. His assessment of Henrician plays in terms of their ability to offer royal counsel anticipates John N. King's chapter, which moves forward by describing changes that Henry's monarchical image underwent following England's break from the Church of Rome. During the second half of Henry's reign, the royal image bears the imprint of Protestant ideology even though the king himself rejected change in official theology. Portraits of Henry transform the king from the representative of devout Christian orthodoxy to the champion of royal authority in both secular and ecclesiastical spheres. This iconographical shift manifests itself in a variety of works of art and literature, most notably in the title pages of the Coverdale Bible (1535) and the Great Bible (1539). King also investigates the divergent ways in which Henry and others at court viewed his authority in specifically biblical terms, on a model derived from interpretation of the Psalms as foreshadowing Henry's own struggles against the papacy.

In bringing this section on evolving views of kingship during Henry's reign to a close, Dale Hoak scrutinizes the king's own opinions on this subject. In doing so, he provides a theoretical foundation for the succeeding chapters. Hoak argues that Henry's own views on kingship provide the starting point for any understanding of his legacy. Hoak complicates received opinion about Henry's gradual decline into tyranny by arguing that from the beginning of his reign the king combined his assumed role as an ideal Renaissance prince with savage cruelty toward anyone who opposed him. Contemporary treatment of Henry's taste, ability, and learning, as well as the magnificence and entertainments of his household and court, exist alongside the king's own self-deception and a self-pity that turned to volcanic anger over his failed marriages. Henry viewed the royal supremacy as his greatest legacy.

Henry VIII loomed sufficiently large in English political culture that the mere fact of his death was not enough to end his daunting presence. Alec Ryrie opens a series of chapters on the king's literary and political afterlives by discussing ways in which Henry gradually came to represent a liability to his successors. Ryrie argues that for Roman Catholics, and indeed for most foreigners, the king remained an icon of lust, greed, and pride, although this was complicated by the need of Mary's regime to derive its legitimacy from him. For the regimes of Edward VI and Elizabeth I, and their servants, on the other hand, Henry remained a father figure, admittedly a highly ambiguous one. Many religious conservatives remembered Henry as a bulwark against heresy and tried to appropriate his memory on behalf of their cause. Conversely, the more radical Protestants whom Henry had intermittently persecuted weaned themselves from their habit of obedience to the old tyrant. Some of those in exile under Mary came to denounce Henry with as much vitriol as any Catholic. Others continued to try to excuse or minimize his failings. Crystallizing Protestant unease about how to deal with his memory, the first edition of John Foxe's *Book of Martyrs* (1563) represents Henry as a uniquely ambiguous figure whom Foxe could not place confidently among either the saved or the damned.

Uniting these diverse strands is an effort to lay Henry VIII to rest and the common inability to do so.

In his investigation of the literary presence of Henry VIII during the reigns of Elizabeth I and James I, Mark Rankin, on the other hand, demonstrates that many writers refused to ignore Henry. They explicitly stirred up paradoxical aspects of his legacy in order to satisfy the demands of patronage or political ambition. Rankin argues that the beginning of Henry's "mythic" status coincides with writers' attempts to use Henry in order to shape the direction of public opinion around debated points of controversy. They ranged from the question of the royal succession under Elizabeth I to the proposed involvement of England in the Thirty Years War under James I. Ronald Paulson carries the investigation of Henry VIII's literary legacy forward into the eighteenth century. Like King's, his chapter explicitly compares Henry's literary representation with that in the graphic arts. Following a revival of Shakespeare's *Henry VIII* in 1727 to accompany the coronation of George II, writers incorporated the king in narratives of patriotism and English nationalism. Enemies to these ideals from Henry's reign included Thomas Wolsey, whose treatment in Johnson's *The Vanity of Human Wishes* (1749) suggests a widespread reluctance to impugn Henry VIII or, by extension, George II for moral and political failings. William Hogarth's 1727–8 illustration of Henry's coronation with Anne Boleyn extends the contemporary analogy between Henry VIII and George II, in this case by focusing on the two kings' sexual activities.

Paulson traces the representation of Henry VIII in both the visual and performing arts across the eighteenth century. Hogarth's illustration for John Gay's *The Beggar's Opera* (1728) established an analogy between Macheath and Robert Walpole that extrapolated and extended the visual iconography of Holbein's Henry VIII. Inaugurating a selection of essays addressing Henry's importance in art and popular culture, Tatiana C. String uses the Holbein codpiece as a point of departure to discuss analogues between this image of Henry's masculinity and Renaissance portraiture more generally. Ideas of Henry's "masculinity" range beyond dynastic iconography alone; individual components in the Holbein portrait comprise a composite whole, in which triangular forms created by the splayed legs and enormous shoulders meet at the codpiece as a focal point. String places Henry VIII and his painter at the center, rather than at the traditional margins, of artistic enterprise in the Renaissance.

Building upon String's findings, Christopher Highley examines the aura of Henry VIII not only through perceptions of his masculinity, but also in his material artifacts themselves. The personal objects that he touched, used, and wore enjoyed a wide circulation. Focusing on Henrician artifacts at the Tower of London, especially the king's talismanic codpiece, Highley shows how extant narratives written by spectators during the seventeenth and eighteenth centuries helped construct Henry as a pivotal figure in the emerging practice of cultural tourism. Beginning in the late sixteenth century, the Tower functioned as a proto-museum in which Henry VIII was a central presence. By considering suits of armor connected with the king at the Tower and the narratives that grew up around them, including stories concerning their codpieces, Highley demonstrates Henry's evolving function as a cultural icon.

Turning from literary and graphic remains to aural ones, Matthew Spring argues that Henry VIII's musical abilities confirmed his reputation as an ideal prince in the minds of his contemporaries. Contemporary evidence documents Henry's reputation as a skilled performer and an able composer, but he went further by reorganizing and expanding musical activities at court. His patronage of continental musicians laid the foundation for the development of polyphonic consort and orchestral music during the eighteenth century. Musicians gained access to the Privy Chamber, and with it a degree of proximity to the monarch, following the establishment of this inner precinct in the Eltham Ordinances of 1526. Musicologists' tendency to praise Henry's musical talents has as much to do with his patronage of musicians as his own musical ability. Although Henry may not have actually composed certain pieces that are commonly attributed to him (such as "Greensleeves"), scholars came to describe his accomplishment according to inflated, alternate criteria.

Tom Betteridge concludes this section with his chapter on Henry VIII in popular culture. Over the course of the last hundred years, popular culture, cinema, prose, and theater have wavered between depicting Henry VIII as a gloriously hearty monarch, on the one hand, and a misogynist and violent tyrant, on the other. Beginning with an investigation of Henry as depicted in the film version of Robert Bolt's play *A Man for All Seasons* (1966), Betteridge discusses the famous BBC series *The Six Wives of Henry VIII* (1970) and other recent fictional accounts of Henry, including Philippa Gregory's *The Other Boleyn Girl* (2002) and the Showtime miniseries *The Tudors*, which is now in its third season. Betteridge detects a direct and uncanny relationship between representations of Henry VIII in these texts and debates within popular culture over the nature of history and, in particular, the interaction between historical action and gender. Henry is a profoundly masculine figure, but, at the same time, Betteridge argues that his having six wives appears at once excessive, comic, and even tragic in these texts.

The final section of this collection revisits the fascinating and problematic topic of the historiography of Henry VIII. In the last decade of the sixteenth century, a powerful wave of politically motivated nostalgia swept over the English imagination. As a part of this tradition, Thomas Nashe's *The Unfortunate Traveller* (1594) and Thomas Deloney's *Jacke of Newbury* (1597) – two early experiments in fiction – idealize an avuncular Henry VIII at the heart of a socially cohesive England. In his chapter, Andrew Fleck argues that these two texts playfully appropriated the markers and tropes of the period's increasingly sophisticated and partisan historiography. Mid-century Tudor chronicles, including Edward Hall's *Union of the Two Noble and Illustrate Families of Lancaster and York* (1548), Thomas Cooper's continuation of Thomas Lanquet's mid-century *Chronicle* (1560), Richard Grafton's *Abridgement* and *Chronicle at Large* (1569), John Stowe's *Summary* (1565) and *Annales* (1592), and *Survey*, and Holinshed's *Chronicle* (1577), provide sources for Nashe's and Deloney's proto-novels. These authors' framing of their fictional tales with historical events concerning Henry VIII jeopardize the stable limits of truth and fact. In doing so, they project generic ambivalence that characterizes the sixteenth-century flowering – and subsequent decline – of the chronicle tradition.

Peter Marshall's concluding chapter on the twentieth-century historiography of Henry VIII brings this collection to a close. Throughout the twentieth century and into the twenty-first, Henry VIII has remained a towering figure in the English historical imagination, one of the very few historical personages of whom almost everyone has heard. Nevertheless, there has been a surprising paucity of modern academic (or even non-academic) biographies that devote themselves to the analysis of the king's life. A. F. Pollard's epic biography of 1902 was in many ways the final crash of a Victorian wave, seeing the king as a patriotic embodiment of England's national will at the threshold of its era of imperial greatness. Most subsequent writers on Tudor England have found less to celebrate unequivocally, and, as a result, many have shied away from the intense personal involvement with Henry that biography demands. It is remarkable that (barring an unusual 1971 offering by Lacey Baldwin Smith), J. J. Scarisbrick's 1968 biography still stands as the standard academic study, and still more remarkable in light of Scarisbrick's complete disavowal of the empathy and admiration a biographer usually evinces for his or her subject. We eagerly anticipate Paul Hammer's new biography, which is forthcoming from Yale University Press.

In examining the twentieth-century historiographical tradition surrounding Henry VIII, Marshall argues that, in a sense, Henry VIII has become an icon without a cult. His exercise of power lacks the allure of Elizabeth I's mastery of gender politics, and gendered analyses of Henry's masculinity – besides those contained within the present volume – are few. His idiosyncratic ecclesiastical policies make him neither the founder of any modern Church nor the beneficiary of any tradition of confessional or apologetic writing. Nor was Henry's exercise of violence sufficiently extreme to turn him into a compelling "portrait of evil." (In contrast, it seems impossible to separate the achievement of his daughter Mary I from the unforgettable sobriquet of "Bloody Mary.") Instead, much of the most important modern work on Henry VIII has come at him obliquely, either through biographies of important contemporaries, such as Thomas Wolsey, Thomas More, and Thomas Crammer, or through small-scale prosopography of his multiple marriage partners. From at least the time of G. R. Elton's controversial thesis concerning the "Tudor Revolution," Henry has also been the main protagonist of rival scholarly interpretations of the workings of Tudor government and politics, pitting advocates of a faction-driven model against those who emphasize the king's mastery and autonomy. In recognizing these disputes, Marshall does not arbitrate them. Instead, he examines and explains the difficulties modern historians have found in producing a rounded, persuasive, and widely accepted portrait of Henry VIII as a monarch, a religious reformer, a husband, and a man.

NOTES

1. We follow Thomas F. Mayer's model of the "life as lived" versus the "life as written" in his study on *Reginald Pole: Prince & Prophet* (Cambridge: Cambridge University Press, 2000).
2. Details in this paragraph draw upon Stephen Greenblatt, *Renaissance Self-Fashioning: From More to Shakespeare* (Chicago: University of Chicago Press, 1980); J. J. Scarisbrick, *Henry VIII* (Berkeley: University of California Press, 1968), 21–4; *Antwerp, Dissident Typographical Centre: The Role of Antwerp Printers in the Religious Conflicts in England (16th Century)* (Antwerp: Snoeck-Ducaju & Zoon for the Plantin-Moretus Museum, 1994), item 3; and Alec Ryrie, *The Gospel and Henry VIII: Evangelicals in the Early English Reformation* (Cambridge: Cambridge University Press, 2003).

3. Studies of Elizabeth's afterlife include Michael Dobson and Nicola J. Watson, *England's Elizabeth: An Afterlife in Fame and Fantasy* (Oxford: Oxford University Press, 2002); Susan Doran and Thomas S. Freeman (eds.), *The Myth of Elizabeth* (Houndmills: Palgrave Macmillan, 2003); Georgianna Ziegler (ed.), *Elizabeth I: Then and Now* (Washington, DC: Folger Shakespeare Library, 2003); and John Watkins, *Representing Elizabeth in Stuart England: Literature, History, Sovereignty* (Cambridge: Cambridge University Press, 2002). The only detailed study to take up Henry's posthumous reputation remains Uwe Baumann (ed.), *Henry VIII in History, Historiography and Literature* (Frankfurt am Main: Peter Lang, 1992). The present volume builds upon Baumann's initial beginning to this subject by expanding its chronological range and appealing to a wider academic audience.

4. James P. Carley (ed.), *The Libraries of King Henry VIII* (London: The British Library in association with the British Academy, 2000); James P. Carley, *The Books of King Henry VIII and His Wives* (London: The British Library, 2004).

5. For detailed analysis of this edition see Greg Walker, *Writing under Tyranny: English Literature and the Henrician Reformation* (Oxford: Oxford University Press, 2005), 29–99.

6. See George F. Warner and Julius P. Gilson, *Catalogue of Western Manuscripts in the Old Royal and King's Collections*, 4 vols. (London: The British Museum, 1921).

7. http://news.bbc.co.uk/2/hi/uk_news/politics/6159957.stm

PART I

Contemporary responses

Henry VIII in the interludes

Peter Happé

In this chapter I shall consider four interludes containing characters who may be identified as representations of Henry VIII. Three of them, John Skelton's *Magnyfycence*, John Heywood's *Play of the Wether*, and the anonymous *Godly Queen Hester*, can be interconnected at the time of Henry's divorce from Catherine of Aragon and his marriage to Anne Boleyn in 1533. The fourth insight into the presence of Henry in interludes comes from John Bale's *King Johan*, where two figures can be identified with him, but the slightly later dates conjectured for its first composition make for differences in the way these two figures are handled.[1]

MAGNYFYCENCE

Skelton's connection with Henry presumably went back to the king's childhood, before he was heir to the throne. Among his activities as tutor Skelton wrote his *Speculum Principis*. A manuscript of this, written out in 1509 possibly for presentation at the time of Henry's accession, but with some later additions, points to two interweaving themes: the necessity of a prince to be learned and virtuous and also to deal wisely with his advisers. "Princes," he writes, "should enlighten their lives both with excellence in learning, which is the property of a noble soul, and with outstanding probity of character." Shortly after this he says of advisers: "they are either learned or ignorant, and the first are indecisive and the others are wrong: you are wise on your own account."[2] This emphasis upon a king's responsibility for his own authority and his appropriate use of advisers is a theme which lasted in Skelton's mind through to *Magnyfycence*, which he probably wrote in about 1519 at the time of the expulsion of the so-called minions, who were misleading the King rather than being of support. It also recurs after his death, as we shall see.

In fact it seems possible that this play was written after the expulsion and that its purpose was to celebrate the King's achievement, and it may well have been written because Skelton had by this time fallen out of favor and was trying to re-establish his former eminence and influence at a court now largely dominated by Wolsey. In presenting his material Skelton was clearly interested in the proper use of the quality of "magnificence" by a king: that is to say the use of royal resources to empower the monarchy and the possible consequences of inappropriate use of them. Much of the action of the play shows how the court vices misused royal wealth to the detriment and humiliation of the kingly figure in the play. Nowhere is this figure specifically identified as King Henry, but Skelton has skilfully adapted the ethical mode of the morality plays, which were focused upon the moral corruption of the central figure. In doing so Skelton has shifted the emphasis notably from purely ethical matters to notions deeply involving the political strength of the king figure. This adaptation reveals Skelton's medieval thinking as well as a newer, presumably Renaissance concern with the political glory of kingship and with the king as an educated and cultivated individual.

But if Skelton was indeed celebrating the downfall of the minions and the triumph of monarchical survival there remains a strong element of advice and a continuing thrust towards giving advice to the king in a way which may revive or develop his own earlier role as educator of princes. The conjunction of medieval with Renaissance ways of thinking is a feature characteristic of much of Skelton's work elsewhere. We can best approach his presentation of King Henry by considering his management of the allegory which is fundamental to the play's structure and design. In doing so I want to concentrate upon the role of Magnyfycence himself rather than attempting a full exposition of the complex allegories in the play.

Magnyfycence's role is arranged into two sequences. At the beginning of the play, before he arrives, there is a philosophical disputation initiated by Felycyte about the importance of controlling Liberty by means of Measure. It illustrates, as Paula Neuss has demonstrated, the proverb "measure is treasure."[3] It is only when this humanist demonstration of virtue has been set up that Magnyfycence's first sequence begins. The following episode (163–395) shows him at first exhibiting wisdom in sustaining the control of Liberty by Measure. But in the process he falls for the tricky language of Fansy, whom he at first rejects. Fansy catches him by means of a counterfeit letter and by using the alias of Largesse, suggesting that extravagant living is the appropriately noble way to use kingly wealth. Magnyfycence then releases Liberty from the control of Measure and gives authority to this deceptive Largesse.

In the following thousand or so lines, during which Magnyfycence is not on stage, Skelton builds up a complex allegory in which court vices go about to deceive Magnyfycence. The names of these vices are notoriously confusing because they are so similar, but as a group they represent the deception and craftiness of court intrigue, each with its own particular characteristics. These characters also take aliases, and it is these renamed figures whom Magnyfycence comes to trust in his second major sequence, which concludes the play (1375–2567).

In pursuing the allegory Skelton relies upon the rise and fall structure of the morality play, but he also draws upon the equally common medieval concept of tragedy as a representation of the falls of princes. Even though Skelton may have had in mind the broader religious or political objectives to which I have referred, there seems little doubt that this presentation of literary values was a part of his humanist agenda, and something which was intended to enhance the appeal of the play as an intellectual and cultural experience.

During Magnyfycence's second sequence the allegory pinpoints his mistakes and his ensuing predicament. He loses control of events with the release of Liberty. The protesting Felycyte is placed under the control of Courtly Abusyon, who uses the alias Lusty Pleasure. Thus the allegory underlines the disastrous concept that Magnyfycence can only be true to his own magnificence if he seeks felicity and liberty through the unreserved pursuit of pleasure, and this involves largess in the use of his wealth. It is a recipe for disaster. At this point, in a method which exploits the multi-layered resources of allegory, Skelton develops further the dual roles of Fansy, already under the alias Lusty Pleasure, and Foly, who becomes Consayte (1310). This shows itself in the extraordinary scene of recognition and brotherhood between these two characters. The source of this particular aspect of the allegorical network is probably Skelton's familiarity with the French *sotties*, part of the humanist culture in France from the later fifteenth century. It is something which also foreshadows the interests of Erasmus and Thomas More, who were both intrigued by the concept of folly.

This consciously literary element is further enlarged by the catastrophe in which Adversyte overwhelms Magnyfycence, and here Skelton deliberately invokes the themes of human impermanence and the *ubi sunt* motif. These are both classical in origin, but they are also part of the medieval concept of tragedy.[4] But for Skelton the didactic stance is always familiar, and the humiliation of Magnyfycence, signified by the sinister figures of Dyspayre and Myschefe, has to be put right by Good Hope and Redresse, who symbolically clothes Magnyfycence in a new garment. Redresse, returning to the primary allegory of the introductory disputation, makes it clear that nobleness or magnificence should have limits:

> For of Noblenesse the chefe point is to be lyberall,
> So that your Largesse be not to prodygall.   (2483–4)

In doing so he emphasizes the need for rulers to follow virtuous paths, especially, he recalls, because the world is carnal and transitory (2506), and flattery, a danger to all rulers, is everywhere.

The presence of these allegorical formulations gives Skelton the means to place the role of the king in a moral context, but one which is not simply aimed at moral perfection. These matters are after all centered upon someone called Magnyfycence, and that very word is morally ambiguous in as much as it refers to the appropriate way for a ruler to behave. It is not a moral abstraction in the sense that vices and virtues essentially are: its focus is rather upon what is appropriate to the role of the ruler. Skelton's motives in creating this portrait of vulnerability and responsibility in the monarch can only be surmised, but I think we ought to try to do so. In some ways he anticipates Bale in *King Johan* because the presentation of the monarch in both plays implies advice and even instruction towards King Henry. But the weight of Skelton's assessment is less directly concerned with a political situation and more a matter of what might be desirable in all kings: that virtue should guide their conduct, and wisdom based upon established principle should be pursued.

However, we now need to consider that Skelton's play had two lives and that the second one was perhaps the more influential, though he did not live to see it. The play was apparently not printed at the time of its composition, around 1519. Possibly it circulated in manuscript and possibly it was performed in or near the court. But Skelton lived for ten or more years, and at this time he was living in London, perhaps becoming known to people around the court. Some of his non-dramatic work indicates that he continued to be opposed to Lollards, as in his *Replycacion Agaynst Certayne Yong Scolers Abjured of Late* directed against Thomas Arthur and Thomas Bilney, and dedicated to Wolsey (printed 1528). His death in 1529 may have brought the manuscript of *Magnyfycence* into the hands of John Rastell. The latter had been quite busy in royal affairs at the Field of Cloth of Gold (1520) and in producing a royal entertainment at Greenwich for the French ambassador in 1527. He had a theatre in his own house in Finsbury Fields from 1524 and was involved in the writing and printing of plays.[5] *Magnyfycence* was printed by Peter

Treveris using some of Rastell's type in 1530, when the divorce, already a public matter for two or three years, was coming to its crisis. Rastell was himself a Catholic at this point and he was related by marriage to both Sir Thomas More and to John Heywood. More became Chancellor in 1529 without supporting the divorce, and he set about vigorously attacking heresy. Now the play might not simply be read as an abstract piece of advice about how a king should behave, but as a warning about virtue and true nobility in a specific new political context. For Catholics it was important to stop the movement towards separation from Rome, and by having it printed at this time Rastell might have hoped to influence the turn of events. Because the play reflects Skelton's Catholic outlook Rastell might have wanted to draw attention to it in this period of growing controversy. Skelton's poem *A Replycacion Agaynst Yong Scolers Abjured of Late*, printed by Pynson in 1528, is further evidence of his reaction against heresy.[6] It is ironic that, having taken this important step, Rastell, backed up, one might suppose, by his printing of some of More's anti-heresy tracts, was himself converted to a Protestant outlook.

At this point I should like to emphasize that London was a very small place, and the court itself could not have involved a large number of individuals. There was every opportunity for interchange about persons and events. Skelton must have achieved a considerable reputation through the quantity and variety of his poetry over many years. Rastell's making use of his work through the publication of *Magnyfycence* was a distinctly public event and one in a specific political context. Whether he was the first to see that printing a play could be a political act I am not sure, but it does seem that others followed in his footsteps. Indeed one of the chief conclusions arising from recent research on the interludes suggests that they came to be widely acknowledged as a political weapon, and accordingly the control and censorship of interludes became a significant preoccupation of the authorities.[7] It is of course possible that this came about because Skelton in his poetry had been such a vigorous commentator upon public life and had used allegories of various kinds as a means of expression. Rastell's move leads us to the next two interludes for consideration here: *Godly Queen Hester* and John Heywood's *The Play of the Wether*. The first survives in a printed edition of 1561, and its date of composition can only be conjectured, but the second, perhaps more significantly, was printed by Rastell's son William in 1533 in a specific context about which we can be fairly sure, and it was one of a number of publications he undertook from a Catholic viewpoint, as he remained within the Church after his father's conversion. Indeed his pro-Catholic publications appear to have come to the attention of Cromwell, who intervened against William in 1534.[8]

The date of the anonymous *Godly Queen Hester* has been a matter of controversy. Though the only surviving edition was printed by William Pickering and Thomas Hacket in 1561, it is now generally accepted that the play's main reference is to the fall of Wolsey in July 1529, and it has been assumed that the play was written at that time, before or after the event.[9] It should be noted, however, that there is a good deal of conjecture in this, and the presumed date has been arrived at as a consequence of the perceived fit between public events surrounding the conflict between Wolsey and Queen Catherine of Aragon and the action of the play, which presents a version of the biblical story of Hester's victory over the ambitious Aman. Using this theory of the origin of the play, we may relate it to the context provided by the printing of *Magnyfycence* a year later and the subsequent printing of John Heywood's plays in the years 1533–4. Unfortunately we do not have positive evidence of specific performances for any of these, and the conclusions have to rely upon the possibility of interrelationship of text rather than enactment.

Nevertheless with regard to the possible performance of *Hester* there are two distinct features. One is that twice there are stage directions requiring many people on the stage: the maidens for the beauty contest (187) and the large number of people who swell Aman's retinue (129). This suggests that performance was not dependent upon a tightly integrated doubling scheme by a small number of players. Interestingly, though the title page appears during the latter half of the sixteenth century, its list of players is not arranged for doubling as had become common by the 1560s. The second feature is the reference to a traverse (635), presumably a curtained space behind which King Assuerus retires at certain points in the action. This has a parallel with Heywood's *Wether*, during which Jupiter withdraws behind a curtain while Merry Report interrogates the suitors about their pleas about weather. The play was probably designed for a hall performance, the hall perhaps being part of a religious house whose residents might be called upon to take part in the crowd scenes. That the action of the play also refers to life in religious houses may sustain this proposition, as indeed does the summoning of a group of singers as a "chapel" (850 and s.d.).

This presumed date and the accompanying performance possibility mean that the play is potentially a contributor to the main preoccupation here, the way in which Henry VIII is used by writers of interludes. Assuerus is not really the center of interest, the characterization and interaction of Hester and her opponent Aman being much more powerful matters, but as most of the characters do refer to him in some way a picture of him emerges. He says enough himself to indicate that he is a character conceived for didactic purposes, and the teaching process seems largely intended to be a form of advice to kings. Rather like Magnyfycence he makes a bad choice in elevating Aman to be his chancellor. The process of choosing, after a careful exposition in council about the necessity for rulers to be virtuous and just to their subjects, is very simple, possibly foolishly so. Aman states his progeny and Assuerus immediately praises his learning, reason, and discretion without apparent evidence (104–7). Unlike Magnyfycence, however, Assuerus is not made to suffer for his mistakes. Aman's avarice affects others more directly, especially the Jews, whom he persecutes and seeks to impoverish for his own gain. His persecution of them forms one of the main strands in the plot: the other is the choice of a wife by Assuerus, which falls upon Hester. She emerges as a powerful and articulate figure who is able to advise the king. Through her exposition the role of the king is reinforced in the play. Perhaps because of the political circumstances which interested the author, she speaks initially of the role of the queen in relation to the king and in doing so apparently vindicates the position of Queen Catherine, who was under pressure from the papal commission, including Wolsey, to resolve the issue of the king's divorce. As Janette Dillon has suggested, some of the details of her presentation to Assuerus may recall the obedient but forthright public appeal to King Henry at one of the sessions of the commission at Blackfriars.[10] This is particularly true of the apology which begins her main speech:

> To speake before a king, it is no childes playe,
> Therfore I aske pardon, of that I shall saye.   (269–70 in 269–95)

Under this obedience she suggests firmly that the king must be content to be counseled by the queen (278), but she also expects that there must always be as much goodness in the king as in the queen (293). Her ideas thus serve two objectives: they outline the requirements for kingship and they create a position in which the queen matches the king in virtue and in authority. The strong position created for Hester in this way is related to the threat from Aman, who attempts to have Mardocheus,

Hester's foster father, executed in his project of persecuting the Jews. If
we take Aman as a representation of Wolsey, the author's assessment of
the role of King Henry becomes relevant to our discussion. It would seem
that although there is good evidence that Hester is behaving in a way
which represents and favors Queen Catherine, the same is not quite true
in relation to Henry. Perhaps there had been moments once when his
closeness to Catherine was evident and a matter for celebration, but at this
critical juncture the implication is that it is not so and that the king has
much to do to make the most of the qualities of his wife. These include a
religious dimension, in that her saving of the Jews has been interpreted as a
critique of Wolsey's interference in the affairs of some religious houses.
From this it follows that if this play were indeed known to King Henry the
author might have recommended that the king cherish his wife and
benefit from her role as virtuous consort. Moreover the dramatist is intent
on vindicating the Church. But the play also echoes the predicament in
Magnyfycence in that the ruler chooses to rely upon an evil lieutenant,
putting the wealth of his kingdom at the disposal of the false servant. The
dramatic structure intensifies this by its recall of the morality-play conventions of allegorical characterization through abstractions. The episode
involving Pride, Ambition, and Adulation, which contributes nothing to
the plot, brings out in a formal way the allegorical point that these abstractions have been impoverished, since Aman has taken away their roles by his
own embodiment of the evils they represent (338–580).

The dramatic consequence of the two strands I have mentioned gives
rise to a peculiar irony. Assuerus, learning of Aman's greed and cruel intent,
orders his execution using the very gallows he had prepared for
Mardocheus. This is a poignant and appropriate event. If the play was
indeed conceived before Wolsey's fall, it would have advocated a strong
demonstration of royal justice. If, otherwise, it follows upon Wolsey's death
as he traveled towards royal retribution, the ironic conclusion would be
a celebration of justice achieved. Either way these would seem to be effective
ways of influencing King Henry and indications of how the author saw the
king. It seems very likely therefore that if the conjectures about this play's
dates are correct this concept of the king might have given a lead to John
Heywood, who in 1529 was already active as a playwright near to the court.

WETHER

Work on Heywood in the past few years has made it impossible to
consider him in the traditional way as merely a witty player of word

games. The studies by Bevington and Walker have elicited many underlying implications relating to the religious and political crisis over the
divorce and Heywood's persistent concern to sustain his lifelong Catholic
beliefs.[11] It is therefore necessary to refer only briefly here to some salient
features of his position in his plays. Before 1529 he was a court musician, but
we can also be reasonably sure of his interest in plays, especially in his
contribution to John Rastell's *Gentleness and Nobility* (1525). His presence
at court cannot be doubted, and he continued to be associated with it until
after Elizabeth I's accession, in 1558. The most striking feature of his work
for this discussion is that at about the same time as the possible creation of
Godly Queen Hester and the printing of *Magnyfycence*, he wrote several
plays which engaged political issues. They were most likely produced for
performance in Tudor halls, and possibly royal palaces, and they were
printed by William Rastell, his brother-in-law, in the years 1533 and 1534.[12]
These were the years when the divorce at last took place, accompanied by
Henry's break with Rome and his assumption of supremacy. We do not
know how far the performance texts were modified for their printing, but
the printed versions show concerns over political and religious matters.

One of their most remarkable aspects, for example, is the changes he
made in *Johan Johan* to the text of *La farce nouvelle du Pasté*, which he
translated. The play was printed in February 1534, but its composition and
perhaps a performance may have occurred at a point in 1533 when Anne
Boleyn's pregnancy must have been manifest and just after the secret
marriage at the end of January. In the first place we should note that the
act of choosing this particular farce was significant, since he must have
perceived that it offered so much about adultery illuminated with sexual
innuendo. But many of his additions give particular emphasis to indications
that Tib, the wife, is actually pregnant. She appears to be suffering from
"morning sickness" as a result of the cure that Sir Johan gave upon a bed.
This sickness is mentioned three times (126, 130, and 145). The "miracles"
mentioned are mostly to do with amazingly short pregnancies, implying
divine interference and resulting in delivery far sooner than expected.
Heywood adds a reference to St. Modwyn (561), to whom pregnant
women customarily prayed. Thus it seems that Heywood was developing
his source very pointedly.[13] How near the performance got to Henry and
Anne must remain speculative, but it seems unlikely that they were actually
present at any performance.[14] The King's presence at a performance of *Witty
and Witless* is a stronger possibility, as indicated by this stage direction:

Thes thre stave next folowyng in the Kyngs absens are voyde. (675 s.d.)

This makes it apparent that certain ideas would be directed specifically to him. These stanzas assert that rulers should show the glory of God and deal charitably with subjects of all ranks.[15]

These two items draw attention to the caution which must have been necessary in approaching matters about which the King might have been sensitive, and it is remarkable that Heywood must have felt that he could get away with commentary on Henry which was in part mockery. At the center of this is Jupiter in *The Play of the Wether*. In the light of what I have suggested about the seminal nature of the printing of *Magnyfycence* it is notable that the link between Henry and Jupiter had already been made by Skelton in *Speke Parott* (1522), and John Rastell had made a pageant of the "Father of Hevin" at Greenwich as recently as 1527.[16] In reviving or exploiting such a link for *Wether* Heywood may well have felt he could rely upon Henry's vanity, and perhaps there was also a capacity in Henry to enjoy a joke against himself.[17] There are two things in *Wether* which seem to have a bearing on this. One is the type of pompous style of speech given to Henry, dressed out in formal rhyme royal.[18] The second factor is the possibility that Heywood played Merry Report himself. Greg Walker has developed the comedy inherent in this by noticing that in a performance Jupiter/Henry would have been a boy and that the contrast between such a player of small stature and light voice with the tall Heywood, who may have played Merry Report, would have given an engaging comic ambience.

Yet such comedy may involve serious matters, and that seems to have been just what Heywood was seeking. Jupiter refers to the recent parliament of the gods early in the play, thus drawing attention to a political context in which he has greater powers. He appoints someone from the assembled company to proclaim his desire to hear representations about the weather (94). The appointment of Merry Report having been made, Jupiter retires with another pompous speech which seems designed to undermine his dignity, as Heywood gives him one of those leashes which work individual words almost to death: "Rejoyce ye is us with joy most joyfully, / And we ourselfe shall joy in our own glory" (184–5).

Once again I should like to pull out two strands from this play regarding the presentation of Henry: the ultimate purpose of the allegory about the weather, and the use of sexual innuendo. The former, it has long been noted, depends upon what one thinks the weather is. This is a very English sort of preoccupation, and Heywood arranges things very tightly around the different needs of the suitors. He does not tell us that the weather stands for anything else, and so to this extent he just seems to be avoiding allegory. I am reminded of Orwell's technique in *Animal Farm*, where one is not told who the pigs or indeed any other animals represent. Yet one begins at some point to suspect, and this process is essentially different from the demonstrative allegories of the morality plays. The upshot is that we come to suspect that much more is meant, and finally we see that Heywood shows Jupiter refusing to choose between the suitors and leaving things as they are. This, presumably, is the didactic point. Heywood does not want the King to follow factions but to assume responsibility himself and to govern as before. Such a piece of advice may indeed recall Skelton's *Speculum Principis* and the follow-up in *Magnyfycence*. It follows that once this has been realized one begins to look at whether the individual suitors can indeed be further identified, which is just what some critics have sought to do.[19] It is also worth noticing that at this time Sir Thomas More, who was related to Heywood by marriage, was waging a bitter polemical campaign against Reformation opinion, and that although Heywood may have been pulling in the same direction his method was distinctly more emollient and entertaining.

The sexual innuendo in the play is partly directed at Jupiter, and this happens markedly as soon as the Gentlewoman enters. Her request "to passe into the god now" sets off a chain of bawdy remarks and suggestions by Merry Report, who is keen to present her as a sexual opportunity for Jupiter: "Here is a derlynge come by Saynt Antony" (a saint tempted by sensuality). Jupiter abruptly reproves him. This leads immediately to the revelation that behind the curtain Jupiter is making a new moon because the old one is wasted and leaky. "This new moone," says Merry Report bawdily, "shal make a thing spryng more in this while / Then a old moone shal while a man may go a mile" (808–9). A few lines later he swears by St. Anne, and this clue perhaps more than others suggests Anne Boleyn as the new moon. Once Jupiter withdraws, Merry Report seeks to enjoy the encounter with the Gentlewoman on his own behalf, but, as he tries to push his luck with a kiss, he is interrupted by the Laundress, whose ribald comments smother the episode in sexual bathos.

We might conclude then that this episode comprises a sexual encounter as a means by which Heywood seeks to focus his allusion to Henry. No doubt it was meant to be entertaining, and maybe the bawdy reduced everyone to stitches. By such comic means Heywood leads us to the immediacy of the Henry–Boleyn marriage and to the ensuing political crisis. It should be added that the recent workshop performance of extracts from this play in the Great Hall at Hampton Court drew attention to the great variety of possibilities in performance which might elicit or encode the implications Heywood sought to generate.[20]

KING JOHAN

Bale's *King Johan* may first be considered in relation to the chronology and the interconnection of the other plays so far discussed. It does not look as though he was closely related to the possible personal links between Skelton, the Rastells, and Heywood.[21] Probably his bibliographical work had hardly begun when he started to write plays, and in the early 1530s he seems to have been occupied away from London. He can hardly be connected with the court or with people of influence there until his collaboration with Leland begins. Another link later in the decade involves Cromwell's recognition of him, as is attested in Bale's letter of 1537 to him. Though we shall have occasion to notice the heavy revisions in the surviving manuscript, there is no certainty that Bale intended to print the play.[22] But it did achieve some prominence by being performed at Cranmer's house in Canterbury in 1538/9. Possibly this occasion was connected with the destruction of Becket's tomb in Canterbury at about the same time.[23] His own reference to Cromwell comes at a time when the latter was overseeing a propaganda campaign in support of Protestant interests.[24]

Bale's Protestant stance, which he began to adopt in the early 1530s when he left the Carmelite order in which had been educated, led him to a different approach to the use of Henry VIII in the interludes from those we have noticed so far. This may be characterized by an interest in persuading the king over certain issues but also an iconic process which sought to enhance the status of a king in Protestant society. From the titles of lost plays that he wrote about the divorce and also about Becket there can be no doubt that he was concerned with the trend of public events surrounding Henry's break with Rome.[25] Among these the unique role of the monarch was a leading theme, possibly connected with the royal supremacy, which became one of Henry's chief means of facilitating the divorce.

In fact the concept of the role of the monarch was so important to Bale that he incorporated two versions of kingship into *King Johan*: the eponymous hero and the figure of Imperial Majesty, who appears near the end of the play. The function of the latter, however, is complicated by the nature and date of Bale's revisions to the existing text. In any case there may have been some necessity to invent Imperial Majesty because the story Bale chose to dramatize includes the death of King Johan, and he might not have wanted to leave the play in the form of a tragedy, even though it has been shown by Dermot Cavanagh that Johan's impotence against the destructive power of the papacy is presented tragically in many respects.[26] There is thus a strong contrast between the two figures of kingship, and both are theatrical realizations of Henry VIII. But we should notice that even the idealized version manifested in Imperial Majesty is not completely flawless, and this suggests that Bale was not entirely satisfied with Henry's manifestation of kingship.

Because the play was so heavily revised we need to consider briefly the differing contexts for which the two versions might have been created.[27] The first of the two versions, the A-text, was probably generated by 1538, in connection with Bale's extensive performing interests with a company of players supported by Cromwell and identifiable as the Lord Privy Seal's players after Cromwell's appointment in July 1536. It is the basis of the existing manuscript, but this fascinating document, written out by an unknown scribe, was then extensively revised by Bale in his own unmistakable handwriting, possibly for his return to England under Edward, and then updated sometime after Elizabeth I's accession in 1558, when Bale returned from his second exile. This revised text, the B-text, has manifestly survived in a complete form. The process of revision involved inserting passages on page, putting in two additional slips of paper, and then finally crossing out some four pages near the end and setting out a new ending in a fair copy.[28] The four surviving cancelled pages indicate that Bale kept very close to his original and incorporated nearly every word from the A-text, but, frustratingly, they do not extend to the old ending of the play.[29] We cannot be sure how drastic were the revisions to the conclusion. But two outstanding facts are relevant here: the A-text told the whole story of King Johan right up to his death speech; and the surviving cancelled sheets of the A-text contain no reference to the dominant role of Imperial Majesty near the end of the play, making it distinctly likely that this character was a later invention, conceived in a different political-religious context from that when Bale first represented the story of King Johan. This would make Bale's decision to write a new fair copy for the ending more explicable.

Looking at the presentation of King Johan in the earlier version, we find evidence of Bale's intentions and interests at that time. There are a number of contemporary themes. One is Johan's initial statement emphasizing the necessity of allegiance to the lawful king, a theme traceable in

Luther's work as well as in William Tyndale's *Obedience of a Christian Man*, a book known to have impressed King Henry (2–6).[30] King Johan also stresses his own imperial inheritance (8–14), thus touching upon a concept of empire which was of importance in the Parliamentary legislation establishing royal supremacy (drafted by Cromwell).[31] As the play develops, Johan shows further thematic links with the Henry of the 1530s. These include a knowledge of scripture (55, 1467), his assertion that his power is of God (223), his interest in the destruction of monks (259), his role in correcting all vice, including evils committed by clerics, whom he would not allow to be defended by special legal favor (1276–7), and his conflict with the Cardinal, who is the representative of the papacy and who sets the bishops against him (1356–77).

But Bale also uses Johan in a tragic mode, as we have noticed, and part of his managing of this character alludes to the tragic death of the saints.[32] Much of the action is concerned with King Johan's attempts to control the three estates, nobility, clergy, and the lawyers (Civil Order). Each of these in different ways is seduced from its proper allegiance to the king, through the treasonous activities of Sedition. This character makes clear his loyalty to the pope (90–1, 181–4), and he also prompts insurrection (1242). But in particular he has a theatrical role and is given much prominence upon the stage. Indeed it seems that he is one of Bale's most significant innovations in that he is a forerunner of the theatrical "Vice" who was to dominate interludes in the second half of the sixteenth century. Bale gives him two notable sequences. The first is his comic double act with Dissimulation in which they prepare their attack upon Johan (639–763). The second is a presentation of allegory in visual terms, clearly a sort of procession (called metatheatrically a "pagent," in line 786) in which Dissimulation "brings in" Private Wealth and Private Wealth then "brings in" Usurped Power (770–87), the phrase being literal as well as allegorical. The application of this figure to Bale's perception of the predicament of King Johan, and beyond him of King Henry, cannot be doubted, as it focuses upon the wealth of the Church and the potential threat this embodied to the authority of the crown. Sedition then adds a further layer to the allegory by demanding that these three now carry him in upon their backs, which they shortly do. Perhaps here Bale is deliberately invoking the custom of ceremonially carrying the pope; but he makes a point of having Sedition mock the process by means of a scabrous joke (803–4). As we shall see, Bale developed Sedition further.

These and other conspiratorial activities, which are often comic in tone, are part of the destructive combination which overwhelms King Johan, but he remains a virtuous figure, and his virtue is sustained when it comes to the capitulation to the reimposition of papal authority. He yields because the threat of war, destruction, and penury is heavy upon his people, and he does not wish them to suffer (1713–22). He dies an admirable king, and it would seem that Bale meant this admiration to be transferred to King Henry. This is particularly evident when he groups a number of kingly figures together. He emphasizes this in the later interpolation of a speech by the Interpreter on a single sheet (p. 26), possibly in a role which he envisaged for himself, as with "Baleus Prolocutor" in the other extant plays (1107–20). This interpolation is prophetic where it is inserted, anticipating the admirable behavior of King Johan in the death sequence.

The material discussed here relating to the 1530s leaves no doubt that in these difficult and changing times, under a monarch who can justly be described as changeable to say the least, the nature of kingship was open to question and redefinition. For Bale circumstances were frequently threatening, and he had to consider changes brought about in the name of the three subsequent monarchs. As already stated, we do not quite know when he made the revisions, but the manuscript shows that he was still revising the play after Elizabeth I's accession.

With Imperial Majesty's arrival the focus shifts away from the historical parallel between King Johan and King Henry to a more distinctly emblematic one. Once again Bale seems to have been interested in morality-play conventions involving abstract characterizations. The action is now confined to the three estates characters, Clergy, Nobility, and Civil Order (lawyers), plus Veritas, Sedition, and Imperial Majesty himself.[33] Veritas begins with praise for the dead monarch, in which he mentions King Johan's valor and godliness. He claims that chronicles have revealed these qualities and rejects the criticism of Polydore Vergil in his *Anglicae Historiae Libri* (1534) (2195–6, 2203–7). He notes how much King Johan has done for London, which includes building London Bridge.

Veritas castigates the three estates for their offenses against King Johan and extracts promises of reform from them (2310, 2312, and 2314). This clears the way for Imperial Majesty, who restates the role of the king under God:

> No man is exempt / from thys God's ordynaunce –
> Bishopp, monke, chanon / priest, cardynall, nor pope.
> All they by Gods lawe / to kynges owe their allegeaunce.   (2380–2)

But Bale immediately works the situation further by having Clergy make a slip in agreeing to exile the pope "If it be your pleasure" (2387). This excites the wrath of Imperial Majesty, for it is not, he claims, a matter of the monarch's pleasure but an aspect of God's truth. The monarch speaks directly from God and not of his own volition. His insistence allows him to press the estates to further action against the papacy, and thus Bale uses the figure of Imperial Majesty as a means of reinforcing the Reformation. Assuming that the B-text was written after Bale went into exile in 1540, it is apparent that Bale was trying to influence King Henry further towards Protestant views. During the 1540s Henry had become conservative in outlook once more, and Bale presumably wanted to counteract that.

One further episode is now necessary, one which is noticeably vigorous theatrically: the punishment of Sedition. Bale's revisions developed this character remarkably, perhaps in part because the Vice convention had grown significantly after the 1530s.[34] In the B-text ending, beyond the overlap, Sedition comes in singing and tries to save himself by using the alias Holy Perfection. During this passage he refers to two items which might well have been in the 1530s version. These are the injunctions he says Imperial Majesty gave, which probably refers to Henry's Second Royal Injunctions of 1538 (1509); and a reference to his attempt to sustain the status of the Church "in the Northe but now of late" (2515), a likely pointer to the Pilgrimage of Grace of 1536. Though we cannot be certain, it looks as though these details survive from the 1530s, even if a new context for them was later generated by the invention of Imperial Majesty. Sedition now admits that he intended to treat Imperial Majesty just as he had treated King Johan, had it not been for the intervention of Veritas (2575–6). This brings down the wrath of Imperial Majesty in a way perhaps reminiscent of King Henry. He orders Sedition to be hanged and quartered at Tyburn and his head to be placed upon London Bridge (2579–84). This prospect makes Sedition aspire to a place in the Litany and the martyr's status of Becket (2589–90). It is not quite clear how much Bale added to Sedition's part in the B-text, but it is striking that Sedition keeps up with the old Catholic ways and seeks martyrdom. Although in his early years, when he was still a Catholic, Bale had studied the lives of the saints, he became very critical of hagiography, especially in his *Acts of English Votaries* (1546). Imperial Majesty is thus shown righteously pursuing Protestant practice as Bale hoped King Henry would. Before he departs, leaving the estates to praise the new queen, Imperial Majesty kisses them as a sign of peace, an action which may be intended to recall and convert the Catholic motif of the kisses exchanged by the Daughters of God into a gesture designed to sustain the royal authority in a reformed world.

The presentations of King Henry in these interludes are partly dependent upon the stance or predicament of the authors. Skelton thought he ought to have a direct influence on Henry because of his role as a tutor, and his play embodies advice related to that. The unknown author of *Godly Queen Hester* distances himself from Henry, and yet he is interested in the dangers of misguided trust in royal servants. Heywood, using bold comic methods, seeks to bring about Catholic support. Finally, Bale saw two Henrys. One was for him on the right lines, a saint-like figure, in his resistance to the papacy, but the second, an idealized figure, also needed persuasion. Perhaps there is here a reflection of Bale's apprehension about Henry, who had Cromwell, Bale's patron, executed, and whose regime forced Bale to weather the last years of Henry's reign in exile.

NOTES

1. Text references for *Magnyfycence* are to my *Four Morality Plays* (Harmondsworth: Penguin, 1979); to my *Complete Plays of John Bale*, 2 vols. (Cambridge: D. S. Brewer, 1985–6); to Richard Axton and Peter Happé (eds.), *The Plays of John Heywood* (Cambridge: D. S. Brewer, 1991); and to W. W. Greg (ed.), *A New Enterlude of Godly Queene Hester*, Materialien zur Kunde des älteren Englischen Dramas 5 (Louvain: Uystpruyst, 1904).

2. For the Latin text, which is not known to have been printed, see F. M. Salter, "Skelton's *Speculum Principis*," *Speculum* 9 (1934), 25–37. The translations here are from David R. Carlson (ed.), "The Latin Writings of John Skelton," *Studies in Philology Texts and Studies* 4 (1991), 39.

3. Paula Neuss (ed.), *Magnificence: John Skelton* (Manchester: Manchester University Press, 1980), 19.

4. See Willard Farnham, *The Medieval Heritage of Elizabethan Tragedy* (Berkeley: University of California Press, 1936), 42 and passim.

5. For Rastell see Richard Axton (ed.), *Three Rastell Plays* (Cambridge: D. S. Brewer, 1979), 8, and for his theater see Janette Dillon, "John Rastell's Stage," *Medieval English Theatre* 18 (1996), 15–45.

6. For Rastell's printing business see J. Christopher Warner, *Henry VIII's Divorce: Literature and the Politics of the Printing Press* (Cambridge: D. S. Brewer, 1998).

7. See for example the essays by Janette Dillon, Greg Walker, Alice Hunt, and David Bevington in Peter Happé and Wim Hüsken (eds.), *Interludes and Early Modern Society: Studies in Gender, Power and Theatricality* (Amsterdam: Rodopi, 2007).

8. James Gairdner (ed.), *Letters and Papers, Foreign and Domestic, of the Reign of Henry VIII* (London: Longman, *et al.*, 1883), vol. VII, p. 61, no. 149.

9. G. W. Bernard, *Power and Politics in Tudor England* (Aldershot: Ashgate, 2000); David Bevington, *Tudor Drama and Politics: A Critical Approach to Topical Meaning* (Cambridge, MA: Harvard University Press, 1968); Greg Walker, *Plays of Persuasion: Drama and Politics at the Court of Henry VIII* (Cambridge: Cambridge University Press, 1991).

10. Janet Dillon, "Powerful Obedience: Godly Queen Hester and Katherine of Aragon," in Happé and Hüsken (eds.), *Interludes and Early Modern Society*, 117–39.

11. Bevington, *Tudor Drama and Politics*; Greg Walker, *Writing under Tyranny: English Literature and the Henrician Reformation* (Oxford: Oxford University Press, 2005); Axton and Happé (eds.), *Plays of John Heywood*, 6, 51–2.

12. It is certain that later Heywood's plays were performed in royal palaces: see Axton and Happé (eds.), *Plays of John Heywood*, 7.

13. See also 584–6 and further details in my "'Rejoice ye in us with joy most joyfully': John Heywood's Plays and the Court," *Cahiers Élisabéthaines* 72 (2007), 1–8.

14. However, these lines mentioning safe passage in delivery might just possibly have a direct reference to Anne, even if she was not actually present: "I wolde eche wyfe that is bounde in maryage / *And that is wedded here within this place* / Myght have as quicke spede in every suche case" (584–6, my emphasis).

15. There may also be a compliment here at lines 685–6 in reference to the title *Fidei Defensor* bestowed by the pope upon Henry in 1521; see Axton and Happé (eds.), *Plays of John Heywood*, 226.

16. Axton and Happé (eds.), *Plays of John Heywood*, 48.

17. One such joke may be the delightful idea that when Heywood's Pardoner visits hell he finds Lucifer celebrating his birthday by playing tennis in his special jacket: see *Four PP*, 881–8, in Axton and Happé (eds.), *Plays of John Heywood*, and see note to 881, p. 259.

18. See, for example, Jupiter's initial and final speeches at 1–97 and 1241–54.

19. As in Lynn Forest-Hill, "Lucian's Satire of Philosophers in Heywood's *Play of the Wether*," *Medieval English Theatre* 18 (1998), 142–60.

20. Thomas Betteridge and Greg Walker, "Performance as Research: Staging John Heywood's *Play of the Wether* at Hampton Court Palace," *Medieval English Theatre* 27 (2005), 86–104.

21. Bale knew of *Wether* by 1548, when he praised the play for its ability to raise laughter. See his *Illustrium maioris Britanniae scriptorium … summarium* (1548), fol. 235.

22. Possibly his close attention to punctuation in the revisions to the text does suggest he was thinking of a printed version, but these revisions come somewhat later, and there is little to suggest that he meant the play to fit into the Skelton–Heywood context.

23. Peter Roberts, "Politics, Drama and the Cult of Thomas Becket in the Sixteenth Century," in Colin Morris and Peter Roberts (eds.), *Pilgrimage: The English Experience from Becket to Bunyan* (Cambridge: Cambridge University Press, 2002), 221–2.

24. For a prompt about polemical plays see the hints in *A Discourse touching the reformation of the lawes of England* attributed to Sir Richard Morison in Sydney Anglo, "An Early Tudor Programme for Plays and other Demonstrations against the Pope," *Journal of the Warburg and Courtauld Institutes* 20 (1957), 176–9.

25. Bale's list of his own plays in his manuscript *Anglorum Heliades* (1536–9: BL, MS Harleian 3838) includes *Super Utroque Regis Coniugo* and *De Traditione Thome Becketi*.

26. "Reforming Sovereignty: John Bale and Tragic Drama," in Happé and Hüsken (eds.), *Interludes and Early Modern Society*, 191–209.

27. The complexities of the manuscript (HL, MS HM3) were first unravelled by J. H. Pafford and W. W. Greg in *King Johan by John Bale*, Malone Society Reprint (Oxford: Oxford University Press, 1931). See also Barry B. Adams (ed.), *John Bale's "King Johan"* (San Marino: Huntington Library, 1969); vol. I of my *The Complete Plays of John Bale*, 2 vols. (Cambridge: D. S. Brewer, 1985–6); and Jeffrey Leininger, "The Dating of Bale's *King Johan*: A Re-Examination," *Medieval English Theatre* 24 (2002), 116–37. Reference to the facsimile is also invaluable: W. Bang (ed.), *Bales Kynge John*, Materialien zur Kunde des älteren Englischen Dramas 25 (Louvain: Uystpruyst, 1909).

28. I have tabulated the interrelationship in *Complete Plays*, vol. I, 100.

29. The overlap of the cancelled sheets and the revised fair copy can be checked for lines 1804–2161. The play ends at line 2691.

30. Honor McCusker, *John Bale: Dramatist and Antiquary* (Bryn Mawr, PA: Bryn Mawr College, 1942), 90–4.

31. See my "Dramatic Images of Kingship in Heywood and Bale," *Studies in English Literature* 39 (1999), 239–53.

32. See my "The Protestant Adaptation of the Saint Play," in Clifford Davidson (ed.), *The Saint Play in Medieval Europe* (Kalamazoo: Medieval Institute, 1986), 205–40.

33. Adams points out that in the cancelled sheets of the A-text the Cardinal is instructed to go out and dress for Nobility. In the cancelled sheets that do survive Nobility does not reappear, but the stage direction makes it very likely that he did come on stage again in the ending, which was recorded in the sheets now lost. *John Bale's "King Johan"*, 6.

34. See my "Sedition in *King Johan*: Bale's Development of a Vice," *Medieval English Theatre* 3 (1981), 3–6.

CHAPTER 2

Henry VIII as David: the king's image and Reformation politics

John N. King

The outbreak of schism between the Church of England and the See of Rome entailed a radical revision of Henry VIII's monarchical image.[1] Until that time the king's portraiture as a devoutly observant Christian was orthodox in the extreme. Little more than one decade earlier, Pope Leo X conferred upon Henry VIII the title of Defender of the Faith, an honor once granted to his father, Henry VII, and retained to the present day by British monarchs. The declaration of the Reformation Parliament that "this realm of England is an empire, and so hath been accepted in the world, governed by one Supreme Head and King" brought an end to the subordination of "the imperial Crown of the same" to the papal Tiara, however, by lodging ecclesiastical and secular authority in Henry VIII.[2] This claim to *imperium* denoted full sovereignty within the realm, rather than a claim to supremacy over other sovereign monarchs.[3] While it is hardly a new development for a politically expedient monarch to adopt a pietistic pose, from this point onward the Henrician image bears the imprint of Protestant ideology even though the king himself rejected change in the official theology and hierarchal structure of church government.[4] We may note this iconographical shift in a variety of works of art and literature that were produced for consumption both inside and outside of the royal court, most notably in the title pages of the Coverdale Bible and the Great Bible.

Hans Holbein the Younger depicted Henry VIII as a powerful Reformation monarch on the title page of the Coverdale Bible (1535).[5] Although this Bible was printed abroad, in all likelihood by the Antwerp printer Merten de Keyser,[6] it was clearly designed for an English readership. A very expensive folio, this large book lacked the unassuming and easily concealed material nature of de Keyser's surreptitious editions of William Tyndale's prohibited translation of the New Testament and related tracts. The title-page woodcut of the Coverdale Bible envisions Henry VIII as a monarch who accepts the free circulation of the first complete English printed Bible (Figure 1). Dissemination of the Bible in the vernacular was a goal that Protestants inherited from Catholic humanists such as Erasmus and More. Although the volume was not formally authorized, it may have circulated under the patronage of Thomas Cromwell, the king's vicegerent in religious affairs. In all likelihood, Holbein received appointment as King's Painter in 1535 after working at the royal court for several years. The artist painted Cromwell's portrait prior to 1534.[7] It may be that Cromwell sponsored the Holbein image as a publicly available means of validating Henry's claim to govern without clerical intercession as the sole intermediary between temporal society and the divine order, an interpretation supported by Miles Coverdale's preface (sig. +2v).[8] Alternative possibilities are that Coverdale or a publisher in Antwerp procured the title-page border. The engagement of the title-page border in an appeal for patronage of the Coverdale Bible is not incompatible with propagandistic glorification of the king's headship of the Church of England. After all, the assertion of royal supremacy represented the "organizing principle, the doctrine around which the rest of the king's religion was arranged" following England's schism from the Church of Rome.[9] It is important to remember, however, that the Henrician Reformation represented an act of state that was political, rather than theological, in nature. Although Henry VIII supplanted the pope as head of the Church of England, theology, ritual, and church polity were unchanged.[10]

The intricately carved compartments and emblazoned texts of Holbein's border portray an ideal of evangelical kingship in terms of the transition from the Law of Moses to that of Christ. The figures of Adam and Eve at the top left prefigure Christ's resurrection at the opposite side. Henry VIII wields the Sword and the Book as a worldly instrument of divine revelation at the bottom.[11] His authority is transmitted to him symbolically from the heavens above via the Old and New Testament models for sacred kingship depicted elsewhere on the page. The composite biblical symbol of the Sword and the Book would play a vital role in a campaign to establish Henry's image as a theocratic ruler capable of unifying ecclesiastical and secular authority. The figures of David and Paul who flank Henry VIII respectively symbolize divine revelation before and after the advent of the Christian dispensation. Whereas the lyre-bearing figure of David serves primarily as a type for Henry VIII's claim to govern by divine sanction, St. Paul's presence denies the papal claim to primacy as an inheritance from St. Peter.[12] Paul's chief attribute of the sword was employed throughout the Middle Ages as a device commemorating his beheading. Protestants revered Paul as the paramount saint for his promulgation of the crucial distinction

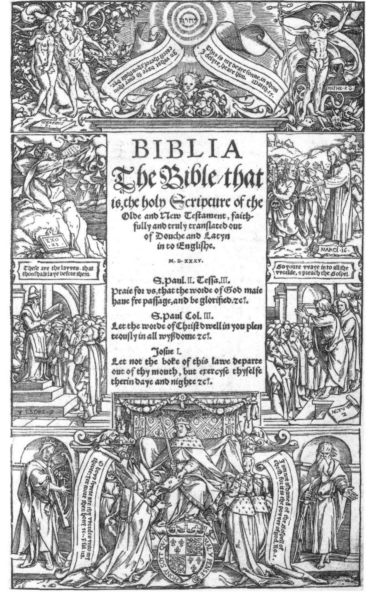

Figure 1. Hans Holbein the Younger, title-page border, Coverdale Bible (1535).

between faith and works, however, rather than for his martyrdom alone. Reformers aligned the sword in Paul's hands not with the means of his decollation, but with "the sword of the Spirit, which is the word of God" (Eph. 6:17).[13] Although the sword in King Henry's hand carries its traditional identification with justice, its proximity to the weapon borne by St. Paul also identifies it with evangelical truth.

The vertical axis that connects the Tetragrammaton above with the king suggests that a line of spiritual authority descends from heaven to earth without intervention from any ecclesiastical authority. Although Henry VIII is portrayed as the conduit through which the Bible descends to the bishops and nobles kneeling beneath him, this scene in the royal presence chamber is modeled on traditional dedication portraits in which donors hand books to patrons or would-be patrons. Given the absence of formal authorization of the Coverdale Bible, the scene suggests a reciprocal interchange in which the king accepts from a prelate, presumably Archbishop Thomas Cranmer, a copy of the English Bible. The side compartments of Holbein's border align his portrayal of Henry VIII with a sequence of key biblical events. Moses' reception of the Ten Commandments at the left side may be interpreted as a type for divinely inspired leadership capable of delivering God's chosen people out of bondage to the tyrannical Pharaoh, whom the reformers interpreted as a figure for the pope. Beneath this scene, Esdras preaches the Mosaic Law. In the balanced New Testament scenes at the right, Christ first commissions the apostles to undertake their ministry in the words of Mark 16:15. With tongues of flame upon their heads, St. Peter and his companions then preach the New Law at Pentecost (Acts 2:3). The keys borne by the apostles in the inset at the right-hand side undermine the papal claim to primacy as the inheritor of the keys of St. Peter.

The prominent quotation of Mark 16:15 suggests that Henry VIII's public image in the Coverdale Bible corresponded to the iconography of works designed for the royal court.[14] At the approximate time that Holbein carved the wooden blocks for the title page, a portrait attributed to Joos van Cleve depicted the monarch holding a scroll bearing the Vulgate version of that scriptural text.[15] We lack information concerning the commissioning of this painting by an artist active in Antwerp during the 1530s. The iconography of this courtly image corresponds to iconoclastic activity in the outward world by appropriating a text in which the Church of Rome had discovered a precedent for the papal claim of apostolic succession from Christ, thus "demolishing" a key claim to Roman supremacy.[16] The painting presumably refers to Henry's adopted role as a latter-day apostle engaged in the evangelical task of propagating the scriptures. Holbein's woodcut portrayal of Henry VIII in the Coverdale Bible is compatible with the private delineation of the monarchical image.

The propagandistic title page of the Great Bible (1539; Figure 2) contains a sophisticated reformulation of the title-page border of the Coverdale Bible. Loosely adapted from the earlier woodcut by a member of the School of Holbein, the Great Bible title page symbolizes royal supremacy over church and state by depicting a graded hierarchy in which the king replaces the pope as the temporal intermediary between heaven and earth. The memorable title page of this officially commissioned edition of the English Bible played a key role in the popular defense of the royal supremacy of Henry VIII over the Church of England. It embodies the establishmentarian belief that the vertical process of reform is a royal prerogative, for the king alone can transmit the Bible to the bishops and magistrates in the second level.[17] The rigid stratification of the scene exemplifies a conflict between freedom and control, because its orderly ranks reflect Henry's cautious retention of traditional doctrine and ritual during the early stages of the English Reformation. The image ambivalently endorses the Protestant commitment to the priesthood of all believers in a realm where the monarch maintained tight control over religion. Accordingly, the bottom compartment portrays members of a congregation hearing the English Bible from the lectern rather than reading it for themselves, for they are still passive recipients of scriptures that are transmitted by a priestly elite operating under political instructions from the crown. The ability of aristocrats to call out the Latin words of homage, "Vivat Rex," distinguishes them as superiors of the tiny, almost childlike figures of commoners, who shout out "God Save the King."

The complicated typology of this woodcut border conveys different scriptural guises of Henry VIII in a heavily layered and overlapping fashion. The most prominent visual allusion is to his instrumental role in the transmission of *Verbum Dei*, an apostolic image for the dissemination of the Bible in the post-Pentecostal world of the early church; it offered Protestants a figure for the renewal of the "true" church during the Reformation. The image of the sacred book, as it descends through various levels of the political and social hierarchy, objectifies the utterance emanating from God in the banderol at the top of the border: "So shall my word be that goes forth from my mouth; it shall not return to me empty, but it shall accomplish that which I purpose" (Isa. 55:11). In the Vulgate New Testament, *Verbum Dei* – "word of God" – refers specifically to the preaching of the divine Word and missionary activity of

Figure 2. School of Holbein, title-page border, Great Bible (1539).

the apostles (Acts 8:14). The prominence of *Verbum Dei* in the title page of the Great Bible provides a visual analogue to the inset scenes in the Coverdale Bible that show Christ's delegation of the disciples and the inspiration of the apostles at Pentecost. Taking on strong Protestant coloration, this tag-phrase corresponds to the manner in which identification of the word of God with the royal supremacy became "the hallmark of Henrician propaganda and preaching in the mid-1530s." By associating Henry VIII with the Bible, religious reformers attempted to identify political obedience with belief in justification by faith alone and other Lutheran doctrines.[18]

Key scriptural texts that are inscribed in sinuous banderols set forth the iconographical program of the woodcut border. Although Henry VIII's pre-eminent role is that of David, he also voices King Darius' acknowledgement of the power of Yahweh and speaks to Cromwell in the voice of Moses and to Thomas Cranmer, Archbishop of Canterbury, through words uttered by St. Paul. With the exception of Darius, all of these regal prototypes also appear in the border of the Coverdale Bible. The praying figure of the king in the upper right corner utters words attributed to David in celebrating the power of the divine Word as a guide for royal conduct: "Thy word is a lamp to my feet" (Ps. 119:105; Vulg. Ps. 118:105). God reciprocates in his selection of Henry as David to govern over England as a new Israel: "I have found in David the son of Jesse a man after my heart, who will do all my will" (Acts 13:22). The largest banderol attributes to Henry's enthroned figure the response of Darius the Mede to the miraculous survival of Daniel in the lion's den, whereby that ruler proclaimed: "I make a decree, that in all my royal dominion men tremble and fear before the God of Daniel, for he is the living God" (Dan. 6:26). The Bible's presentation of the unhistorical figure of Darius as the conqueror of Babylon may be interpreted as a prefiguration of the English king's rejection of the authority of papal Rome.

Henry VIII's balanced actions at the right and left sides of the border present him as a figure who unifies the roles of Moses, as one who imparts law to judges, and St. Paul, as a clerical authority who offers counsel to an apostle on the conduct of Christian missions to the Gentiles. In the border's second register, Cranmer's empowerment to "command and teach" religious doctrine (I Tim. 4:11) casts him in the role of a new Timothy who, as the favored colleague of the Pauline Henry, is entrusted with the task of instructing the English in an evangelical religious program. Cromwell in turn receives a Mosaic charge to "judge righteously" and to "hear the small and the great alike" (Deut. 1:16–17). In the third register these servants of the crown transmit *Verbum Dei* respectively to figures representative of the clergy and magistracy. Cranmer instructs the cleric at the left by repeating

St. Peter's injunction that pastors fulfill their obligation to "Tend the flock of God" (I Pet. 5:2); according to Protestant teaching, the Bible is the worldly source of spiritual "feeding." Cromwell outlines the responsibility of civil authorities by quoting from Psalm 34:14 (Vulg. Ps. 33:15): "Depart from evil and do good; seek peace and pursue it." The congregation representative of the English people at the base of the title page hears a biblical text that was interpreted as a foundation of the political doctrine that subjects must obey royal authority. The cleric enjoins them to pray for "kings and all who are in high positions" (I Tim. 2:1–2).

The title pages of the Coverdale Bible and the Great Bible typify the incorporation of reformist ideology into royal images during the 1530s. Members of court who had reformist sympathies could now appropriate pre-existing regal iconography by flattering the king as a new Moses for delivering the English people or as a new David for establishing control over a unified church and state. Henry's apologists and those who sought royal patronage created courtly works of art and literature that contained flattering portrayals of the king that corresponded to his published images. In some cases these compliments were doubtless designed to encourage the monarch to satisfy expectations for an evangelical government to which the king had a lukewarm commitment, if he supported them at all.[19]

Medieval and Renaissance rulers had frequently been envisioned in the image of Moses, but Tudor iconography reinterpreted the Israelite leader as a personal figure for Henry VIII as the initiator of the English Reformation. The association of Henry VIII with Moses on the title pages of the 1535 and 1539 Bibles suggests that the schism from the Church of Rome is a providential event akin to the Israelites' Exodus out of the land of Egypt. Moses' combined role as both leader of the Chosen People and recipient of the Ten Commandments furnishes a precedent for Henry VIII's reputed deliverance of England out of bondage in papal Egypt and for his authorization of the vernacular Bible. The vignette in the Coverdale Bible that portrays Moses receiving the divine Word from its transcendent author identifies worldly sovereignty with an external and universal source of spiritual power, thus validating its temporal authority.

In line with this view, Catherine Parr, the king's last wife, praises him as a new Moses in *The lamentacion of a sinner* (1547), a set of pietistic meditations drawn from the scriptures. Her complex figure compares the pope to the tyrannical Pharaoh from whom the Israelites fled:

But our Moyses, a moste godly, wise governer and kyng hath delivered us oute of the captivitie and bondage of Pharao. I mene by this Moyses Kyng Henry the eight, my most soverayne favourable lorde and husband. One (If Moyses had figured any mo[re] then Christ) through the excellent grace of god, mete to be an other expressed veritie of Moses conqueste over Pharao. And I mene by this Pharao the bishop of Rome, who hath bene and is a greater persecutor of all true christians, then ever was Pharao, of the children of Israel. (sig. E1r–v)[20]

Catherine Parr's compliment suggests that praise of Henry as a Mosaic king was fashionable at the royal court after the break from Rome, because her works circulated in manuscript within royal circles before they appeared in print. The continuing currency of the Moses epithet at the Reformation court may be noted in Miles Coverdale's praise of Edward VI as a new Moses in his dedication for the "second tome" of Erasmus' *Paraphrases on the New Testament* (1549).

A different representation of the royal court during this period of religious unrest is provided by miniatures portraying the king as a new David in "Henry VIII's Psalter," a Latin manuscript written for presentation to him by the French courtier Jean Mallard.[21] Although David had served as a regal prototype throughout the Middle Ages in illustrations for royal psalters and other works, Mallard (or an artist whom he may have commissioned to illustrate the volume) adapts traditional iconography to suit contemporary circumstances by portraying Henry VIII in the guise of David.[22] Both donor and recipient share the prevailing assumption of their time that the Psalms represent an autobiographical collection of lyric songs composed by King David. The portrayal of King Henry playing his lyre in the guise of King David (Figure 3; fol. 63v) provides a close analogue to the vignette at the lower left of the Coverdale Bible title page (Figure 1). Holbein's inclusion of David as a type for Reformation kingship may well have derived from Henrician court circles, where volumes like the Mallard psalter circulated, particularly if Cromwell was the effective patron of that Bible translation.[23]

Mallard's miniature fuses type and antitype within a single monarchical image. (Holbein's woodcut border depicts David as a separate figure, on the other hand, albeit one that flanks the central figure of the Tudor king.) The specific image of David with his lyre is associated by convention with David's reputed authorship of the Psalms. Portrayal of the royal fool, Will Sommers, at the left of the lyre-playing king provides an amusing illustration for Psalm 53 (Vulg. Ps. 52; "The fool says in his heart, 'There is no God'"). Mallard's portrait of Henry seated at a table while playing the lyre in a private chamber of a royal palace may also allude to the king's well-known reputation as a musician and composer of both sacred and profane music (see Spring, chapter 9 in this volume).[24] According to George Puttenham, the king was fond of hearing English versifications of the Psalms sung by

in confpectu fanctorum tuorum Gloria
patri S icut erat .

Di xit infipies in corde fuo no est Des G or= rupti fut

Figure 3. Henry VIII as David with Lyre, "Henry VIII's Psalter" (*c.* 1530–40).

Thomas Sternhold, who received appointment as Groom of the Privy Chamber as a reward for turning out ballad versions of the biblical poems.[25]

Henry appears as both David and one of his lyric subjects in illustrations for two other Psalms, whose appeal for deliverance from external enemies and false accusers is altogether appropriate to the self-image of the Reformation king and his court.[26] The manuscript thus identifies the English king as both the subject and the object of a collection of lyrics that was traditionally taken to be an autobiographical work by King David. Henry plays the learned and pious role of "the man who walks not in the counsel of the wicked" in the miniature for Psalm 1 that portrays him reading a book in his bedchamber, with two books on the floor beside him (fol. 3). In this scene Henry has withdrawn from the active world portrayed beyond the portal of the elegantly furnished room into introspective contemplation.[27] A miniature for Psalm 69 (Vulg. Ps. 68) portrays the king praying for deliverance from enemies; with his crown at his feet in a setting of classical ruins, he kneels beneath an angel who has a sword, a skull, and a rod (fol. 79). His plight recalls an outcry attributed to David: "More in number than the hairs of my head are those who hate me without cause; mighty are those who would destroy me, those who attack me with lies" (Ps. 69:4). This verse would have taken on a special meaning during the 1530s and 1540s, when England experienced a sense of encirclement by hostile Catholic powers including the Hapsburg emperor and the French king.

The king received this psalter with approval, because he kept the gift among his private books and accepted Mallard's view that the Psalms constitute a *speculum principis* concerning ideal kingship. Annotations that appear throughout the text in Henry's heavy swashing handwriting designate particular Psalms as advice on government and religion. By noting "officiu[m] regi[s]" ("the king's office") beside Psalm 72:4 (Vulg. Ps. 71:4), Henry styles himself as a godly king in response to Mallard's view that the hymn was written "De regno christi et gentium vocatione" ("concerning the kingdom of Christ and the calling of the people"). The king indicates his concern with matters of faith by drawing attention to a passage "de idolatria" ("concerning idolatry") in Psalm 44:20 (Vulg. Ps. 43:21). Henry's note "de rege" ("concerning the king") accords with the donor's comment on Psalm 63:11 (Vulg. Ps. 62:12) as an utterance concerning regal piety. The note "de regib[us]" ("about kings") endorses Mallard's view that Psalm 21 (Vulg. Ps. 20) concerns the triumph of Christ through the agency of Christian kings. Henry VIII similarly reads Psalm 20:9 (Vulg. Ps. 19:10) as "pro rege oratorio" ("a prayer for the king").

Jottings independent of Mallard's commentary provide even greater insight into Henry VIII's private interpretation of the Psalms by showing how he applies specific passages to his own conduct as king. Sometimes he merely brackets verses or indicates passages of particular importance with the designations "n[ota] bene" or "bene n[ota]." Many notations indicate that Henry assumes the Davidic role of a righteous man who sings praise to the Lord for delivering him from the hands of his enemies. The 1530s context of the psalter suggests that these perceived threats may have come both from foreign enemies of Henry's policy of religious reform and also from domestic opponents whose hostility to the Cromwellian regime led to the rebellious Pilgrimage of Grace in 1536. The king's annotations furnish a written analogue to the miniature that portrays him as David pleading for divine assistance against enemies (Ps. 69). Thus his "n[ota] bene" beside Psalms 11:6 and 41:11 (Vulg. Ps. 10:7 and 40:12) exults that God will uphold him and direct "fire and brimstone" against the wicked. His annotations on Psalms 18:20–24 and 62:12 (Vulg. Ps. 17:21–25 and 61:13) claim that God will reward him and punish his enemies. Exclamation marks alongside Psalm

34:7, 9 (Vulg. Ps. 33:8, 10) call attention to promises that those who fear the Lord will receive divine protection. Notes on passages in Psalm 37:28, 38, and 39 (Vulg. Ps. 36:28, 38, and 39) that refer to damnation and salvation comment on the meting out of divine penalties "de iniustis et impijs" ("concerning the unjust and impious") and rewards "de iustis" ("concerning the just").

In reading this collection of divine poems as a royal text, Henry VIII joins Jean Mallard in suppressing reference to David's flaws as an adulterer. The king pointedly ignores his Hebrew predecessor's longstanding reputation as an archetype for the repentant sinner in the Seven Penitential Psalms (6, 32, 38, 51, 102, 130, and 143; Vulg. 6, 31, 37, 50, 101, 129, and 142). In contrast to the annotations in which Henry clearly stresses David's status as a model for regal strength rather than personal weakness, avoidance of the psalms of repentance represents a truly significant absence at a time when the king brutally set aside four wives during his search for a legitimate male heir.[28]

Henry's subjects would not so conveniently ignore the negative potential for blame that is inherent within any praise of the king as a latter-day David. Indeed, Miles Coverdale tempers his flattery of Henry VIII in the preliminary matter of the Coverdale Bible by citing Nathan the prophet, who "'spared not to rebuke … [David], and that right sharply, when he fell from the word of God into adultery and manslaughter,' offences for which Henry was already known."[29] (Hugh Latimer was to emulate Nathan's role in his sermons before Edward VI, in which he lodged oblique blame of the late king for setting a bad example for his heir.)[30] When Sir Thomas Wyatt versified the Penitential Psalms against the contemporary backdrop of Henrician politics, he wrote as one thoroughly familiar with the infidelities and intrigue that permeated the royal court. Although any personal allusions in this poetic sequence would appear to be directed to the circumstances of Wyatt's own life,[31] one may not deny that the poet attaches Protestant associations to a group of Psalms that were "essentially and unavoidably controversial" at the time that he versified them (*c.* 1534–42). If Wyatt wrote them soon after Anne Boleyn's execution in 1536, he may even "glance, slyly and indirectly, at Henry VIII," who would therefore receive advice that he should imitate the Hebrew king "and repent his own scandalous abuse of power in the service of his lust."[32] The likelihood of critical reference to King Henry is even greater in the sonnet in praise of "Wyates Psalmes" in which the earl of Surrey notes that "Rewlers may se in a myrrour clere / The bitter frewte of false concupiscence." In reading the Penitential Psalms as a hybridization of a *speculum principis* and a *de remedia amoris*, Surrey discovers a providential warning for lustful monarchs: "In

Prynces hartes Goddes scourge yprinted depe / Myght them awake out of their synfull slepe."[33]

In contrast to the private record of Henry VIII's envisagement of himself as David in his manuscript psalter, *The Exposition and Declaration of the Psalme, Deus ultionum Dominus* (1539) by Henry Parker, eighth Baron Morley, embodies a representation of the king that originated within courtly circles before it was published for popular consumption. The commentator originally prepared his manuscript and dedicated it to the king in 1534, at the approximate time when the Reformation Parliament proclaimed the king to be supreme head of the Church of England. (He had already been declared *de facto* head of the Church by the Act in Restraint of Appeals of the previous year.) Publication of Parker's text by the King's Printer, Thomas Berthelet, suggests that Henry VIII favored its dissemination. The patriotic fervor of the baron's interpretation of Psalm 94 (Vulg. Ps. 93) displays the Erastianism that enabled him to survive so many twists and turns in religious policy during the reigns of Henry and his offspring, Edward VI and Mary I. Parker's praise of Henry as a modern version of "the royall kyng David" (sig. A7r) or "the excellente kynge and prophete David" (sig. B8r) corresponds to the juxtaposition of Henry VIII and David in the Coverdale Bible border (Figure 1). By emphasizing the role of David not as the psalmist, but as the youthful victor against Goliath, Parker cries out against the violence and arrogance of tyrants and treats Psalm 94 as a prayer to God, the Lord of Vengeance, and as a prophecy of Henry VIII's liberation of England from the pope, the "gre[a]t Golyas [Goliath]" (sig. A7r–v). Complimenting the king as a second Moses leading England as a new Israel out of bondage (sig. A5v), this text also contains hyperbolic appeals for vengeance "ageynst this serpent," the pope, and the liberation of England from its "captivite Babylonical" (sig. A3v, A5r).

Solomon was second only to David as an enduring biblical type for Tudor kingship, one that is rooted in the princely iconography of western Europe and Byzantium. The relationship of the Hebrew monarchs could readily support the Tudor claim to legitimate dynastic descent by tracing out the lineage from Davidic father to Solomonic son. Like his father, Henry VIII received praise as a second Solomon[34] in a doubling of regal prototypes that produced comparisons to both the father and the son who were regarded as paramount among the rulers of ancient Israel. These comparisons were adapted to different purposes, however: David was remembered largely for authorship of the Psalms, slaying of Goliath, establishing the united kingdom of Israel and Judah, and governing as the ideal king who was viewed by Christians as a prototype of the Messiah. By tradition, Solomon was the greatest of the Hebrew kings, one whose stature as a sacred ruler was marked by the erection of the Temple in Jerusalem; for Christians the construction of the Temple was a prototype for the foundation of the "true" church during the early Christian period; for Protestants this architectural event betokened the renewal of the church during the Reformation. Solomon's reputation for unparalleled wisdom and prudence was associated with Israel's period of greatest material wealth and well-being. It is important to remember that pre-existing iconography of this kind was applied to the particular claims of all the Tudors to govern as Christian monarchs, regardless of whether they embraced orthodox or reformist religious positions.

At about the same time that Holbein juxtaposed Henry and David in the title-page border of the Coverdale Bible, he composed a portrait on vellum showing the king as Solomon receiving the gifts of the Queen of Sheba, who kneels at the head of her retinue.[35] This miniature appears to have been designed as a gift for presentation to the monarch.[36] The composition of this miniature in the same period as the break with Rome and at the time when Holbein began to receive patronage from the king suggests an allusion to the royal supremacy. After all, the Queen of Sheba is a traditional type for the church, and her kneeling homage and submission to an omnicompetent monarch carry every suggestion that the picture commemorates the recent submission of the Church of England to Henry as the head of the church. The opulent attire of the crowded courtiers and the rich offerings borne by the queen's attendants enhance the glory of the king. This scene functions as an epiphany of sacred majesty, in response to which the queen averts her head as a mark of homage. The artist executed a design that reinterprets the queen's visitation (I Kings 10:1–13, II Chron. 9:1–13) in accordance with an understanding of Solomon's wisdom as a type of divine revelation through scripture.

Solomon's stance loosely resembles that of King Henry on the Coverdale Bible title page (Figure 1). The full frontal view of the Hebrew king, who sits enthroned, wearing a crown and holding a scepter beneath an arch at the top of a high dais, dominates the scene, in which the Queen of Sheba meets him and exclaims: "Happy are these your servants, who continually stand before you and hear your wisdom! Blessed be the LORD your God, who has delighted in you and set you on his throne as king" (II Chron. 9:7–8). Inscribed on the wall and canopy behind the king, the Latin version of her salutation most likely alludes to the Reformation Parliament's replacement of the pope with Henry as Supreme Head of the Church of England; this text suggests that both Henry and Solomon are responsible to God alone and to no other worldly power. The inscription on the base of the throne articulates the queen's response to their meeting: "VICISTI FAMAM VIRTVTIBVS TVIS" ("By your virtues you have won fame").[37]

Scriptural texts or images of books symbolic of the Bible were widely employed in royal portraits after Henry VIII's breach with Rome in the 1530s. Hans Holbein the Younger created a familiar image in defense of royal supremacy in ecclesiastical affairs when he portrayed the enthroned figure of the English king wielding the sword symbolic of justice and the divine Word as he transmits the book representative of the divine Word on the title page of the Coverdale Bible, the first vernacular translation of the scriptures to circulate with the tacit permission of the British Crown. This scene underwent variation during the 1530s, notably in the title page for the Great Bible that was modeled upon Holbein's original design, and it corresponded to portrayals of Henry VIII in coterie works such as the miniature that portrays the king in the guise of Solomon receiving the Queen of Sheba, and in a manuscript psalter in which illuminations conferred Henry's image on King David and in which the English king inscribed marginalia in the manner of a latter-day David. Images of this kind would undergo transmutation until the end of the Tudor dynasty as iconographical symbols for governance by a line of "godly" rulers. The envisionment of Henry VIII as a "godly" ruler is at one and the same time a conventional means by which artists envisioned Henry VIII and a vehicle for dissemination of images of regal piety both inside and outside of the royal court.

NOTES

1. In revised and augmented form, the present essay incorporates findings presented in John N. King, *Tudor Royal Iconography: Literature and Art in an Age of Religious Crisis* (Princeton: Princeton University Press, 1989), chap. 2. See also my "Henry VIII as David: The King's Image and Reformation Politics," in Peter C. Herman (ed.), *Rethinking the Henrician Era: Essays on Early Tudor Texts and Contexts* (Urbana: University of Illinois Press, 1993), 78–97. Unless otherwise noted, scriptural texts are from the Revised Standard Version, including those that are offered without notice in place of the original Vulgate quotations.

2. Act in Restraint of Appeals, 24 Hen. VII, c. 12, in G. R. Elton (ed.), *The Tudor Constitution: Documents and Commentary* (Cambridge: Cambridge University Press, 2nd edn., 1982), 353–8. Roy C. Strong notes the "far-reaching" impact of this legislation in *Holbein and Henry VIII* (London: Routledge & Kegan Paul, 1967), 6. See also J.J. Scarisbrick, *Henry VIII* (Berkeley: University of California Press, 1968), 116–17.

3. Richard Koebner, "'The Imperial Crown of this Realm': Henry VIII, Constantine the Great, and Polydore Vergil," *Bulletin of the Institute of Historical Research* 26 (1953), 51.

4. In *Persuasive Fictions: Faction, Faith, and Political Culture in the Reign of Henry VIII* (Aldershot: Scolar Press, 1996), 95, Greg Walker concludes that "the images of Henry VIII's reign appear much less as revolutionary breaks with convention and far more as simply milestones in a long tradition of royal portraiture." In doing so, he conflates views that I have stated with separate arguments by Roy Strong in *Holbein and Henry VIII* and Simon Thurley, "Henry VIII: The Tudor Dynasty and the Church," in Christopher Lloyd and Simon Thurley (eds.), *Henry VIII: Images of a Tudor King* (London: Phaidon Press, 1990), 9–40. Although Walker does lodge persuasive counter-arguments to Strong's claim that the Whitehall Palace mural painted by Hans Holbein the Younger exemplifies a new "use of royal portraiture in England as propaganda in the modern sense of the word" (Strong 44; Walker 75) and Thurley's view that portraits of Henry VIII in Royal Plea Rolls of the 1530s attest to an abrupt break with tradition (Thurley 33, 36; Walker 76–8), he offers no evidence in opposition to my demonstration that the exploitation of biblical typology in portrayals of Henry VIII's newly assumed headship of the Church of England represents a departure from pre-existing iconography. Indeed, iconographical applications of this kind would have made no sense prior to Parliamentary passage of the Act of Supremacy (1534). It is important to note that royal iconography and ceremonial remained profoundly traditional in other areas, as in the case of spectacle and pageantry associated with the coronation and funeral of Henry VIII. See Jennifer Loach, "The Function of Ceremonial in the Reign of Henry VIII," *Past and Present* 142 (1994), 43–68.

5. Strong, *Holbein and Henry VIII*, 14. See also J. B. Trapp and Hubertus S. Herbrüggen, *"The King's Good Servant": Sir Thomas More, 1477/8–1535* (London: National Portrait Gallery, 1977), no. 144.

6. Guido Latré, "The 1535 Coverdale Bible and Its Antwerp Origins," in Orlaith O'Sullivan and Ellen N. Herron (eds.), *The Bible as Book: The Reformation* (London: The British Library and Oak Knoll Press, 2000), 89–102.

7. Susan Foister, "Holbein, Hans, The Younger," *ODNB* (online edition).

8. Tatiana C. String claims that Miles Coverdale commissioned this title page as an appeal for royal approval in "Henry VIII's Illuminated 'Great Bible'," *Journal of the Warburg and Courtauld Institutes* 59 (1996), 319. It is by no means certain, however, that Coverdale functioned as a publisher who invested capital in the publication of this book. According to David Daniel an Antwerp merchant named Jacob Van Meteren, who engaged in trade with England, sponsored this project (*ODNB*). Greg Walker rightly indicates that Coverdale's dedication represented "an attempt rather to prompt and pre-empt royal policy on biblical translation than to follow it" (*Persuasive Fictions*, 85). He asserts that the title page functions as a petition for royal assent to publication of this Bible, in the manner of a traditional dedication portrait, and also adduces evidence that Cromwell underwrote this venture (87, 97n34). Given Cromwell's prior patronage of both Coverdale and Holbein, and his collaboration with Cranmer in attempting to secure royal approval for publication and dissemination of an English Bible, it seems plausible that the

king's chief minister and vicegerent for religious affairs played a central role in this venture.

9. Alec Ryrie, "Divine Kingship and Royal Theology in Henry VIII's Reformation," *Reformation* 7 (2002), 54.

10. Christopher Haigh, *The English Reformations: Religion, Politics, and Society under the Tudors* (Oxford: Clarendon Press, 1993), 14, and passim.

11. This "image … was to be a definitive one for the Tudor and Stuart Kings" according to Strong, *Holbein and Henry VIII*, 14.

12. On the medieval origins of praising monarchs as recollections of David or Solomon and the relationship of these *topoi* to the figure of the Sword and the Book, see King, *Tudor Royal Iconography*, 56–7, 60. As a variation of the *Tolle Lege*, the conventional scene in which Christ confers keys upon Peter and a book symbolic of the scriptures upon Paul, Holbein's image portrays David as an implicit "replacement of Peter, obviously out of favour on account of his association with the Papacy," according to Pamela Tudor-Craig, "Henry VIII and King David," in Daniel Williams (ed.), *Early Tudor England: Proceedings of the 1987 Harlaxton Symposium* (Woodbridge: Boydell Press, 1989), 193. On the association of Davidic iconography with reformist or Protestant rulers, see Edward A. Gosselin, *The King's Progress to Jerusalem: Some Interpretations of David during the Reformation Period and Their Patristic and Medieval Background*, Humana Civilitas: Sources and Studies Relating to the Middle Ages and the Renaissance, vol. II (Malibu: Undena Publications, 1976), 67–8; Anne Lake Prescott, "Musical Strains: Marot's Double Role as Psalmist and Courtier," in Marie-Rose Logan and Peter L. Rudnytsky (eds.), *Contending Kingdoms* (Detroit: Wayne State University Press, 1991); and her "Evil Tongues at the Court of Saul: The Renaissance David as a Slandered Courtier," *Journal of Medieval and Renaissance Studies* 21 (1991), 163–86.

13. Although he emphasizes classical antecedents, Roy Strong acknowledges the "overtly reformist" bias of the iconography of the title page of the Coverdale Bible (*Holbein and Henry VIII*, 14–16). For centuries the sword had symbolized the monarchical claim to independence from clerical overlordship (see Koebner, "Imperial Crown," 37).

14. The repeated claims of Greg Walker to the contrary, earlier formulations of arguments presented in the present essay lodged no claim that coterie works at the royal court functioned within a "royal propaganda machine" aimed at the public at large. See his *Persuasive Fictions*, 93, and passim.

15. See King, *Tudor Royal Iconography*, fig. 10.

16. Roy Strong, *Tudor and Jacobean Portraits*, 2 vols., National Portrait Gallery catalogue (London: Her Majesty's Stationery Office, 1969), I, 158; II, pl. 299. See also Strong, *Holbein and Henry VIII*, 8; and Trapp and Herbrüggen, *King's Good Servant*, no. 202.

17. String observes that this is the outstanding visual "statement of Henry's Royal Supremacy" in "Henry VIII's Illuminated 'Great Bible'," 319.

18. Richard Rex, "The Crisis of Obedience: God's Word and Henry's Reformation," *Historical Journal* 39 (1996), 889–90, et seq.

19. On a like-minded strategy of Davidic praise under Elizabeth I, see Margaret P. Hannay, *Philip's Phoenix: Mary Sidney, Countess of Pembroke* (Oxford: Oxford University Press, 1990), 91–5.

20. Catherine Parr, *The lamentacion of a sinner* (1547), sig. E1r–v. RSTC 4827.

21. BL, MS Royal 2 A. XVI. According to King, *Tudor Royal Iconography*, 76 and n. 21, this manuscript predates the fifth session of the Reformation Parliament (1534), which ratified England's break from the Church of Rome with the Act of Supremacy; Henry VIII's marginalia postdate that session. Tudor-Craig argues that "Henry VIII's Psalter" is a *c.* 1540 manuscript that entered the royal library in early 1542, "two months after he had heard of Queen Catherine Howard's infidelities, and thirty-seven days before her execution" ("Henry VIII and King David," 194). She weakens her case, however, with a questionable identification of this Latin manuscript as the "psalter in Englishe and Latyne covered w[i]th crimoysyn satyne" that may be dated by reference to a royal inventory (p. 193). It seems unlikely that the miniature for Psalm 82 (Vulg. Ps. 81; fol. 98v) in Mallard's psalter, a presentation manuscript expressly designed for Henry VIII, would portray God wearing a papal tiara as late as 1540, years after the king led England into schism from the Church of Rome. It remains possible, however, that Henry entered some or all of his marginalia into MS Royal 2 A. XVI as late as 1542. Tudor-Craig rightly notes that Jean Mallard served in the royal household in 1540–1 as "orator in the French tongue" (p. 196). She and I agree that Mallard's styling of Henry VIII as David is aligned with the envisionment of the king that flourished in England between 1534 and 1539.

22. On the earlier portrayal of François Ier as David, see Tudor-Craig, "Henry VIII and King David," 197 and n. 62.

23. Greg Walker collapses together separate arguments concerning public and private portrayals of the king when he claims that scholars have "read the Psalter as furthering the iconographic glorification of the King begun by Holbein" and that it is difficult to envision the miniature for Psalm 1 "as contributing to a cult of Henry the magnificent, still less to see it as part of a campaign of visual propaganda" in *Persuasive Fictions*, 80.

24. Scarisbrick, *Henry VIII*, 15–16.

25. See Puttenham's *The Arte of English Poesie*, in G. G. Smith (ed.), *Elizabethan Critical Essays*, 2 vols. (Oxford: Clarendon Press, 1904), II, 17. On the corresponding, albeit more sophisticated role of Clément Marot at the court of François Ier, see Prescott, "Musical Strains."

26. Yet another miniature, that for Psalm 27 (Vulg. Ps. 26), portrays King Henry as David slaying Goliath (see Tudor-Craig, "Henry VIII and King David," 197). See below for discussion of Henry Parker's application of this figure to the king's conflict with the papacy in a 1534 manuscript dedication.

27. "Henry is himself the Blessed Man" of Psalm 1:1 according to Tudor-Craig, "Henry VIII and King David," 197.

28. Portrayal of "David in penance" in the miniature for Psalm 69 points toward a cleavage between respective portrayals of Henry VIII and François Ier in Mallard's psalter and a French book of hours (see Tudor-Craig, "Henry VIII

and King David," 198). Although Bathsheba is portrayed in close proximity to François in his prayer book, she appears in no illustration for MS Royal 2 A. XVI, possibly because the story of David and Bathsheba suggested too close an analogy to Henry's troubled marital life.

29. Hannay, *Philip's Phoenix*, 91.

30. Allan G. Chester (ed.), *Select Sermons of Hugh Latimer* (Charlottesville: University Press of Virginia for the Folger Shakespeare Library, 1968), 79. Edward's pre-coronation pageantry associates the Davidic Henry with "hethen rites and detestable idolatrye" when ancient Truth proclaims to Henry's heir: "Then shall England, committed to your gard, / rejoyce in God, which hath geven her nation, / after old David, a yonge kynge Salomon." Quoted from John Gough Nichols (ed.), *Literary Remains of King Edward the Sixth*, 2 vols. (London: Roxburghe Club, 1857), I, ccxci.

31. Alistair Fox, *Politics and Literature in the Reigns of Henry VII and Henry VIII* (Oxford: Basil Blackwell, 1989), 280–5.

32. Stephen Greenblatt, *Renaissance Self-Fashioning: From More to Shakespeare*, (Chicago: University of Chicago Press, 1980), 115, 121. Alexandra Halasz contends that Wyatt's psalms point "toward political allegory" in "Wyatt's David," *Texas Studies in Language and Literature*, 30 (1988), 342. On the vexed issue of dating Wyatt's Penitential Psalms, see R. A. Rebholz (ed.), *Sir Thomas Wyatt: The Complete Poems* (New Haven: Yale University Press, 1981), 455–6.

33. Henry Howard, earl of Surrey, *Poems*, ed. Emrys Jones (Oxford: Clarendon Press, 1964), no. 31 ("The great Macedon that out of Perse chasyd"). The note on lines 13–14 mentions the possibility of "covert allusion to Henry VIII." This poem was inserted into BL, MS Egerton 2711, as a preface to Wyatt's holograph text of his version Penitential Psalms (Halasz, "Wyatt's David," 320 and n. 1).

34. E.g., CUL, MS Dd. 7. 3, fol. 295v.

35. See King, *Tudor Royal Iconography*, fig. 18.

36. *Holbein and the Court of Henry VIII*, The Queen's Gallery exhibition catalogue (London: Buckingham Palace, 1978), no. 88.

37. Michael Levey, *Painting at Court* (New York: New York University Press, 1971), 95 and fig. 77. The Latin text from II Chronicles 9:7–8 reads: "Beati viri tui et beati servi hi tui qui assistant coram te omni t[em]p[or]e et avdivnt sapientiam tuam. Sit dominus deus benedictvs, cui complacit in te, ut poneret te super thronvm, vt esses rex constitutvs domino deo tvo." See *Holbein and the Court of Henry VIII*, no. 88. This entry mistakenly claims that this Holbein miniature is "the first known example of Solomon being given a contemporary likeness in such a representation." For discussion of the earlier portrayal of Henry as Solomon in a stained-glass window at King's College Chapel at Cambridge University, see King, *Tudor Royal Iconography*, 85–9.

CHAPTER 3

The legacy of Henry VIII

Dale Hoak

Henry VIII is the first person in English history whose visage has become universally well known, thanks to reproductions of Hans Holbein's portraits of him. The most familiar of these is the image of a bejeweled, richly clothed king striking an aggressively proud, bold-legged stance, a theatrical, artificial pose which the king himself chose in 1537 as part of what he intended as the supreme artistic statement of his reign, a mural of the Tudor dynasty for the south wall of the Privy Chamber at Whitehall (frontispiece).[1] The king's collaboration in the composition of Holbein's mural should put us on guard: after more than four and a half centuries, Henry VIII is still manipulating the perception of his official persona. This is, of course, one of his legacies, the shaping of an iconic image of his kingship, an image which, thanks to the proliferation of numerous contemporary copies, quickly acquired the status of a stereotype.

How this artistic legacy affects the way we remember Henry VIII is itself a complex and important historical problem. But the question of Henry's legacy begs another that must first be resolved: by what criteria – by whose criteria – should we judge him? This chapter approaches the problem from three angles. The first part of the essay traces two aspects of political and cultural "modernity" to the decade of the 1530s. The second part takes "magnificence" as a measure of the way Henry VIII and his contemporaries would have judged both the king and his court, especially during the first two decades of his reign. The third section considers how the familiar record of his behavior as king – his wars, marriages, and judicial murders, for example – should be understood as expressions of character traits that remained consistent throughout his reign. What deductions might twenty-first-century observers draw from Henry's actions, and what do those tell us about his legacy? In the concluding section I return to the Whitehall mural of 1537 for an assessment of what Henry himself believed was his greatest legacy.

"MODERNITY"

J. J. Scarisbrick concluded his magisterial study of the king with the statement that Henry's reign "left deeper marks on the mind, heart, and face
of England than did any event in English history between the coming of
the Normans and the coming of the factory."[2] Two of those "marks" were
the break with Rome and the dissolution of the monasteries, both of which
are said to have furthered England's transition to political and cultural
"modernity."

   The politically modern state was the product of three interconnected
developments, legal, financial, and technological. A modern state claims in
law an absolute sovereignty over its subjects or citizens. Two of Henry VIII's
parliamentary statutes together defined such sovereignty, the Act in Restraint
of Appeals (1533) and the Act of Supremacy (1534). Sir Thomas More's trial of
July 1535 underscored the significance of that definition: More was a martyr
not to freedom of "conscience" but to the supremacy of the laws of Henry's
"imperial" monarchy.[3]

   A modern polity is also bureaucratically organized; it identifies its citizens
by number, collecting, storing, and manipulating data relating to them on
a statistical basis. From the state's point of view, the most important type
of data is a person's tax liability. Although Henry VIII's England was
obviously not a tax-collecting bureaucracy, Wolsey's innovative tax schemes
of the 1520s pointed in that direction. The cardinal's taxes on incomes and
possessions, spelled out in a series of parliamentary subsidies, hit every adult
in the country.[4] Administratively, the assessment and collection of those
taxes anticipated the statistically based methods of Sir William Petty's
"political arithmetic" of the 1660s.

   Wolsey's subsidies were driven by the cost and timing of Henry VIII's
first two wars against France; in Western Europe the drive towards political
modernity was chiefly a product of the exigencies of warfare and its costly
technologies. Technologically advanced states are permanently armed; their
standing police and military forces give them, vis-à-vis their subjects, a
virtual monopoly of the means of violence. Although the economy of Tudor
England was still that of a traditional society, Henry VIII's navy, numbering
thirty ships by 1514, was the first standing military force of its kind in the
West. His flagship, the 1,500-ton *Henry Imperial*, was launched in February
or March 1513 at a cost of £8,000. Renamed the *Henry Grace à Dieu*, it
"was the most powerful warship the world had ever seen."[5] The appointment in 1537 of Sir John Dudley as vice-admiral "for the keeping of the
seas" represented a "new departure" in peacetime naval strategy, one of

"long-term significance." Dudley's creation of the Council of Marine Causes (1545–6) put the Henrician naval revolution on a permanent administrative footing.[6]

A very different measure of modernity comprehends mentality: modern persons exhibit an essentially materialist, skeptical outlook on the world, which is to say that they do not accept supernatural explanations of everyday events. Two aspects of Henry VIII's Reformation, Cromwell's injunctions to the clergy of 1538 and the dissolution of the monasteries, helped dissolve traditional attitudes toward the supernatural. Cromwell's injunctions rendered relics and religious images "superstitious"; by destroying the rationale for monastic endowments – the singing of masses for the souls of deceased donors – the dissolution undercut belief in purgatory.[7]

Locating the origins of political and cultural modernity in Henry VIII's England is, however, a product of historical hindsight which runs the risk of anachronism, as none of our terms of analysis would have made any sense to contemporaries. If we wish to understand Henry VIII, the better approach is to grasp the king's own self-conscious preoccupations at the outset of his reign, his insistent desire to display the magnificence of his person and court and to achieve in war the honor and glory that he believed was his due.

MAGNIFICENCE

Although born in an era that witnessed a great Renaissance of letters, Henry VIII was in reality "the last of the troubadours and the heir of Burgundian chivalry."[8] None the less, by intelligence, taste, and training, and in the record of his princely pursuits, the king well fulfilled Castiglione's prescription for the accomplished courtier: one has only to consider the extraordinary range of Henry's ability in music and theology, dancing, tennis, and disguising, the arts of conversing and writing well in French and Latin, not to mention his remarkable athleticism and skill in shooting, riding, and wrestling. Henry excelled at feats of arms on foot and horseback. His breathtaking equestrian performances were up to modern Olympic standards. In the company of foreign princes, prelates, and ambassadors he clearly exhibited what contemporaries prized most highly, a noble "courtesy."

Henry also understood the requirements of princely magnificence, and in this he followed the formula Sir John Fortescue had set down in *The Governance of England* (1470–1), an advice book written for Edward IV in reaction to Henry VI's impoverished display, especially his notoriously shabby attire. A magnificent prince, Fortescue had written, must "bie hym

[self] riche clothes, riche furres" ... [and] "rich stones."[9] Court dress was of the greatest importance to Henry VIII, for he knew that costly attire was central to royal image-making. In order to project an illusion of personal grandeur, a truly magnificent king must clothe himself in the finest fabrics, jewels, and furs.

What is remarkable about Henry VIII is not only his early self-awareness of the significance of court dress, but also how swiftly as king he exploited the illusionistic potential of royal attire in promoting the "cult" of sacred kingship he had inherited from his father. Consider the semi-religious spectacle of his coronation in June 1509. Henry VIII's anointing and crowning required that he wear vestments which, because they were holy relics, invested him with priest-like qualities and associated him symbolically with Edward the Confessor's sainthood. In his burning jewels, crimson silks, and cloth of gold, Henry VIII at his coronation became, at the age of eighteen, a sacred, living icon, a moment marking what Roy Strong has rightly termed the young king's "epiphany."[10] Henry VIII's consciousness of this rendered him charismatic in a way that transcended even his magnificence, as the reaction of others soon indicated. "His Highness does not seem a person of this world, but one descended from Heaven," gasped an awe-struck foreigner in 1513.[11]

If Henry VII can be said to have inaugurated a "theater" of Tudor majesty, Henry VIII took the development of this type of royalist political drama to new heights. Diplomatic receptions in the Presence Chamber were carefully staged in order to present the magnificently attired young king to foreign ambassadors in the most visually striking, dramatic way. An early example is the reception of the Venetian, Piero Pasqualigo, at Richmond Palace on April 23, 1515, a reception scheduled to coincide with the installation of the knights of the Garter in order "to render it more pompous." Pasqualigo beheld Henry "leaning against his gilt throne" beneath a Florentine canopy of cloth of gold, "the most costly thing I ever witnessed." The king wore a purple velvet mantle; a French bonnet of crimson velvet, its brim looped with gold lacets and gold enameled tags; a doublet of white and crimson satin (striped "in the Swiss fashion"); and scarlet hose "all slashed from the knee upwards." Around his neck was a gold collar "from which there hung a round-cut diamond, the size of the largest walnut I ever saw." Henry's hand lay on a dagger sheathed in cloth of gold; his fingers were a "mass of jeweled rings."[12]

By 1519 such reports had established Henry VIII's reputation as "the best dressed sovereign in the world"; his clothes, reported another Venetian, Sebastiano Justinian, were "the richest and most superb that can be imagined."[13] Henry was able to admire a reflection of the richly clothed figure that Pasqualigo and Justinian described, for there was no room or closet, it seems, in any of the royal palaces without a looking-glass of some kind: the king owned more than two hundred mirrors of all types and sizes, hand-held, framed, and standing.[14] Had he admired himself in a standing mirror before posing for Holbein's Whitehall mural?[15]

Henry VIII's consumption of costly attire was part of what Sydney Anglo called "a policy of deliberate ostentation."[16] In respect of the king's clothes, it was a policy that came at a staggering price. In a typical year Henry VIII spent at least £3,000 for court dress and often more – £8,335 in 1511–12 and £7,263 in 1542–3 – or roughly £173,000 for the whole of his thirty-eight-year reign. By contrast, he paid his tailor, John Malt, a salary of £18 5s a year.[17]

Luxurious dress was only one aspect of Henry VIII's desire to impress foreign envoys with the wealth of his court. The policy also required magnificent entertainment, which usually meant a tournament accompanied by elaborate "disguisings." Such types of merriment had occasionally been staged at Henry VII's court. Henry VIII's accession witnessed a spectacular, sustained outburst of such activities and more: until the late 1520s, *every* major event at court – a christening, ambassadorial reception, or celebration of the signing of a treaty, for example – was marked by a major entertainment of *unprecedented* cost and splendor.[18] And at the center of these entertainments was England's magnificent young king, proudly displaying unsurpassed energy and skill as combatant, singer, dancer, and musician.

Anglo has described the tournament as a complex, multiform spectacle that combined over a period of two or three days combat on foot and horseback; pageants of portable scenery, including (until they were abandoned after 1512) great wheeled cars painted to resemble ships or fountains or castles, astonishing contraptions akin to modern-day floats; music, both vocal and instrumental; poetry recited by actors; a dramatic presentation in the form of a debate or mock argument between two speakers; intricate dancing, some of it performed by companies of skilled amateurs (the forerunner of *ballet de cour*); and a lavish banquet.[19]

Eye-witness accounts of the pageants accompanying Henry VIII's early tournaments testify not only to his success in projecting to an elite audience the magnificence of his court but also in binding his ordinary subjects to his monarchy. The scenes of revelry at Whitehall Palace on February 12, 1511 following a pageant to which commoners had been admitted would have been inconceivable in an earlier reign. Henry allowed Londoners of the "rude" sort playfully to rip off his expensive clothes into which the most costly souvenirs had been sewn – 887 pieces of gold. Stripped down to his doublet and hose, the rambunctious nineteen-year-old king retreated to his chambers, where, over wine, he laughed off his losses, saying they were but for "honor, and larges." The people picked up his unmistakable signal. There had never been such a king of England: crowds of 25,000 and 50,000 thronged the tournaments of May Day 1515 and July 1, 1517 to catch a glimpse of their astonishing king, who, having returned victorious from French lists and sieges in 1513, had achieved in English eyes the status of an international super-star.[20]

Henry VIII's striking success in using court spectacle and pageantry to win the adulation of his subjects so quickly, a success apparently without parallel among princes of his era, was explained by Robert Fabyan, wealthy cloth merchant, former master of the Draper's Company, alderman, and sometime sheriff of London. Fabyan witnessed the tournament and pageantry of February 12–13, 1511. A seasoned, hard-headed man of business who had been "at the forefront of civic affairs" for almost forty years, Fabyan was not given to exaggeration or hyperbole. There were two significant reasons, he thought, why the spectacle of February 1511 was the finest that had ever been seen in England. First was the "excellency of the king's person," which surpassed that of every English monarch before him. Second was "the exceeding cost" of the pageant cars, pavilions, and costumes, which topped £20,000.[21] The MS Great Tournament Roll of Westminster, specially painted on the occasion, preserves something of the magnificence of the spectacle described by Fabyan (Figure 4).[22]

Fortescue had also said that a magnificent prince must "make new bildynges" and "bie rich hangynges and other apparel ffor his howses," not only for his own pleasure but also in order to entertain foreign guests in splendor.[23] For the reception of the French ambassadors who arrived at Greenwich Palace on May 5, 1527 to sign the treaty of Westminster, Henry built a special banqueting house and theater as part of the Greenwich tiltyard complex. Artistically, the Greenwich reception was the most brilliant and original of the early Tudor court spectacles. Taken together, the jousts, banquet, and disguisings held on Monday, May 6, were the most lavish ever mounted in Renaissance England.[24]

The walls of the banqueting house were hung with a set of ten Flemish tapestries that Henry had ordered from Brussels for the special pavilion built at Guines in 1520 on the Field of Cloth of Gold. More than any other form of Renaissance art, tapestry, as Thomas Campbell has shown, projected the majesty of royal magnificence. This dazzling set, illustrating the life of David and woven with gold and silk and showing patterned flowers of silver satin on a ground of cloth of gold, was described in 1527 by Gasparo Spinelli, the Venetian ambassador, as "the most costly tapestry in England." In fact, the tapestries making up this set were among the finest and most costly ever woven. Although Henry's artistic taste ran the gamut from metalwork to jewelry and painting, he took special pride in the decorations of the banqueting house, ordering that the tapestries be left hanging for several days so that people might appreciate the magnificence of his court, "a vivid demonstration of the king's self-conscious display" of the unmatched splendor of the house of Tudor. If tapestries be taken as the truest measure of such display, it was magnificence beyond compare: Henry VIII's collection of 2,450 tapestry wall hangings was the greatest ever assembled by any human being in history.[25]

Henry VIII had already won renown for his elaborate, showy banquets, and the one served to the French in the new banqueting house on May 6, 1527 confirmed what the papal nuncio, Chieregato, had reported in July 1517, that all of the wealth and civility of Europe seemed to be on display at Henry's feasts. In 1527 the chronicler Hall remembered the great cupboards in the banqueting house, each groaning under the weight of huge standing cups and bowls and flagons and pots "all of fyne gold" or silver, and all for display only. Chieregato too had been stunned by the vast treasure littering Henry's table, "all the small platters used for table-service … the dishes, basins, plates, saltcellars, and goblets … all of pure gold."[26]

Following the great banquet of May 6, 1527 Henry's French guests were led to the disguising house, where, over their heads, they would have been treated to the artistic spectacle of Holbein's remarkable ceiling, a tour de force of theatrical cosmography. Covering the entire surface of an area perhaps as large as 110 by 30 feet was a representation on painted cloth of "the whole earth enuironed with the Sea, like a very Mappe or Carte." Suspended beneath this was another cloth, apparently a filmy, translucent scrim on which Holbein had carefully positioned representations of the constellations and signs of the zodiac, such that viewers below saw "the zodiacke by means of the xii. Signes" superimposed "on the earth and water" of the map above. Exactly how this illusion was achieved remains unclear. Did it, as Susan Foister has speculated, rely on special lighting effects?[27]

The composition of the ceiling, requiring specialized geographical and astronomical knowledge, fell to Holbein's German collaborator, Nicholas Kratzer, the king's astronomer and instrument maker. Holbein's portrait of Kratzer, painted the next year, shows the sitter with instruments Kratzer lent Holbein in 1533 for the artist's double portrait of *The Ambassadors* (see Figure 13). The point about the fruitful collaboration of Holbein and

Kratzer, as Willem Hackmann has noted, is that Kratzer brought to Henry VIII's court in 1521 the most advanced scientific learning and technical arts of the German Renaissance.[28] Although Henry VIII's appreciation of those arts was conditioned by their military application – he certainly possessed a professional's grasp of military engineering and cartography, for example – his collection of globes, maps, charts, and "Instrumentes of Astronomye" suggests his serious interest in contemporary cosmography.[29]

MARRIAGE, TERROR, AND WAR

If Henry VIII set an exceptionally high standard of courtly conduct, at least in contemporary terms, what of his character? Henry's marriages – why he married and how he dealt with marital failure – arguably reveal much about his personality. David Starkey observed that Henry's motives for marrying were highly unusual for a king – "love, and an insistent, child-like desire to be happy." Henry took his marriages seriously, expecting them to make him happy, and when they "made him unhappy, he wanted out." In this respect, Henry's "attitude was curiously modern." And, unlike previous royal marriages, all of Henry's were conducted in private, as Starkey noted. Although Henry VIII's marriages had public, political consequences, he refused to see them in other than private, personal terms.[30]

Starkey's observations are important, for they point to several debilitating aspects of Henry's character, his willful self-deception and self-pity: these were his responses to marital failure, reactions that led him to divorce Catherine of Aragon and destroy Anne Boleyn and Catherine Howard. The anger that sprang from self-pity often transformed him; without warning he suddenly became a petulant bully, ordering the beheading, hanging, or burning of anyone who he felt had betrayed his trust or rightful demands. The record of those he destroyed by judicial murder runs like a red, spreading stain across the whole of his reign. The list includes two of his wives and one of the most able royal servants of the whole century, Thomas Cromwell; his lord chancellor, Thomas More, one of the most celebrated men of European letters; John Fisher, the first bishop in English history to be executed for treason; a duke, a marquess, an earl, a countess, a viscount, a viscountess, and four barons. Hundreds more were dispatched for their resistance to the royal supremacy: Geoffrey Elton calculated that of 883 persons accused under the laws of treason between 1532 and 1540, 308 were executed,[31] a number that does not include untold others executed by martial law for their rebellion against royal authority.

It is sometimes thought that at court, the pattern of Henry's destructive behavior against his wives, courtiers, and royal officers was first set in May 1521 with the execution of Henry Stafford, duke of Buckingham. In fact the king's capacity to destroy others was revealed at the outset of his reign, when he was persuaded by the members of his father's council, all of whom were now his own advisers, to order the arrest of Sir Richard Empson and Edmund Dudley on trumped-up charges of treason. The accused were victims of a conspiracy hatched without Henry's knowledge; the ringleaders of the conspiracy had discovered that concealed beneath Henry's bonhomie and learning lay a strain of monstrous cruelty that masked a deep insecurity. By exploiting this weakness, they were able to bend him to their purpose and will, convincing him (in August 1510) that he must sign writs for Empson and Dudley's beheading.[32] The timing of this action is instructive: it came without warning amidst the most pleasurable distractions of the king's first summer progress. After signing the writs as requested, Henry resumed his carefree rounds of dancing and feasting and "huntyng, hawkyng and shotyng."[33]

Does Henry VIII's willful, occasionally unpredictable destruction of so many persons describe the actions of a tyrant? Some of Henry's subjects certainly said so, as government sources show. By 1538 Henry's official apologists were defending him against anyone "who can fynd in his hart … to think … [the king] a tyrant."[34] Never mind that Henry cloaked his tyranny in the mantle of the law. *Terror* underlay "thadministracion of [his] Justice vnder the Law," as Sir William Paget averred in 1549. Paget was Henry VIII's secretary of state and confidant and one of those closest to the king at the time of his death. When Henry died Paget helped organize the coup that made the duke of Somerset England's Lord Protector. In the summer of 1549, when Somerset's government faced massive popular rebellions, Paget reminded the duke how Henry VIII had dealt with popular resistance. Not with leniency and sympathy, but "by force and terrour." Under King Henry, wrote Paget, dissension "was by feare kept in and constrayned." This lesson Henry "had learned of his father." Hence, "at the furst sturre" of rebellion, the right way, following the example of Henry VIII, was to strike down the leaders "to the terrour" of others. "By this meanes youe shall be dradde" [dreaded].[35]

Henry VIII followed up his suppression of the insurrections of 1536–7 with measures designed to integrate the region north of the River Trent more fully into his realm. These moves, like the assimilation of Wales in the Acts of Union of 1536 and the imposition of royal authority in Ireland, have traditionally been seen as *unrelated* developments "arising out of

Henry VIII's centralizing policies in response to the Reformation crisis." In fact, as Steven Ellis has shown, the origins of Henrician governmental policy in the Tudor "frontiers" are to be found in the king's paranoid fear, visible in mid-1534, that "disaffected nobles" in Ireland, Wales, and the North were plotting against him. If administratively and legally, the result by 1540 was more centralized rule from London, the achievement left a fateful legacy. In Ireland, Henry's arrest of the earl of Kildare sparked a rebellion which, although crushed, ignited a slow-burning war of Gaelic resistance. This war persuaded the governments of Edward VI and Elizabeth I to embark on a ruinous policy of conquest and colonization.[36]

If there can no longer be any doubt that Henry VIII was "the greatest of … English … tyrants," there is as yet no systematic study of the political and cultural effects of Henrician "terror," though Greg Walker has shown how the literature produced by court office-holders reflected the authors' adaptation to a regime of fear and intimidation.[37] In this regard, English political life changed fundamentally after Henry VIII's death. By 1558, after the depredations of Northumberland's regime (1549–53) and Mary I's burnings (1555–8), no English monarch practiced government by terror. Whatever else one might say of Elizabeth I – despite her willingness to use force on a scale of which her father would have approved[38] – terror born of fear was not an instrument of her rule.

Ultimately, the human and material costs of Henry's destructiveness are to be measured by his French wars of 1512–13, 1522–4, and 1544, all of them the expression of his chivalric pride. War enabled him to display his magnificence; he thought of his first French war "as a large-scale dramatic entertainment with Europe as its *mise en scène*."[39] War was also a matter of honor: a prince's true glory was to be won in war. It has been said that Renaissance monarchies were essentially "machines built for the battle-field,"[40] and in this respect Henry's monarchy was no different than that of Francis I or Charles V. The distinctive political culture of English king-ship also shaped Henry's attitude towards war: war-making in pursuit of the crown of France was his *raison d'être*, and had it not been for the distraction of the first divorce case he probably would have tried to invade France again in the early 1530s.[41]

At eighteen Henry had begun talking of war and preparing for it in feats of arms on the mock-battlefields of his palace tiltyards: the great tourna-ment of February 1511 was really a dress rehearsal for his invasion of France in 1513. Thanks to his boundless self-pride, the MS Great Tournament Roll of Westminster preserves in the scenes of Henry jousting a unique work of art which is indispensable for the study of his early kingship: it is

Figure 4. A live-action "snapshot" of Henry VIII jousting in full armor on February 12, 1511 in the tournament held at Westminster Palace, February 12–13, in celebration of the birth of his short-lived son. The king fights as the good knight, *Cueur Loyal*, before his lady, the queen, whose red-gold scarf he wears attached to his helmet. (The combatants' silver-white armor has blackened with age.) Catherine is shown seated beneath a golden canopy in a castle-like pavilion, an ornate viewing gallery covered with tapestries and cloth of gold and decorated with royal badges. Flanking her are ladies and gentlemen of the court, all, like the liveried footmen in the foreground, wearing heavy gold chains. The artist has sought to portray Henry at the most dramatic possible moment, just as he has scored a perfect hit by breaking his lance on an opponent's helmet. The queen applauds his feat.

"the chivalric self-portrait" that he "wished to bequeath to posterity" (Figure 4).[42]

Henry never let go of the image of himself as the all-conquering, would-be warrior of 1511–13. In 1527 he commissioned Holbein to paint on canvas a huge picture of his victory over Louis XII at the battle of Thérouanne in 1513. This canvas, now lost, decorated one side of the great arch separating the Greenwich banqueting house from a gallery leading to the disguising house. After the banquet of May 6, 1527, Henry pointedly invited his French guests to study the painting. Their reactions have gone unrecorded. Did they humor Henry in his vain belief that at Thérouanne he had relived the glory of Henry V at Agincourt? By 1527 Henry's "Great Enterprise" in France lay in ruin. But no matter: when, obese and tottering, he invaded France for a third time in 1544 he commissioned two enormous paintings of episodes in the campaigns of 1513, including one of *The Battle of the Spurs*, evidence (if one needed it) of by how much Henry VIII still dreamed of war as youthful chivalry.[43]

Henry's war-making in pursuit of glory was inextricably linked to the dissolution of the monasteries. It was only the wealth of the abbeys, after all, that enabled him to return to war in 1544, a war that left the Crown virtually bankrupt at the time of his death in 1547. Lansdowne Charter 14 in the British Library is a manuscript roll listing every ha'penny that Henry VIII spent from his secret treasury at Westminster Palace during the period of the third French war. It shows that of the colossal sums Henry diverted from the abbeys directly into his own coffers – the total ran to just over £246,000 – he spent nearly half on garrisons and "Ingynes made for Warre," and this is not counting the money that flowed out of other royal treasuries for military purposes.[44] Persuaded that he must shore up his defenses against a possible invasion of Franco-Imperial armies in 1538–9, he disbursed £376,000 in that year alone on fortifying the south coast, the northern border, and Calais. The result was the greatest system of national fortifications before the industrial era.[45]

Henry's obsession with war is central to an understanding of his reign, as Richard Hoyle has convincingly demonstrated. Henry had wanted to attack Boulogne ever since 1509. He funded the war of 1512–14 from the huge surpluses in Henry VII's privy coffers, and that of 1522–4 almost entirely from extraordinary income. But the financial lesson of 1522–4 had been that loans and subsidies were inadequate for protracted campaigns. The French pension, amounting annually to about one fifth of Henry's ordinary revenues, 1527–33, kept the king afloat after 1527, but surpluses in the coffers were practically nil by 1529, and the pension ceased by 1533. Clerical property became the obvious target; the king's new jurisdiction, the royal supremacy of the crown imperial, allowed him to gain access to it. In short, the financial effects of Henry's first two French wars helped propel him towards his Reformation, a Reformation which rewarded him with the spoils of the abbeys. But by selling off monastic property he destroyed the future financial fortunes of the monarchy, another fateful legacy of his rule. (Such sales were not Cromwell's policy, as John Guy has noted; maximizing the Crown's long-term income was.) Moreover, the debasement of the coinage that masqueraded as war finance in the 1540s brought unemployment, inflation, and finally depression, economic after-shocks of war which with only slight hyperbole one might regard as Henry VIII's "crimes" against the English people.[46]

The dissolution of the monasteries and Henry's investment in war underscore what he did *not* do with his new-found wealth – build hospitals, libraries, and schools, to name only three things that evangelicals and reformers, including Queen Anne Boleyn, had urged him to do. It is true that war-making and the financial demands of royal magnificence, both essential to the pursuit of glory, strained his resources. But Henry VIII's failure to invest in charitable and educational causes on a scale made possible by the dissolution throws into sharper relief the king's undisguised appetite for coin. French diplomats in London called Henry "an old wolf" whose greed for gold was matchless.[47] The inventories taken after his death describe the staggering scale of his avarice and acquisitiveness. The contents of all of the chambers, closets, cupboards, and drawers and storerooms in his sixty palaces show that by 1547 Henry VIII had accumulated more costly things than any king in English history.

ART, FAITH, AND RELIGION

Henry VIII was many things: a romantic who failed in marriage; a cruel bully who was capable of destroying those he loved and most favored; a war-monger who impoverished his subjects and his realm. The mask of royalty was that of a magnificent prince of the Renaissance, a mask that he wore proudly. A final reckoning of the legacy of Henry VIII rests on how he himself wished to be remembered, and for this we possess two artistic images, which if placed together form a royal diptych of sorts. One is the 1511 image of the king at nineteen breaking his lance on an opponent's helmet: here is the knight errant, a living embodiment of Renaissance chivalry (Figure 4). It is the Henry of the first half of the reign. The other image is that of the Tudor colossus in the Whitehall mural, the king of the second half of the reign. It is Henry's own statement of his legacy (frontispiece).

The original mural was destroyed in a fire at Whitehall in 1698 – only Holbein's cartoon of the left-hand section survives, the section showing Henry and his father – but thanks to Remigius van Leemput's copy, which Charles II commissioned in 1667, we have the full text of the Latin inscription which appeared on a stone plinth in the center of the composition (Figure 5). The inscription takes the form of elegiac couplets that Henry either dictated or himself composed (see also String, chapter 7 in this volume). The first verses ask the viewer to look upon the figures of those "illustrious … heroes," Henry VII and Henry VIII; "no painting ever bore greater." "The great question is whether the father or the son" was more victorious, "for both indeed are supreme." Henry VII "overcame his enemies" and extinguished the "fires" of civil war, thereby giving peace to England.

Henry VIII, on the other hand, was "born indeed for greater tasks." He first "removed the unworthy" from "the altar," "the unworthy" being the pope or anyone who had denied the king's new ecclesiastical authority, for what follows hammers home the overpowering, climactic theme of the last four lines:

Figure 5. Hans Holbein's large (*c.* 12 feet × 9 feet) 1537 mural for Henry VIII's Privy Chamber at Whitehall was destroyed by fire in 1698 and so is known now only from a much smaller (88.9 cm. × 98.7 cm.) oil-on-canvas copy made in 1667 for Charles II by Remigius van Leemput, one of Sir Anthony van Dyck's Flemish assistants. Van Leemput's reduced, inferior copy hardly begins to convey the optical power of Holbein's original, which created a stunning *trompe-l'oeil* effect, as if the life-size figures of Henry VIII and Henry VII (on the left) and their queens, Jane Seymour and Elizabeth of York (on the right), actually were standing in front of the southern, end wall of the room. Startled viewers found the effect literally overwhelming. One described Henry VIII as "so lifelike" that he felt "abashed" and "annihilated in his presence," even "stricken with fear."

> The presumption of Popes has yielded to unerring virtue,
> And so long as Henry the Eighth carries the scepter in his hand,
> Religion is renewed, and during his reign
> The doctrines of God have begun to be held in his honor.[48]

There can be no doubt that Henry VIII thought the royal supremacy his greatest achievement: he had restored True Religion to the true church, the Church of England, *his* Church. There exists an important piece of evidence confirming that he intended that church to remain so after his death. This was his exclusion of two of his greatest officers and servants, the duke of Norfolk and Stephen Gardiner, bishop of Winchester, from the regency council he named in his last will and testament. He excluded them because he thought them "much bent to the popish party" and opposed to his "proceedings" in religion, as Paget later reported to John Foxe.[49]

Henry VIII's supremacy outlived him; Queen Elizabeth II is still Supreme Governor of the Church of England, just as she inherited what remains of Henry's palaces, tapestries, and other works of art. But Henry's absolutist pretensions to an "imperial" authority died with him, rejected by Edward VI's councillors in favor of a type of government that was essentially a parliamentary monarchy. Henry himself had unwittingly sown the seeds of such a monarchy: in order to enforce his Reformation, he had grounded the royal supremacy on statute, with the result that his greatest political legacy remains the supremacy not of the monarchy but of parliamentary law.[50]

By 1544–5 religion, as much as the Great Enterprise in France, was still central to Henry VIII's image of himself. The marginal notations in his illuminated psalter show that even as an old man he still identified strongly with the young King David, and that like a David who had taken down the Goliath of Rome, he stood among the righteous whom God would not forsake (see King, chapter 2 in this volume). Or so he thought. In practice, royal religious strategy remained a balancing act reflecting a perilous divide in Henry's own mind. Convinced of his unique relationship with God, he had abandoned purgatory without finding, despite the urgings of Archbishop Thomas Cranmer, an alternative path to salvation.[51] At the end Henry VIII had changed his world irrevocably, as only a king could have done. Thinking he had restored the true church and True Religion, had he lost his own way?

ACKNOWLEDGEMENTS

The author wishes to thank the members of the Bishop James Madison Society (founded 1812) for the honor of their invitation to present this essay as "The Last Lecture" in the Great Hall of the Sir Christopher Wren Building, College of William & Mary, November 12, 2008.

NOTES

1. The original survives as a life-size cartoon, or preparatory drawing, for the lost mural. For discussions of the cartoon and mural, see the following: Susan Foister, *Holbein and England* (New Haven and London: Yale University Press, 2004), 175–96, especially 181–3 and 190–1; Xanthe Brooke and David Crombie,

Henry VIII Revealed: Holbein's Portrait and Its Legacy (London: Paul Holberton, 2004), 23–35; Simon Thurley, *Whitehall Palace: An Architectural History of the Royal Apartments, 1240–1698* (New Haven and London: Yale University Press, 1999), 48–9; Roy Strong, *The Tudor and Stuart Monarchy: Pageantry, Painting, Iconography*, vol. I, *Tudor* (Woodbridge: The Boydell Press, 1995), 1–54, a reprint of Strong, *Holbein and Henry VIII* (London: Routledge & Kegan Paul, 1967); and John Rowlands, *The Paintings of Hans Holbein the Younger* (Boston: David R. Godine, 1985), 224–5. Foister's discussion is now the most authoritative.

2. J. J. Scarisbrick, *Henry VIII* (Berkeley: University of California, 1968).

3. The Act of Appeals (1533: 24 Henry VIII, c. 12) and Act of Supremacy (1534: 26 Henry VIII, c. 1) are printed in *The Statutes of the Realm*, 12 vols. (London: Record Commission, 1810–28), III, 427–9, and III, 492, respectively, and are conveniently extracted in G. R. Elton (ed.), *The Tudor Constitution: Documents and Commentary* (Cambridge: Cambridge University Press, 2nd. edn. 1982), 353–8 and 364–5, respectively.

4. The acts were drafted under Wolsey's supervision by John Hales (d. 1539), a baron of the exchequer from 1522; Roger Schofield, "Taxation and the Political Limits of the Tudor State," in Claire Cross, David Loades, and J. J. Scarisbrick (eds.), *Law and Government under the Tudors. Essays Presented to Sir Geoffrey Elton on His Retirement* (Cambridge: Cambridge University Press, 1988), 232–3.

5. David Loades, *The Tudor Navy: An Administrative, Political and Military History* (Aldershot: Scolar Press, 1992), 62 and 67. Fifteen ships of the royal navy, including the *Henry Grace à Dieu*, appear in the large painting of *c.* 1545 of *Henry VIII's Embarkation at Dover* in 1520 (Royal Collection). The *Henry Grace à Dieu* appears at the head of a unique pictorial survey of the entire navy compiled in 1546: C. S. Knighton and David Loades (eds.), *The Anthony Roll of Henry VIII's Navy. Pepys Library 2991 and British Library Additional MS 22047 with related documents*, ed. C. S. Knighton and D. M. Loades (Aldershot: Ashgate Publishing Company for the Navy Records Society, 2000), 40–1 and 163.

6. David Loades, *John Dudley, Duke of Northumberland 1504–1553* (Oxford: Clarendon Press, 1996), 34.

7. Cromwell's Injunctions of 1538 are printed in Gerald Bray (ed.), *Documents of the English Reformation* (Minneapolis: Fortress Press, 1994), 179–83.

8. Scarisbrick, *Henry VIII*, 16.

9. Sir John Fortescue, *The Governance of England: otherwise called The Difference between an Absolute and a Limited Monarchy*, ed. Charles Plummer (Oxford: Oxford University Press, 1885; reprinted, London: Humphrey Milford, 1926), 125.

10. Roy Strong, *Coronation: A History of Kingship and the British Monarchy* (London: HarperCollins, 2005), 170–1, 211.

11. *Calendar of State Papers and Manuscripts, relating to English affairs, existing in the archives and collections of Venice, and in other libraries of Northern Italy*, ed. Rawdon Brown (London, 1867; reprinted, Nendeln, Liechtenstein: Kraus Reprint, 1970), II, no. 336. Hereafter cited as *CSP Ven.*

12. Piero Pasqualigo to an unknown correspondent, April 30, 1515: *Four Years at the Court of Henry VIII: Selection of Despatches written by the Venetian ambassador, Sebastian Justinian*, ed. and trans. Rawdon Brown, 2 vols. (London: Smith, Elder, and Co., 1854; reprinted, New York: AMS Press, 1970), I, 85–6.

13. Ibid., 313.

14. See the entries under "Mirrors" in David Starkey (ed.), *The Inventory of Henry VIII: The Transcript* (London: Harvey Miller Publishers, 1998).

15. Between the preparatory drawing and the finished mural, Holbein turned Henry's head from a three-quarter pose to a full-faced, frontal one, as if the king were looking straight into a mirror placed where the viewer would be standing. On this change of pose, see Foister, *Holbein and England*, 190–1.

16. Sydney Anglo, *Spectacle, Pageantry and Early Tudor Policy*, 2nd edn. (Oxford: Clarendon Press, 1997), 123.

17. The total for the whole reign is based on my calculation of an annual average of £4,576, which I derived from the list of known royal expenditures, 1511–44, in Maria Hayward, *Dress at the Court of Henry VIII* (Leeds: Maney Publishing, 2007), table 3.2, p. 32.

18. Anglo, *Spectacle*, 123, 108.

19. Ibid., 118, 121–2.

20. *Four Years at the Court of Henry VIII*, I, 79–81 and II, 101–2; *The Great Chronicle of London*, ed. A. H. Thomas and I. D. Thornley (London: George W. Jones, 1938), 374; Edward Hall, *Chronicle*, ed. Henry Ellis (London: J. Johnson, *et al.*, 1809), 519; Sydney Anglo, *The Great Tournament Roll of Westminster* (Oxford: Clarendon Press, 1968), 55–8.

21. *Chronicle of London*, 374; M-R. McLaren, "Fabyan, Robert (d. 1513)," *ODNB*.

22. The manuscript at the College of Arms in London consists of thirty-six painted membranes of vellum almost sixty feet long portraying scenes from the jousts and the closing procession on February 13, 1511. For a discussion of the manuscript and a collotype reproduction, see Anglo, *Great Tournament Roll of Westminster*.

23. Fortescue, *Governance*, 125.

24. For discussions of the Greenwich revels of May 1527 and the banqueting house and disguising house, see Hall, *Chronicle*, 722–3; Foister, *Holbein and England*, 121–8; Anglo, *Spectacle*, 209–24; and David Starkey (ed.), *Henry VIII: A European Court in England* (London: Collins & Brown in association with the National Maritime Museum, Greenwich, 1991), 54–69, a section of pages which contain essays by Susan Foister on "Holbein as Court Painter" (58–63) and Simon Thurley on "The Banqueting and Disguising Houses of 1527" (64–9).

25. Thomas P. Campbell, *Henry VIII and the Art of Majesty: Tapestries at the Tudor Court* (New Haven and London: Yale University Press, 2007), 175 (where Spinelli is quoted) and 317. A virtually identical set of ten tapestries on the David theme which Henry purchased in October 1528 "for the extraordinarily high sum of £1,548" survives at the Musée National de la Renaissance, Château d'Écouen. The set, covering a total of 418 square yards (each tapestry measures about 450 cm. × 815 cm.) constitutes "one of the finest examples in the world of pre-1530 weaving"; photographs of five from the set appear in ibid., figs. 10.5

to 10.10, pp. 178–86. See also Thomas P. Campbell, *Tapestry in the Renaissance: Art and Magnificence* (New York: The Metropolitan Museum of Art; New Haven and London: Yale University Press, 2002).

26. Francesco Chieregato to Isabella d'Este, from London, July 10, 1517: *CSP Ven.*, II, no. 918 (p. 400); Hall, *Chronicle*, 722.

27. Hall, *Chronicle*, 723. On the ceiling of the disguising house see Foister, *Holbein and England*, 123–8; Anglo, *Spectacle*, 217–19; Starkey (ed.), *Henry VIII: A European Court*, 68–9; and Susan Foister, "Holbein's Paintings on Canvas: The Greenwich Festivities of 1527," in Mark Roskell and John Oliver Hand (eds.), *Hans Holbein: Paintings, Prints, and Reception* (Washington, DC: National Gallery of Art, 2001), 109–24, especially 111–12.

28. Willem Hackmann, "Nicholas Kratzer: The King's Astronomer and Renaissance Instrument-Maker," in Starkey (ed.), *Henry VIII: A European Court*, 70–3; Günther Oestmann, "Kratzer, Nicholaus (b. 1486/7, d. after 1550)," *ODNB*. On Kratzer and Holbein, see John North, *The Ambassadors' Secret: Holbein and the World of the Renaissance* (London and New York: Hambledon and London, 2002).

29. Henry possessed at least ten terrestrial and celestial globes and spheres of metal, paper or "paste": Starkey (ed.), *Inventory of Henry VIII*, no. 15420 ("a rounde Globe of thole wourlde"), for example.

30. David Starkey, *Six Wives: The Queens of Henry VIII* (London: Chatto and Windus, 2003), xxviii, 6–8.

31. G. R. Elton, *Policy and Police: The Enforcement of the Reformation in the Age of Thomas Cromwell* (Cambridge: Cambridge University Press, 1972), 388–400, especially 389.

32. This paragraph outlines the thesis set out in "The Downfall of Empson and Dudley," a chapter in my *Henry VIII* (forthcoming, Palgrave Macmillan). It is based chiefly on *The Anglica Historia of Polydore Vergil*, ed. and trans. Dennis Hay (London: Camden Society, 3rd ser., vol. LXXIV, 1950), 131, 151–3; Hall, *Chronicle*, 502, 503, 505, 515; S. J. Gunn, "The Accession of Henry VIII," *Historical Research* 64 (1991), 279–88; S. J. Gunn, "Dudley, Edmund (c. 1462–1510)," *ODNB*; and M. M. Condon, "Empson, Sir Richard (c. 1450–1510)," *ODNB*.

33. Hall, *Chronicle*, 515.

34. Quoted from TNA, SP 1/143, fo. 9v, in G. W. Bernard, "The Tyranny of Henry VIII," in G. W. Bernard and S. J. Gunn (eds.), *Authority and Consent in Tudor England: Essays presented to C. S. L. Davies* (Aldershot: Ashgate, 2002), 114.

35. Paget's words quoted here are from confidential letters he wrote to Somerset on December 25, 1548, and July 7 and August 28, 1549; Northamptonshire Record Office, Fitzwilliam (Milton) MS C.21, cited and quoted in D. E. Hoak, *The King's Council in the Reign of Edward VI* (Cambridge: Cambridge University Press, 1976; reprinted 2008), 180–3 and 189.

36. Steven G. Ellis, *Tudor Frontiers and Noble Power: The Making of the British State* (Oxford: Clarendon Press, 1995), 173–7; Steven G. Ellis, *Ireland in the Age of the Tudors 1447–1603: English Expansion and the End of Gaelic Rule* (London and New York: Longman, 1998), 131–43, 354–8.

37. Greg Walker, *Writing under Tyranny: English Literature and the Henrician Reformation* (Oxford: Oxford University Press, 2005), where the remark about Henry VIII is quoted on 433 from Maurice Latey, *Tyranny: A Study in the Abuse of Power* (London: Macmillan, 1969), 195.

38. Among participants in the rebellions of 1536–7 about one man in 3,500 was executed. Elizabeth I ordered the executions of three times as many in the northern rebellion of 1569; G. R. Elton, *Policy and Police*, 389 n. 1, citing J. B. Black, *The Reign of Elizabeth, 1558–1603* (Oxford: Oxford University Press, 1936), 111–12.

39. Anglo, *Great Tournament Roll*, 60.

40. Perry Anderson, as quoted by David Potter, "Foreign Policy," in Diarmaid MacCulloch (ed.), *The Reign of Henry VIII: Politics, Policy and Piety* (New York: St. Martin's Press, 1995), 112.

41. On Henry VIII's wars see, S. J. Gunn, "The French Wars of Henry VIII," in J. Black (ed.), *The Origins of War in Early Modern Europe* (Edinburgh: John Donald Publishers Ltd, 1987), 28–47; C. S. L. Davies, "Henry VIII and Henry V: The Wars in France," in John Watts (ed.), *The End of the Middle Ages? England in the Fifteenth and Sixteenth Centuries* (Stroud: Sutton, 1998), 235–62; Glenn Richardson, "Eternal Peace, Occasional War: Anglo-French Relations under Henry VIII," in Susan Doran and Glenn Richardson (eds.), *Tudor England and Its Neighbors* (Basingstoke: Palgrave Macmillan, 2005), 44–69; and Glenn Richardson, *Renaissance Monarchy: The Reigns of Henry VIII, Francis I, and Charles V* (London: Arnold, 2002), 36–62.

42. College of Arms, London, MS Great Tournament Roll of Westminster, membrane 25; Anglo, *Spectacle*, 112. A volume containing a collotype reproduction of the MS Great Tournament Roll accompanies Anglo's *Great Tournament Roll*.

43. On Holbein's lost painting of the battle of Thérouanne, see Foister, *Holbein and England*, 121–3, and Hall, *Chronicle*, 722. On the paintings of the mid-1540s commemorating the English campaigns of 1513, see Oliver Millar, *The Tudor, Stuart and Early Georgian Pictures in the Collection of Her Majesty the Queen* (London: Phaidon, 1963), nos. 22 and 23, p. 54 (and plates 8 and 9).

44. BL, Lansdowne Roll 14, was first described and analyzed in Dale Hoak, "The Secret History of the Tudor Court: The King's Coffers and the King's Purse, 1542–1553," *Journal of British Studies* 26 (1987), 208–31. The MS has been published in *The 1542 Inventory of Whitehall: The Palace and Its Keeper*, transcribed and edited by Maria Hayward (London: Illuminata Publishers, 2004), vol. II, *The Transcripts*, 285–305.

45. John Guy, "Thomas Wolsey, Thomas Cromwell and the Reform of Henrician Government," in MacCulloch (ed.), *Reign of Henry VIII*, 46.

46. This paragraph first appeared in substantially the same form in my review of MacCulloch (ed.), *Reign of Henry VIII* in *Albion* 28 (1996), 686–7. The paragraph is my synthesis of arguments and information in three articles in MacCulloch (ed.), *Reign of Henry VIII*: Potter, "Foreign Policy," 113, 121–2, 125 (where the French are quoted), 126; Richard Hoyle, "War and Public

Finance," 82–3, 85, 87, 91, 95–9; and Guy, "Reform of Henrician Government," 46–7.

47. Louis de Perreau, sieur de Castillon, called him a ruler "who loves gold and silver more than any prince I know," "one of the most avaricious princes in the world"; quoted by Potter, "Foreign Policy," in MacCulloch (ed.), *Reign of Henry VIII*, 125.

48. Rowlands, *Paintings of Hans Holbein*, 225, for both the full Latin text of the inscription and Rowlands's translation. Richard Morison, employed by Henry to defend the break with Rome, may have composed the inscription. Morison composed the Latin inscription in Holbein's 1539 portrait of the infant Prince Edward.

49. E. W. Ives, "Henry VIII's Will – A Forensic Conundrum," *Historical Journal* 35 (1992), 797.

50. G. R. Elton, "*Lex Terrae Victrix*: The Triumph of Parliamentary Law in the Sixteenth Century," in G. R. Elton, *Studies in Tudor and Stuart Politics and Government*, vol. IV (Cambridge: Cambridge University Press, 1992), 37–57; Dale Hoak, "Sir William Cecil, Sir Thomas Smith, and the Monarchical Republic of Tudor England," in John F. McDiarmid (ed.), *The Monarchical Republic of Early Modern England: Essays in Response to Patrick Collinson* (Aldershot: Ashgate Publishing Ltd, 2007), 37–54.

51. Diarmaid MacCulloch, "Henry VIII and the Reform of the Church," in MacCulloch (ed.), *Reign of Henry VIII*, 176–80.

PART II

Henry VIII's literary and political afterlives

CHAPTER 4

The slow death of a tyrant: learning to live without Henry VIII, 1547–1563

Alec Ryrie

Henry VIII stopped breathing on January 28, 1547, but although his body died, his political power did not. When such a political colossus finally topples, the resulting vacuum is disorientating to his allies and enemies alike. Politics cannot swiftly return to normal, if only because no one knows what "normal" is. In modern times, the examples of leaders as diverse as Franklin Roosevelt, Joseph Stalin or Margaret Thatcher demonstrate how bewildering the sudden departure of a dominant political figure can be, as well as the potential potency of their political afterlives. And so it was with Henry VIII, a king who had made himself the sun around which England's political and religious universe turned. He might be gone, but the planets which orbited him had still to continue in their courses.

But even political giants die eventually, and the aftershocks of their fall fade. This chapter is an attempt to trace how Henry VIII's subjects, neighbors, friends and enemies came to terms with his absence in the decade and a half after his death, through to the early years of his younger daughter's reign. It will argue that the loyal consensus that Henry had successfully forced on his people broke down only slowly, and that his memory continued to be politically potent. Evangelicals and conservatives alike tried to conscript the dead king to support their cause under Edward VI, but this contest was won decisively by the evangelicals; their successful co-option of Henry VIII was vital to their Edwardian triumph. Thereafter, both Catholics and Protestants became much more willing to dissociate themselves from the old tyrant, but he remained politically vital, an irreplaceable source of legitimacy and authority for both Mary I's and Elizabeth I's regimes – however uneasy those regimes may have been at the association.

PRAISE AND VILIFICATION: VIEWS OF HENRY VIII BY THE TIME OF HIS DEATH

By 1547, most of Christendom had come to one of two polarized views on Henry VIII. He was, according to taste, an egomaniacal, sacrilegious tyrant; or the rightful Supreme Head of his subjects' church, defending it from papal usurpation and heretical error alike.

The first view was Europe's conventional wisdom. It was widespread amongst Protestants: Martin Luther's antagonism towards Henry VIII had been obvious since their pamphlet dispute of the early 1520s, and was only inflamed by the English king's subsequent matrimonial and religious adventures. Although European Protestants recognized the magnitude of the religious changes Henry had imposed on England, the failure of the attempts to forge an alliance in the 1530s and the limits of Henry's reforms left few with illusions about the English king. The English agent in Bremen in 1546 summed up what his hosts thought of Henry: he "has put awaye the divyll but his ma^te has his dam & his dyvylysh sermonyes styll vssed w^t in hys realme w^t dyvers other thynges wch I dare not wrytte."[1] A few English reformers were willing to assert such views on their own account. In 1542 the radical Henry Brinklow wrote (in an anonymous pamphlet which he had smuggled to printers in Antwerp) that "if it be so that GOD throughe the Kyng hath cast oute the deuell oute of this realme … yet both he and we supp of the broth in which the deuell was sodden."[2]

For those loyal to the papacy, of course, no such equivocation was necessary. From 1534 down to the present, the orthodox Roman Catholic view of Henry VIII has been very straightforward: he was an excommunicate, a schismatic, an adulterer, and a murderer. He had profaned holy places, desecrated sacred relics, destroyed true religion, and claimed a blasphemous degree of authority for himself. Many of his subjects – we cannot know how many – silently entertained such thoughts, or whispered them to their neighbors. Only a few said such things aloud, and faced grim coercion or exile as a consequence.[3] But amongst their co-religionists elsewhere in Europe, this view was universal. In 1547 William Thomas, an English evangelical who had fled to Italy to escape charges of theft from his former master, wrote a treatise, "Peregrine," defending his recently deceased king against such perceived slanders. In it he gives us a neat summary of the common Italian view of Henry VIII. It was not a positive one. "Cicero his elloquence should not suffice to defend him of his Tyrany, since he hath ben knowne, and noted ouer all, to be the greatest Tyrant that euer was in England." Heading the charge sheet were four executions. The deaths of Thomas More and John Fisher had shocked the continent and were still remembered; Henry could not have chosen two better-known subjects to kill. And the executions of his second and fifth wives had already made him notorious as a wife-killer. One of Thomas's

Italians asked, "did he nott choppe, change, and behead them [his wives], as his horse coueted new pasture"? Here, undoubted fact was bolstered by rumors that Catherine of Aragon had been poisoned, and that Jane Seymour had died from callous neglect (or worse). But these judicial murders were only the showpiece accusations against a king accused of ransacking the English Church and debasing his country's coinage from mere avarice, and of conducting a generalized campaign of terror against his own people in the process. Thomas's Italians told him that

yor kinge beinge invironed wth the ocean sea, thought it impossible that the fame of his wicked lyfe & doinges should passe into the firme lande of other Countryes … but … not only his generall proceedinges but euery particuler & privat parte thereof was better knowne in Itallye then in his owne dominions, where for feare no man durst either speake or winke.[4]

Very similar charges were echoed from the opposite end of the continent. In 1549 the Scottish judge William Lamb wrote a passionate denunciation of English conduct towards Scotland, in which he dwelt at length on the iniquities of the dead English king. The new English king, Edward VI, is a

bastard seid … and quhat his father wes I traist þe wallis of every guid toun will tell quhar abbayis stuid. I will no*ch*t z*ou*r lordis and ladyis reherss, quhilkis for þe trew*th* wes miserablie murdreit, þair airis disherist, the spuilze of z*ou*r kirkis, the extorsioun of þe yemanrie and gentillmen; as concerny*ng* the faith and religioun, thair actis and proclamatiounis zeirlie ane aganis ane vthir will speik quhone we be gane.

He made a virtue of the fact that King James V of Scots – Henry's nephew – had refused even to meet this "kyng seuerit fra societie of Christin men." He too deplored Henry's matrimonial history, explicitly accusing him of poisoning Catherine of Aragon, mocking his frequent changes to the English succession "als oft as Protheus did change formis," and, worst of all, compelling all his subjects to swear to the new order "no*ch*t without greit periure of all þe haill realme." And there was blunter tyranny, too. Henry "wes no*ch*t saciate in vij. or viij. zeris persecutioun and scheddin of his awin subdittis bluid."[5] Another Scot, Robert Wedderburn, not only detailed Henry's brutal persecution of his clergy (many of whom had taken refuge in Scotland), but drew particular attention to how this Welsh king had oppressed his own countrymen: "the pepil of valis ar in sic subiectione that thai dar neuer ryde bot iiij to gidder."[6]

These were to remain constant themes of Henry's reputation down to modern times, especially but not exclusively from Catholics. They were, in his own lifetime and immediately afterwards, matched by an obvious mirror-image, an image which reflected Henry's own preferred view.

In this he was Imperial Majesty, a new David, a new Solomon, a new Hezekiah, whose martial glory was matched by his achievement in liberating his crown and his people from papal tyranny, and who had used his rightful power as the Supreme Head of the English Church to drive out error and corruption. Henry's subjects competed with one another to praise him in these terms. Sometimes they did so with a little unease: evangelicals, for example, might observe that the king was not responsible for everything done in his name, or pray that he might finish the Reformation which he had begun. But such caution was hardly typical.[7] More common is the attitude of a priest named Edward Leibowrne, who, in the late 1530s or early 1540s, dedicated a verse paraphrase of Psalm 21 to the king. Leibowrne declared that the description of kingship in the psalm has not "represented ony kingis behaviour soo constantlye / Sence Dauid wrote it as it does nowe our owne kinge henry." Before Henry's reign, Leibowrne lamented, the English were imprisoned in darkness by covetous prelates; now Henry "hath eradicatt by the roote*s* mooste of these myscheves / And moo will herafter by scriptur*es* supportacyon."[8] Or again, in 1539 an Essex lawyer named John Pylbarough published an excruciating panegyric to Henry based loosely on the *Benedictus*. For Pylbarough, Henry's title of Supreme Head was only the beginning, and even the sacred kingship of the Old Testament did not quite go far enough. Remarking how the Jews had been promised a savior born of David's line, he observes that for England (the true Israel, or "vs moste christian englyshe people"), God has "raysed vp to vs thy peculyar people, a godly dewe power of helthe, our naturall most soueraygne lorde kynge HENRY the VIII" from "the moste noble house of his moste famous progenitours." Henry is therefore "thyne holy enoynted, immediate minyster, and vicar ouer us … to whom also we owe only to haue recourse as unto thy chiefe herdeman." He did not quite dare claim that Henry VIII is the Second Coming, but he did add that Henry "ought to be estemed of vs an other John Baptist, and holy prophete of the mooste hyghest god."[9]

Of course, sycophantic praise directed at a vain and capricious tyrant should not be taken at face value. Nor, however, should we dismiss it entirely, for one of the features of a successful tyranny is that its subjects are brought to believe in it. Ethan Shagan's study of what he calls "popular politics" under Henry VIII has made it plain how far the king's subjects were brought to consent to his actions, rather than merely being coerced into accepting them.[10] In modern terms, this was a regime adept at the use of soft power. When Henry VIII begged his subjects for unity at

Christmas 1545, he could reduce the parliament house to tears: tears no less genuine for being politic, for in such a world, both the safest and the easiest course is to let oneself believe the slogans one is compelled to parrot. William Petre, as flint-faced a Tudor bureaucrat as one might hope to find, delighted that on that occasion his king had spoken with "such a gravity so sententiously, so Kingly, or rather fatherly," and added that it "was such a Joy and marvellous comfort, as I reckon this day one of the happiest of my life."[11]

And indeed, it is one of Henry VIII's few real achievements that, while he lived, most of his subjects were successfully united by this rhetoric. The shibboleth that kept them so was the royal supremacy. From staunch religious conservatives, through the religiously compliant, confused or uninterested, to most (but not all) of the king's evangelical subjects, assent to the king's self-awarded title of Supreme Head controlled the views they could hold about his rule. In the decade and a half following Henry's death, however, this artificial unity fractured under its own internal pressures, as the medicines, or poisons, which were Henry VIII's legacy worked their way through England's body politic. The emergence of a range of views of the old king himself is one of the clearest signs of those changes.

"A FATHER YET BREATHING IN HIS SON": HENRY VIII IN THE REIGN OF EDWARD VI

The battle lines of the struggle for Henry VIII's legacy in Edwardian England were quickly drawn. It was, and remained thereafter, a battle of due process against political substance. And as usual in English politics, due process won decisively.

At the heart of the battle were two old colleagues and opponents, the bishops Thomas Cranmer and Stephen Gardiner.[12] It was Gardiner who swiftly developed the most dangerous and effective critique which Edward VI's regime's faced: that the young king's regents had no right to overturn his father's settled will in matters of religion.[13] It was a powerful argument, for two reasons. First, the appeal to Henry VIII packed a powerful emotional punch. Appealing to Henry's final and most authoritative statement of doctrine, the *King's Book* of 1543, Gardiner insisted that "the King my late sovereign lord, in his book, taught a true doctrine," and reacted angrily to Cranmer's crass suggestion that Henry had been "seduced" from the truth.

I will defend his wisdome and learnyng in these matters to be greater then it may seemly be said of hym by any man that he was seduced … These words, my Lord, to say, "the King our late sovereign lord was seduced in his book," be words to be spoken by them that durst not or would not shew the truth in his tyme, and not of your Grace, which can professe neither the one in respect of your selfe, ne the other in respect of him; who made you as you are, and left you his executour to maintayne his acts and laws and not impugne them … Although hys body lvyeth no longer amonge us, yet hys memory should … continew in honour and reverence.[14]

Second, Gardiner's factual claims were undoubtedly and obviously right. Cranmer had argued with his old master for years over the doctrine of justification, with no success whatsoever. Henry's implacable opposition to the Protestant view of this matter was encoded in the *King's Book*, and as such had been given statutory force. As Gardiner put it, "if such as travaile in the doctrine of 'fayth only' brought their water pott to the Kinges booke, they were lyke to go thence with out lycquour." And as Gardiner also pointed out, he himself had had nothing to do with this. "In this, our late soveraigne lordes resolution, I was no doer, but a folower, accepting the treuth concluded, as became me."[15] Yet within months of Henry's death, and while the laws mandating the *King's Book* were as yet unrepealed, Cranmer's newly published homilies were officially teaching the doctrine which Henry had so abhorred.

For Gardiner, and for many other religious conservatives in Edward VI's reign, Henry VIII became a totem of everything which they fought to protect, or whose passing they mourned.[16] In 1549 the Kentish schoolmaster John Proctor lamented the passing of "that Noble Henrye, Kynge of Kynges," urging his ungrateful subjects: "Deceaue not the louyng expect-acion of so hygh and fatherly a Prince conceyued of you, do not frustrate his traueil and labours."[17] In the same year, William Lamb's diatribe against Henry recognized that pious English conservatives still respected him. One of the characters in Lamb's dialogue, the "guid man of Syon," laments Henry's death, "for than I think þe court sall nocht onlie þe new leirnyng for to incresche amangis þe nobillis and commonis of Ingland, bot als able to renew þe auld philosophouris opinionis." The worst he would say of Henry was that his "naturale guidnes wes oftymes alterat be counsel" (a clause much used by all sides to exculpate Henry).[18] Deep loyalty to the old king was matched by expediency. Henry's memory was perhaps the only defensible line against runaway religious change, since the papacy had been so comprehensively renounced. In particular, the 1539 Act of Six Articles became an emblem of the orthodoxy which Henry VIII had defended. When Bishop Hooper listed the signs of popery which his visitation of 1552 was to stamp out, heading the list was "the Six Articles."[19] Three years earlier, the south-western rebels of 1549 had demanded Henry's "Lawes … concernynge the syxe articles, to be in vse again, as in hys tyme they were."[20] Even Reginald Pole believed that the Act had been "the best thing [Henry] ever did in this world."[21]

This argument – that since Henry VIII had repeatedly condemned the new regime's policies as rank heresy, the regime could hardly claim his mantle – may have seemed powerful to those, like the south-western rebels, who were innocent of how the Tudor state functioned. But Gardiner, at least, will have been aware of how dangerous this gambit was. For if Henry VIII had been plain in his loathing of perceived heresy, he had been plainer still in his determination to maintain the absolute temporal and spiritual authority of the Crown. If the substance of the new regime's religious policy was innovative, the political theory behind it was largely unchanged.[22] Edward VI, as the new Supreme Head of the Church, wielded his father's authority. As Gardiner himself put it, Henry was "a father most unfortunately reft from us, yet breathing in his son."[23] Gardiner's argument, of course, turned on the new king's age, pointing out that the new policies were not his own but his regents'. While undeniably true, this was – as Gardiner of all people will have known – legally almost unthinkable. If accepted, his argument threatened systematically to undermine the authority of this and of any regency government. The logical consequence would have been something like the situation in Scotland, where regents' acts and grants were provisional and legally revocable upon a monarch attaining majority – a level of uncertainty which England's rigid legal structure could never have tolerated. It is easy enough to see why Gardiner's attack alarmed Edward's regents, but it is hard to see how it could possibly have succeeded.

Instead, the Edwardian conservatives' appeal to Henry VIII's memory rebounded on them, in two ways. First, and more importantly, to wrap oneself in Henrician loyalty ruled out any attack on the royal supremacy, the fundamental motor of the Edwardian Reformation. Gardiner's own attacks on the Edwardian regime started to falter by the end of 1547, when that regime's policies began to be backed up by parliamentary legislation. He even found himself forced to concede the 1549 Prayer Book, much to his distaste. The regime and its allies were quick to cite Henry as "evident profe" that true spiritual authority was vested in the temporal power, a proof which carried emotional as well as logical force.[24] The Henrician orthodoxy which Gardiner and others tried to defend had been a splendid edifice, but it turned out to be built on sand, and it crumbled under the Edwardian assault; for it was built specifically to repel the one weapon which could have defended it, the papacy. After six years of hard doctrinal pounding from 1547 to 1553, there was not much left.

Second, and more immediately, the conservatives' argument was based on a false premise – one which seemed plausible enough in 1547 but which was becoming threadbare by 1553: namely, that the young king did not really approve of the policies being enacted in his name. Henry VIII had persuaded Gardiner and other religious conservatives to accept the royal supremacy on the grounds that it was a bulwark against real heresy, and during his lifetime he had more or less kept to that promise. It was a promise bolstered by the almost numinous faith in good kingship which England had long enjoyed and which Henry himself had so ruthlessly exploited. But none of this could rule out the ghastly possibility that an English king might become a heretic himself, and by the early 1550s there was no concealing that this was happening. Many conservatives continued to believe that – as John Bale put it – "when [Edward] cometh of age, he will see another rule, and hang up a hundred of such heretic knaves."[25] But it was becoming plain that Edward shared those heretic knaves' convictions. These hopes inclined conservatives to wait patiently while their Church was destroyed around them, clinging to an increasingly transparent fantasy of rescue rather than acting to defend what was left of their Church.

"THIS MONSTROUS BOAR": HENRY VIII IN MARIAN ENGLAND

Edward VI's death, the Jane Grey fiasco and the accession of Mary threw the battle to claim, and to escape, Henry VIII's legacy into a new phase.

It is not always appreciated how far Henry himself was responsible for the bizarre dynastic crisis of July 1553.[26] This is not merely because of his colorful matrimonial history, nor because of his serial inconsistency on the subject of the succession. The order which was left in the 1543 Succession Act and in his own will was certainly very odd indeed: two daughters, whose claims were in logic mutually exclusive and both of whom remained legally illegitimate, were placed in the order of succession by a sheer assertion of the royal will. But the real problem was the precedent this set, which again pitted political substance against political process. Henry's will expressed the substance of his policy clearly enough. But the process he used apparently established that English monarchs might settle the succession according to their own wills, rather than submitting to inexorable laws of inheritance. Elizabeth I's reign was largely consumed by her refusal to follow her father's example in this regard. This was precisely what Edward VI's "devise" for the succession in 1553 was trying to do, and if (especially in its final form) it was short on dynastic logic and long on expediency, it remained more consistent than Henry's order. All it lacked was a parliamentary rubber-stamp. In this case, however, substance trumped process, as good luck and good judgment enabled Mary to raise a successful rebellion. This matters because, on any reading, Henry VIII's will and Mary's perceived legitimacy were crucial to her victory. Henry had overruled his son from beyond the grave. The new queen owed her throne to him but also reviled his central legacy to her. This paradox was to snap at her heels throughout her reign.

In one sense, of course, Mary's decision to return England to papal obedience rescued English Catholicism from the horns of its Henrician dilemma. Where English Catholics had been paralyzed by the royal supremacy, they could now once again ground their faith firmly on St. Peter's throne. Yet Henry VIII's legacy was not so easily shaken off. The new regime was willing enough to denounce him. Court preachers apparently inveighed against both Henry and Edward in the first few months of the reign.[27] Above all, Reginald Pole was unswerving in his condemnation of his old master, whose name was "notorious throughout the Christian world like no other for centuries."[28] Pole's view of England's troubles was unambiguous. Within days of his hearing of Mary's accession, he wrote to her in blunt terms:

Her Majesty will perceive that the beginning and cause of all the evil, commenced at the time when the perpetual adversary of the human race placed in the heart of the King her father the perverse desire to make the divorce from the blessed Queen her mother … From this iniquitous and impious seed there subsequently sprang up those pestiferous fruits which have so corrupted every part of the kingdom.[29]

Yet this could not be the last word on Henry VIII, and Pole knew it. Months later he was reproaching Mary for having referred to her father as "*regem piisimae memoriae.*" Her duty as a daughter to honor her father, he warned, was trumped by Christ's injunction to hate one's parents for the sake of the Gospel. He pointed out, with perfect logic, that if Henry were to be remembered as pious, that those such as Thomas More, John Fisher, Catherine of Aragon and indeed Pole himself, who had resisted his tyranny, must be condemned. Yet this logic was too sharp for the Marian regime to accept, and even Pole himself quailed at it, going on to emphasize his own love for the dead king. "There was never mother mourned her only child as I mourned him … I never saw the time but I would have been content to have lost my life corporal to have saved his soul."[30] Even Pole could not simply abandon Henry to the devil.

For those whose personal histories were less heroically consistent – a group which included the queen – matters were more complicated still. In the battle between political substance and political process, the competing parties had changed ends. Now it was the newly empowered religious conservatives who wished radically to change the policies they had inherited, but who had to do so using the existing machinery of state. The irony of Mary's having been, in law, Supreme Head of the Church is well enough known, but she was plainly determined to rid herself of the title as quickly as possible. She could not, however, shake off the fact that her claim to the throne derived from her father. Nor was this a merely technical, legal connection. Henry had so transformed the authority of the English throne that her authority was inescapably linked to, and built upon, his. Those of her subjects who had tried to reconcile Catholicism with the royal supremacy under Edward were now ready to celebrate her accession, but also to remind her to whom she owed her throne. Thomas Paynell twice dedicated translations to Mary, both times emphasizing that she was "daughter vnto the moost victorious and mooste noble prynce, kinge Henry the viii. kynge of Englande, Fraunce and Ireland."[31] Her own chaplain, John Angell, praised God for sending England "a newe Iudith, by whose godlines the trewe light and knowledge of Goddes worde is nowe by her broughte agayne, whiche frome the death of that noble prince her father Henry yᵉ viii. was here in this realme extincte" – a radically different diagnosis of England's ills from that which Pole had offered.[32]

Marian Protestants, of course, were aware of this discomfort and did their best to exploit it, positioning themselves as Henry's true heirs in exactly the same way Gardiner had done in the previous reign. Princess Elizabeth, under house arrest at Woodstock, asked to be allowed to use the 1544 English litany, on the grounds that it "was set forth in the kyng my Father hys dayes."[33] She was of course refused, but she was not the only person to recognize the 1544 Litany's potential to unsettle the Marian regime. It was the only part of the Prayer Book service whose authorized use dated to Henry's reign, and its regular use for nearly a decade had ingrained it into most English memories. In 1554, the tough conservative William Chedsay, interrogating the Protestant Thomas Hawkes, asked

Hawkes for his view of the Pope. Hawkes replied by quoting the Litany: "From him and all his detestable enormities good Lorde deliuer vs." Chedsay was stung into a revealing response: "Mary so may wee saye from king Henry the eight, and all his detestable enormities, good Lord deliuer vs."[34]

Not all his colleagues would have said Amen to that. In the same year, by his own account, Nicholas Ridley used the issue to set his interrogators by the ears. When John Feckenham put it to Ridley that forty years previously, all Christendom had accepted transubstantiation (a variant of the classic "where was your Church before Luther?" argument), Ridley replied that forty years previously, all Christendom had accepted papal supremacy. Feckenham, a conservative cleric of Pole and Chedsay's school, could only agree, but one of the other interrogators present, Sir John Bourne (the queen's principal secretary), found himself discomfited. Bourne was a stout Catholic but, as a recent study of his career suggests, "he was more plain English than ultramontanist."[35] Papal supremacy was, he now said, "but a positive law." Ridley pounced, pointing out the papacy's claims to have been instituted by Christ. "Tush, it was not counted an article … of our faith," Bourne replied, much to Feckenham's horror. A third man present, the former Lord Chief Justice, Roger Chomley, weighed in on Bourne's behalf, "and told a long tale what laws were of Kings of England made against the Bishop of Rome, and was vehement to tell how they alway of the clergy did fly to him." This was singing an old Henrician song. The argument became so heated that Chomley "thought himself much wronged, that he could not be suffered to speak, the rest were so ready to interrupt him." Meanwhile Ridley, supposedly the subject of the interrogation, needed only to sit on the sidelines and watch as the tensions between clergy and laity, and between theological and legal certainties, played themselves out.[36]

However, Marian Protestants were themselves subject to a parallel set of tensions. Those who continued to appeal to Henry's legacy – whether cynically or sincerely – found themselves trapped by the same logic which had troubled Gardiner and the Edwardian conservatives. If they recognized the royal supremacy, how could they oppose the queen's proceedings? It was a criticism made all the more powerful by the twin fiascos of Jane Grey's abortive reign and of Wyatt's rebellion, a rebellion which the regime quickly (and misleadingly) painted as a Protestant plot. Protestants were left vulnerable, and sensitive, to the charge of sedition. John Proctor, who had lamented Henry's passing in 1549, now used some very Henrician rhetoric to argue that heresy was inherently treacherous and corrosive of good order.[37] The effect was to herd Marian Protestants into affirming their loyalty to the queen, so making their continued defiance of her religion uncomfortable. Famously, Thomas Cranmer was trapped by this dilemma, forced by his exceptionally high doctrine of the royal supremacy into accepting that the queen might authoritatively deny her own supremacy. The tale is that he was shocked out of his recantations in part by a dream in which Henry VIII spoke to him and rejected him. If true, it is eloquent testimony to how the dead king continued to weigh heavily on his subjects' hearts.[38]

Cranmer's position was extreme, however, and by this time most Protestants had already begun to put a little distance between themselves and their former master. The record of Protestant unease towards Henry during his own lifetime helped here, and as his memory receded the reformers became bolder. Hugh Latimer, who had reason to remember both the kindness and the severity of his former patron and gaoler, recalled the bloody atmosphere of Henry's reign when preaching before King Edward in 1549: "It was, as ye know, a dangerous world, for it might soon cost a man his life for a word speaking."[39] William Turner, in exile in the mid-1540s, had been one of the bolder Protestant voices criticizing Henry during his own lifetime. In particular, he was openly uneasy about the royal supremacy, anticipating Elizabeth by trying to recast Henry as "Supreme Governor."[40] By 1554, this had grown into a more comprehensive critique, whose key points were Henry's marriages and his looting of church property. Turner now lambasted "King Henry the eight, [who] … toke all the goodes of the abbayes," and compared Henry to Ananias, struck dead by God for trying to steal from the Church. "The same Kinge spoiled againe all honestie and goddes forbid." Turner still, however, put most of the blame on Henry's "couetous counsell," who not only swallowed up all the stolen wealth, but also "suffred the Kinge and diuers Lordes of the realme to put away and take as many wiues as they liste."[41]

The longest journey of disillusionment which we can document was that of Anthony Gilby. In a tract of 1548 against Gardiner, Gilby was referring to "the noble kynge Henrie the eight (whom surely God appoynted to beat downe poperie and Idolatrie, long preserued him from your manifolde treasones, and at the length now whan hys good wyll was: hath taken hym to hys mercies)."[42] Ten years later, in 1558, that year of printed bitterness from British Protestant exiles, Gilby wrote an *Admonition to England and Scotland to call them to repentance*. This was bound with the work of his newfound friend John Knox, whose prophetic denunciations it echoed. From Gilby's new perspective, Henry appeared less noble. "There was no reformation, but a deformation, in the tyme of that tyrant and lecherous monster." He admitted that Henry had torn down many popish institutions:

The bore [Henry] I grant was busie wrooting and digging in the earth, and all his pigges that folowed him. But they sought only for the pleasant frutes that they winded with their longe snowtes; and for their own bellies sake, they wrooted up many weeds; but they turned the grounde so, mingling good and badd togither … that no good thing could grow, but by great miracle, under such Gardners.

His bloody persecution of Catholics and evangelicals alike "doth clearly paynt his beastlynes, that he cared for no maner of religion." Noting that he had written both against Luther and the Pope, Gilby concluded that

this bore raged against God, against Devill, against Christ, and against Antichrist … This monstrous bore, for al this, must nedys be called Head of the Churche in paine of treason, displacing Christ, our onlie Head, who oght alone to have this title … In his best time, nothing was hard but the Kinges booke, and the Kinges procedings; the Kinges Homelies in the churches, where Goddes word should onely have bene preached. So made you your King a god, beleving nothing but that he alowed.

More than merely a covetous, adulterous murderer, Henry was now given an almost apocalyptic significance, as a monster whose wickedness equalled that of the papacy itself.[43]

"PUISSANT PRINCE ROYAL": THE TAMING OF HENRY VIII'S MEMORY

After years of obedient sycophancy, one can understand that Gilby's wild language might seem cathartic, an act of iconoclasm directed at Tudor England's most insidious idol. Yet for the sober Protestants who reinherited England's governance in 1558, such language was quite impossible. Other ways had to be found of domesticating Henry VIII's memory. For the new queen, too, owed her claim to the throne, and indeed the fact of her survival during her sister's reign, to her father. A pamphlet celebrating her recalled that some had called for her execution in 1554, and wondered that

> those mad men did not knowe
> That ye were doughter vnto King Hary
> And a princesse of birth, one of the noblest on earth,
> And sister vnto Quene Mary.[44]

Yet Mary and King Philip did know it, and for that and other reasons had not only allowed the young princess to live, but allowed Henry VIII's illogical order for the succession to stand. Henry's paternity and his will trumped illegitimacy and partisan religious concerns.

The new Elizabethan establishment found two ways of managing this awkward inheritance: one subtle and at least partly honest, the other disingenuous and effective. The honest approach is that which was canonized for the Protestant establishment by John Foxe. Foxe inherited the Marian exiles' growing willingness to distance themselves from Henry, but it was politic to be more diplomatic than Turner, and his own conscience would have revolted at Gilby's language. The natural response, then, was to portray Henry as an innocent scarcely in control of his own court, swayed by his councillors and easily led astray. It was an interpretation with good precedents, even in Henry's own reign.[45] In 1546 George Joye had described Henry as a "weake faithed king" who was "demented and bewitched" by his wicked advisers, comparing him to King Darius, who had been duped into persecuting the prophet Daniel.[46] If this was hardly the unvarnished truth, it did provide an explanation of sorts for Henry's apparently erratic behavior, and it is not too far distant from some modern interpretations of Henry's reign, which have depicted him as the plaything of faction.[47] However, where Joye's portrait of Henry had emphasized the king's innocence, Foxe's was more openly ambiguous. In the first, 1563 edition of his *Actes and Monuments* (known then and since as the *Book of Martyrs*), Foxe interrupted his narrative of the case of John Lambert with an "apost[r]ophe to king Henrye."[48] The Lambert case was a particularly uncomfortable episode for Foxe. Lambert was burned for denying Christ's presence in the Eucharist in 1538, following a show trial at which Henry VIII presided in person, and in which an array of evangelicals from Robert Barnes to Thomas Cranmer participated. Foxe dealt with this in part by trying to blame the entire episode on the arch-villain Stephen Gardiner, an accusation which seemed highly plausible to him and to most other evangelicals, but for which he had no evidence whatsoever.[49] However, it also forced him (or gave him an opportunity) to confront the question of King Henry's own role head-on.

He addressed his remarks to the king directly, "where so euer thou arte": a telling declaration of ignorance, as Foxe could confidently place virtually all of his other characters firmly in Heaven or Hell. It was true, he admitted, that Lambert's death was primarily due to Gardiner's "malityous and crafty subtilty." Yet nothinge seemed more vnworthye, then the vndecent and the vncomelye behauiour of the kinges maiestye at that daye … Howe muche more commendable had it beene for thee, O kynge Henry … if thou haddest ayded and holpen the poore litle sheape … and haddest graunted hym rather thy autoritye to vse the same for his sauegarde, rather then vnto the other to abuse it vnto slaughter.

He made no bones as to what this might mean for Henry's soul. "The time shall once come, when as ye shall geue accompt of all the offences whiche ye haue eyther committed by your owne fault, or by the Councell or aduise of others." And he imagined Henry being judged by the apostles and martyrs, some of whom were martyrs of his own making. "With what hart wil ye implore their mercy, which so vnmercifully reiected and cast them of, when they fled vnto your pity and mercy?"[50]

And yet, for all this, Foxe maintained that the Lambert trial, and all the others that went with it, were in some sense aberrations. "O kynge Henrye, I knowe you did not follow your owne nature there in, but the pernitious councels of the b[i]shoppe of Wynchester."[51] Did Foxe genuinely believe this, or was it a convenient way of avoiding a blunt condemnation of his queen's father and his Reformation's founder? It does not matter, for he and the entire Elizabethan Protestant establishment shared the same dilemma here, and as such would have shied away from any attempt to resolve the question. The careful ambiguity of Foxe's stance, which blended a godly nature and an uncertain eternal fate into its stern condemnations, served its purpose. It meant that, whether Henry was in Heaven or Hell, he could at least be safely confined to his grave.

Even so, for most political purposes, this cut altogether too close to the knuckle. The Elizabethan establishment's mainstream view of Henry VIII picked up on another, rather older set of traditions, whose key feature was that they studiously ignored his religious policy altogether.

The concentration on Henry's religious and matrimonial misadventures in the last part of his life and in the years following his death is understandable enough, but it can obscure the fact that Henry had spent the first half of his reign constructing another image for himself: the Renaissance warrior-king, Great Harry, a king whose astonishing political charisma was not bounded by his somewhat limited real achievements (see Hoak, chapter 3 in this volume). However soured and vitiated by the events of his last two decades, this older image had one great advantage: it was safe. During his own lifetime, it was recovered by foreign observers who wished to maintain good terms despite his religious proceedings. The anonymous "Spanish Chronicler" who wrote up an account of Henry's reign in about 1550 was as unforgiving as any Spaniard of Henry's treatment of his first wife and of her supporters, but as his account moves on its tone changes. The king's dalliances with heresy are (once again) sloughed off onto his ministers, notably Cranmer. Instead, the Spaniard focused on Henry's larger-than-life personality. Literally: "The King was so stout that such a man has never been seen. Three of the biggest men that could be found could get inside his doublet." And he had Anne of Cleves say of Katherine Parr, at the time of her marriage, "A fine burthen Madam Katherine has taken on herself!" He had much to say about Henry's expensive and ultimately futile French war of 1544–6, and in particular commended his generosity to Spanish soldiers. "Oh! good King! how liberal thou wert to everyone, and particularly to Spaniards!" And he had Henry dying a stereotypically good death, reconciled to his eldest daughter and receiving the sacrament on his deathbed. "Truly the English lost much on the day that the valiant King Henry VIII died."[52]

To call Henry "valiant" was to stretch the truth, but to do so in an uncontroversial direction. One of the earliest depictions of Henry in Elizabeth's reign was in *A brief abstract of the genealogie of all the kynges of England*, which provided crude portraits and brief verse summaries of the reigns of each of the new queen's predecessors. The image of Henry was a simple copy of the already-iconic Holbein portrait. The verse beneath it described him as a "puissant prince royall … whose martiall actes be knowen abroad right well." It named three particular achievements: the capture of Tournai (in 1513) and of Boulogne (in 1544), and the creation of the kingdom of Ireland in 1541. The only religious reference of any kind was the claim that Henry departed life "very godly." This was not because the anonymous author was uninterested in such matters: Edward VI is noted as a king "who punished vice and wickedness abhorred" and who was a precocious Solomon, while Philip and Mary "allowed the Popes authoritie / Erecting eke all Papistry agayne."[53] But the simplest way of dealing with Henry VIII was to pretend he was merely a martial hero, and to efface his Reformation entirely.

This approach, which together with Foxe's cool agnosticism formed the Elizabethan orthodoxy, was the final victory of process over policy. The specifics of Henry's own religious policy were only of use to one party in Elizabethan England: papal loyalists, who could happily denounce the schismatic king and his bastard daughter. For everyone else, the old king's proceedings were an embarrassment. His function became simply to provide legitimacy to his daughter, while retreating to become as much of a stock figure of kingship as possible. That way, even if he could never again be the focus of unity he had been in his lifetime, he could at least cease to be so divisive. In this manner, his bereaved subjects slowly learned to live with, and without, Henry VIII.

NOTES

1. TNA, SP 1/222, fo. 79r (*LP* XXI (i) 1331).
2. Henry Brinklow, *The lamentacion of a christian, against the citie of London, made by R. Mors* (*RSTC* 3764. Bonn, 1542), sig. B2r.
3. Peter Marshall, *Religious Identities in Henry VIII's England* (Aldershot: Ashgate, 2006), chapter 11.
4. BL, MS Harleian 353, fos. 10r–11v; cf. BL, MS Cottonian Vespasian D.xviii, and J. A. Froude (ed.), *The Pilgrim: A Dialogue on the Life and Actions of King Henry the Eighth* (London: Parker, Son and Bourn, 1861).
5. William Lamb, *Ane Resonyng of ane Scottis and Inglis Merchand betuix Rowand and Lionis*, ed. Roderick J. Lyall (Aberdeen: Aberdeen University Press, 1985), 35, 39, 41, 45.
6. Robert Wedderburn, *The Complaynt of Scotland*, ed. A. M. Stewart (Edinburgh: Scottish Text Society, 4th series, no. 11, 1979), 74–5, 128.
7. Ryrie, *The Gospel and Henry VIII*: Evangelicals and the Early English Reformation (Cambridge: Cambridge University Press, 2003), 61–7.
8. BL, MS Royal 7.F.xiv, fos. 53r–55r.
9. John Pylbarough, *A commemoration of the inestimable graces and benefites of God* (*RSTC* 20521. London, 1540), sigs. A4r–v, B2v–3r, D4v.
10. Ethan Shagan, *Popular Politics and the English Reformation* (Cambridge: Cambridge University Press, 2002).
11. TNA, SP 1/212 fo. 111r (*LP* XX (ii) 1030).
12. Diarmaid MacCulloch, "Two Dons in Politics: Thomas Cranmer and Stephen Gardiner, 1503–33," *The Historical Journal* 37 (1994), 1–22.
13. Stephen Alford, *Kingship and Politics in the Reign of Edward VI* (Cambridge: Cambridge University Press, 2002), 57.
14. James Arthur Muller (ed.), *The Letters of Stephen Gardiner* (Cambridge: Cambridge University Press, 1933), 301.
15. Ibid., 338, 365.
16. This paragraph draws on the argument made in Alec Ryrie, "Paths Not Taken in the British Reformations," *The Historical Journal* 52 (2009), 1–22.
17. John Proctor, *The fal of the late Arrian* (*RSTC* 20406. London, 1549), sigs. B3r, C4v.
18. Lamb, *Ane Resonyng*, 169–71.
19. John Hooper, *The Later Writings of Bishop Hooper*, ed. Charles Nevinson (Cambridge: Parker Society, 1852), 129.
20. *A Copye of a letter contaynyng certayne newes, & the articles or requestes of the Deuonshyre & Cornyshe rebelles* (*RSTC* 15109.3. London, 1549), sig. B6r.
21. *Calendar of State Papers and Manuscripts existing in the archives and collections of Venice*, vol. V (1534–54), ed. Rawdon Brown (London, 1873), no. 575.
22. Alford, *Kingship*, 58–63.

23. Muller (ed.), *Letters of Stephen Gardiner*, 322.

24. William Baldwin, *The canticles or balades of Salomon, phraselyke declared in Englysh metres* (*RSTC* 2768. London, 1549), sig. A3r.

25. John Bale, *An expostulation or complaynte agaynste the blasphemyes of a franticke papyst of Hamshyre* (*RSTC* 1294. London, 1552), sig. B1r.

26. I am grateful to Eric Ives for discussions on this point.

27. Thomas S. Freeman, "'As True a Subiect being Prysoner': John Foxe's Notes on the Imprisonment of Princess Elizabeth, 1554–5," *English Historical Review* 117 (2002), 104–16, p. 105.

28. Thomas F. Mayer (ed.), *The Correspondence of Reginald Pole*, vol. II, *A Calendar, 1547–1554: A Power in Rome* (Aldershot: Ashgate, 2003), 107.

29. *Calendar of State Papers … Venice*, vol. V (1534–54), no. 766.

30. Mayer (ed.), *Correspondence of Pole*, II, 236–7.

31. St. Augustine, *Twelue sermons of Saynt Augustine, now lately translated into English by Tho. Paynel*, trans. Thomas Paynell (*RSTC* 923. London, 1553); cf. Cuthbert Tunstall, *Certaine godly and deuout prayers*, trans. Thomas Paynell (*RSTC* 24318. London, 1558).

32. John Angell, *The agrement of the holye fathers, and Doctors of the churche, vpon the cheifest articles of Christian religion, as appeareth on the nexte syde folowing, very necessary for all curates. Gathered together by Iohn Aungell preist, one of the Quenes maiesties Chapleyns* (*RSTC* 634. London, 1555?), sig. A3r.

33. Freeman, "'As True a Subiect'," 115.

34. John Foxe, *Actes and monuments of matters most speciall in the church* (*RSTC* 11225. London, 1583), 1589.

35. L. M. Hill, "The Marian 'Experience of Defeat': The Case of Sir John Bourne," *Sixteenth Century Journal* 25 (1994), 531–58, p. 536.

36. Nicholas Ridley, *The Works of Nicholas Ridley, DD*, ed. Henry Christmas (Cambridge: Parker Society, 1853), 163–5.

37. John Proctor, *The historie of Wyates rebellion* (*RSTC* 20407. London, 1554).

38. Diarmaid MacCulloch, *Thomas Cranmer: A Life* (New Haven and London: Yale University Press, 1996), 598.

39. Hugh Latimer, *Sermons by Hugh Latimer*, ed. George Elwes Corrie (Cambridge: Parker Society, 1844), 149.

40. William Turner, *The rescuynge of the Romishe fox other vvyse called the examination of the hunter … The seconde course of the hunter at the romishe fox* (*RSTC* 24355. Bonn, 1545), sigs. C1v–3v.

41. William Turner, *The huntyng of the romyshe vuolfe* (*RSTC* 24356. Emden, 1555), sigs. D6r–v; cf. Acts 5:1–11.

42. Anthony Gilby, *An answer to the deuillish detection of S. Gardiner* (*RSTC* 11884. London?, 1548), fo. 23r.

43. Anthony Gilby, "An Admonition to England and Scotland, to Call them to Repentance," in David Laing (ed.), *The Works of John Knox*, vol. IV (Edinburgh, 1895), 563–4.

44. William Birche, *A songe betwene the Quenes maiestie and Englande* (*RSTC* 3079. London, 1564). This broadsheet was first entered into the Stationer's Register for a different printer in 1558–9, presumably indicating a lost edition.

45. Ryrie, *The Gospel and Henry VIII*, 64–7.

46. George Joye, *The exposicion of Daniel the prophete* (*RSTC* 14823. Antwerp, 1545), fos. 90r–91v.

47. A view associated particularly with Eric W. Ives. See his survey of the debate in "Stress, Faction and Ideology in Early-Tudor England," *Historical Journal* 34 (1991), 193–202.

48. John Foxe, *Actes and monuments of these latter and perillous dayes, touching matters of the church* (*RSTC* 11222. London, 1563), 533.

49. Michael Riordan and Alec Ryrie, "Stephen Gardiner and the Making of a Protestant Villain," *Sixteenth Century Journal* 34 (2003), 1039–63.

50. Foxe, *Actes and monuments* (1563), 533–4.

51. Ibid., 533.

52. Martin A. Sharp Hume (ed. and trans.), *Chronicle of King Henry VIII of England. Being a Contemporary Record of some of the Principal Events of the Reigns of Henry VIII. and Edward VI. Written in Spanish* (London: George Bell and Sons, 1889), 106, 108, 127, 151–2,

53. *Beholde here (gentle reader) a brief abstract of the genealogie of all the kynges of England* (*RSTC* 10022. London, 1560?).

CHAPTER 5

The literary afterlife of Henry VIII, 1558–1625

Mark Rankin

Written representations of Henry VIII continued to appear during the time spanned by the accession of Elizabeth I in 1558, when Henry was still very much a figure of living memory, and the death of James I in 1625. By that point, a greater degree of interpretive freedom characterized these portrayals, because sufficient historical distance had intervened between Henry's death and writers' reimagining of him. All of these representations are acutely politicized. I am concerned particularly with writings by the courtier poets of this age and, more generally, "poets" loosely connected to elite power centers.[1] Their preoccupation with the legacy of Henry VIII coincides with – and inaugurates – Henry's emergence as a mythic figure. Writers attempted to use Henry VIII to shape the direction of public discussion about controversial issues, including the royal succession and England's relationship with its foreign neighbors. Ongoing comment about Henry displays the widely held belief that his posthumous reputation remained malleable and applicable to the most important political and religious debates of the age. Somewhat paradoxically, it is in this very specific topical application of the Henry VIII legacy that the king's image transformed into a universal symbol of English identity within the national imagination.

Earlier representations of Henry VIII provide important analogues to works considered here. Henry's reign undeniably fostered the literary output of succeeding decades. It witnessed the advent of new forms of humanistic study, for example, that infused the dialogue form with new layers of complexity. The translation into the vernacular of classical and continental books advanced under the humanist program to re-establish the primacy of textual sources. Desiderius Erasmus's landmark facing-column Latin-Greek edition of the New Testament, the *Novum Instrumentum* (1516), opened the door for William Tyndale to translate the scripture into English directly from the Koiné Greek for the first time. His English New Testament appeared in 1526. Lyric poetry attained new levels of sophistication, particularly in verse by Sir Thomas Wyatt and Henry Howard, earl of Surrey. The writings of

Chaucer and other medieval authors appeared in deluxe printed editions. The commitment of humanism to textual studies shaped historical writing by encouraging authors to seek causes of events and explain their ongoing importance. Prominent histories by Robert Fabyan, Edward Hall, and Polydore Vergil circulated in manuscript as well as printed copy.

The full influence of this material upon subsequent output cannot be measured here. My goal is to delineate the shared interpretive tendencies and representational motifs that emerge in a wide body of writing concerned with the figure of Henry himself. Contrary to what might initially appear, the number of those who commented on the king exceeds Nashe and Shakespeare, whose investigation of Henry VIII is now best known from this period. Rather than address their portrayals (which receive attention elsewhere in this volume), I seek to understand the broader rhetorical and generic backdrop to their representations. In fact, writers during this era consistently cite Henry VIII with both tendentious skepticism and opportunism. Their representations employ subtle shifts in expression in response to pressures of patronage and political ambition. As the Henry figure is imagined and reimagined, he not only evolves as an important precedent for ongoing action, but also apotheosizes into a full-scale mythic and cultural phenomenon.

Elizabeth's accession year of 1558 produced a remarkable revisionist account of Henry VIII. The courtier-poet William Forrest rewrote the medieval Griselda motif, which he derived from *The Canterbury Tales*, as an allegory of Henry's divorce from Catherine of Aragon. Forrest offered a magnificent copy of his narrative poem *The History of Grisild the Second* to Queen Mary on June 25, 1558 in a bid for patronage. He composed in rhyme royal, a form that George Gascoigne and George Puttenham identified as the English stanza of choice for serious verse.[2] By presenting the queen with a copy of his poem written on vellum and bound in costly black velvet, Forrest emphasized the capacity of Henry VIII to serve as a moralistic *exemplum* for the elite. The handsome appearance of this manuscript accords with Forrest's decision to cast Catherine as the saintly Griselda and Henry as her unfaithful husband, Walter, in order to commemorate Catherine as a latter-day martyr and praise the rule of Mary as a return to "true" religion in England.[3]

Forrest's amalgamation of disparate historical material from Henry's and Mary's reigns into a clearly defined metaphorical and allegorical frame foreshadows subsequent treatment of this subject: Henry VIII takes on larger-than-life associations through his very application to specific political milieux. With Elizabeth on the throne, writers widely distributed polemics on Henry VIII similar to Forrest's in conception as well as execution. Highly biased treatments of this king gain in intensity throughout the reign. As Henry remains applicable to political issues, such as the royal succession, in these writings, he simultaneously takes on more sophisticated mythic associations. By the accession of James VI and I in 1603, Henry has emerged in the national imagination as a powerfully transcendent figure, but also a surprisingly topical one. The representations of Henry VIII range from cheaply printed ephemera to full-length treatises, verse panegyrics, quasi-fictional "histories," and more. Historical and biographical studies are certainly important: George Cavendish produced his *Life and Death of Cardinal Wolsey* during the mid-1550s, and William Roper penned *The Life of Sir Thomas More*. Both works circulated in manuscript throughout our period. They contain stylized accounts of Henry's acts, but their focus on Henry VIII remains secondary. Catholic readers were sympathetic to the treatment of Wolsey, More, and others whom Henry executed, but their resentment of Henry VIII falls outside the scope of this study.[4]

Publication of Richard Tottel's *Songs and Sonnets* (1557) established a precedent for viewing Elizabethan political realities in Henrician terms. The king's appearance as an imagined persona in these poems explores the potentially sensitive uncertainties of living under this mercurial monarch. This collection demonstrated how Henry's reputation could undergo inter-rogation in verse without inviting harsh reprisal. Moreover, by framing the writings of the Henrician poets, Thomas Wyatt and Henry Howard, earl of Surrey, for popular consumption, Tottel's compilation offers a selective reading of Henrician literary production.[5] This verse anthology established models of versification that would shape Sidney, Spenser, and Shakespeare.[6] In terms of content, selected poems in Tottel's collection describe Henry as presiding over a court in which political realities overrule alternative forms of obligation, including personal or kinship relations. Through this unique blend of political content and formalistic innovation, Henry VIII emerges as a fabulous figure.

Surrey's poem "Of Sardanapalus dishonorable life, and miserable death," for instance, probably alludes to Henry VIII as a latter-day Assyrian despot. The link to Sardanapalus remains only allusive in the poem, particularly because Surrey's monarch perishes in a suicide. The comparison to Henry's marital adventures, however, is suggestive of how Surrey blends imagined and actual realities into a single coherent representation. The speaker chides "Thassirian king" who, instead of pursuing martial achievement, cultivates the "foule desire / And filthy lustes" that will prove his ruin. This monarch "scace [i.e., scarce] the name of manhode did retain, / Drenched in slouth, and womanish delight."[7] Surrey developed a somewhat brash outlook that accords with his royal criticism. He took very seriously his own genealogical pedigree, which connected him to the royal line via Edward III, Henry's grandfather six generations removed. When Surrey quartered his armorial crest with the heraldic designs of Edward the Confessor, Henry reacted forcefully. The poet went to the executioner's block in 1547 only days before the king himself died.[8] Describing Henry VIII as a latter-day Sardanapalus enables Surrey to offer politically charged comment while simultaneously placing Henry into a figurative realm.

In similar fashion, Wyatt diffuses harsh political realities through the use of figurative description. The poem "Of the courtiers life written to Jhon Poins," evokes the Henrician court as an undesirable habitation from which the speaker flees. "[F]le the prease [i.e., press] of courtes," he memorably urges.[9] Tottel does not print "Who list his wealth and ease retain," a poem said to describe Wyatt's imprisonment in 1536 in the Tower of London, when he witnessed the execution of Anne Boleyn.[10] Proximity to Henry VIII, who appears here in the guise of Jupiter, is highly dangerous for the speaker of this poem. Drawing upon Seneca's *Phaedra*, the speaker advises readers to remain unknown at court in order to avoid Henry's thunderous anger. The distinctive phrase *circa regna tonat* (i.e., he [Jupiter] thunders around thrones) forms an ongoing refrain.[11] One is tempted to wonder whether Wyatt had in mind John Heywood's *Play of the Wether* (1533), which also evokes Henry under the guise of Jupiter (see Happé, chapter 1 in this volume). In any event, this verse emerged from direct engagement with Henry's perceived tyrannies.[12] Later anti-courtly poems, such as Ralegh's "The Lie" or Spenser's *Faerie Queene*, which obliquely incorporates anti-court discourse, build upon this Henrician theme.

These poems' vision of an implacable Henry VIII provided subsequent writers with a complex paradigm for the paradoxes of the Tudor court. The writers reimagined Henry in such a way that described political issues with greater focus. These issues included a fervid Protestant nationalism that Henry VIII was supposed to have embodied. Henry helped give shape to a vigorous tradition of pro-Tudor propaganda, for example, in which his persona takes on both wondrous and ineffable attributes. Ulpian Fulwell and Edmund Harman's pseudo-biography *The Flower of Fame* (1575), the first Protestant attempt to digest the king's lifetime achievement in print, affords a case in point.[13] A minor playwright and satirist, Fulwell dedicated this panegyric to William Cecil, Lord Burghley. It goes beyond standard chronicle treatment, according to its title, in discussing Henry's military successes, "matters, by the rest of our Cronographers overpassed." More fundamentally, and tonally not unlike Shakespeare's well-known concluding description of Queen Elizabeth in *Henry VIII*, the queen fully encompasses her father's image. She "doth [Henry] so revyve, / as though the Father were alyve." Henry himself, however, becomes transcendent – a "rare spectacle of Humanitie," a "speciall paterne of Clemencie and moderation" and a "bottomlesse spring of larges and benignitie."[14] As Fulwell and Harman's lively sobriquets display such grand and heroic enthusiasm, actual political circumstances fade almost beyond detection. Elizabeth embodies Henrician traits that acquire persuasive force specifically because they cannot be applied to an actual historical Henry VIII.

Henry VIII takes on mythic dimensions in these Elizabethan treatises, which simultaneously respond to real political commitments. Like most myths, Henry's persona encourages disparate interpretation and evolves into a kind of venerable institution over time. The impetus toward both patronage and royal counsel lies at the heart of these treatments. On the eve of Elizabeth's coronation, for instance, we detect Henry's emergence as a phenomenon at the dawn of the new regime. The queen's coronation procession through London locates the imagined representation of Henry's accomplishment within a particular discussion over the future of the realm. At Gracechurch Street, the queen viewed a dynastic tableau in which her father, "crowned w^t a crowne imperiall," joined her mother, Anne Boleyn, and her paternal grandparents, Henry VII and Elizabeth of York. The queen receives imperial authority from Henry VIII in particular, as Richard Mulcaster, author of the official account of these proceedings, makes clear:

at the verie remembraunce of her fathers name [she] toke so great a joy, y^t all men may well thinke, that as she rejoysed at his name whom this realme doth holde of so woorthie memorie: so in her doinges she will resemble the same.[15]

This account attempts to build unanimity for the new queen among the governing elite while repressing localized differences between the two regimes. It does so by offering an imagined narrative centered on Henry VIII of harmonious relations between the crown and the city, which funded these proceedings. In reality, London aldermen wished to remind Elizabeth of their own interests and concerns.[16]

The Elizabethan myth of Henry VIII emerges as a powerful, indeed paradoxical, legitimating narrative that effortlessly reconciles competing positions. Henry conveys meaning by straddling historical and fictional realms of representation. Writers consistently demand fluency concerning Henry's actual deeds among viewers and readers, who are then told to anticipate sequels of these acts in the deeds of Elizabeth. During the queen's progress to Oxford in 1592, for instance, academics disagreed with Elizabeth over the particular uses of Henry's memory. Roger Jones of New College discussed the extent to which Henrician precedent should influence the university's autonomy from the crown decades later. His treatise, "An Apology for ye gouerm^t of ye Uniu[er]sitie of Oxon against Henry the 8th" (1597), emphasizes Henry's unscrupulous methods of extracting the support of Oxford theologians for his divorce from Catherine of Aragon.[17] Elizabeth unwittingly plays the role of successor to Henry VIII in this warning against unnecessary royal administrative oversight of the university. The queen was certainly no stranger to this kind of appeal. During her first visit to the city, in 1566, George Etherege, the former Regius Professor of Greek, presented her with elegiac verse praising her father, together with a Latin prose argument and a Greek prose inscription to her.[18] Etherege states that his book "encloses the right healthy praise of the most invincible king, Henry VIII" and notes that "his great acts of generosity to both universities are enumerated."[19] He encourages Elizabeth to emulate Henry's supposed virtues through financial largess toward the university. "With all these things having to this point been enumerated," he writes,

the author himself congratulates the country and republic, that the illustrious queen depends upon these virtues, and she follows in the footsteps of her father toward the achievement of similar eternal glory.[20]

In Etherege's biased representation, Henry overshadows the fiscal policies of the regime even from the grave. The king's shadow, though, is only distinguishable when framed by current issues.

   Ambivalence of this kind may verge on anachronism and is the hallmark of Elizabethan writers' representation of Henry VIII. A number of scholars have examined the Elizabethan "public sphere," in which virtually any writer might hope to shape public opinion on matters of national or international significance.[21] Henry's impressionable reputation becomes inherently topical under such wide-ranging conditions. Arguments concerning the royal succession, for example, relied upon the malleability of the king's reputation – and its ability to evolve under changed circumstances – for their persuasive force. The parliamentarian Thomas Norton, besides co-authoring the succession play *Gorboduc* (1561), received a commission from Francis Walsingham, the queen's personal secretary, to write "Of the v periodes of 500 yeares." This unpublished prose treatise equates Henry's eviction of papal authority with the inauguration of the apocalypse.²² Norton's tract attributes quasi-biblical significance to Henry's rule. The queen need not concern herself with the royal succession, Norton argues, given the impending advent of Doomsday.

Representations of Henry VIII here and elsewhere certainly constitute a collective rhetorical projection. During these years portrayals of Henry gravitated from one set of concerns to the next with surprising regularity. As a governing paradigm, the Elizabethan succession crisis was the catalyst that accelerated Henry's growth into a cultural phenomenon. Representations of Henry VIII during the crisis consistently employ deferral techniques in order to re-envision the king as a kind of prophylactic figure who guards against the dangers of an uncertain succession. Sir Thomas Chaloner, an ambassador under four Tudor monarchs, contrived just such an overblown Henry in his revision of verse panegyric on the king, which he offered to Elizabeth in 1560 as a New Year's gift. Chaloner had written the work during the 1540s to celebrate Henry's victories over the French at Boulogne. In his updated dedication to the queen, Chaloner says of Henry that "no greater king ever ruled in our shores" and encourages Elizabeth that "nothing will be more worthy than for you, descended from a noble lineage, to be like your noble father." Nevertheless, he wryly enjoins Elizabeth to "bestow the bonds of your modesty on a husband" so that "then a little Henry will play in the palace for us, a handsome child who happily will bring to mind his grandfather, than whom no man was ever more handsome or more outstanding for handsome deeds."²³ Chaloner's boldly ironic counsel challenges the queen's reluctance to entertain public debate on her marital status. John Leslie, bishop of Ross, went so far as to argue that Elizabeth should not emulate Henry's own failure clearly to delineate the succession. Her father's error profited England no better than the quasi-historical monarchs Lear and Gorboduc, whose disastrous succession policies inaugurated periods of civil war.²⁴

The boundary between political and mythic representation of Henry VIII was both rigid and fluid. Elizabethan writers grappled with the intractable problem of how to counsel or even simply to describe the sitting monarch in terms of Henry's own accomplishment. The stakes reached a fever pitch amid debate concerning the queen's proposed marriage to François, duc d'Alençon. In his notorious tract *The Discovery of a Gaping Gulf* (1579), John Stubbes proposes Henry VIII as a corrective against Elizabeth's apparent hasty willingness to marry d'Alençon. Stubbes includes a discussion of "Example auncient" of disastrous French marriages by English monarchs dating back to King Henry I. He says that Elizabeth's father wisely chose to avoid a French marriage for himself:

I might set dowue [*sic*] all such [French] matches, as unhappy ones: and contrariwise those matches nothing so unhappy, but for the most parte prosperous, which were made eyther at home or in other places, as weren al those mariages made … by her majesties graundfather and by her father.

Stubbes goes on to suggest, sardonically, that Elizabeth actually marry Alençon in order to keep Henry's line from dying out.[25] Even though Stubbs lost his hand as punishment for publishing this unsolicited advice on this subject, the acceptable limits under which Henry VIII could galvanize political opposition to the marriage were wide ranging. Others opposed to it included his printer, Hugh Singleton. He had published Edmund Spenser's influential pastoral poem, *The Shepheardes Calendar* (1579), which also criticized the match. Spenser shared a political agenda with Robert Dudley, earl of Leicester, into whose service he had entered the previous year. Dudley may have viewed himself as a possible candidate for the queen prior to the Alençon negotiations. But it fell to Spenser to develop the most sophisticated representation of Henry VIII as a figurative stakeholder in these proceedings.

Spenser relishes the opportunity to delineate nuanced shades of meaning in his investigation of the Henry-myth. His treatment of Henry and the dissolution of the monasteries affords one instance of his ability to combine seemingly contradictory interpretations into a single complex precedent for current practice. In Spenser's dialogue on the "problem" of English occupation in Ireland, which he composed during the 1590s, the character Irenæus explains to his companion Eudoxus why ruined Irish towns are typically not rebuilt. Those with ample means deceptively obtain charters "under colour to repaire them" only to take "all meanes" to "keepe them waste." The case is "much like as in those old monuments of abbeyes, and religious houses," he continues. "For which cause it is judged that King Henry the Eight bestowed them … conceiving that thereby they should never bee able to rise againe."[26] Irenæus, of course, wishes that the towns be repaired in order to support his schemes for the "civilizing" of Irish society. Spenser sees Henry colluding with those who receive grants of former monastic lands in order to keep them suppressed. This collusion echoes fraudulent charter schemes linked to ruined Irish towns.

Spenser views this particular moment of Henrician history in poetic terms in the *View of Ireland*; as would be expected given Henry VIII's evolving mythic status, the king takes on increased representational flexibility as a result. Spenser makes explicit his conflation of the genres of history and poetry in Irenæus's justification of his narrative to Eudoxus: "Thus I have, Eudoxus … run through the state of that whole country, both to let you see what it now is, and also what it may bee by good care and amendment." Irenæus follows Sidney's *Defense of Poesy*, which argues that the "peerless poet" performs the functions of both philosopher and historian: "[F]or whatsoever the philosopher saith should be done, he [the poet] giveth a perfect picture of it in someone by whom he presupposeth it was done, so as he coupleth the general notion with the particular example."[27] On this model Henry – the alleged "perfect picture" – acquires both universal and specific applicability, not only here but throughout Spenser's writings. It is important to realize that this applicability is contingent upon the constant refashioning of Henry's image in response to a localized set of concerns. Moreover, incorporating both universal and specific aspects into this representation of Henry VIII directs the reader in divergent directions. Henry's suppression of monastic lands affords Irenæus a *negative* example, just moments before this peroration. In his effort to reconcile this divergence, Spenser elsewhere incorporates Henry into his overall project to construct a *viable* foundation for moral awareness.

The Henry myth attains its greatest degree of complexity in Spenser's *Faerie Queene* (1590–6). The poet's preoccupation in that work with the "false" appearance of Duessa, who signifies the Roman Catholic Church, is well known; but his interest in interrogating issues of representational "truth," "falsehood," and "transcendence" surrounding Henry VIII is less often remarked. As we have seen, the king's decision to sequester the monasteries as a strategy to keep them ruined shapes Irenæus's plans to reconstruct Irish towns. This seemingly paradoxical association invites readers to investigate the broader hermeneutical contexts on which this analogy is based.

The dissolution becomes a focal point for Spenser's working out difficulties associated with representing Henry VIII. Spenser elsewhere emphasizes, for example, the alleged capacity of monastic foundations to *damage* the cohesion of society, in opposition to Irenæus's proffered theory. In these moments the poem's narrator implicitly suggests the desirability of disillusion rather than evoke its inauspicious properties, and Henry's response to the monasteries takes on either auspicious or inauspicious associations as a moveable trope. At the conclusion to Book 6, Calidore, the knight of Courtesy, must pursue the Blatant Beast to "a Monastere," where "he him found despoyling all with maine and might."[28] This monastery ironically thrives not by fostering religious devotion, but rather by nurturing the Blatant Beast, whose name derives from the Latin *blatare*, which signifies vain babble. Spenser does not propose the Blatant Beast as justification for Henry VIII's action against monastic foundations, preferring instead to criticize them on grounds of the alleged shallowness of their devotion.

Spenser encodes Henry VIII and the dissolution more explicitly in the Lion whom Una, his figure for the "true" church, tames. The Lion slays Kirkrapine, who brings goods stolen from churches to the house of Abessa, "[w]ith whom he whoredome vsd" (1.3.18.5). Her name signifies the "blindness" of monastic devotion that suffers setback via association with the slain Kirkrapine. Given the extensive regal imagery associated with the lion in the Bible,[29] Spenser's possible link to Henry as an opponent of "false" monastic religiosity acquires rich possibilities. In these examples, then, Henry takes on an unstable, shifting position. On the one hand, he implicitly supports Spenser's polemical arguments in favor of "true" religion against "false" monastic abuses, but, on the other hand, when monasteries endure or even thrive, Henry's support for Spenser's agenda is more reserved and opaque.

Writing during the 1590s, Spenser imagines and reimagines Henry's intervention in religious debate, but in response to topical issues that are foreign to Henry's own time. Spenser's approach to the royal succession in *The Faerie Queene* develops Henry as an anachronistic precedent most explicitly. By equating Henrician and Elizabethan England, Spenser has Elizabeth's paternity legitimize her moral authority as a perpetual virgin in *The Faerie Queene*. Notably, the poet's treatment of Henry differs from that of those who urged Elizabeth to marry, on her father's example, in order to achieve stability. Now, according to Spenser, stability will prevail only if Elizabeth refuses to marry. Such stability ironically – and tendentiously – emerges as a direct consequence of the Henry figure's representational flexibility. This attribute appears in Book 2 after Guyon and Arthur arrive at the Castle of Temperance, where they read the overlapping histories of Britain and Faerie. Paradoxically, these "rolls, / And old records from auncient times deriud" are "all worm eaten, and full of canker holes" (2.9.57.6–7, 9) despite the fact that they break off as recently as Henry's reign. According to this historiography, Gloriana, the Fairy Queen, descends lineally from Oberon, a fairy king. Because of Elizabeth's own associations with the poem's titular monarch, Oberon comes to signify Henry VIII. "Great was his power and glorie ouer all, / Which him before, that sacred seate did fill, / That yet remaines his wide memoriall," Spenser claims concerning the queen's father (2.10.76.1–3). The throne itself commemorates Henry VIII because Elizabeth, his successor, occupies it. Henry's triumph nullifies any contrary interpretations, which undermine the king's place in the historical record in the manner of canker worms. Spenser wishes to set the record straight, as it were, concerning Henry's complex posthumous story, a process which begins with correcting those who have misread its meaning. This particular device echoes the apotheosizing function of *The Flower of Fame*, for "[f]airer and nobler liueth none this howre" than Elizabeth (2.10.76.6).

Ironically, however, Spenser's version of events remains just one facet of the Henry myth. Elizabeth's purported "fairness" derives explicitly from her virgin status as daughter of Henry VIII. Spenser's detractors are those contemporary readers who describe Henry as the supposed originator of their troubles. Spenser's comment on the paternity of Belphoebe, another of the poem's Elizabeth figures, responds especially to these hostile readers. Raised within "saluage forests" (3.6.1.4), Belphoebe is sister to Amoret, whom Busirane captures to provoke Sir Scudamore's quest in Book 3. In a remarkable passage concerning Belphoebe's supposed immaculate conception, Spenser rehabilitates Elizabeth's reputation and, implicitly, Henry's, from critics:

> Her berth was of the wombe of Morning dew,
> And her conception of the ioyous Prime,
> And all her whole creation did her shew
> Pure and vnspotted from all loathly crime
> That is ingenerate in fleshly slime.
> So was this virgin borne, so was she bred,
> So was she trained vp from time to time,
> In all chaste virtue, and true bounty-hed
> Till to her dew perfection she was ripened.   (3.6.1–9)

Spenser's claim that Belphoebe/Elizabeth is immaculately conceived affords an ironic rebuttal to those who would oppose this reading, since, as a Protestant, Spenser rejected this doctrine. The poet may have in mind Nicholas Sander's *De origine ac progressu schismatis anglicani* (1585). Sander argued that the queen descended from the incestuous union of Henry and Anne Boleyn, whom, according to Sander, Henry had fathered *and* wed.[30] Belphoebe and Henry both avoid such "fleshly slime" and the "loathly crime" with which Elizabeth has been maligned. Instead, the queen's virginity becomes the defining mark of her virtue, which remains intelligible only within this contrived paternal context.[31]

Elizabeth's paternity legitimizes Spenser's use of Henry as a motivating framework for political action. Spenser shares this principle with Stubbes, even if he employs more sophisticated formal ironies. In the "April" eclogue to *The Shepeardes Calendar*, we discover Hobbinol, a shepherd poet, who praises Elizabeth as the scion of virtuous classical prototypes that double for her own parents. "[S]hee is *Syrinx* daughter without spotte, / Which *Pan* the shepheards God of her begot."[32] In his accompanying prose commentary,

Spenser's anonymous commentator, E. K., who probably doubles for Spenser himself, identifies Anne Boleyn as Syrinx and Henry VIII as Pan: "[B]y Pan is here meant the most famous and victorious King, her highnesse Father, late of worthy memorye K. Henry the eyght … And in some place Christ himself, who is the verye Pan and god of Shepheardes."[33]

When read against Spenser's larger *oeuvre*, explicit incongruities unsurprisingly abound in this account. They reveal some of the representational challenges associated with employing the Henry myth. Like Mulcaster's, this portrayal of the queen verbalizes late medieval dynastic ceremonial tableaux.[34] Henry takes on quasi-religious properties as the messianic forebear of the Elizabethan establishment. Pan assumes a dual role in this eclogue as both Henry VIII and Christ himself. E. K. suggests this linkage as a means of dignifying Elizabeth's genealogical pedigree and reimagining Henry as the guarantor of political orthodoxy. As an irrefutable argument concerning Henry's ongoing vitality to the Elizabethan regime, though, this logic is flawed, because Pan's ability to occupy a shared middle ground between Henry and Christ does not necessarily produce the conclusion that Henry takes on Christ-like attributes. In *The Faerie Queene*, the poet forces Henry VIII to occupy this same paradoxical signifying position. In Merlin's Prophecy to Britomart, another Elizabeth figure, in Book 3, the queen's grandfather, Henry VII, reclaims the crown for the Britons. "Then shall a royall Virgin raine, which shall / Stretch her white rod over the *Belgicke* shore," prophesies Merlin (3.3.49.6–7). Spenser was not ignorant of the controversy surrounding English Protestant involvement in the Low Countries. His highly wrought description of this intervention figuratively emerges within the context of English incursion into the so-called British "fringe" of Wales and Ireland, where he resided while writing the poem. Henry provides the impetus and pseudo-mythical grounds on which Spenser builds his position. The father's martial accomplishment works in tandem with the daughter's sexual restraint to bring success to a cosmopolitan nation. In terms of their historical veracity, none of these attributes bears more than an indirect link to the politics from which they evolve. Nevertheless, they assume an important political function within the poem. In his prophecy to Britomart, Merlin evokes the Act of Union (1536), which provided Henry VIII with the legal justification to incorporate Wales under English jurisprudence. "Thenceforth eternall union shall be made / Betweene the nations different afore" (3.3.49.1–2).

Representations of Henry VIII took on imagined characteristics of universality combined with specific applicability in Elizabethan writing about this king. What, then, of James I? Henry certainly represented a problematic precursor to James's use of the royal prerogative. James's wide literary interests represented a distinct departure from Elizabeth, who was fluent in several languages but failed to articulate a systematic vision of royal authority with the degree of nuance employed by James. James and other members of the royal family could not avoid Henry's shadow, despite the king's attempts to keep Henry at a distance.[35] The pressures of the topical could sometimes overwhelm the equally powerful trend toward transcendence in Jacobean representations of Henry VIII. Following the discovery of the Gunpowder Plot to blow up Parliament in the fall of 1605, for example, satire concerning Henry circulated.[36] Henry proved particularly germane to James's contribution to this discussion, given the Tudor king's dealings with the papacy. The ironies of this representation of Henry VIII, however, were lost on the king, who failed to understand the extent to which Henry VIII adhered to a theologically orthodox outlook. The Italian Cardinal Robert Bellarmine urged George Blackwell, the leader of the English secular Catholic clergy, against professing allegiance to the crown in the aftermath of the plot. James's *Triplici Nodo, Triplex Cuneus. Or an Apology for the Oath of Allegiance* (1607) responds to Bellarmine and two papal proclamations by demonstrating ways in which English Catholics may swear temporal obedience without jeopardizing their religious allegiance to Rome.[37]

In this revival of the Henry myth in the wake of the Gunpowder Plot, the royal supremacy acquires demonic overtones. Bellarmine brings Henry into the debate by contrasting papal authority with the presumed "false" authority of the English Church. In his letter to Blackwell, which James reprints along with his reply, Bellarmine describes James's insistence that Catholics renounce obedience to the pope as "nothing else, but sleights and subtilties of Satan." The Jacobean Oath of Allegiance "tends to this end, that the authoritie of the head of the Church in England, may bee transferred from the successour of S[aint] Peter, to the successour of King Henry the eight."[38] Bellarmine explicitly describes James as a latter-day Henry VIII who offends loyal Catholics and the memory of honored Henrician martyrs. "Neither can you be ignorant, that these most holy and learned men, John bishop of Rochester, and Tho[mas] More, within our memory, for this one most weighty head of doctrine, led the way to martyrdom" (101–2). The alleged Satanic nature of James's oath fits hand-in-glove with Henry's earlier persecution of these Catholics. Bellarmine's accusation forces James into a difficult conceptual position. The king needed Henry's signifying potential but did not wish to be linked too closely with his predecessor's improprieties. In his reply James strongly denies that the successions of St. Peter and Henry VIII are comparable. To this "unapt and unmannerly similitude," James retorts:

For as to King Henries Successour (which hee meaneth by mee) as I, I say, never did, nor will presume to create any Article of Faith, or to bee judge thereof; but to submit my exemplarie obedience unto them, in as great humilitie as the meanest of the land. (110)

This exchange, then, suggests some of the ways in which James drew upon Henry for his ideas of royal authority. As long as the king does not define doctrine, he believes that he may govern as Henry did. This position strikes the modern reader as somewhat disingenuous, since James did not avoid doctrinal debates. In any event, the exchange reveals ways in which James struggled to maintain control of the representation of his Tudor predecessor.

In Jacobean representations of Henry VIII, the king reacts to and frames focused topical associations. Henry persists decisively as a gauge for measuring the operations of Jacobean politics in representations of the royal family beyond James himself. The courtier poet Henry Peacham, for instance, employs iconography associated with Henry VIII to represent James's heir, Henry Frederick. Peacham's goal is to encourage Henry Frederick to embrace an evangelical position by emulating Henry VIII. Seeking royal patronage, Peacham incorporated elements of Tudor dynastic iconography into a series of manuscript emblem books that he presented both to James and Henry Frederick between 1603 and 1610. These books adapt James's *Basilicon Doron* (1599), a book of fatherly advice that James had offered to guide the education of his son.[39] Peacham undertook the first of these volumes, *ΒΑΣΙΛΙΚΟΝ ΔΩΡΟΝ In Heroica Emblemata resolutum* (1603–4), as an expression of gratitude "to the most serene prince Henry Frederick."[40] The eighteenth emblem in this volume employs the familiar Protestant image of the Sword and Book, which had appeared in connection with Henry VIII on earlier texts. Peacham incorporates this device to praise Prince Henry as the Protestant fulfillment of a decisively Protestant and thoroughly anachronistic version of Henry VIII.

In his drawing Peacham places a perpendicular sword propping open a book with its hilt. The attached feathers of the Principality of Wales emphasize a direct link from this device to the prince. Peacham instructs his dedicatee in virtuous governance in a manner not dissimilar to the image's appearance on the title-page border of the Coverdale Bible (1535) (see King, chapter 2 in this volume). Perhaps as an encouragement to the prince to model himself after Henry VIII, this emblem signifies "the praise of virtue in action" since "it is not enough that yee have and retaine (as prisoners) within your self never so many good qualities and Virtues except yee imploy them, and set them on work, for the weale of them that are committed to your charge."[41] The third, much expanded version of this book,

ΒΑΣΙΛΙΚΟΝ ΔΩΡΟΝ in *Basilica Emblemata totum versum ... donata* (1610), confirms the Sword and Book design as a specific link between the two Henrys. In this instance, the inscription "Biblia" identifies the book as a Bible and recalls Henry VIII's appearance within this scheme on the title pages of sixteenth-century vernacular Bibles (Figure 6).[42] This inscription, which does not appear in the first two versions of this device, signifies royal authority explicitly derived from Henry VIII. In these emblems, Peacham encourages Henry Frederick to rule in the manner of forward Protestant engagement supposedly represented by Henry VIII.

Jacobean treatises like Peacham's combine figurative argument concerning Henry VIII with royal counsel more forcefully than do their Elizabethan predecessors. The greater historical distance separating Jacobean England from Henry's own reign meant that writers could comment on Henry more freely than even Spenser could. Their representations accordingly become more extravagant, iconic, and contrived. Following the onset of the Thirty Years War in 1618, Henry VIII appears as a mediator amid Stuart royal intrigue in *Vox Coeli, or News from Heaven* (1624). In this remarkable allegorical treatise, the controversialist John Reynolds demands that England intervene on behalf of continental Protestants in their struggle against Spain.[43] Reynolds records a fictitious debate in heaven among England's deceased monarchs about the dangers to the nation of Prince Charles's proposed marriage to Maria, the daughter of Philip III of Spain. Significantly, this work appeared from the presses the year after Charles's unsuccessful courtship journey to Spain. Even though the Spanish marriage was no longer a real possibility, Reynolds probably wrote in 1623, at a time when he might have hoped to shape public opinion against the proposed match.[44] After Charles's return, *Vox Coeli* would have had the more general effect of utilizing anti-Spanish sentiment to foment opposition to Hapsburg incursion into the Low Countries.

Reynolds gathers an unlikely cohort of royal worthies to analyze not only the prince's Spanish marriage, but also Anglo-Spanish relations as they had evolved since the Armada of 1588. Henry VIII leads this group and presides over the meeting, which discusses, according to the work's title, "Spain's ambition and treacheries to most kingdoms and free estates of Europe." Joining him are Edward VI and Queen Elizabeth, who offer decidedly Protestant commentary. Prince Henry, who had died unexpectedly in 1612, and Anne of Denmark, James's late wife, are also present. Completing their number is Mary Tudor, who is allowed to attend only because the group believes "that from her innate and inveterate malice to England, she might ... bewray something that might turne and redound to the good of England."[45]

4

Initium sapientiæ.

Squammiger in gyros gladio se colligit anguis
   Naturam signant quæ Politéia tuam
Effera Iustitia est, Prudentia vana Solonis
   Hæc nisi sustentent Biblia sacra Dei

Figure 6. Henry Peacham, *Initium sapientiae*. From *ΒΑΣΙΛΙΚΟΝ ΔΩΡΟΝ in Basilica*
Emblemata totum versum (detail).

This collection of royal figures engages in a full-scale reshaping of James's royal ancestor.

In his capacity as moderator, Henry VIII admits that his descendants have more experience than he does in dealing with Spain. This is ironic, of course, given his first marriage to Catherine of Aragon. When Henry opens proceedings by calling for a summary of Spain's relations with various European nations over the past century, Mary defends Spanish occupation of Navarre: "sith they are the Catholique kings, they cannot be irreligious much lesse uncharitable." Henry rejoins, "they are only Catholique in title, not in effect, much lesse in heart or soule, for if usurpation be religion, I know not what is heresie" (7). Henry ironically alludes to his own practice of styling himself an explicitly Catholic monarch in order to reinforce his brand of religious orthodoxy as definitively non-papal. To Henry VIII, the pope could never be a Catholic.[46] The king's remark also echoes the representational paradoxes explored by Spenser and others. According to the king's formulation, usurpation is implicitly heretical, if not seditious, but Mary threatens to overturn this equation by blurring the boundary between heresy and revolt. For Reynolds, Hapsburg incursion embodies Henry's concern over the semantics of orthodoxy. Reynolds transforms the king from a monarch whose religious policies had themselves changed from anti-Lutheran defense of Roman Catholicism during the 1520s to a retrenched advocacy of conservative doctrines during the 1540s. Henry reproves Mary for espousing the very shift in religious perspective that the historical Henry had himself approved.

Reynolds presents Henry VIII as the benevolent defender of English Protestant nationalism that he never actually was. The process whereby Henry VIII – and not one of the other monarchs present – comes to embody this position is shrouded with mystery. This mystery, however, constitutes an important component of his posthumous legacy. After describing various Spanish atrocities against the native inhabitants of North America, Henry attests how "religion must still bee the pretext, and cloke" of Spanish usurpation (9). When objecting to Spain's possession of the Portuguese crown, the king affirms, "to a prince and people so greedy and ambitious of empire as is Spain, all fish is good that comes to his hooke or net" (14). When Mary argues that the assassination of Henri III of France, on August 1, 1589, was providentially ordained, Henry retorts,

You are deceived daughter, for it was a good king, and a bade fryer (or rather a divill in a fryers weede) to set handes on the Lords anoynted, but this arrow came out of the quiver of Spain, and hell, for that bloudie and execrable murther was no sooner perpetrated, but then instantly followed the proposition of the Infantas title to France, which apparantly makes the murther to be Spaynes. (28–9)

If a thin veneer of religion veils Spain's desire for domination and usurpation, Reynolds imagines England still practicing "true" religion as embodied by Henry VIII. The historical irony is, of course, that Henry himself had exploited ecclesiastical wealth in an effort to sustain military domination on the continent.

By the time Reynolds is writing, the king had long since abandoned his tyrannical moorings and entered the realm of representation. Whether alive or dead, he had, in fact, always occupied this realm. Somewhat paradoxically, he succeeds so spectacularly in achieving a kind of universal meaning here because of the magnitude of his actual historical importance. In Reynolds's book, topicality and figurative transcendence struggle in order best to describe Henry VIII. From the perspective of both the topical and the universal, Henry solidified his place as a mythic symbol for Protestant factionalism and English accomplishment. It is a stance that his posthumous persona has not yet relinquished.

NOTES

1. I follow Sidney's notion of the poet as a "maker" who writes with a view toward moral edification, although not necessarily exclusively in verse. Sir Philip Sidney, *The Defence of Poesy*, in Gavin Alexander (ed.), *Sidney's "The Defence of Poesy" and Selected Renaissance Literary Criticism* (London: Penguin, 2004), 8–11.
2. Alex Preminger (ed.), *Encyclopedia of Poetry and Poetics* (Princeton: Princeton University Press, 1965), 710.
3. Bodl., MS Wood empt. 2. W. D. Macray published an edition for the Roxburghe Club in 1875. See Madan, vol. II, part ii, 1198.
4. My essay on "Typology and Tyranny in Roman Catholic Histories of Henry VIII" is forthcoming.
5. Richard Tottel (ed.), *Songs and Sonnets, written by Henry Howard Late Earl of Surrey, and Other* (London: Richard Tottel, 1557). *RSTC* 13861.
6. Arthur Marotti, *Manuscript, Print, and the English Renaissance Lyric* (Ithaca and London: Cornell University Press, 1995).
7. Tottel (ed.), *Songs and Sonnets*, sig. E1v.
8. W. A. Sessions, *Henry Howard, the Poet Earl of Surrey: A Life* (Oxford: Oxford University Press, 1999).
9. *Songs and Sonnets*, Tottel (ed.), sig M2v–3v.
10. The poem is known from the Blage manuscript.
11. R. A. Rebholz (ed.), *Sir Thomas Wyatt: The Complete Poems* (New Haven: Yale University Press, 1981), 155.
12. John Heywood, *The Play of the Wether* (1533). *RSTC* 13305. See also Greg Walker, *Plays of Persuasion: Drama and Politics at the Court of Henry VIII* (Cambridge: Cambridge University Press, 1991) and Greg Walker, *Writing under Tyranny: English Literature and the Henrician Reformation* (Oxford: Oxford University Press, 2005).

13. Ulpian Fulwell, *The Flower of Fame* (London: W. Hoskins, 1575), *RSTC* 11475. Fulwell's dedication reveals Harman as his collaborator.

14. Fulwell, *The Flower of Fame*, sigs. C1v, C4r.

15. *The Passage of our Most Drad Sovereign Lady Queen Elizabeth through the City of London to Westminster the Day before her Coronation* (London, 1558). *RSTC* 7590.

16. Susan Frye, *Elizabeth I: The Competition for Representation* (Oxford: Oxford University Press, 1993). See also Dale Hoak, "The Coronations of Edward VI, Mary I, and Elizabeth I, and the Transformation of the Tudor Monarchy," in C. S. Knighton and Richard Mortimer (eds.), *Westminster Abbey Reformed: 1540–1640* (Aldershot: Ashgate, 2003), 114–51.

17. "An Apology for ye gouerm^t of ye Uniu[er]sitie of Oxon against Henry the 8th," Bodl., MS Wood D 18. See Madan, vol. II, part ii, 1183–5.

18. BL, MS Royal 16.C.x. Warner and Gilson, II, 183. See also Jayne Elisabeth Archer and Sarah Knight, "Elizabetha Triumphans," in Jayne Elisabeth Archer, Elizabeth Goldring, and Sarah Knight (eds.), *The Progresses, Pageants, and Entertainments of Queen Elizabeth I* (Oxford: Oxford University Press, 2007), 14–16.

19. "rectem sanem Encomium Inuictissimi Regis Henrici Octaui, hic libellus continet"; "summa eius in utramq*ue* Academiam Oxoniam et Cantabrigiam beneficia recensentur." BL, MS Royal 16.C.x., fo. 5r.

20. Ibid., fo. 5v: "His omnibus adhunc modum enumeratis, author ipse patriae ac Reipublicae gratulatur, quod has virtutes Regina illustrissima initetur, et ad similes hoc est aeternas laudes parandas paternis vestigiis insistat." I am grateful to Chris Warner for assisting with Etherege's Latin.

21. Natalie Mears, "Counsel, Public Debate, and Queenship: John Stubbes's *The Discoverie of a Gaping Gulf*, 1579," *Historical Journal* 44 (2001), 629–50; Peter Lake and Michael Questier, "Puritans, Papists, and the 'Public Sphere' in Early Modern England: The Edmund Campion Affair in Context," *Journal of Modern History* 72 (2000), 587–627.

22. BL, MS Cottonian Titus F3. See Barry Shaw, "Thomas Norton's 'Devices' for a Godly Realm: An Elizabethan Vision for the Future," *Sixteenth Century Journal* 22 (1991), 495–509.

23. John B. Gabel and Carl C. Schlam (eds. and trans.), *Thomas Chaloner's* In Laudem Henrici Octavi (Lawrence, KS: Coronado Press, 1979), 25 and 99.

24. John Leslie, *Treatise Concerning the Defence of the Honor of the Right High, Mighty and Noble Princesse, Mary Queene of Scotland … With a Declaration … of her Right, Title, and Interest, to the Succession of the Crowne of England* (1569). *RSTC* 15505. See Marie Axton, "The Influence of Edmund Plowden's Succession Treatise," *Huntington Library Quarterly* 37 (1974), 209–26; and Marie Axton, *The Queen's Two Bodies: Drama and the Elizabethan Succession* (London: The Royal Historical Society, 1977), 35–7.

25. John Stubbes, *The Discovery of a Gaping Gulf Whereunto England is Like to be Swallowed by another French Marriage* (London, 1579), 37–40. *RSTC* 23400.

26. Edmund Spenser, *A View of the State of Ireland*, ed. Andrew Hadfield and Willy Maley (Oxford: Blackwell, 1997), 158.

27. Ibid., 160; Sidney, *The Defence of Poesy*, 16.

28. Edmund Spenser, *The Faerie Queene*, 2nd edn., ed. A. C. Hamilton (Harlow: Pearson Education, 2007), 6.12.23.8–9. All citations to this edition will be cited parenthetically.

29. See, for example, Revelation 5:5.

30. Christopher Highley, "'A Pestilent and Seditious Book': Nicholas Sander's *Schismatis Anglicani* and Catholic Histories of the Reformation," *Huntington Library Quarterly* 68 (2005), 151–71.

31. The preceding discussion is indebted to theories concerning the Cult of Elizabeth as both a marriageable and unmarriageable virgin. See Susan Doran, "Juno Versus Diana: The Treatment of Elizabeth I's Marriage in Plays and Entertainments, 1561–1581," *Historical Journal* 38 (1995), 257–74; and John N. King, "Queen Elizabeth I: Representations of the Virgin Queen," *Renaissance Quarterly* 43 (1990), 30–74.

32. William Oram, *et al.* (eds.), *The Yale Edition of the Shorter Poems of Edmund Spenser* (New Haven and London: Yale University Press, 1989), *The Shepheardes Calender* "April," lines 50–1.

33. Ibid., 67–8, glossing line 50.

34. Sydney Anglo, *Spectacle, Pageantry, and Early Tudor Policy,* 2nd edn. (Oxford: Clarendon Press, 1997). See also John N. King, *Spenser's Poetry and the Reformation Tradition* (Princeton: Princeton University Press, 1990), 154–5.

35. For an overview of historiography on the reign of James, see Ralph Houlbrooke, "James's Reputation, 1625–2005," in Ralph Houlbrooke (ed.), *James VI and I: Ideas, Authority, and Government* (Aldershot: Ashgate, 2006), 167–90.

36. Richard F. Hardin, "The Early Poetry of the Gunpowder Plot: Myth in the Making," *English Literary Renaissance* 22 (1992), 62–79.

37. *RSTC* 14400.

38. Johann P. Sommerville (ed.), *King James VI and I: Political Writings* (Cambridge: Cambridge University Press, 1994), 99. Further citations to this edition will appear parenthetically within the text. On the oath see 3 & 4 Jac. I, c. 4.

39. James I, *Basilicon Doron* (Edinburgh: Robert Waldegrave, 1599), *RSTC* 14348. This edition was issued in just seven copies specifically for the prince's use. It appeared in a new edition four years later: *Basilicon Doron. Or, His Majesty's Instructions to his Dearest Son, Henry the Prince* (Edinburgh, Robert Waldegrave, 1603), *RSTC* 14349. See James Doelman, *King James I and the Religious Culture of England* (Cambridge: D. S. Brewer, 2000), 23, 62.

40. Bodl., MS. Rawl. poet. 146. The opening of the dedication reads, "in gratiam serenissimi principis Henrici Frederici."

41. Bodl., MS Rawl. Poet 146 fo. 17v: "Virtutis Laus in actione." Madan, III, 313–14.

42. BL, MS Royal 12 A lxvi, fo. 4r. Warner and Gilson, II, 9. Peacham's second manuscript emblem book, BL, MS Harleian 6855, art. 13, is described in the *Catalogue of the Harleian Manuscripts, in The British Museum, with Indexes of Persons, Places, and Matters*, vol. III (London, 1808), 441. For dating the emblem books, see the *ODNB* on Peacham.

43. *RSTC* 22094.

44. Thomas Cogswell, *The Blessed Revolution: English Politics and the Coming of War, 1621–1624* (Cambridge: Cambridge University Press, 1989), 290.

45. John Reynolds, *Vox Coeli, or News from Heaven* (London, 1624), 4. RSTC 20946.4. Subsequent references to this work will be cited parenthetically.

46. Peter Marshall, "Is the Pope Catholic? Henry VIII and the Semantics of Schism," in Ethan Shagan (ed.), *Catholics and the "Protestant Nation": Religious Politics and Identity in Early Modern England* (Manchester: Manchester University Press, 2005), 22–48.

CHAPTER 6

The Henry VIII story in the eighteenth century: words and images

Ronald Paulson

What did Henry VIII mean to the eighteenth century? The immediately significant monarch, still affecting politics, was Henry's daughter Elizabeth I, of the Tudors the heroic figure. His other daughter Mary only recalled popery and burnings, although Henry was responsible for at least as many, and his son Edward VI was a shadow. In the anti-papist Gordon Riots of 1780, for example, there were slogans against Bloody Mary and for Queen Bess but no mention of Henry VIII. Except for historians, writers let Henry keep a low profile. As a progenitor of Protestant England he was not as respectable or unambiguous as Elizabeth. It was safer to allude to him in the form of graphic images – the heavy Holbein figure, legs outspread like the Colossus of Rhodes.

Henry VIII reached the eighteenth century as a figure, physically and politically, of concentrated and absolute power – partly the result of the effective work of Thomas Cromwell and his propagandists and partly the memory of many beheadings. This was the Henry whom Geoffrey Hill has called "this king of bloody trunks."[1]

Not a very sympathetic figure, though the grimness of the royal image is domesticated in the jolly, bluff Harry, the gormandizer, hunter, and womanizer, six feet tall with a fifty-four-inch girth, who ran through (in some cases fatally) six wives. This was the Henry who, in the popular Restoration satire of travesty (*Dido talks and acts like a fishwife*), broke with Rome – who used this break to consolidate his own power, the principle of his personal supremacy – simply in order to get himself the body of Anne Boleyn.

> As old Babylon saith:
> The protestant faith
> Took deep root from the codpiece of Harry.[2]

In folklore Henry was, on the one hand, the animated codpiece (emphatic in the Holbein full-length portrait; see frontispiece), and, on the other, the cheerful (comic in the sense of repetitive) beheader of wives, or perhaps of anyone. The nursery rhyme that begins "Oranges and lemons, / Say the bells of St. Clements," ends with the mock-sinister couplet: "Here comes a candle to light you to bed, / Here comes a chopper to chop off your head" – which has been associated by some folklorists with England's most famous head-chopper.[3] I have sometimes wondered if the common shopsign of "The Good Woman," which shows a headless woman – as in Hogarth's *Times of the Day*, Plate 2 – had a source in the commonsense justification of Henry's treatment of his wives. This Henry VIII is still recalled, in *Alice in Wonderland*, in the Queen of Spades' order "Off with their heads" – Carroll's playful irony in that, while the King of Hearts sports a suspiciously Henrician beard, the command comes from the queen.[4]

Henry, in his youth a patron of More, Erasmus, Colet, and the humanists, was remembered more for his execution of More and Surrey. For the satirists, Whig and Tory, it was still the martyred Charles I who mattered, and the Protestant Succession that followed 1688. Charles II tended to absorb the bawdy aspect of Henry VIII.

Henry was most available in one graphic and one literary source: the portrait by Holbein that everyone seemed to know through copies in oil or other media and the play by Shakespeare, produced seventy-two times in the century.[5]

HOLBEIN

There had been earlier portraits, of the (according to contemporary accounts) dazzling, handsome young king, but only around 1536, in his mid-forties, was he, as David Piper has put it, "ripe for Holbein": "he had divorced Catherine of Aragon, challenged the Pope and the whole of Catholic Europe, and set up his own Church with himself as its Supreme Head."[6] He had also beheaded another queen and was marrying for the third time, about to produce the wished-for male heir. He was at this point, in the popishly inclined Bishop Gardiner's words, a king who claimed to be "in this world present the person of God."[7]

The visual image of Henry VIII (Holbein's only full-length portrait among his many English subjects), the stance, swagger, even the little piggy eyes, was the primary source of response in the eighteenth century. Its contemporary importance had been as imperial propaganda, borne out by the many copies and derivatives, the stance subsequently carried on to the legs-astride pose of Henry's son Edward VI and then (skipping the two intervening queens) Prince Henry.[8] It was copied and reproduced sufficiently to be familiar – for example, on the title page of Samuel Rowley's play *When*

You See Me, You Know Me. Or the famous Chronicle Historie of King Henrie the Eight (1605) – and the Holbein Henry apparently served actors as their model for Shakespeare's stage Henry. In the frontispiece to Nicholas Rowe's 1709 edition of *Henry VIII* the actor Thomas Betterton plays Henry in the Holbein pose and costume, though the actors in the background are in contemporary dress. The portrait was for the English public iconic and for its artists a part of the English visual vocabulary (which included both the high art of the Raphael Cartoons at Hampton Court and the low art of shopsigns showing crude copies of Holbein's "King's Head").[9] We can assume that the artists who used the image of Henry – not only William Hogarth but Sir Joshua Reynolds – were aware not only of its cultural significance, but of the sheer quality of Holbein's portrait.

SHAKESPEARE

In literature, the negative aspects of Henry VIII were displaced to the other, safer characters of his story – prime minister, queen, and mistress. Shakespeare's play, *The History of Henry VIII* (1613), based on the life in Holinshed's *Chronicle*, focused on the period just prior to the time of Holbein's portrait, and so on Cardinal Wolsey, Queen Catherine, Anne Boleyn, and the Reformation – but only two of the six wives and none of their beheadings. The prologue (lines 14–17) sets this play off as serious history from the "merry, bawdy play" of Rowley's *When You See Me* and the carnivalesque figure of the bluff King Harry.

What Henry signifies in the play – as opposed to Wolsey, Queen Catherine, Buckingham, Anne, and Cromwell – is simply, in Geoffrey Bullough's words, "a man of sensual lust and self-will."[10] He is a relatively normative figure of kingship in a patriotic English context, though at the end he is set off against Archbishop Cranmer, who emerges as the significant spiritual (as opposed to Henry's physical) progenitor of Queen Elizabeth, the true telos of the drama. Shakespeare's psychological emphasis is on Henry's need for an heir, and this takes the form of a threat to his masculinity (see String, chapter 7 in this volume).[11]

The play was popular throughout the century, probably because it reiterated the crucial story of Protestant England, and the popularity peaked at royal coronations, in particular that of George II in 1727. *Henry VIII* had played frequently at John Rich's Lincoln's Inn Fields Theatre, and as recently as February 1727;[12] but then, following the coronation on June 11, on October 26 Colley Cibber revived the play at Drury Lane with a spectacularly expanded coronation scene. This was so successful that

Rich produced a rival coronation scene of his own. The popularity of the production brought out other Henry VIII pieces, including four days later *Poems on Several Occasions. With Anne Boleyn to King Henry VIII. An Epistle.* And on November 13 the *Daily Post* reported that the play "still continues to draw numerous Audiences, which is owing to the Excellency of the Performance, and the extraordinary Grandeur of the Decorations." The royal family attended the play on November 7.[13]

And on November 22 Cibber revived another Henry VIII play, John Banks' *Virtue Betray'd: or, Anna Bullen, a Tragedy* (first produced in 1682), a staple of the Drury Lane repertory. In both plays Barton Booth and Cibber played Henry and Wolsey and Mrs. Porter played Anne Boleyn. But in Banks' play Henry is simply, to set off the virtuous Anne, lustful and inconstant – "the amorous King," "the vext and passionate King."[14]

WOLSEY

From early on, spectators had read contemporary parallels into the play: George Villiers, duke of Buckingham, in 1628, had sponsored a production of the play and walked out after his namesake is beheaded. Robert Cell, in a letter, remarked that "Some say, he should rather have seen ye fall of Cardinall Woolsey, who was a more lively type of himself," but, as the Arden editor, Gordon McMullan, notes, he was showing "that his name-sake in the play died as a result of being framed. Walking out of the theatre at the moment of the Duke's assertion of his innocence would thus serve both to imply that the charges against him were false and to ensure that the audience ignored the rest of the play, including the possible comparisons with Wolsey."[15] Again in 1717, at a performance for George I at Hampton Court, courtiers laughed at evident analogies between Wolsey and "minis-terial craft," and the king "joined in a hearty laugh of approbation."[16]

Cibber, who played Wolsey in the 1727 production, tells the story of how George II so enjoyed the analogy between Wolsey and his father's chief minister, Sir Robert Walpole – observed by Cibber when he spoke Wolsey's lines in 1.2.103–8, where he takes credit for Henry's lifting of taxes he had himself imposed – "that it may be no wonder why his Majesty's Particular Taste for it, should have commanded it three several times in one Winter."[17]

Horace Walpole, in his *Memoirs of King George II* (publ. 1822) saw the comparison of the kings, George and Henry, as mock-heroic; the former "had the haughtiness of Henry the Eighth without his spirit."[18] No one, however, intended a parallel between George II and Henry VIII. The operative analogy, always on a lower level, was between Wolsey and Sir Robert

Walpole at the moment when Henry dismissed Wolsey. The opposition journal the *Craftsman*, reviewing the play on November 18, drew attention to the resemblance between "The Character of this ambitious, wealthy, bad *Minister*," Cardinal Wolsey, and Sir Robert Walpole; and anti-Walpole poems appeared in subsequent issues.[19] The issue of December 3 adds the theatrical and (with it) the *de casibus* topos with the example of Wolsey, repeated in the next issue in an essay on "Great Men" (a code for Walpole). Richard Fiddes' *Life of Cardinal Wolsey* of 1726 was reissued, and in the *Daily Journal* for November 15 a pamphlet, obviously extending the parallel, was announced: *The History of the Fall of Count Olivarez, sole Minister to Philip IV, King of Spain.*[20]

Not only the king, however, but the circumstances were different: George II had just ascended the throne, and shortly thereafter, discovering that Walpole was financially indispensable, reappointed him – and so John Gay, at the beginning of the next year, in his ballad-opera *The Beggar's Opera* (February 1728), continued the story by having his Walpole analogue, Captain Macheath, just before he is hanged, granted a royal reprieve.

The analogy survived. The opposition continued to entertain hopes that the new king, George II, would follow Henry's example and dismiss Walpole. A decade later, in his journal the *Champion*, on December 8, 1739, Henry Fielding applied the term "Greatness," associated with Walpole, not only with Wolsey but "King *Henry* himself," thereby invoking his repudiation of Catherine and execution of Anne Boleyn. Discussing prime ministers, in the *Champion* for May 8, 1740, he cited Wolsey–Walpole, who "from the meanest Extraction, with such dissolute and scandalous Morals, that he was publicly set in the Stocks, was by a *Conflux of fortunate Accidents* advanced (if I may say so) above his Sovereign; so that Dukes and Earls held his Towel and Bason for him when he washed."[21]

HOGARTH

Hogarth's earliest reference to Henry VIII is in one of his large *Hudibras* plates of 1726, *Burning the Rumps at Temple Bar*: the figure on the shopsign above the head of the Puritan MP who is being hanged in effigy appears to be Henry, here the patron saint of the Reformation, the *reductio ad absurdum* of which was the Rump Parliament, now in the process of demise.[22]

At the time of the 1727 production of *Henry VIII*, Hogarth engraved a scene he entitled *Henry VIII and Anne Boleyn* (Figure 7). It is a satire on Wolsey–Walpole, with significant verses to underline the meaning. The engraving was later copied in a painting that hung in Vauxhall Gardens,

Here Struts old Pious Harry, once the Great,
Reformer of the English Church and State;
Twas thus he stood, when Anna Bullen's Charms,
Allur'd th'Amorous Monarch to her Arms,
With his Right hand he leads her as his own,
To place this matchless Beauty on his Throne.

Whilst Kate & Piercy mourn their wretched Fate,
And view the Royal Pair with equal State;
Reflecting on the Pomp of glittering Crowns,
And, Arbitrary Power that knows no Bounds.

Whilst Woolsey leaning on his Throne of State,
Through this unhappy change foresees his Fate,
Contemplates wisely upon worldly Things,
The Cheat of Grandeur & the Faith of Kings.

Figure 7. William Hogarth, *Henry VIII and Anne Boleyn*,
etching and engraving, 1727–8.

as Horace Walpole noted, "in the portico of the old great room on the right
hand as you enter the garden" – a place that made it part of the visual
experience of middle-class Londoners.[23] But a fledgling painter, Hogarth
also assimilates the scene to the conversation piece genre he was beginning

to explore.[24] In this sense, his intimate scene may have served as a corrective to the spectacle being emphasized in contemporary productions of the play – as it certainly did to the grand Van Dyck-style portraits of the time. Relying on the circumstantial realism associated with the French genre, he produced a costume conversation piece, with the same tensions between groups he showed in *The Cholmondeley Family* and other conversations: there, the parents are contrasted with the children, order with disorder; here, the relationship of Henry and Anne Boleyn on the left is set against Cardinal Wolsey on the right, and between them, Queen Catherine and Anne's former lover, Henry Percy. Wolsey's apprehensive expression illustrates the lines describing him in 3.2.112.

Percy is not a character in Shakespeare's play. He is, however, a leading character in Banks' *Virtue Betray'd*, which was as popular a play in the 1720s as *Henry VIII*. Hogarth is conflating the two plays – the story of Henry and the fall of Wolsey with the story of Henry–Anne–Catherine–Percy and the villainy of Wolsey.

The analogy between the coronation of George II and Queen Caroline and Henry VIII–Anne must have been suggestive, especially since it was only the queen who was crowned in Shakespeare's play.[25] Henrietta Howard (later Lady Suffolk) was the king's *maîtresse en titre*, but also, in the complicated world of the conversation piece, Queen Caroline's Woman of the Bed Chamber, and she divided her day between ceremonious duties to the queen and physical ones to the king. The analogies were picked up again a decade later and applied to Prince Frederick's court.

The Holbein Henry apparently served Davenant for the stage Henry, and, in the 1727 production, the actor Barton Booth; it serves Hogarth for his illustration, copied and reversed in the engraving (as was usual with Hogarth), and we can see the general stance returned in the Macheath of his several *Beggar's Opera* paintings (1728; Figure 8). In this instance his arms are raised and crossed: the figure is stronger, supported solidly on his two legs, which looked spindly in *Henry VIII and Anne Boleyn*. Furthermore, all three – Macheath, Henry, and Walpole – shared the wife–mistress problem, and Macheath's pardoning parallels Walpole's dismissal and subsequent reappointment.

It is an image of Walpole as Holbein's Henry that Hogarth could already have seen in the painting by John Wootton and Jonathan Richardson (Figure 9), which shows Squire Walpole in a hunting scene – an analogy Walpole seems to have encouraged. With the memory of Holbein's Henry VIII, Hogarth slides the analogy from Wolsey to Henry himself: by this time it was clear, says Hogarth, as the Macheath–Walpole analogy

Figure 8. William Hogarth, *The Beggar's Opera*, oil on canvas, 1728.

shows, George was not going to drop Walpole; Walpole had in effect replaced the monarch, and by implication become monarch-as-tyrant. Thus the Holbein image of Henry, legs wide apart, projecting authority and power once associated with the monarch, now designates his prime minister.

The exchange is already predicted in *Henry VIII and Anne Boleyn*, which places Wolsey on the throne (in the accompanying verse, "Whilst Woolsey leaning on the Throne of State"). Stuart Sillars takes the canopy to be an allusion to Hogarth's *Paradise Lost* illustration of 1725 showing Satan ruling over Pandemonium: "Walpole's presiding over parliament is an exact parallel to Satan's hold over the rebel angels, and both are figured meta- phorically in Wolsey's doomed over-reaching."[26] In Banks' *Virtue Betray'd*, Hogarth could have found a further source for the throne of Lucifer: Elizabeth Blunt, Henry's earlier mistress, predicts for Wolsey, when he is dead, "a mighty throne, as high / As was great *Lucifer's* before his fall" (30).

Now when the Wolsey figure becomes the Holbein Henry the result is not just satire but a historic truth: the power *was* in the eighteenth century seen to be shifting from the king to his chief minister – and even the "fall" of

Figure 9. John Wootton and Jonathan Richardson, *Sir Robert Walpole*, oil on canvas, 1740.

Walpole (finally, in 1742) proved to be a mask for the continuation of his policies in the hands of his epigones.

Two decades later, proceeding from politics to aesthetics, Hogarth uses the Holbein portrait of Henry VIII again in the second plate of his *Analysis of Beauty*, published in 1753.[27] In this plate (Figure 10), the graphic text that supplements the verbal, Henry is set off from the action in a niche (no. 72),[28] rather like an icon, as was of course the result of his iconoclasm (images

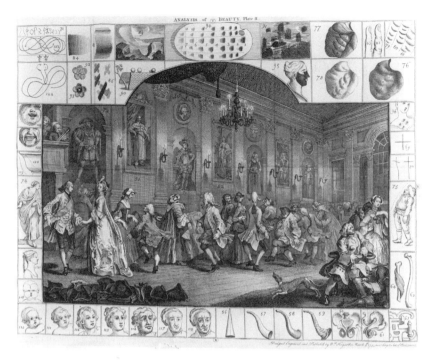

Figure 10. William Hogarth, *The Analysis of Beauty*, Plate 2, etching and engraving, 1753.

of Henry replacing pope, saints, and deity); and in the adjacent niches are
Edward VI (no. 73) and Queen Elizabeth (unnumbered). The significance of
the trio (Henry, Edward, and Elizabeth) for the fulfillment of the Reformation was stressed by most historians, most recently by David Hume. In terms
of his immediate environment – within and without the design – Henry is
associated with the New Testament Woman of Samaria (no. 74), who had six
husbands corresponding to Henry's six wives (John 4), and across the print, in
the margin opposite her (but consecutively numbered, 75), is Sancho Panza
showing surprise either at the Woman of Samaria opposite or at the adulterous triangle immediately in front of him within the frame. Beneath the statue
of Henry is a man pointing out his codpiece to his female friend. The
sequence of numbers ties together these disparate figures and the identifying
elements of Henry VIII.

   Just before this, nos. 56–9 and 69–70, are figures of various horns and
crosses. In the context of Henry, the juxtaposition seems appropriate: the
origin of the Protestant Reformation in adultery and cuckoldry. The
crosses, variations on Greek and Roman crosses, one of them transformed

into Hogarth's serpentine Line of Beauty, draw attention also to the close connection for him between religion and aesthetics, one the replacement of the other. The horns were part of the Henry story in the accusations of adultery made against Anne at her trial; these were immediately accessible in the productions of *Virtue Betray'd* ("I have more horns than any Forrest yields," says Henry, "Than *Finsbury*, or all the City Musters / Upon a Training, or a Lord Mayors-Day," 60).

In the verbal text of *The Analysis*, Holbein's Henry is an example of *uniformity* – full frontal instead of profile, one side balanced by the other; the aesthetic pleasure, Hogarth explains, derives from the qualities of fitness, design, regularity, and utility: "the front of a building, with all its equalities and parallelisms," to disrupt which one would like to throw a tree or the shadow of a cloud "or some other object that may answer the same purpose of adding variety" – that is, to reduce the uniformity. And yet, on the positive side, Henry's uniformity as stability, "the idea of firmness in standing," is contrasted with delicate serpentine figures by Guido and Correggio, as "necessary, in some degree, to give the idea of rest and motion. But when any such purposes can be as well affected by more irregular parts, the eye is always better pleased on the account of variety."[29]

Henry VIII "makes a perfect X," Hogarth writes, "with his legs and arms," and he notes the progression from Henry to Charles I and Edward VI in the direction of variety (though Elizabeth is a mere wooden figure that seems a regression to the unity and stability of Henry). This is also Hogarth's interpretation of the Holbein portrait as it embodies the power and stability of Henry's reign and the effect it (the Protestant Reformation) has had on England.

Behind the Holbein Henry, Hogarth has figured the qualities of strength, power, and sexual potency. Sir Joshua Reynolds, in his painting *Master Crewe as Henry VIII* of 1776 (Figure 11), has domesticated and trivialized these qualities by painting a child posed and costumed as Henry, in a mock-heroic fiction – something easy to accept because it is droll; and yet, as often in Reynolds' children's portraits (as St. John, Samuel Johnson, etc.), there is something sinister – for example, in the aspect of sexual potency or promiscuity – which seems to have been a private Reynolds joke (see *Cupid as a Link Boy* or *The Strawberry Girl*).[30]

Another coronation brought Shakespeare's *Henry VIII* again to prominence, although the play had never been off the stage for long. George III was crowned on September 22, 1761, followed on the 30th by David Garrick's production of the play, again at Drury Lane, with an even more elaborate coronation scene, repeated "for near forty nights successively"

Figure 11. Sir Joshua Reynolds, *Master Crewe as Henry VIII*, painting,
engraving by J. R. Smith, 1776.

according to Thomas Davies. In fact, it ran for eight more performances into
November, but enough to associate Henry VIII and George III in the minds
of the public.[31] Having now become a Tory, Hogarth shows, in *The Times*,
Plate 1 (an overtly partisan political print published in September of 1762)
Holbein's Henry VIII standing on stilts, fanning the fire that is burning up

Figure 12. William Hogarth, *The Times*, Plate 1, etching and engraving, 1762, first state.

England; and, in the second state, the figure of Henry is a mask for William Pitt, the prime minister-as-tyrant (Figure 12).[32]

In 1759, the "Year of Wonders," when Canada and India became English satraps, Hogarth would have detected again an analogy between Henry's Wolsey and George II's Pitt, and again the minister seeing himself as king, or indeed replacing the king. George III had ascended the throne, Pitt had resigned in 1761 (to some he was forced to resign), but unlike Walpole, instead of being reinstated, Pitt had gone into opposition, opposing peace negotiations – and so Hogarth, in *The Times*, Plate 1, associates him with the imagery of riot and revolution.

Between Hogarth's Henry VIII in *Analysis*, Plate 2, of 1753 and his Henry VIII in *The Times*, Plate 1, of 1762 had appeared Edmund Burke's aesthetic treatise (in some ways an attempt to correct Hogarth's) *A Philosophical Enquiry into the Origin of our Ideas of the Sublime and Beautiful* (1757). Burke never mentions Henry VIII, but the elements he employs to define the sublime are the power and terror associated by the writers and artists we have discussed with Henry. The sublime derives from the "fear being an apprehension of pain or death ... it is impossible to look on any thing as trifling, or contemptible, that may be dangerous"; and pain is "always inflicted by a power in some way superior" – examples of which begin with animals (lion, tiger, panther) but ascend to "kings and commanders ... sovereigns," who, however, are passed over for the supreme power of God. The effect of power is destruction, ranging from a state execution to "a conflagration or an earthquake," and including, for example, the "ruins" of London, "images of a tower, an archangel, the sun rising through mists, or in an eclipse, the ruin of monarchs, and the revolutions of kingdoms," imagery Hogarth materialized in *The Times*, Plate 1 and his last print, *Finis, or The Bathos* (1764).[33]

SWIFT

The historical Henry VIII in the eighteenth century was based on memories of Holinshed's Elizabethan *Chronicles* and, more recently, *The Life and Raigne of Henry VIII* (1649) by Edward Herbert, Lord Cherbury, of 1649, Gilbert Burnet's *History of the Reformation* of 1679 and 1681, and David Hume's *History of the Tudors*, published in 1759. These historians agree in general that Henry was a cruel, capricious, and despotic king but that in the long run his acts were justified by the triumph of English Protestantism. Bishop Burnet was no defender of Henry's cruelty, but he concludes that

if we consider the great things that were done by him, we must acknowledge that there was a signal providence of God, in raising up a king of his temper, for clearing the way to that blessed work that followed: and that could hardly have been done but by a man of his humour; so that I may very fitly apply to him the witty simile of an ingenious writer, who compares Luther to a postilion in his waxed boots and oiled coat, lashing his horses through thick and thin, and bespattering all about him.[34]

Like most writers on Henry, Burnet presents him as a man of great flaws ("great blemishes") who, however, as a result of these vary flaws ("his humours"), was instrumental in creating English Protestantism, Liberty, and the rest. Burnet's argument was that Henry's divorce was the occasion but not the cause of the Reformation – though he admitted that Anne's behavior itself lacked decency and discretion. The issue depended on whether Henry's meeting with Anne was before or after he had begun to contemplate a divorce.

It is hard to see much difference between Burnet's and Jonathan Swift's Henry VIII except for the primary colors used by Swift, who is less uncritical of Henry's so-called Reformation. Swift makes Burnet into the defender of an egregious Henry, therefore himself egregious. For Swift, Henry, the progenitor of the Reformation, is the great villain, but even Swift was prudent in committing his thoughts to paper. He published only the one diatribe, which used Henry to attack Burnet, started a second but left off in mid-sentence, and confined a third to the marginalia of Herbert of Cherbury's biography of Henry. It is through, or against, Burnet's eyes that Swift sees Henry, in his *Preface to the Bishop of Sarum's* [Burnet's] *Introduction to the Third Volume of the History of the Reformation of the Church of England* (1712).[35] What disgusts him in Burnet's (and Whig) "Histories of those Times" is "to see one of the worst Princes of any Age or Country, celebrated as an Instrument in that glorious Work of the Reformation." The only virtue he will assign Henry is "personal Courage" (Burnet's "humours"), which in his case took the form of ruthlessness.[36]

In the Whig *Tatler* no. 220 (September 5, 1710), Henry VIII is referred to as the "Religious Prince [who] put some to Death for owning the Pope's Supremacy, and others for denying Transubstantiation."[37] This was a faint shadow of Swift's Henry, the "reformer" who only usurped ecclesiastical power from pope and priests but kept the popish doctrine. That is, Henry remained a papist except "in the Point of Obedience to the see of *Rome*": "Henry VIII. had no Manner of Intention to change Religion in his Kingdom; he continued to persecute and burn Protestants after he had cast off the *Pope's* Supremacy: And, I suppose, his Seizure of Ecclesiastical Revenue … cannot be reckoned as a Mark of the Church's *Liberty*." It is the clergy Swift has in mind, their submission to Henry and his seizure of their lands and revenues, and the present uncorrected situation of the oppressed state of the lower clergy – not the rich bishops:

The Reformation owed nothing to the good Intentions of King *Henry*: He was only an Instrument of it, (as the Logicians speak) by Accident; nor doth he appear throughout his whole Reign, to have had any other Views, than those of gratifying his insatiable Love of Power, cruelty, Oppression, and other irregular Appetites …. he made no other Step, than rejecting the *Pope's* Supremacy, as a Clog upon his own Power and Passions; but retained every Corruption beside, and became a cruel Persecutor, as well of those who denied his own Supremacy, as of all others who professed any Protestant Doctrine.

Swift's was an extreme expression of the commonly held Protestant view that Henry did not go far enough with the doctrinal reformation.[38] Henry was the root of the evil, and the root can be traced back, Swift argues (as in the semen adust that motivates the French Henry IV to declare war in *A Tale of a Tub*), to his concupiscence.

In an unfinished essay dated May 24, 1736, Swift continued the diatribe, seeking an explanation "Concerning that Universal Hatred which Prevails against the Clergy," blamed on "that Monster and Tyrant, Henry VIII. who took away from them, against law, reason, and justice, at least two thirds of their legal possessions." The "reformation" carried out by this "detestable Tyrant"

was the mere effect of his irregular appetite, to divorce himself from a wife he was weary of, for a younger and more beautiful woman, whom he afterwards beheaded. But, at the same time, he was an entire defender of all the Popish doctrines, even those which were the most absurd. And, while he put people to death for denying him to be head of the church, he burned every offender against the doctrines of the Roman faith.

He adds the execution of Sir Thomas More, "a person of the greatest virtue this kingdom ever produced, for not directly owning him to be head of the church," and concludes that "Among all the princes who ever reigned in the world there was never so infernal a beast as Henry the VIII. in every vice of the most odious kind, without any open appearance of virtue: But cruelty, lust, rapine, and atheism, were his peculiar talents."[39] After a few pages he returns to Henry, explaining how "with great dexterity, [he] discovered an invention to gratify his insatiable thirst for blood, on both religions …" at which juncture he breaks off, as if realizing that his rage is in excess of its objective correlative – or out of prudence.[40]

After this, he confined his feelings about Henry VIII to the marginalia of his copy of Herbert of Cherbury's 1649 *The Life and Raigne of Henry VIII.*[41] He takes Cherbury's *Life* to be as unbalanced an analysis as Burnet's, and even the mildest remarks elicit "Dog of a King" or, extending Henry to all kings, "A Dog, a true King," a "Bloody inhuman Hell-hound of a King," and (against a reference to his son by Elizabeth Blunt) "The profligate Dog of a King." Opposite Cherbury's conclusion about Henry's divorce, that "nothing but desire of giving satisfaction to his Conscience, and care of establishing the Succession to the Crown … had first procur'd him to controvert this Marriage," Swift comments: "An impudent perjured true King," and opposite the conclusion that Anne Boleyn "had rather be that Lords Wife than a Kings Mistres," he writes simply: "whore."

As Cherbury approaches Henry's death, referring to his condemnation of the duke of Norfolk, Swift responds: "The Brute of a King deserved to dye in blood as he had lived,"[42] and when Cherbury sums up, wishing to end "without either presuming audaciously to condemn a Prince, heretofore Sovereign of our Kingdom, or omitting the just freedom of a Historian …"

Swift adds: "where is the Presumption? Nero was Emperor of Rome, and was a Saint in comparison of this dying dog Henry." When Cherbury appears to palliate Henry's cruelty, Swift adds, "Does the Author question this monster's cruelty?" And of his death: "And I wish he had been Flead, his skin stuffed and hangd on a Gibbet, His bulky guts and Flesh left to be devoured by Birds and Beasts for a warning to his Successors for ever. Amen."[43]

Fielding, an oppositional Whig, in *The Vernoniad* (1741) explains Henry's motivation for reform in more measured terms: "Of partial *Harry* and his Pope disdain'd; / The Love bestow'd on beauteous *Bullen*'s Face": as W. B. Coley's note points out, "partial in two senses: unduly favouring one party or side in a suit or controversy (*OED*, I.i), and favouring a particular person excessively (I.i.a)" – i.e., for Anne Boleyn. In the *Champion* (September 8, 1739) he suggests that the Herculean club of the Vinegars (in this case, of Major Hannibal Vinegar) was often called for in the reign of Henry VIII – the corrector of vicious actions.[44]

HUME

In his *History of the Tudors* (1759), David Hume explains Henry's "Humours" in terms of his psychology. Even the reports of the young Henry as the ideal prince conceal for Hume the fact that he was from the start, before he became the bloody killer, subject to his emotions – "heedless, inconsiderate, capricious, impolitic; guided by his passions or his favorite; vain, imperious, haughty; sometimes actuated by friendship for foreign powers, oftener by resentment, seldom by his true interest." Hume refers to "his usual openness and freedom," "his usual violence." "His frankness, his sincerity, his magnificence, his generosity, were virtues which counterbalanced his violence, cruelty, and impetuosity." He was "that furious monarch," often out of control, with a "temper, equally violent and superstitious" – "a prince so violent and capricious in his humor," "so much governed by passion."[45]

The gist is that Henry's passion was driven by his need for an heir as well as his sexual attraction to Anne Boleyn, these tending toward a focusing of his own power, while retaining the old beliefs ("superstitions"). His "violent temper" explains why he is "desirous of striking a terror into the whole nation," and explains the bloody acts from the executions of Fisher and More to that of the Countess of Salisbury and Henry Howard, earl of Surrey. But in fact he was vacillating: the reformers, "by their opposition to the pope, seconded the king's ambition and love of power"; the papists, "by maintaining the ancient theological tenets, were more conformable to his speculative principles: and both of them had alternately the advantage of gaining on his humor, by which he was more governed than by either of these motives" (232)

In Hume's palliative survey, the "catalogue of [Henry's] vices would comprehend many of the worst qualities incident to human nature: violence, cruelty, profusion, rapacity, injustice, obstinacy, arrogance, bigotry, presumption, caprice: but neither was he subject to all these vices in the most extreme degree, nor was he, at intervals, altogether destitute of virtues: he was sincere, open, gallant, liberal, and capable at least of a temporary friendship and attachment" (309).

Hume employs the Enlightenment way of dealing with evidence. He notes that the picture of Henry as monster had its origin in the propaganda of Rome (Swift used the same terms) – "comparing him to Caligula, Nero, Domitian, and all the most unrelenting tyrants of antiquity" – and it is admitted "the treatment which he met with from the court of Rome provoked him to violence; the danger of a revolt from his superstitious subjects seemed to require the most extreme severity" (212, 309). Hume's use of the word "superstitious," which would not have appeared in Swift (except of dissenters), points to the Enlightenment bias against the church itself.

Even Wolsey is distinguished from the mythological Wolsey, and made to fit into the picture of the uncontrollable Henry: "when we consider, that the subsequent part of Henry's reign was much more criminal than that which had been directed by Wolsey's counsels, we shall be inclined to suspect those historians of partiality, who have endeavored to load the memory of this minister with such violent reproaches" (186). Hume's Wolsey is another example, like Henry, of *concordia discors*: "Insatiable in his acquisitions, but still more magnificent in his expense: of extensive capacity, but still more desirous of glory: ... haughty to his equals, but affable to his dependants; oppressive to the people, but liberal to his friends; more generous than grateful; less moved by injuries than by contempt" (94).

Wolsey, more than Henry, was being reassessed in the eighteenth century. Bishop Burnet, who shows that Wolsey actually in a number of ways anticipated Henry's Reformation, through his dissolution of monasteries and his training of his secretary, Thomas Cromwell, makes the point, repeated throughout the century, that Henry was "a prince who upon the slightest pretences threw down those whom he had most advanced" (I: xiv).

It is strange that the one person in the Henry story for whom Swift has a good word is Wolsey. When he refers to Wolsey, in a marginal note in his copy of William Howells' *Medulla Historiae Anglicanae* (ninth edn., 1734), it is to defend him against the accusation that he was only the son of a butcher. His father, Swift insists, was a gentleman. Did Swift associate himself, in his own days of power, with the Cardinal? (Hume confirms that the father was a butcher.)[46]

Samuel Johnson's *Vanity of Human Wishes* (1749) presented the definitive image of Wolsey, still retaining memories of Walpole from the Wolsey–Walpole analogy of the 1720s. Walpole had finally fallen in 1742 and died in 1745, and Johnson published *The Vanity of Human Wishes* in 1749. Johnson conflates "the sinking Statesman" (79) with the Wolsey–Henry VIII–Holbein (Macheath–Walpole) associations of the first line: "In full-blown Dignity, see *Wolsey* stand" (99). His is the sympathetic Wolsey of Shakespeare's scene of the fall, not Banks' Machiavellian villain.[47] Wolsey is simply a more glaring, better-known example of a particular form of *de casibus*, that of the king's minister, with the implied and crucial figure of Henry VIII – and the parallel cases Johnson gives of James I's Buckingham, Queen Anne's Harley, Charles I's Strafford, and Charles II's Clarendon: To be "By Kings protected, and to Kings ally'd" is the fatal wish (in the terms of Juvenal's Tenth Satire, which Johnson is imitating); "What but their Wish indulg'd in Courts to shine, / And Pow'r too great to keep or to resign" (132–4). Where Hogarth sees Wolsey becoming Henry, Johnson, echoing Bishop Burnet, sympathizes with the downfall of the chief minister at the monarch's whim.

THE WIVES

The Whig *Spectator* (1709–12), that enormously influential journal, says little about Henry, although he represents (as Burnet demonstrated) Whiggish values – church reform, secularization, and "modern" thought; but the *Spectator* does make reference to Wolsey – egotism and ambition – and, with great warmth, to Anne. *Spectator* no. 397 (June 5, 1712) prints Anne's last letter to Henry in its entirety, making her another of those unfortunate young women Steele in particular likes to think about. Joseph Addison (the author of this *Spectator*) says he can think of no "Modern Story more affecting than" this letter. By implication, as so often in the eighteenth century, behind this letter and this figure of female love and distress is the dark shadow of the king, her lover and destroyer.

The other play about Henry, also in the Drury Lane repertory in the 1720s, was John Banks' *Virtue Betray'd: or, Anna Bullen, a Tragedy* (1682), an early she-tragedy (Banks also wrote one on Lady Jane Grey) which anticipated Nicholas Rowe's tragedies of Jane Shore and Jane Grey. John Rich, at Lincoln's Inn Fields Theatre, countered Drury Lane's *Virtue Betray'd* with a burlesque afterpiece, *Harlequin Anna Bullen*, running through December.[48] This was presumably a burlesque of the Drury Lane play. In Banks' *Anna Bullen*, Anne is a Protestant martyr traduced by the papists, in particular by a resurrected Cardinal Wolsey ("the proud-imperious Cardinal"). Anne's tragedy is to be tricked (by her brother, father, etc.) into marrying "one she cannot love" (2) and losing the one man, Percy, she does love.

In 1743, Sarah Fielding added a chapter to her brother's *Journey from this World to the Next* in the second volume of his *Miscellanies*, which was essentially a burlesque of the Anne of Banks' tragedy, a reprise of her life from the prospect of the underworld, as in one of Lucian's *Dialogues of the Dead*.[49] Henry is simply "the amorous King" (123), the same phrase Banks applied to him; as in Banks' play, he is the unloved – from his point of view, Anne is cold (she's in love with Percy); from hers, in the Fielding narrative, Henry is gross and unpleasing, "a Man who liked me, and for whom I not only did not care, but had an utter Aversion to," "the Man I hated" – and she adds a simile that sounds like Henry Fielding himself:

I often used to think myself in the case of the Fox-hunter, who when he has soiled and sweated all day in the Chace, as if some unheard-of Blessing was to crown his Success, finds at last, all he has got by his Labour is a stinking nauseous Animal. But my condition was yet worse than his; for he leaves the loathsome Wretch to be torn by his Hounds, whilst I was obliged to fondle mine, and meanly pretend him to be the Object of my Love. (123, 126, 125)

Sarah's Anne is essentially the Anne of the Old Lady's response in Shakespeare's play (2.3), not the virtuous young lady herself; she is a device that owes something not only to the Lucianic genre but to her brother's theatrical burlesques and in particular to *Jonathan Wild*.[50]

Sarah's contribution lies in the analysis of female psychology that distinguishes the story from her brother's burlesque writings. And unlike the tragically trapped Anne of Banks' play, Sarah's Anne is the reality of a flighty young girl, who given the chance of rising in the world, goes along with her elders' plot, although she finds the king disgusting, and gets in deeper than she anticipated.

The woman, by mid century, had become the center of attention in the novel (Pamela, Clarissa) and in the drama (Calista, Lady Jane Grey, Jane Shore), with Henry VIII recalled only in the secondary role of the male threat. The scenes of Shakespeare's *Henry VIII* that were illustrated in the paintings of *Boydell's Shakespeare* (the Shakespeare Gallery, 1789; the book, 1805) reflected the stage history of the play.[51] One focuses on Anne (Henry is subordinated and shown in the unusual position of three-quarter-turned suitor), a second on Catherine facing down Wolsey and Campeius, a third on Wolsey, taken in by the Abbot of Leicester, and only in the fourth, on the christening of Elizabeth, does Holbein's Henry return, balancing Anne and the baby Elizabeth.

AUSTEN

The young Jane Austen, in a MS she called *The History of England*, dated 1791, a chronicle of the monarchs running from Henry IV through Charles I, summed up Henry VIII: "The Crimes and Cruelties of this Prince, were too numerous to be mentioned," the "principal events which marked his reign" being: "Cardinal Wolsey's telling the father Abbott of Leicester Abbey" that "he was come to lay his bones among them," the reformation in Religion, and "the King's riding through the streets of London with Ann Bullen."[52] Once again, Henry VIII means Cardinal Wolsey, the English Reformation, and Anne Boleyn. As the quotation suggests, Austen is remembering Shakespeare's *Henry VIII*: Wolsey "Is come to lay his weary bones among ye" (4.2.22), though the fact that she omits "weary" suggests that she may herself have read Holinshed.[53]

Austen's *History* is a document of the 1790s, for she is writing in the mode of *Northanger Abbey* (written around the same time), assuming the persona of a Catherine Morland, a lover of Gothic romance, a mock-supporter of the old Roman religion, the Stuart cause, and especially persecuted maidens. She deplores Henry's dissolution of the monasteries but concedes that, as a result, he produced many sublime Gothic ruins. His chief crime was the murder of his wives, but she detests him most because he produced Elizabeth, the *bête noir* who (with her chief ministers, she adds) killed her heroine, the Catholic and doomed Mary, Queen of Scots. She returned to Shakespeare's play in *Mansfield Park* (1814). In Chapter 3 of Volume III, Fanny Price is reading to Lady Bertram a speech from *Henry VIII*, perhaps the famous Wolsey speech she had referred to in her *History*, perhaps his farewell at the end of Act 3 ("Had I but served my God," from Cavendish's *Life*).[54] Fanny would have read it because it recalls the passage about Wolsey in Johnson's *Vanity of Human Wishes*, a poem the pious Fanny would have appreciated. In Johnson's terms, the "Wish indulg'd in Courts to shine, / And Pow'r too great to keep or to resign" (132–4) is applicable to Fanny's situation in the Bertram family at Mansfield Park.

But Henry Crawford, entering, picks up the book, finds the passage, and goes on to play all the characters – "the King, the Queen, Buckingham, Wolsey, Cromwell, all were given in turn … It was truly dramatic."[55] But

Austen's list mysteriously excludes Anne Boleyn. The scene characterizes Crawford, who is assiduously courting Fanny, showing off, specifically as a play-actor. But it extends the context to the whole of Shakespeare's play. The scene of Henry's play-acting is followed by his discussion with Edmund of the differences between an actor delivering his lines and a clergyman delivering his sermon.

Why *Henry VIII*? Partly, once again, because of its popularity in the eighteenth century. But the play – to Austen if not Henry – would have suggested parallels similar to those earlier obvious in *Lover's Vows*: between Fanny and Queen Catherine – the latter abandoned by Henry for Anne Boleyn as Fanny has been abandoned by Edmund for Mary Crawford. It is possible that Henry Crawford (or, before him, Fanny) read Catherine's final speech, more applicable to Fanny than Wolsey's.[56] Like Catherine, Fanny is, at the moment of reading, resisting a marriage as Catherine resisted a divorce. Given Henry's claim that he had seen the play on the stage, and the emphasis on play-performance in the novel, a reader would have recalled Kemble's production with Sarah Siddons as Catherine. Siddons' spectacular performance in the Drury Lane revival of 1788, the power of her performance attested to by many contemporaries, had made Catherine the dominant figure.[57] In Henry Fuseli's painting, *Queen Katherine's Dream* (1781), available in Francesco Bartolozzi's engraving of the same year, she is stretched out on a divan with her left arm crooked, recalling Titian's *Venus and Cupid with an Organist*, the other arm raised to contact the dreamy angels hovering over her, making her an avatar of Venus in which, to quote Stuart Sillars, "Agape displaces Eros, and the heroic female virtues of tenderness and passivity are made explicit." This is a reading that corresponds to Austen's idea of Fanny in love with Edmund Bertram as opposed to Henry Crawford.[58]

Connecting the Henry VIII of Austen's *History of England* with *Mansfield Park* was General Tilney of *Northanger Abbey*, who lives in one of Henry VIII's ruined abbeys and, as seen by Catherine Morland, who "meditated, by turns, on broken promises and broken arches," is imperious, impatient ("he pulled the ball with violence"), and presumptively the murderer of his wife. The "dreaded figure of the General" draws, of course, on Mrs. Radcliffe's Montoni, but his physique and stance go with his title and anticipate, with his peremptory dismissal of poor Catherine, the autocratic *pater familias* Sir Thomas Bertram. Sir Thomas' return to Mansfield Park is "[t]o the greater number [of his family] … a moment of absolute horror" – "appalling" and "terrible." Fanny's "dread" of her uncle, who is repeatedly shown exercising his "will" upon his family, is accompanied by "excessive trembling" (175–6).

Compared to the scandalous, unsanctioned performance of *Lovers' Vows*, the "performance" of *Henry VIII* is normative, authorized by Sir Thomas, and as such it acts as a template for the novel *Mansfield Park*. Austen sees Shakespeare's play as, in Gordon McMullan's words, a meditation "on the progress of the Reformation in England, reading English life since Henry VIII's day as a series of bewildering changes in national and personal allegiance" (6). Or, in Isobel Armstrong's formulation, Shakespeare is himself normative of Englishness in the novel, and the play *Henry VIII*, a chronicle of English history, can be said to reprise the novel's issues of "authority, delegation, the rights of citizens and the power, or lack of it, vested in women," in the particular terms (given Edmund–Fanny) of the religious settlement.[59] *Henry VIII* figures, as it does through the century, a new settlement – in England of the Protestant Reformation and in Mansfield Park an analogous reformation of structure and alliances, a new balance of power, premised on Fanny–Elizabeth. If Fanny begins as the Catherine of Shakespeare's play, including the issue of her "legitimacy," she ends as the Elizabeth of Cranmer's speech in the final scene.

NOTES

1. Geoffrey Hill, *A Treatise of Civil Power* (London: Penguin, 2007).
2. George de Forest Lord (ed.), *Poems on Affairs of State*, 7 vols. (New Haven: Yale University Press, 1963–1975), V, 315; also XVI, 73, I, 209; 1674, I, 244; 1682, III, 229. The story is occasionally expanded, e.g., to include the deaths of Empson and Dudley (1684, III, 515).
3. Iona and Peter Opie (eds.), *The Oxford Dictionary of Nursery Rhymes* (Oxford: Clarendon Press, 1952), no. 392. It makes sense to read the verses as the way to death/execution, but the death-by-beheading is particularly Henrician.
4. Terence Gray's production of 1931 has his characters wearing Carrollesque playing-card costumes. The line, of course, is Shakespearean (*Richard III*).
5. Robert Hume, *The London Theatre World, 1660–1800* (Carbondale, IL: Southern Illinois University Press, 1980), 197.
6. David Piper, *The English Face* (London: National Portrait Gallery, 1978), 46–9.
7. Stephen Gardiner, *Obedience in Church and State: Three Political Tracts*, ed. P. Janelle (Cambridge: Cambridge University Press, 1930), 96–7.
8. Roy C. Strong, *Holbein and Henry VIII* (London: Routledge & Kegan Paul, 1967), 4.
9. Ibid., 44, plates 39, 40.
10. Geoffrey Bullough (ed.), *Narrative and Dramatic Sources of Shakespeare* (Cambridge: Cambridge University Press, 1962), IV, 450.
11. On Henry's sexual problems, see Gordon McMullan (ed.), *Henry VIII*, The Arden Shakespeare (London: Thomson Learning, 2000), 80–3.
12. Emmett L. Avery (ed.), *The London Stage 1660–1800: Part 2: 1700–1729* (Carbondale, IL: Southern Illinois University Press, 1960), II, 906.

13. Ibid., II, 940–6.

14. John Banks, *Vertue Betray'd: or, Anna Bullen, a Tragedy*, ed. Diane Dreher, Augustan Reprints (Los Angeles: William Andrews Clark Memorial Library, 1891), 30, 31.

15. Robert Gell, letter to Sir Martyn Stuteville, August 9, 1628, BL, MS Harleian 383, fo. 65; cited in McMullan (ed.), *Henry VIII*, 15–17.

16. Cumberland Clark, *A Study of Shakespeare's Henry VIII* (1931, revised 1938), cited McMullan (ed.), *Henry VIII*, 17. Banks' *Vertue Betray'd* of 1682 made his lustful Henry the analogue for Charles II as Dryden's David was the analogue for Charles II in *Absalom and Achitophel* of the same year. The difference was that Banks was on the side of the opposition, and Wolsey's plot was the equivalent of the Popish Plot as seen by Shaftesbury–Achitophel. Another example: William the Conqueror was invoked by satirists, for example by Pope in *Windsor Forest* (1714), as an analogue for the more recent foreign monarch, William III.

17. Colly Cibber, *An Apology for the Life of Mr. Colley Cibber*, ed. B. R. S. Fone (Ann Arbor: University of Michigan Press, 1968), 299–300.

18. Horace Walpole, *Memoirs of King George II*, ed. John Brooke (New Haven: Yale University Press, 1985), 120.

19. April 6 and 13, May 25, July 20, 1728; February 8, March 15, 1728/9. See also *Mist's Journal*, March 1, 1727/8, et seq.

20. *Craftsman*, March 2, 1727/8; *Daily Journal*, November 15, 1727.

21. Henry Fielding, *Contributions to The Champion and Related Writings*, ed. W. B. Coley (Oxford: Clarendon Press, 2003), 52, 310–11; also 451.

22. See Ronald Paulson, *Hogarth's Graphic Works* (New Haven: Yale University Press, 1965, 1979; London: The Print Room, 1989).

23. Letter to John Nichols, October 31, 1781. *Horace Walpole's Miscellaneous Correspondence*, ed. W. S. Lewis and John Riely (New Haven: Yale University Press, 1980), II, 451.

24. See Paulson, *Hogarth's Graphic Works*, no. 116; Ronald Paulson, *Hogarth: The Making of the Modern Moral Subject* (New Brunswick, NJ: Rutgers University Press, 1991), 164–72; Stuart Sillars, *Painting Shakespeare: The Artist as Critic, 1720–1820* (Cambridge University Press, 2006), 42–5.

25. The 1727 production emphasized the coronation scene, but Hogarth did not, for obvious reasons, including the fact that the king was not present at the coronation of Anne Boleyn, portray it. Queen consorts were crowned separately. Henry is absent in Shakespeare's scene; in reality he observed the procession from a hidden window in Westminster Abbey.

26. Sillars, *Painting Shakespeare*, 45.

27. There were, incidentally, seven productions of *Henry VIII* at Drury Lane in 1753: *The London Stage 1660–1800: Part IV: 1747–1776*, ed. George Winchester Stone, Jr. (Carbondale, IL: Southern Illinois University Press, 1962), I, 350, 354, 368, 382, 383, 390, 397.

28. The Holbein Henry is in this case the sculptural figure over the gate of St. Bartholomew's Hospital, Smithfield, a place of personal and professional

importance to Hogarth, reminding us of his great history paintings that decorate the staircase.

29. William Hogarth, *The Analysis of Beauty* (1753), ed. Ronald Paulson (New Haven: Yale University Press, 1997), 29–30.

30. See Ronald Paulson, *Emblem and Expression: Meaning in English Art of the Eighteenth Century* (London: Thames and Hudson; Cambridge, MA: Harvard University Press, 1975), 88–90.

31. There had been performances that included the coronation scene in April and May of 1760 and May and June of 1761, but the timely series following the coronation of George III began on September 30, 1761 and continued on October 2, 3, 5, 6, 8, 9, and 23 and November 2 (*London Stage*: *Part 4*, II, 751, 783, 798, 863, 869–71, 892–5, 898, 900); Thomas Davies, *Memoirs of the Life of David Garrick, Esq.* (1753), I, 365–6.

32. There were rival performances of the coronation scene at John Rich's Covent Garden Theatre, but of course there was no reason why Rich would have included Henry, who was not present.

33. Edmund Burke, *A Philosophical Enquiry into the Origin of our Ideas of the Sublime and Beautiful*, ed. J. T. Boulton (London: Routledge, 1958), 57, 65, 67, 62.

34. Gilbert Burnet, *The History of the Reformation of the Church of England* (London: Henry G. Bohn, 1857), I, xv.

35. For background on Swift–Burnet, see Irvin Ehrenpreis, *Swift: The Man, His Works, and the Age* (Cambridge, MA: Harvard University Press, 1962), II, 84–90; on the *Preface*, see Louis Landa (ed.), *A Proposal for Correcting the English Tongue* (Oxford: Basil Blackwell, 1973), xx–xxviii, and Ehrenpreis, *Swift*, II, 692–6.

36. Jonathan Swift, *A Preface to the B – p of S-r-m's Introduction*, in Jonathan Swift, *A Proposal for Correcting the English Tongue, Polite Conversation, etc.*, ed. Herbert Davis and Louis Landa (Oxford: Blackwell, 1964), 72–3.

37. Donald F. Bond (ed.), *The Tatler* (Oxford: Clarendon Press, 1987), III, 148.

38. See, e.g., John Foxe, *Acts and Monuments* (1563), 675. RSTC 11222.

39. Jonathan Swift, "Concerning that Universal Hatred, which prevails against the Clergy," in Jonathan Swift, *Directions to Servants and Miscellaneous Pieces 1733–1742*, ed. Herbert Davis (Oxford: Blackwell, 1959), 123.

40. Ibid., 126.

41. Edward Herbert, Baron Herbert of Cherbury, *The Life and Raigne of Henry VIII* (1649). Jonathan Swift, *Miscellaneous and Autobiographical Pieces, Fragments and Marginalia*, ed. Herbert Davis (Oxford: Blackwell, 1962), 247–51.

42. I have corrected Davis' reading, *desired*.

43. Swift, *Miscellaneous and Autobiographical Pieces*, 247–51.

44. Henry Fielding, *The Vernoniad* (1741), and *The Champion*, December 8, 1739, in W. B. Coley (ed.), *Contributions to* The Champion *and Related Writings* (Oxford: Clarendon Press, 2003), 560, 52.

45. David Hume, *History of the Tudors* (1759), in *The History of England* (Boston, 1853), III, 121, 213, 217, 223, 230, 250, etc. Subsequent references will appear parenthetically in the text.

46. Swift, *Miscellaneous and Autobiographical Pieces*, 263: "Wolsey's Father was no Butcher, but a private Gentleman."

47. The Shakespeare allusion could have been reinforced for Johnson by the quotation of the scene in Robert Dodsley's *Preceptor* (April 7, 1749), I, 70–3. For a discussion of the poem, see C. B. Ricks, "Wolsey in *The Vanity of Human Wishes*," *Modern Language Notes* 73 (1958), 563–8.

48. December 11–16 and 19, 1727; Avery (ed.), *The London Stage*, II, cxix, 949–51.

49. For the question of authorship, see Bertrand A. Goldgar (ed.), *Henry Fielding Miscellanies* (Oxford: Clarendon Press, 1993), II, xxxiv–xxxv.

50. Ibid., 113–28.

51. John Boydell, *Collection of Prints, from Pictures painted for the Purpose of Illustrating the Dramatic Works of Shakespeare* (London, 1805).

52. *The Works of Jane Austen*, ed. R. W. Chapman, vol. VI, *Minor Works* (London: Oxford University Press, 1954), 142–3.

53. She had read both Hume and Goldsmith (both in the library at Steventon).

54. See, e.g., *Spectator* (IV, 434).

55. *Works of Jane Austen*, III, *Mansfield Park*, 337.

56. See Isobel Armstrong on the function of *Henry VIII* in *Mansfield Park*: *Jane Austen: Mansfield Park*, Penguin Critical Studies (Harmondsworth: Penguin, 1988), 2–89.

57. McMullan (ed.), *Henry VIII*, 27–8.

58. Sillars, *Painting Shakespeare*, 120, and plates 34–6.

59. I base this final paragraph on Armstrong's reading in *Jane Austen: Mansfield Park*, 59, 85.

PART III

Henry VIII in art and popular culture

CHAPTER 7

Projecting masculinity: Henry VIII's codpiece

Tatiana C. String

The image of Henry VIII is surely the most familiar and instantly recognizable referent of all English kings and of royalty generally. It has been reproduced in countless copies, caricatures, and derivations beginning in the sixteenth century and continuing until the present day. The silhouette created by Holbein of Henry's distinctive shape (see frontispiece) has become synonymous with power, force, and aggression, all terms that have also been linked to the concept of masculinity as it manifested itself in the elite culture of the early modern period.[1] "Masculinity" is a modern notion, of course, but one with multiple retroactive applications: as a term it is elastic enough to insert itself into a host of social and cultural situations – virtually any interaction, in fact, with a gendered dimension. Masculinity must be distinguished from straightforward "maleness," which is a biological fact; masculinity, instead, can be understood in terms of the performance of agreed, conventional, or internalized social roles.[2] But does this make "masculinity" too broad or too blunt a category of analysis? What particular facets, or inflections, of communicated gendered identity, of masculinity, emerge from an analysis of Holbein's Henry? This chapter will argue that it is possible to interrogate what it meant to be masculine in the Renaissance through close study of Holbein's portrait of Henry VIII.[3]

One obvious but necessary point to make from the outset: Henry surely did not constantly strike the pose so familiar from Holbein's depiction, as if frozen by a photograph, despite the ways in which actors as different as Charles Laughton, Robert Shaw, Keith Michell, Ray Winstone, and Eric Bana have sought to imitate Henry in these terms. So it follows that the portrait was not just an opportunity for Holbein to display his technical virtuosity. It was his job to anticipate his patron's expectations and needs. Henry may not have had a specific model in mind when he commissioned Holbein to paint this portrait or have been able to articulate what he wanted in detail, but he would have expected to know it when he saw it. This necessarily took Holbein, and takes us, into a consideration of the expectations, the codes and norms, which would have permitted Henry to read his masculinity into the image unproblematically while also holding up a mirror to his individual sense of aggrandized selfhood. In other words, what was Holbein's range of possibilities? What motifs were at his disposal? And were these manipulated, individually and in combination, in ways that permit us to speak of masculinity as the underlying, unifying frame of reference? As we shall see, Holbein crafted the image based on his knowledge, and/or Henry's, of other images of strong, militaristic men. This meant that the visual language and codes of male monarchic behavior deployed by the artist, in the full awareness of his patron's aspirations for this work, were able to communicate strong and intelligible messages about masculinity and power.[4] What intellectual and visual sources did Holbein draw upon for this ultra-powerful representation? I will argue that Holbein's portrait is the site of many then-current ideas about gendered identity, ideas that permit us to speak of "masculinity" as their organizational principle.

The portrait of Henry VIII was part of a larger image painted by Holbein on one wall of the Privy Chamber in Whitehall Palace in 1537.[5] The mural would have measured approximately 9 feet high × 12 feet wide, and the figures within it would have been about life size.[6] Henry is shown with his father, Henry VII, his mother, Elizabeth of York, and his third wife, Jane Seymour. The mural was destroyed in the 1698 Whitehall Palace fire, but evidence for the composition survives in two principal forms: Holbein's original cartoon for the left part of the painting, now in the National Portrait Gallery (frontispiece); and a copy of the mural undertaken by Remigius van Leemput (see Figure 5). This latter was commissioned by Charles II in 1667 because the mural was beginning to deteriorate; today it can be seen at Hampton Court. We have further evidence for the mural portrait of Henry VIII thanks to a number of life-size copies that can be seen in the Walker Art Gallery in Liverpool, at Chatsworth, at Petworth House, and at Trinity College, Cambridge.[7] These copies, which are all quite early, sixteenth century, and closely resemble each other and the original in their dimensions, attest to the authoritative status that the original swiftly acquired. The Whitehall mural was not Holbein's first portrait of Henry VIII: a small-scale panel was made a year or two earlier recording the king's head and upper body, a painting that can be seen in the Thyssen Collection in Madrid. Holbein had also portrayed Henry in his printed title page of the Coverdale Bible, which dates from 1535 (see Figure 1). Holbein, therefore, was already a practiced portraitist as far as Henry's likeness was concerned. Indeed, his familiarity with the material is evident in his ability to make a late change to the mural. For it is clear from comparing the cartoon to the copy by Leemput that Holbein made a significant alteration at the final stage of the painting by adjusting Henry's head to face the viewer fully.

What I propose to do in this chapter is to examine the Whitehall image of Henry body-part by body-part, focusing on what they can reveal about contemporary attitudes to masculinity, as refracted through Henry's own self-image and Holbein's understanding of visual communication in the service of the royal regime.

LEGS

In any analysis of the painting, the first observation always made by writers on this portrait is that Henry stands legs astride, arms akimbo.[8] True, his legs are spread apart, one facing outwards towards the viewer, the other displayed in a three-quarters view. Henry was evidently proud of his legs, to judge from the remarks of the Venetian ambassador in 1515:

His majesty came into our arbour, and, addressing me in French, said: "Talk with me awhile! The King of France, is he as tall as I am?" I told him there was but little difference. He continued, "Is he as stout?" I said he was not; then he inquired, "What sort of legs has he?" I replied, "Spare." Whereupon he opened the front of his doublet, and placing his hand on his thigh, said, "Look here! And I have also a good calf to my leg."[9]

In Holbein's depiction, Henry's legs' muscularity is accentuated by placing them in the two different positions, frontal and three-quarters, to be admired in their various dimensions. Roy Strong in 1967 noticed that the feet astride posture in this portrait was related to other male depictions: Donatello's St. George (originally Orsanmichele, Florence, *c.* 1416) and Perugino's St. Michael (National Gallery, London, *c.* 1499).[10] While Holbein was almost certainly not quoting the pose directly from either of these sources, it is clear that this was a posture appropriate for representations of assertive soldiers and knights, and, by extension, rulers. St. George, St. Michael, and St. Demetrius, God's military heroes, are often shown in this way. The same pose can also be found in portraits of contemporary men, for example Andrea del Castagno's *Pippo Spano* in the fresco cycle of famous men and women in the Villa Carducci, Legnaia (1448), and later in Carpaccio's *Portrait of a Young Knight in a Landscape* (Thyssen-Bornemiza Collection, Madrid, 1510). Interestingly, in a woodcut title page published in 1518, Hans Holbein's brother Ambrosius used the legs astride pose for his representation of the ancient German chieftain Arminius defeating the Romans in the Teutoburg forest (Universitäts-Bibliothek, Basel).[11]

In this way, then, Holbein has conflated Henry's pose with that of military heroes, and although the king wears no armor, the visual language of this recognizable posture unproblematically takes on the resonance of this physical, combative identity. More specifically, part of the explanation for the straddled legs may reside in the dimensions and shapes of armour designed to be worn by those on horseback. And here we might think of Charles V's position in the 1548 portrait by Titian as evidence for this (Museo del Prado, Madrid). Viewers would thus be able to read Henry's pose as a militaristic, powerful stance associated with men and their armor, as known from depictions in the tradition of images described above.

We may pause here to note how constructed and formulaic was Holbein's rendering of Henry's masculinity through the reuse of poses and motifs

Figure 13. Hans Holbein the Younger, *The Ambassadors*, oil on panel, 1533.

from other portraits of other men and on the basis of knowledge of other traditions. The stance has become synonymous with Henry, but it was in fact a far more generic posture than we have perhaps realized. This generic quality is neatly illustrated by the fact that Holbein himself had used a very similar formula within his own *oeuvre* for Jean de Dinteville in *The Ambassadors* (National Gallery, London, 1533) (Figure 13) before applying it to Henry. It is reasonable to suppose that such a posture was also meant to be read into the half-length portraits of Charles de Solier (Gemäldegalerie, Dresden, 1535) and Sir Henry Guildford (Royal Collection, Windsor, 1527), whose weights are firmly planted on both legs. This body shape is not a classical pose with weight shifted onto one hip, but one in which weight is evenly distributed.[12] In this context it is worth noting Umberto Eco's argument that the Renaissance canon of male beauty was not simply a slavish rendering of the classical norms, but one which celebrated big, powerful figures presented in postures that emphasized balanced, planted, potential energy.[13] The "legs astride" pose supports Eco's argument convincingly – and indeed suggests that we can extend it from the realm of the beautiful male to that of the masculine male.

SHOULDERS

One of the areas where the physique was potentially most distorted, or enhanced by clothing, especially given emerging Mannerist conventions, was the shoulders. The extremely broad shoulders, exaggerated by the huge puffed sleeves of the gown, are one of the image's foregrounded elements. Holbein has exploited the potential within current men's fashion for accentuation of Henry's physique.[14] In this, his is of a piece with many other images, including portraits of Henry's contemporary monarchs, Francis I (Jean Clouet, Musée du Louvre, Paris, 1525–30) and Charles V (Jacob Seissenegger, Kunsthistorisches Museum, Vienna, 1532). These rulers, too, would have sought to have their physical strength emphasized, and idealized, in portraiture. Shoulders metaphorically bear weight and assume burdens. And beyond this they permit a vivid contrast to be made with the other figures in the composition: in the first instance Jane Seymour's small, closed form and sloping shoulders, then by extension Elizabeth of York, and finally even Henry VII, whose posture and physical projection more closely resembles those of the two female figures than those of his son. Henry VII's posture is again an adaptation of one Holbein had prepared earlier, the figure of Georges de Selve from *The Ambassadors* (Figure 13), whose closed form contrasts with the open form of Jean de Dinteville.

ARMS/ELBOW

As with the shoulders and legs, so too with the arms. The arrangement of Henry's arms is also highly conventional, composing them in a way as to be one example of what has been referred to as "the Renaissance elbow."[15] Joaneath Spicer has observed that depictions of males in masculine roles in the sixteenth and seventeenth centuries are frequently configured with this thrusting elbow, which works as a ready sign of assertion, power, and masculinity. In Henry's case, Holbein created the thrusting elbow by arranging one arm at around hip height, the other more extended. The higher, right hand holds a pair of leather gloves, the lower, left hand fingers the cord of his dagger. So when Henry's pose is described, as it almost always is, as standing with his arms "akimbo," which properly means hands on hips, this is not quite right. Once more Holbein was in familiar terrain. He had used precisely this arrangement of arms and hands in the portraits of Charles de Solier and Henry Guildford. Significantly, the stance was later appropriated by a Flemish artist for the Prince of Wales, the future Edward VI (Royal Collection, Windsor, c. 1546–7), in order to assimilate the images of father and son – in other words, to effect the sort of blurring of identities that Henry had denied his own father in the mural.[16]

Overall, then, we can begin to say that in a number of respects Henry's body is arranged in the Holbein mural in accordance with conventional norms for the expression of masculinity in portraits. This is not to say that Henry wished to be portrayed as a conventionally masculine figure, simply that Holbein was carefully accumulating motifs with readily understood associations. This is not a cryptic image to be puzzled over and decoded.

CODPIECE

That said, the effect of this calculated arrangement of the body was clearly something more significant and complex than a simple aggregation of individual masculinity-bearing elements. This reading of the image emerges distinctly from a consideration of a further feature of Henry's physique and dress, one that is worth discussing at some length and proves central to the whole illocutionary act of Henry's image. Composition provides the first pointer. Holbein's composition (see frontispiece) creates two triangles which meet, visually, at the codpiece. The splayed legs and the distance between the feet create the first; the shoulders are an equal width and form one side of the second triangle with the bent, right arm acting as the second side and the left arm the third. Holbein has, thereby, created a clear focal point at the groin, one which forces his viewers to confront, no holds barred, the large, protruding codpiece and to imagine, or even fantasize about, the phallus contained within. The very three-dimensional, sculpturesque rendering of the codpiece, which projects from beneath Henry's jerkin and doublet, emphasizes its importance in the messages intended by its maker. Holbein understood the importance of the codpiece to Henry VIII, and it is thus constructed visually at the meeting of the two triangular shapes of Henry's upper and lower halves, in a rounded, volumetric form. Given Holbein's use of this visual emphasis, it is worth pondering in some detail the codpiece as depicted object, fashion item, and cultural signifier in sixteenth-century Europe.

Codpieces are visible in a number of contemporary portraits in Italy and Germany. Witness the very large one in Bronzino's portrait of Guidobaldo II della Rovere which dates from 1531/2 (Galleria Palatina, Florence), or the portrait of Ludovico Capponi by the same artist in 1551 (Frick Collection, New York). Large, bulging codpieces are frequently depicted in representations of German mercenary soldiers, the Landsknechte.[17] In each of these cases the codpiece seems to be positioned well above horizontal, upright, suggesting an erect penis inside, though we may note that Henry's is more overtly, thrustingly signaled than those in the other examples.

The fashion for codpieces seems to have reached a high point towards the middle of the sixteenth century.[18] Henry's codpiece, as depicted here, is a padded case or box in which the genitals rest. The derivation of the term "codpiece" lies in the Middle English word "cod," slang for the scrotum. Codpieces were originally just material flaps, or "brays," which could be undone to allow urination, but they became increasingly more fully formed and textured in the sixteenth century in the dress of aristocratic men.[19] The codpiece would have been attached to the hose and doublet by means of laces or sewn directly onto the hose. In the fifteenth century, genitalia had often not been covered by the hose or short jerkins; this had increasingly become the subject of disapproving moralizing comment and, eventually, prescriptions on dress in some parts of Europe.[20] Codpieces thus performed a double role: they were meant to avert the danger of immodest exposure but simultaneously confirm the viewer's gaze upon the source of potential immodesty. In addition to the obvious practical function of sheathing the phallus for modesty, warmth, and protection, there is anecdotal evidence that codpieces were also used like pockets in which to store snacks and trinkets.[21]

Interestingly, the thrusting quality of the Whitehall mural's codpiece is absent from one of the early copies of the Holbein prototype, the half-length portrait in the Galleria Nazionale, Rome (Palazzo Barberini). Here the artist has neglected this essential component in Henry VIII's masculine identity. The codpiece simply forms one part of the flat pattern of the elaborate costume. Since Holbein would not have overlooked this element, it seems reasonable to reattribute the Rome painting to a follower of Holbein, and not Holbein himself as is sometimes claimed.[22]

Holbein's emphasis on the codpiece invites the viewer to think about the portrait as a conspicuously masculine, virile image. This is reinforced by the other types of codes used by Holbein, and beyond the image in Henry VIII's behavior and self-fashioning.[23] In fact, the connections were not asking too much of the viewer. The vast majority of the elite viewers of this painting, if not all, would have been male, themselves practicing forms of masculine behavior as members of the Henrician privy council, or as foreign diplomats familiar with Renaissance courtly male roles. The mural was painted in the Privy Chamber, a semi-private space in which matters of state amongst the very highest level of councillors or ambassadors, all men, would have been conducted. In this environment, the codpiece was obvious as a signifier of virility and fertility: in the specific context of the Whitehall mural it further indicated Henry's ability to continue the Tudor dynasty by impregnating Jane Seymour.[24] The mural bears the date 1537, the year in which Prince Edward was conceived and born. Jane Seymour, who is shown in the right half of the mural, was referred to by Henry as his "true wife" because it was through penetrative sex with her that he was able to father an apparently healthy, male child and heir (presumed at the point of the commissioning and painting of the Whitehall mural). Everything Henry had worked for in striving for the divorce, removing papal authority from England, reforming the Church, had been about this moment. His quest to fulfill his masculine role is thus visually constructed and vindicated by Holbein.

The fact that the codpiece is so prominent and constructed with such artifice suggests that it is not simply a portrait feature, but a fashioned element in the projection of Henry VIII's masculinity. Patricia Simons has memorably argued that in Italy in this period "cocks and politics" were conflated: that the codpiece was a "surrogate political weapon" in a phallogocentric cultural universe.[25] There are a number of intriguing late medieval and early modern accounts which reveal a fascination with men with oversized penises. Simons posits the idea that the size of a penis was enough to chase off rivals in the case of a husband brandishing a huge penis and keeping would-be competitors away from his wife. A similar impulse is evident in our English scene (see Figure 5), a signal of potency directed towards rivals for power and authority. There are constant references to huge penises and magnificent codpieces in Rabelais' *Gargantua and Pantagruel*, including a chapter in Book Three entitled "Why the codpiece is held to be the chief piece of armour amongst warriors."[26] And here we might think of an actual equivalent to the size and three-dimensionality of the codpiece in the Whitehall mural, which is the accompaniment for a suit of armor made for Henry in 1540 (Royal Armouries, HM Tower of London) which admittedly has a more practical function, although its over-length is not strictly necessary except in the terms we have been discussing (see also Highley, chapter 8 in this volume).

BEARD

In addition to these fashioned elements, what else does an examination of Henry's portrait reveal? A further aspect, Henry's beard, both illustrates Holbein's intention to compress multiple masculinity traits within a single image and serves as a useful springboard for a wider consideration of Henry's cultural self-fashioning, his physical behavior, and the public enactment of masculinity as political instrument.[27] As an expression of masculinity in the mid-sixteenth century, beards were worn by elite men across Europe: Henry VIII, Francis I, Charles V, Julius II and Castiglione, to name just a few.[28] In 1533 Valeriano's *Pro Sacerdotum Barbis* was translated into English, defending the fashion for wearing beards among priests by calling attention to the great men of the past who wore beards, including Roman emperors, but especially Christ.[29] It has been argued that beards were intentionally worn to emphasize contrasts with women, whose predominant aesthetic required pallid smoothness.[30] Further, as a sign of the achievement of manhood, beards served to contrast men with boys as an emblem of virility.[31] The Whitehall mural thus exploits both binaries. In the more straightforward one, Henry VIII's beard differentiates him from the two female figures. But more subtly, in an inversion of the father–son, man–boy nexus, a point about different generations is being made. Henry VII does not wear a beard, and in some ways his closed, passive posture in the Whitehall mural casts him more in the role of other, like the women.

The wearing of beards was not just fashionable, but can also be understood as an expression of homosocial bonds: in one particularly clear example, Henry and Francis I of France, when both in their late twenties, agreed that they would grow their beards as a sign of friendship and not shave until they met, for the first time, at the Field of Cloth of Gold in 1520.[32] This meeting near Calais was the ultimate demonstration of these homosocial bonds: Henry and Francis spent two weeks in the performance of masculinity, literally. They jousted against one another, they wrestled each other, they dallied with each other's wives, they danced, masked, and played games, they dressed up in their finest, most luxurious and expensive clothes, and they lavishly displayed their wealth and magnificence. This was, of course, a surrogate for making war against one another, which happened in much the same vein, in the spirit of male-on-male suprem-acy.[33] Henry and Francis referred to each other as "brother" monarchs – and their features were duly morphed into virtually indistinguishable masks of Renaissance monarchy. In double portraits of Henry and Francis, for example, the manuscript illumination of a peace treaty in 1527 (Museum of the Public Record Office, London), or in the relief carving commemo-rating the Field of Cloth of Gold, at the Hôtel Bourgtheroulde in Rouen, the features of the two men are made to look intentionally similar to stress their likenesses, as opposed to their differences. Interestingly, this can also be seen in a double portrait of Henry with Charles V, which probably dates from 1522 (Private Collection), another commemoration of the signing of a peace treaty.[34] Here Charles, on the left, and Henry, on the right, are clearly intended to be read as closely similar in look and fashion, a reflection of their common thinking and the bonds of friendship between these two men who are emblematic of their polities.

Physical strength, sexual potency, the ability to produce an heir, the power to rule over his people, the friendships or rivalries with other powerful men: these are the socially modeled conceptions of heterosexual masculinity in the early sixteenth century, and Henry played them out better than most. The urgency with which he sought the divorce speaks to this: he would stop at nothing to effect the conditions that could allow him to produce an heir, and Henry's aim was effectively to assert himself as the "prime alpha male" who could achieve these results in order to fulfill the cultural and political expectations of his gendered role as king in a highly competitive environment.[35]

COMPETITION

In both the mural and in Henry's lived experience, competition played a significant role. When discussing his legs, we noted that Henry's rivalry with Francis I was personally registered in a comparison of physical appear-ance: Henry wanted to learn whether he was taller and broader than his new French counterpart and whether his legs were finer. When they finally met face to face in 1520 at the Field of Cloth of Gold, Henry and Francis engaged in all sorts of competitive, physically demanding sports. Men who "do things" with their bodies are enacting male social roles.[36] In these instances the competition was personalized, man to man, but this would eventually translate into militaristic rivalry in a number of confrontations between the English and French later in the reigns of Henry and Francis – an indication, perhaps, of the instability of sublimating war and diplomacy, the stuff of early modern statecraft, within personalized encounters heavy on masculinity.

Henry's competition with two key figures, his father, Henry VII, and the pope, are registered in the Latin inscription of the Whitehall mural (see Figure 5). Here again, by looking at the inscription, we are reminded of Holbein's tendency to draw on sources in his own work: the inscription placed at the center of the composition is comparable to the centrally placed objects in the *Ambassadors* (see Figure 13). The centrality of the monument on which the inscription is "carved" demands the viewer's interaction. By engaging the viewer full face, Henry acts as the focalizer for the imagined space and as the one figure who prompts the viewer to the action that is demanded, the reading of the inscription. In fact, the messages communicated verbally by the inscription must be seen in tandem with the visual language we have explored within the masculine portrait features of Henry's body. The Latin text translates as:

> If you enjoy seeing the illustrious figures of heroes,
> Look on these; no painting ever bore greater.
> The great debate, the competition,
> The great question is whether the father
> Or the son is the victor. For both indeed are supreme.
> The former often overcame his enemies and the fires of his country,
> And finally gave peace to its citizens.
>
> The son, born indeed for greater tasks, from the altar
> Removed the unworthy, and put worthy men in their place.
> To unerring virtue, the presumption of the Popes has yielded
> And so long as Henry the Eighth carries the sceptre in his hand,
> Religion is renewed, and during his reign
> The doctrines of God have begun to be held in his honour.[37]

Both oppositional figures yield to Henry VIII in their mobilization of masculine traits. In the case of the pope, Henry's personal strength prevails in his firm grip on the scepter. The contrast with Henry VII is even more freighted with masculine competitiveness.[38] While Henry VII's deeds, essentially ending the Wars of the Roses, obviously represented an important achievement, Henry VIII's triumph over the pope is explicitly rendered as having greater consequences than the work of his father. In the visual depiction, Henry is clearly shown outshining his father. Everything about his taut figure contrasts with the languid features of Henry VII behind him. One may perhaps attempt an oedipal reading of this rivalry, but more straightforwardly it is clear that the competition of son with father will more often than not be played out in terms of male attributes and thus become a contest over, and about, masculinity.

It is noteworthy that the motif of intergenerational competition was resumed less than two years after the completion of the mural, in the inscription that forms part of the portrait of Henry's son, the young Prince Edward, that Holbein made as a New Year's gift to the king in 1539 (National Gallery of Art, Washington, DC). Although Edward was only a toddler, the theme of competition was still considered appropriate. The humanist and political apologist Richard Morison's inscription, which is seemingly tacked onto the surface of the painting, seeks to guide the behavior of the infant prince:

Little one, imitate your father and be the heir of his virtue; the world contains nothing greater. Heaven and earth could scarcely produce a son whose glory would surpass that of such a father. Only equal the deeds of your parent and men can wish for no more. Surpass him and you have surpassed all the kings the world ever revered and none will surpass you.[39]

The implication is, of course, that Henry, the individual vicariously but necessarily addressed in the inscription, will not be surpassed. Here, then, we have two images, close in time, both with Henry as the primary viewer, employing a rhetoric of relative accomplishment and achievement mapped onto a competitive discourse of especial appeal to elite male viewers.

PERFORMANCE OF MASCULINITY

If we step back a little from these images themselves, two broader considerations suggest themselves about Henry as king and Holbein as artist. First, there is the idea of gender as performance. As Judith Butler, for one, has argued, both the notion of performativity of gender and the social construction of gender roles are found in the reiteration of sets of recognized behavioral norms.[40] This model readily applies to Henry VIII, unique as his royal status was. Not that Henry woke up every morning and made a conscious decision to play an overtly male role. Rather, everything in his enacted state would have been grounded in cognitive assumptions born of constantly reiterated and reinforced norms. In short, Henry was involved in an unremitting process of masculine assertiveness that satisfied the expectations of appropriate role playing: in choosing and dominating women, in marrying, procreating, building, spending, hunting, jousting, governing through the domination of tight, enclosed male spaces such as the site of the mural, and waging war in expansive public spaces.

Second, both Holbein's technical skill and sensitivity to a patron's needs register themselves in his construction of a particularly overt, concentrated illocution of masculine value. In the Whitehall mural, unlike many other images of the period, nothing is occluded, or allusive, or buried underneath ritual. The concatenation of masculine signifiers is not an unusually compacted rehearsal of visual clichés. Holbein was breaking new ground, not ticking the boxes, in this unusually intensive concentration of masculinity. Masculinity was typically nuanced and inflected, selectively or discretely rendered. But Holbein's construction permitted no ambiguity in the viewer's response to Henry's evident and maximal self-fashioning in masculine terms that fully personalized the exercise of political power.

Thus Henry was portrayed as physically imposing and powerful even to the extent of anatomical distortion in the width of his shoulders and the length of his arms, because he was strong enough to rule effectively. The political culture that Henry embodies and sustains is efficiently deconstructed into a series of polarities: male/female, activity/passivity, open/closed, bearded/smooth, brown/white, strong/weak, and, especially, protruding phallus/enfolded vulva. The codpiece is central, literally and conceptually: Henry was by no means the only male to be depicted with a codpiece, but what is significant is how prominent it is compared to most other portraits of this period. They have codpieces, but they are not as integral to the narrative surrounding the subject. This brings us back to the Whitehall mural image itself. Holbein and Henry VIII are condemned to be locked together in the popular imagination. But it is easy to exaggerate the intensity of that relationship or the homogeneity of its artistic issue. Not all Holbeins were the same. It was not everyday that one had a Whitehall mural painted. Its form imparted a permanence to its messages, and would have made it a constant in the daily routine of the king in ways very different from the commissioning of a panel painting, which, however finely executed, was moveable and thus unlikely to attract as much political and personal investment.

The significance, finally, of the image that Holbein fashioned for Henry can perhaps be illustrated in a series of codas. One is the success of the image, as I pointed out earlier, in becoming the default index of royal power. Another, equally germane to the subject of this chapter, is the image's proven ability to break out of its royal associations and to sustain itself as a fundamental masculine signifier. For illustrations of this enduring model, one need look no further than borrowings in the depictions of über-masculine action heroes Superman and Batman.

A third, and perhaps the most telling point, is the capacity of the codpiece to cross gender boundaries in the interests of communicating Tudor dynastic continuity and capacity to rule. In the Armada portrait of Henry's daughter Elizabeth (William Tyrwhitt-Drake Collection, *c.* 1588), the codpiece is replaced by a pearl that quotes directly from Holbein's image.[41] The queen who had the body of a woman here has a small but potent part of the body of a man, not just any man but her father. This was not a regular motif in portraits of Elizabeth, so it is significant that it should appear in the image that overtly celebrated military success and invited reflection on her ability to transcend gender roles.

NOTES

1. See, for example, Stephen M. Whitehead, *Men and Masculinities* (Cambridge: Cambridge University Press, 2002), 15: "The aristocratic Renaissance man of the sixteenth century … was typified by King Henry VIII himself. Here was a man, the very 'symbol of English nationhood,' ruthless and at times brutal, who also displayed an overtly emotional side." Whitehead is here exploring the malleability of definitions of masculinity, contrasting the complexities of the "Renaissance man" with more idealized and one-dimensional views of what men should be (i.e., not like women) in the late nineteenth century. Studies of masculinity as it was constructed in the sixteenth century are relatively rare, but the most significant are cited in the notes that follow.

2. John Beynon, *Masculinities and Culture* (Philadelphia: Open University Press, 2002), 2, writes that "if maleness is biological, masculinity is cultural." Beynon stresses that a man is not born with masculinity, it is acculturated and indexical of culture. He notes that "masculinity can never float free of culture: it is the child of culture."

3. Stephen Orgel, "Idols of the Gallery," in Peter Erickson and Clark Hulse (eds.), *Early Modern Visual Culture: Representation, Race, and Empire in Renaissance England* (Philadelphia: University of Pennsylvania Press, 2000), 251–83, argues that the most revealing Renaissance paintings were portraits commissioned by the monarch: "those specific manifestations of their view of themselves"; these reveal more about the individual than do the works in his collection (266).

4. For discussion of communication and visual language in Henry VIII's reign, see Tatiana C. String, *Art and Communication in the Reign of Henry VIII* (Aldershot: Ashgate, 2008).

5. For recent discussion of the mural, see Susan Foister, *Holbein and England* (New Haven and London: Yale University Press, 2004), 175–96; Susan Foister, *Holbein in England*, exhibition catalogue (London: Tate Britain,

2006), 94; Stephanie Buck, *Holbein am Hofe Heinrichs VIII* (Berlin: Reimer, 1997), 103–95; and Stephanie Buck, *Hans Holbein, 1497/98–1543* (Cologne: Könemann, 1999), 112–19.

6. For the measurements of the Whitehall Mural, see Simon Thurley, *Whitehall Palace: An Architectural History of the Royal Apartments, 1240–1698* (New Haven and London: Yale University Press, 1999), 49.

7. For the copies of the figure of Henry VIII, see Xanthe Brooke and David Crombie, *Henry VIII Revealed: Holbein's Portrait and its Legacy* (London: Paul Holberton, 2004).

8. See, for example, Andrew Belsey and Catherine Belsey, "Icons of Divinity: Portraits of Queen Elizabeth I," in Lucy Gent and Nigel Llewellyn (eds.), *Renaissance Bodies: The Human Figure in English Culture c. 1540–1660* (London: Reaktion Books, 1990), 11–35, citing 11. The most extensive early discussion of Henry's pose and of the Whitehall mural generally is Roy C. Strong, *Holbein and Henry VIII* (London: Routledge & Kegan Paul, 1967).

9. This exchange is recorded by Piero Pasqualigo, the Venetian Ambassador Extraordinary, in a letter (May 3, 1515) to his master in Venice and published in *Four Years at the Court of Henry VIII: Selection of Despatches written by the Venetian ambassador, Sebastian Justinian*, ed. and trans. Rawdon Brown, 2 vols. (London, 1854; reprinted, New York: AMS Press, 1970), I, 90–4.

10. Strong, *Holbein and Henry VIII*, 42; see also Cecil Gould, *An Introduction to Italian Renaissance Painting* (London: Phaidon, 1957), 19, as cited by Strong.

11. Ambrosius Holbein's title page is illustrated in Oskar Bätschmann and Pascal Griener, *Hans Holbein* (London: Reaktion Books, 1997), 26.

12. For examples of Renaissance portraits of men in the weight-shifted posture, see Lorne Campbell, *Renaissance Portraits* (New Haven and London: Yale University Press, 1990), 94: "a standing male whose legs were visible was usually shown resting his weight on one leg and bending the other at the knee."

13. Umberto Eco, *On Beauty* (London: Secker & Warburg, 2004), 200–5.

14. For discussions of the ways in which costume accentuated men's physique in this period, see Aileen Ribeiro and Valerie Cumming, *The Visual History of Costume* (London: B. T. Batsford, 1989), 77; Geoffrey Squire, *Dress and Society, 1560–1970* (New York: Viking Press, 1974), 45–8; and François Boucher, *A History of Costume in the West*, 2nd edn. (London: Thames and Hudson; New York: H. N. Abrams, 1987), 242–4.

15. Joaneath Spicer, "The Renaissance Elbow," in Jan N. Bremmer and Herman Roodenburg (eds.), *A Cultural History of Gesture* (Cambridge: Cambridge University Press, 1991), 84–128.

16. For the portrait of Edward, see Karen Hearn (ed.), *Dynasties: Painting in Tudor and Jacobean England, 1530–1630*, exhibition catalogue (London: Tate Gallery, 1995), 49–50.

17. On the representation of codpieces in depictions of German Landsknechte, and more widely, see Gundula Wolter, *Die Verpackung des männlichen Geschlects: Eine illustriete Kulturgeschichte der Hose* (Marburg: Jonas, 1991).

18. The significance of the codpiece as part of male dress in the late medieval and early modern periods is considered in Thomas Lüttenberg, "The Cod-piece – A Renaissance Fashion between Sign and Artefact," *The Medieval History Journal* 8:1 (2005), 49–81; and Jeffery C. Persels, "Bragueta Humanistica, or Humanism's Codpiece," *Sixteenth Century Journal* 28 (1997), 79–99. For the codpiece in England, see Maria Hayward, *Dress at the Court of King Henry VIII* (Leeds: Maney Publishing, 2007), 100–3; and Will Fisher, *Materializing Gender in Early Modern English Literature and Culture* (Cambridge: Cambridge University Press, 2006), 59–82.

19. For this, see Grace Q. Vicary, "Visual Art as Social Data: The Renaissance Codpiece," *Cultural Anthropology* 4:1 (1989), 3–25, esp. 3–10.

20. Vicary, "Visual Art," 8; Lüttenberg, "The Cod-piece," 60.

21. Vicary, "Visual Art," 15–17, provides a number of references to the codpiece as a storage compartment for food, coins, amulets, and handkerchiefs.

22. Both Paul Ganz, *The Paintings of Hans Holbein: First Complete Edition* (London: Phaidon Press, 1956), 251 (cat. 106) and John Rowlands, *The Paintings of Hans Holbein the Younger* (Boston: David R. Godine, 1985), 226 (cat. L.14c), exclude this painting from their authoritative lists of authentic works and reclassify it instead as the work of a "close follower" owing to "occasional clumsiness in the rendering of detail." However, the Galleria Nazionale d'Arte Antica, Rome (Palazzo Barberini) continues to attribute the work to Holbein.

23. This phrase and its conceptual understandings is consciously derived from Greenblatt in his foundational study, *Renaissance Self-Fashioning: From More to Shakespeare* (Chicago: University of Chicago Press, 1980).

24. See the comments by Louis Adrian Montrose, "The Elizabethan Subject and the Spenserian Text," in Patricia Parker and David Quint (eds.), *Literary Theory/Renaissance Texts* (Baltimore: Johns Hopkins University Press, 1986), 303–40, esp. 312–15.

25. Patricia Simons, "Alert and Erect: Masculinity in Some Italian Renaissance Portraits of Fathers and Sons," in Richard C. Trexler (ed.), *Gender Rhetorics: Postures of Dominance and Submission in History* (Binghamton, NY: Medieval & Renaissance Texts & Studies, 1994), 163–86, quotations on 172, 175. See also D. Vance Smith, "Body Doubles: Producing the Masculine Corpus," in Jeffrey Jerome Cohen and Bonnie Wheeler (eds.), *Becoming Male in the Middle Ages* (New York: Garland, 1997), 3–19 for an interesting exploration of the body as a metaphor for the world.

26. For the codpiece in Rabelais, see Persels, "Bragueta Humanistica," esp. 79–81, 89–99.

27. For this, see Will Fisher, "The Renaissance Beard: Masculinity in Early Modern England," *Renaissance Quarterly* 54 (2001), 155–87. See now also Fisher, *Materializing Gender*, esp. 83–128.

28. Mark J. Zucker, "Raphael and the Beard of Julius II," *The Art Bulletin* 59:4 (1977), 524–33, esp. 532.

29. Zucker, "Raphael and the Beard," 532; Fisher, "Renaissance Beard," 167–9.

30. Fisher, 'Renaissance Beard', esp. 166–9.

31. Ibid., 175–84.

32. For a very full description of the event, see Joycelyne Gledhill Russell, *The Field of Cloth of Gold, Men and Manners in 1520* (London: Routledge & Kegan Paul, 1969). Edward Hall's contemporary account may be found in a new edition: Janet Dillon (ed.), *Performance and Spectacle in Hall's Chronicle* (London: Society for Theatre Research, 2002), 71–96.

33. For relations between the *dramatis personae*, see Glenn Richardson, *Renaissance Monarchy: The Reigns of Henry VIII, Francis I, and Charles V* (London: Arnold, 2002).

34. The image is included in David Starkey (ed.), *Henry VIII: A European Court in England* (London: Collins & Brown in association with the National Maritime Museum, Greenwich, 1991), 56; and in String, *Art and Communication*, 64.

35. Derek Neal, "Masculine Identity in Late Medieval English Society and Culture," in Nancy F. Partner (ed.), *Writing Medieval History* (London: Hodder Arnold, 2005), 171–88.

36. Ibid., 175.

37. Translation from Rowlands, *The Paintings of Hans Holbein the Younger*, 225.

38. For father/son relations, see William Morton Aird, "Frustrated Masculinity: The Relationship between William the Conqueror and His Eldest Son," in Dawn M. Hadley (ed.), *Masculinity in Medieval Europe* (London and New York: Longman, 1999), 39–55; and Simons, "Masculinity in Some Italian Renaissance Portraits."

39. Translation from Arthur B. Chamberlain, *Hans Holbein the Younger*, 2 vols. (London: G. Allen & Co, 1913), II, 165.

40. Judith Butler, *Bodies that Matter* (New York and London: Routledge, 1993), 12.

41. See Belsey and Belsey, "Icons of Divinity," 12–13, citing the observations of Montrose, "Elizabethan Subject," 312–15.

CHAPTER 8

The remains of Henry VIII

Christopher Highley

BENEDICK: [Claudio] would have walked ten mile afoot to
see a good armour
Much Ado About Nothing, 2.3.14–15

When we think of the personal remains of Elizabeth I, her textual traces
immediately come to mind – the poems, speeches, and letters that have
been collected and edited since her death because they seem to offer
privileged access to the queen's inner life. Accounts of the queen's remains
have focused on her own writings and pronouncements rather than on
the personal artifacts like her riding saddle, riding boots, gloves, and musical
instruments. Many of these items, including the sun hat and lace gloves
preserved at Hatfield House or the christening robe at Sudeley, are of
dubious provenance and owe their identity to unexamined "traditions."[1]
With a few exceptions, her most spectacular personal possessions – the
dresses and jewels that appear in her portraits – no longer survive. They
passed after Elizabeth's death to Anne of Denmark, who, instead of preserving the old queen's wardrobe, either sold or adapted its contents to suit
her own tastes and changing fashions.[2]

In contrast to our perceptions of Elizabeth, we tend to assess Henry VIII's
remains not in terms of his textual traces but of other non-written material
artifacts. Although a thousand or so of Henry's personal and official letters
survive, along with the *Assertio septem sacramentorum* (1521), and miscellaneous speeches and songs, his literary remains have never received the same
editorial attention as Elizabeth's.[3] Many of Henry's possessions as well as
objects that were touched by the royal body were preserved after the king's
death, first by his children and then by his Stuart heirs. Simon Thurley has
recently argued that James I and Charles I maintained the royal palace at
Hampton Court as "something of a museum" to Henry VIII. Instead of
decorating it with their newly commissioned paintings and recently acquired
furniture, they reserved it for Old Master paintings and Tudor antiques like

Henry's tapestries, royal canopies, and great beds, as well as more personal bodily items like his "cap, hawking bag, spurs and stirrups." These "relics of King Hal" at Hampton Court made the palace, in the words of the Venetian ambassador in 1618, "no ordinary memorial" to the late Tudor monarch.[4]

Hampton Court was not the only royal residence that preserved artifacts connected to Henry VIII. When Thomas Platter visited England in 1599 he stopped at the royal manor of Woodstock, where he saw "King Henry VIII's bathing-tub and bathing room, also a large square lead cistern full of water in which he bathed." In 1600, another tourist, Baron Waldstein, stopped at Windsor where he marveled at the beds in the royal apartments: "one of them," he wrote in his diary, "was 12 feet wide and is said to have been Henry VIII's." Perhaps this same bed, "eleven feet square, and covered with quilts shining with gold and silver" was also the one shown to Paul Hentzner when he visited Windsor in 1598.[5]

THE TOWER

Next to Hampton Court, the Tower of London was the most important repository of Henry's remains and a key site in shaping the king's image in the national imagination. For foreign visitors like Platter, Waldstein, and Hentzner, the Tower was – along with Westminster Abbey and the South Bank ampitheaters – one of the must-see attractions of London and often the initial destination on an itinerary that took them from Greenwich in the east to Windsor in the west. On his visit to the Tower, Platter entered a room full of tapestries, where there "stood a heavy iron chair which belonged to Henry VIII." But it was, of course, the arms and armors of Henry that the Tower was to become famous for – the kinds of objects that the visitor to Hampton Court would not have seen. Platter records seeing at the Tower "two great wooden pieces which King Henry VIII had had placed in France in a marshy spot before Boulogne" – a reference to the ferocious-looking "dummy" cannons that persuaded the French town to surrender to the English in 1544. Platter also noted "the ten span long barrel which belonged to the late King Henry, the queen's father, likewise the pistol which he carried on his saddle." In 1592 Jacob Rathger, secretary to Frederick, duke of Wirtemberg, had also noticed "the long barrel and stock which belonged to Henry VIII father of her present Majesty; this he is said to have carried on his saddle and it may be compared to a musket; also his lance or spear which a man has enough to do to lift."[6]

This essay focuses specifically on Henry's armors, their history at the Tower and elsewhere, and the stories they helped tell about the king in the posthumous process of royal myth-making. All the early visitors' accounts of the Tower mention Henry's armors, although like Hentzner's, which records "the body-armour of Henry VIII," they often lack enlivening detail.[7] The more effusive Platter was apparently able to handle the armor. He noted "King Henry's shield [the actual armour of King Henry] which was mighty heavy, also his iron helmet, breast plate [placket] and yellow gauntlets." "Soon after we saw a shield [suit of armour] which had also belonged to King Henry VIII, on which was a pistol which could be discharged with one finger."[8] Philip Julius, duke of Stettin-Pomerania, remarked in his travelogue that "The armour of King Henricus octavus was covered with red satin, and splendidly embroidered with gold."[9]

For Platter and most early observers, Henry's armors were part of a relatively unproblematic narrative that constructed the Tudor king as a warrior prince, a man of strength and action whose greatest deeds were siring the equally resolute Elizabeth, repudiating the pope, and declaring himself head of the Church of England. The notion of Henry as England's masculine ruler par excellence never entirely disappears from later visions and re-visions of the king, but it is modified in surprisingly complex ways across the course of the seventeenth and eighteenth centuries. Along with later literary and visual representations of Henry, his armors were to play a curiously resonant role in the cultural reimagining of the king. Like all material artifacts, Henry's armors have "life-histories" or "biographies" that can be carefully reconstructed.[10] "Cultural artifacts," as Stephen Greenblatt has written, "do not stay still ... they exist in time ... they are bound up with personal and institutional conflicts, negotiations, and appropriations." Greenblatt gives the example of Cardinal Wolsey's priest's hat that shifts its identity over time from an ecclesiastical garment to a theatrical prop to a tourist exhibit in Christ Church, Oxford.[11] Henry's armors were similarly itinerant, circulating across both institutions and discourses and accumulating new meanings and values as their histories unfolded.

Were the arms and armors of Henry VIII as recorded by early visitors to the Tower part of a coordinated display open to a privileged audience only or were they simply in storage there? The original Latin of Hentzner's text, as Albert Way observes, suggests "that various other remarkable armours for man and horse were then in the 'armamentarium' at the Tower" alongside Henry VIII's equipment. "The phrase 'arma multa et egregia, tam pro viris, quam pro equis, in equestri pugna,' ambiguously rendered 'many and very beautiful arms,' in the English translation, may suffice to prove that some of the suits of armour, cap-a-pie, with horse furniture of the same ... formed, as early as the forty-first year of Elizabeth's reign, part of the display in the

Tower armory."[12] Moreover, a letter of 1578 from the Privy Council to the Lieutenant of the Tower and the officers of the Ordinance and Armory indicates that it had become customary well before the end of Elizabeth's reign to grant privileged visitors access to the amory: A "Monsieur Kentell, gentleman of High Almagnye" was to be shown the Tower "and suche thinges as are *usuallie shewed* therin" (my emphasis).[13] Yet if Henry's military remains were indeed "on display" in the Tower, their presentation did not impress all visitors. Rathger/Wirtemberg observed in 1592 that the Tower armory was "not indeed to be compared with the German Armouries … although there are many fine cannon in it, yet they are full of dust and stand about in the greatest confusion and disorder."[14] And early in the next century, Henry Peacham judged the sights of the Tower – which also boasted Henry VIII's "slip-shoes" [slippers] – to be among London's "trifles and toyes not worthy the viewing."[15]

GREENWICH

The story of Henry's armors, however, begins not at the Tower but at Greenwich. In the postmortem inventory made of the king's possessions in 1547, most of the armors identifiable as Henry's personal harnesses are listed at Greenwich rather than the Tower, which functioned at this time as a storehouse for armaments and munitions.[16] Indeed, even in 1601 most of Henry's surviving armors remained at Greenwich. In that year, Sir Henry Lee, the Master of the Armories, informed Sir John Stanhope, Elizabeth's Vice-Chamberlain, that:

there is a little room, joining to the green Gallery wherein was placed such armours as served the person of King Henry VIII., kept in the same place ever since his giving up of arms, as a show of the goodliness of his person and the greatness of his mind. A monument it was of both, and long time after his death showed to such strangers as came to that place. So it was continued [to] the time of his son, of Queen Mary, and these forty and three years, and ever maintained in her Majesty's time that now is.[17]

The idea that Henry's collected armors at Greenwich formed a "monument" to the late king's memory resonates with the Venetian ambassador's remark that Hampton Court Palace represented "no ordinary memorial" to the king. Both comments take on added significance when we remember that Henry's children failed to erect an official funeral monument to their father either in Westminster Abbey or on his tomb in St. George's Chapel, Windsor. For the likes of Lee, who owed his early formation as a gentleman to Henry's favor, this notable absence was perplexing.[18] After all, as Henry's propagandist, Edward Hall, wrote in the dedication of *The union of the two noble and illustre famelies of Lancastre [and] Yorke* (1548) to Edward VI, "what diversitie is betwene a noble prince & a poore begger, ye a reasonable man and a brute beast, if after their death there be left of them no remembrance or token [?]"[19] Elizabeth I, passing through Cheapside on her coronation procession from the Tower to Westminster, was called upon by someone in the crowd "to Remember old King Henry the VIII," but in England during the generations after his death there were few public memorials that could help to stimulate this memory.[20]

That Lee could think of the Greenwich room that housed his old master's armor as a kind of cenotaph to Henry is connected to the close association between armor and early modern memorializing practices. The ancient aristocratic custom of displaying the deceased's trophies, swords, helm, breastplate, gauntlets, etc. over his tomb persisted through the seventeenth century.[21] Although no monument to Henry was ever completed, one especially ambitious plan – authorized by the king himself – called, not for the display of Henry's heraldic trophies, but for a life-size "Image of the King on Horsebacke, livelie in Armor like a King after the Antique maner shewing in countenance and looking on the said two Images lying on the said Tombes." In other words, this armored and mounted figure of Henry was to be depicted gazing down magisterially on the recumbent figures of himself and his last queen, Catherine Parr.[22]

As Master of the Armories and former Queen's Champion, Lee was a key figure in the revival of the cult of chivalry at the Elizabethan court – a cult that stressed the symbolic importance of ceremonial armor at the annual accession day tilts. Lee's investment in the creation and display of high-quality armor extended beyond his own elaborately wrought suits to the preservation of Henry VIII's historic armors.[23] Lee thus complained bitterly when he heard that Henry's Greenwich suits had been "thrown into a corner, taken from their place of so long continuance, thrown upon heaps, and without my knowledge or what might be said therein, or her Majesty's consent, I take it a wrong to the dead and to her Majesty."[24] Because Lee equates Henry's armors with the king's sacred remains, their mishandling represents a sacrilege, whose desecration insults not only Henry's memory but the dignity of the Tudor dynasty.

Greenwich is central to the story of Henry's personal armors because it was here, on the site of the rambling Tudor palace, that the king established the first royal armor workshop in the kingdom in 1515. Henry depended heavily at first upon foreign craftsmen from Germany and the Low

Countries who could design, build, and decorate/enrich fine armors that might rival those produced on the continent for the likes of François I and the Emperors Maximilian and Charles V.[25] In setting up the so-called "Almain" armory under the eventual mastership of Erasmus Kyrkenar, Henry was asserting the cultural prestige of his court and bidding for the "magnificence" befitting an ambitious ruler (see Hoak, chapter 3 in this volume).[26] Henry's investment in the production of high-quality armor for himself and select noblemen was thus consistent with his other cultural projects – including the building of fine palaces – that were all meant to raise the young king's visibility and prestige on the European stage.[27]

Henry's delight in acquiring fine armor from overseas and commissioning suits from his Greenwich craftsmen reminds us of the high value placed on ornate arms and armor by early modern Europe's rulers and aristocrats. Marina Belozerskaya argues that in court and elite circles, elaborately decorated armors, along with other luxury artifacts like tapestries, silverware, and goldwork, were more highly esteemed than paintings. The work of the best Italian armorers, she claims, was more sought after than the work of Italian painters and sculptors.[28]

Princes and aristocrats desired armor not just for the practical purpose of protection on the battlefield or at the tournament, but for the symbolic messages it encoded about the wearer's masculinity, status, and power. The wearing of full body armor was closely bound up with "the constitution of the aristocrat and the honour of a gentleman," insofar as armor embodied an ideal "stiffness of masculinity." Stripped of armor, as many a knight errant in Spenser's *Faerie Queene* discovers, the male self is disarmed, rendered vulnerable to a host of dangers, many of which are gendered female.[29] All the great courtiers of Elizabeth's reign had one or more specially tailored harnesses that could be adapted for various uses in battle, tournament, or parade. The master workman at Greenwich, Jacob Halder, created a manuscript album that contains line-and-wash illustrations of many of these armors (Sir Henry Lee's; the earl of Worcester's; Robert Dudley's, etc.). The collection may have served as a sort of pattern book or color catalogue that was shown to customers choosing a decorative scheme for their own armors.[30]

Henry's eventual ability to home-produce fine armor at Greenwich also served him politically in more tactical ways, since gifts of armor were used to grease the wheels of international diplomacy and domestic patronage relations. Early in his reign, Henry was at a disadvantage because he was unable to repay in kind gifts of armor, like the magnificent harness made for him by Maximilian's court armorer, Konrad Seusenhofer, at Innsbruck.[31]

Foreign rulers wishing to ingratiate themselves with Henry were advised to send him as gifts "arms of various kinds."[32] With the Greenwich workshop operational, Henry was finally able to offer gifts of armor befitting a powerful European prince, including his own previously worn harnesses. Thus in 1527 the French ambassadors returned home from celebrations in England marking an Anglo-French peace treaty with "greate rewards," including possibly a "newe harness all gilte of a strange fashion" in which Henry himself had tilted.[33] On other occasions, Henry sent Greenwich suits as gifts to allies and potential allies like the French admiral, Philippe de Chabot, and Sir Laurence Steyber, the German prince. Another "one of the King's harness complete, fit for the King's use three years past," was recycled and dispatched as a gift in 1534 to the German Marcus Meyer, whose anti-papal attitudes Henry hoped to exploit.[34]

Henry also made loans and gifts of armor to his own subjects. When the courtier John Asteley arranged to engage in judicial combat against "a Knighte straunger" in front of Henry, the king authorized the Royal Wardrobe to loan Asteley various pieces of armor.[35] The chronicler Edward Hall reports that at Henry's coronation, the King's Champion was entitled by custom to take for his own use from the royal armory the monarch's second-best harness, bases, plumes, and other accessories.[36] Even after Henry's death, the king's armors continued to circulate among his erstwhile subjects. Mary Tudor gave one of her father's armors to William Herbert, earl of Pembroke, presumably in recognition of his continuing services to the Tudor regime. The armor is recorded in a 1558 inventory of the Wilton armory (the Herbert family seat) as "a felde armor graven and gilte that was Kinge Henry theightes."[37]

The Wilton armory was perhaps the most famous private collection in early modern England, although by no means the only one. During Henry VIII's reign, Thomas Cromwell showed his own armory to the French ambassador and "tolde hym that there were other particular armaryes of the lordes and gentilmen of this Royaulme more then the nombre of Twenty aswell or better furnyshed then myn was wherat he woundred and sayd that he thought your grace the prince best furnished thereof in Christendom."[38] If Cromwell's armory was open only to elite guests, the Wilton armory apparently welcomed less prestigious visitors. Thus in 1635 a Captain of the Train Bands traveled from his home in Norwich to Wilton near Salisbury, where he saw the earl of Pembroke's "most gallant Armory" about which he "had heard a great report." The armory was "60 yards in Length" and contained enough weaponry to equip over 1,000 soldiers and horses. But what most impressed the captain were the "speciall rich Armes ... of great esteeme" that were specially partitioned off from the rest of the collection. Here were displayed suits belonging to Henry VIII, Edward VI, and several members of the Herbert family, as well as Henry VIII's "Leading Staffe, and his Warlike Scepter."[39] After the civil wars, the antiquarian John Aubrey also visited the Wilton armory, but lamented that during "the late warres much of the armour was imbecill'd [embezzled]." Still, the "rich gilt and engraved armour of Henry VIII [and] the like rich armour of Edward VI" remained intact.[40]

The remarks of Aubrey and the anonymous captain suggest that although only rulers and aristocrats could afford suits of armor that were designed, built, and decorated specifically for them by some of the most skilled craftsmen of the day, the non-elite were no less fascinated by the wealth and glamour of "a good armor." The willingness of the young soldier Claudio in Shakespeare's *Much Ado about Nothing* to walk "ten mile afoot to see a good armour," reflects an interest shared by many ordinary people in early modern England.[41] Armor aficionados of all backgrounds enjoyed an unusual opportunity both to view and (if they were wealthy enough) acquire fine armor in 1586 when a public lottery was held in Paul's Churchyard for "marvellous rich and beautifull armor." The collection included swords, decorated shields, and "graven" and "gilte" harnesses and corslets, and was valued at over £5,000. Armor historian Francis Cripps-Day speculates that many of these items were gifts to Henry VIII from fellow princes, François I, the Emperor Maximilian, and Charles V. Although there is no record of who entered or won the lottery, its location in St. Paul's Churchyard, one of London's central public spaces, suggests that the organizers were trying to attract a large audience.[42]

HENRY'S ARMORS IN THE SEVENTEENTH CENTURY

Beginning in the early 1640s, Henry VIII's armors at Greenwich were transferred along with other fine armors to the Guildhall and the Tower of London. During the 1620s, the Greenwich armory had become increasingly disorderly and the armors poorly maintained, and in "the late distracions" of the civil war much of the armor was looted.[43] In 1649, parliament instructed Edward Annesley, the Clerk of the Tower armory, "to search for, and seize the rich armours of the late King," Charles I. Charles's armors – with the exception of one "Rich Guilt Armor" that was sent to Oliver Cromwell – were delivered to the Tower along with other armors that Annesley associated with Henry VIII, James I, Prince Henry Stuart, and the future Charles II. In 1660, when the transfer from Greenwich (and St. James's Palace) to the Tower was complete, Annesley claimed "he hath bin very insttrumentall in preserving many rich Armors of his late Majestyes, brought from Greenwich, and also hath preserved to his greate Expence a Ritch Armor of great vallue of his late Majestyes owne Person."[44]

By 1660, then, the Tower housed the following armors of Henry VIII:[45]

• The Silvered and Engraved armor – for a long time misidentified as belonging to Henry VII and described in the 1660 inventory as a "Masking Armor compleat reported to be made for King Henry VII." This is a parade armor, made at Greenwich and designed not for combat but for ceremonial occasions. Its extensive etched decorations include the figures of St. George and St. Barbara, scenes from the lives of the saints, and floral designs featuring pomegranates and Tudor roses. These latter symbols suggest that the armor was built at the time of Henry's first marriage to Catherine of Aragon, whose symbol was the pomegranate.[46] This possibility is confirmed by the design of interlocking letters "H" and "K" around the bottom edge of the wide base (or skirt) that was "made in imitation of the fabric *bases* worn with both the civil and military dress of the period."[47] The armor, originally covered totally in silver and gilt, was a spectacular embodiment of the high fashion, wealth, and grandeur of its wearer.

• The Tonlet armor, designed for Henry to wear at his meeting with François I of France at the Field of Cloth of Gold in 1520.[48] In the 1547 inventory of Henry's possessions, the armor is listed at Greenwich as a "Tunlett ... parcel [i.e., partly] guilte with A Basenett complete Lackinge one gauntlett." Sometime in the 1640s the armor was moved to the Tower, before reappearing in the historical record in 1823. The Tonlet (Tunlett, Trundlett) armor is so-called for its distinctive, "almost knee-length, flaring, circular, hooped, skirt of steel" that was meant to protect its wearer during one-on-one foot combat by deflecting an opponent's blows[49](Figure 14).

• A Foot Combat armor, described in the 1660 survey as an "Armour of King Henry 8[ts]. cap-a-pe, being rough from the hammer" – that is, never completed or decorated. The armor was originally designed for Henry's use at the Field of Cloth of Gold[50] (Figure 15).

• A "Big" armor of Henry VIII, "cap-a-pe, white and guilt." This was one of several Greenwich armors built for the obese king in the 1540s (hence "Big")[51] (Figure 16).

Following the Restoration of the monarchy in 1660, officers in the Tower armory made the first systematic attempt to display the armors and weapons for the benefit of visitors.[52] Part of this reorganization involved setting up

Figure 14. Henry VIII's Tonlet armor. II.7.

Figure 15. Henry VIII's Foot Combat armor. II.6.

Figure 16. Henry VIII's "Big" armor for field and tournament. II.8.

a series of royal and noble armor-clad figures mounted on wooden horses. In 1661, the Dutch visitor William Schellinks, after inspecting several rooms full of armaments, including "the carbine, fowling piece, and pistol of Henry VIII," was shown into

a long room, in which behind a rail the body armour of several Kings and their horses' armour are lined up in a row, of very ancient and uncommon fashion, but all well looked after and kept polished. According to the keeper, there is the armour of Prince Henry, King Henry VIII, King Henry VII, Edward III, Charles I, Edward IV, Henry VI, the Duke of Gloucester [actually the Earl of Leicester], Charles Brandon, Duke of Suffolk, and that of William the Conqueror.[53]

The setting up of what, by the end of the century, had become known as the Line of Kings was part of a Restoration cultural project to reassert the legitimacy of the monarchy after the upheaval of the revolutionary years, by presenting England's history in terms of a succession of heroic royal warriors. Alan Borg observes that "the restored Stuart monarchy appears to have grasped the potential propaganda value of a national museum, which would glorify the nation and its rulers at the same time, and to have set about developing the Tower Armouries as a shrine commemorating the military achievements of king and country."[54] After the Restoration, visitors to the Tower would also have seen the so-called Spanish Armoury: a collection of weapons, armor, and other paraphernalia purportedly captured from the Spanish Armada of 1588.[55]

As an avowedly political display, the historical authenticity of the Line of Kings hardly mattered. Even after the Line was improved and expanded between 1685 and 1690, when the mounted figures were arranged chronologically, most of the royal effigies wore composite armors comprising pieces from different garnitures that were produced long after the reign of the monarch depicted.[56] The figure of William the Conqueror, for example, was presented "in a plain, bright Greenwich armour of the sixteenth century" and anachronistically carrying a musket; Edward I was equipped with a sixteenth-century armor originally designed for the earl of Worcester; and Edward III was dressed in one of Henry VIII's "Big" armors. The figure of Henry VIII himself in the Line of Kings was accurately depicted wearing another of the "Big" armors.[57]

To a large extent, the Tower armory in the later seventeenth and eighteenth centuries was organized around Henry VIII – a figure who was central to the nation's Protestant triumphalist narrative, but whose reputation and associations were always complex and even contradictory (see Rankin, chapter 5 in this volume).[58] Henry's central presence in the Tower was partly a consequence of the sheer quantity of his armor and equipment, even though some of the armors were for a long time misattributed to other historical figures. Henry VIII's Silvered and Engraved armor, for instance, adorned the figure of Henry's father until another major reorganization of the display in the early nineteenth century restored the suit to its rightful owner.[59]

OLD HARRY'S CODPIECE

The armors of Henry VIII are the consistent focus of attention in the accounts of post-Restoration visitors to the Tower armory. In 1710, Zacharias Conrad Von Uffenbach remarked that of all the "armour[s] of all the old kings of England … on full-sized wooden figures with the faces painted in colours from life … The most notable is King Henry VIII at the front near the door, whose armour is of a prodigious size. The headpiece, like the stomach piece and breeches, is lined with red velvet."[60] One part of Henry's armors in particular caught the attention of visitors. Among the "thousand pretty things to amuse" Tower visitors in the mid-eighteenth century, Horace Walpole included "the lions, the armoury, the crown, [the axe that beheaded Anna Bullen] and King Harry's codpiece."[61] This codpiece, moreover, was the focus of a peculiar ritual which Von Uffenbach hints at when he explains how "For a jest countless pins have been stuck into [the velvet lined breeches], and any young persons, especially females, who come here, are presented with one, because they are supposed to be a charm against impotency and barrenness."[62]

This custom of sticking pins into the velvet lining of Henry's armor was not new in 1710.[63] Some fifty years earlier, Schellinks recorded the same practice but was more specific about where the pins were inserted: "They also show here a peculiar relic, King Henry VIII's swansdown coverlet, which he used to wear over his codpiece, into which the English girls and women as an obeisance stick a pin and remove it and take it with them as a titillating keepsake."[64] Ned Ward, another Tower visitor before the end of the seventeenth century, further elaborated on this practice of pricking the royal prick case: "King Henry the Eighths codpiece," says Ward in *The London Spy* (1703), "was Lin'd with Red, and hung Gaping like … a Maiden-Head upon full stretch, just consenting to be Ravish'd: This [says the Tower guide] is the codpiece of that Great Prince, who never spar'd woman in his lust, nor man in his anger; and in it to this day remains this virtue, that if any married woman tho' she has for many years been barren, if she sticks but a pin in this member-case, the next time she uses proper means, let her but think of her Tower Pin Cushion, and she need not fear conception."[65]

The cultural implications of this pinpricking custom take on different implications depending on which codpiece and which harness of Henry's was used. Although Schellinks does not explicitly mention a codpiece, it is hard to imagine that between 1661 and 1698 the custom of sticking in pins had migrated from any part of the harness to only the codpiece. Also puzzling is why in Schellinks's account the implied codpiece is part of a whole-body armor, whereas in the other two accounts the codpiece seems to exist as an object in its own right, unattached to any harness. When the codpiece is alluded to again in César de Saussure's account of 1725, it is an integral part of the king's harness: "near the entrance to the hall is the figure of Henry VIII; he is represented standing in his royal robes, with a sceptre in his hand, and this is said to be a good likeness of this celebrated king. If you press a spot on the floor with your feet you will see something surprising with regard to this figure; but I will not say more, and leave you to guess what it is."[66] As in Schellinks's account, de Saussure refrains from actually naming the codpiece, instead relying on the reader's imagination. Although the use of a mechanical, visitor-operated device to reveal the royal codpiece is not discussed in any other text I am aware of, the same frisson of delight at its unexpected revelation appears in a text of 1730. The narrator of *The Country Spy* describes a newlywed woman, "eaten up with the *Vapours* and *Green-Sickness*," who goes to stick a pin in Henry's codpiece in hopes of conceiving. When she stands before the king's figure, "the Wardour, on a sudden, lift up the Piece of Armour that reached to the King's Knees, which discovered the Representation of what the young Lady wanted; it had such an effect upon her … that she fell in a Swoon."[67]

The Tower warder's *coup de théâtre* achieved by "lift[ing] up the Piece of Armour that reached to the King's Knees" is puzzling because none of the Henry armors in the Tower at this time that sported codpieces – the Foot Combat armor and the "Big" armors – were equipped with any kind of base or metal skirt that could be raised in this way. We know, however, that by 1682 the Tower had acquired a separate "codpiece of Henry VIII. parcel gilt" that was not part of a harness.[68] Perhaps an enterprising officer of the Tower had attached this codpiece to another armor that allowed for the act of lifting. Such an effect could have been achieved, for example, by attaching the codpiece to Henry's Silver and Engraved armor and by covering "the deep arched cut-out" at the front of this armor's base with some kind of flap. Whatever the case, the figure of Henry that visitors "operated" by treading "a spot on the floor" was closely related to the mechanized waxwork figures that started to appear in London in the early eighteenth century. The most famous such figure was perhaps "Old Mother Shipton the Famous English

Prophetess," who featured in Mrs. Salmon's waxworks. Richard Altick explains that this figure "administered a farewell kick to Mrs. Salmon's patrons as they left. The floor of the exhibition was booby-trapped with hidden treadles, which, when stepped on, not only set Mother Shipton kicking but threw another figure into a threatening attitude with an uplifted broom."[69]

These anecdotes of the codpiece reveal that in the public imagination of late seventeenth-century England, Henry VIII was not simply a revered historical figure but a larger-than-life, mythical persona of serio-comic dimensions. As a metonymy for Henry's own prodigious desires, the codpiece registers a wayward virility that reached far beyond his six wives and that had long been a part of a folkloric view of the king. A ballad of 1620, for example, sang

> To the praise of old king harry
> But hee would sware, and he would stare
> And lay hand on his dagger
> And would swive while hee was a live
> From the Queene unto the begger
> Then lett him alone he's dead and gone
> And wee have in his place
> Our noble king of him letts sing
> God save King James his grace.[70]

These lines establish Henry VIII's impetuous violence and promiscuity as a foil to James I's controlled dignity. Later, at the Restoration, Henry's reputation as a rake was used to comment satirically on Charles II's sexual excesses. The narrator of a Samuel Butler poem, for example, deems "Old *Harry's* C – piece in the Tower, / That once contain'd such fleshly Power" to be "but a Bauble" in comparison to Charles's "*tarriwag*." Henry's codpiece, moreover, was

> A Case that would not half inclose
> [Charles's] Scepter, all the Kingdom knows:
> No! *Harry's* C – piece must knock under
> Thine merits fifty times the wonder;
> And has ejected twice the Force,
> That e'er leap'd out of *Trojan* Horse;
> For tho' thou hadst but one good Wife
> To recreate thee in thy Life,
> And he had six yet thou hadst more
> Of other Mens, by twice a Score.[71]

The hold on the English imagination of Henry's lusts and changing connubial alliances contrasts with his notorious difficulty in fathering legitimate male children. Hence the oddity of women visitors to the Tower treating his codpiece as a kind of "fertility talisman" that would help them become pregnant. For the women participants, the pinpricking ritual's appeal surely lay in the vicarious and intimate contact it gave them with the body of England's most formidable male ruler.[72] By thrusting their pins into Henry's codpiece, moreover, the women appropriated the male sexual prerogative of penetration while at the same time transforming the seat of Henry's male potency into a pincushion – a domestic object of haberdashery.[73] In their own way, ordinary women were demystifying the memory of Henry VIII, reducing a public exhibition of male potency and chivalry to the level of a Bartholomew Fair show. No wonder, given the Tower armory's aim after the Restoration of rekindling respect for Britain's monarchy, that Archbishop Secker of Canterbury eventually ordered "decent alterations" be made to the interactive contraption which revealed the lewd representation of the royal member.[74]

The Archbishop's intervention, however, was too late to prevent the Tower codpiece(s) from contributing to a proverbial identification of king and codpiece during the eighteenth century in phrases like "old cod-piece Harry."[75] This idea of Henry's codpiece as a metonymy of his insatiable lust was no doubt also inspired by the prominent codpiece that appeared in Holbein's oft-reproduced iconic portrait of the king (see frontispiece). The codpiece, then, was more than Henry VIII's signature fashion accessory: it was an essential part of his identity. And it was a potent rhetorical weapon in political and religious debates of the seventeenth and eighteenth centuries. One Protestant observer lamented "that well known Reflection upon the Reformation here in England, by some loose Persons, viz. That it came from Henry VIII's Codpiece, which opprobrious saying, was probably invented by Enemies to our Religion."[76]

<h3 style="text-align:center">THE HORNED HELMET</h3>

The cultural reimagining of Henry VIII after his death took many forms. In the pre-revolutionary decades, Henry was frequently constructed as the sentimental embodiment of a vanished merry England (see Fleck, chapter 11 in this volume). As Charles I's personal rule increasingly polarized the political nation in the 1630s, the figure of Henry VIII could conjure up a happier and simpler age in which ruler and subject were at ease with each other and the nation was united under a benevolent monarch. This image of the good-natured "bluff king Hal" is recorded in the ballads, chapbooks, and jestbooks of the period.[77] *The History of the King and Cobler* (Edinburgh, 1634), for example, describes the adventures of Harry Tudor among his ordinary subjects. In this tale, the disguised Henry enjoys the "Jolly humour" of an unsuspecting cobbler who entertains the king in his cellar. The prankster Henry then lures the cobbler and his shrewish wife to court, where the couple are the source of much humor. The tale ends with the cobbler receiving an annuity and a place at court from the jovial king.[78]

Henry's good nature is also celebrated in popular seventeenth-century tales about the king's exploits with his jester Will Sommers. The jestbook *A pleasant history of the life and death of Will Summers* (1637) narrates the freedom of this "all-licensed fool" to criticize Henry, and Henry's good humor in accepting such criticism.[79] For the narrator, however, this convivial banter between king and clown is now, lamentably, a thing of the past: "These homely Jests might passe in those dayes, though the refinednesse of these our times will neither admit such coursnesse of language, nor such boldnesse with Princes."[80] This nostalgia for the supposedly honest, plain-spoken days of Henry VIII is captured in a flagrantly anachronistic image in the text that depicts Henry as a "dead ringer" for Charles I, with a narrow, elongated face, small pointed beard, and broad-brimmed hat with feather.[81] Given the wide availability in popular print culture at this time of the iconic image of Henry VIII derived from Holbein's original Whitehall mural, readers of *A pleasant history* could hardly overlook the woodcut's implied message that Charles would benefit from a Henrician "makeover" – by taking on the positive attributes of his legendary Tudor forebear.[82] The pamphlet ends by implicitly faulting Charles for employing not an audacious jester like Sommers, but a "drone" like "the late Archer" or Archie Armstrong. As seventeenth-century readers of the pamphlet would have known, Armstrong was "late" because Charles had recently dismissed him for insulting Archbishop Laud.[83]

The narrator of *A pleasant history* makes the further intriguing observation that Will Sommers, "Going over with the king to Bulleine … had compleat armour made for him, from head to foote." This armor, moreover, could now "bee seene within the Tower at London."[84] This may be the earliest reference to the display in the Tower of an unusual armor identified as belonging to Sommers. In the year following the publication of *A pleasant history*, a foreign visitor to the Tower recorded seeing there the armor of a fool.[85] After this, nothing more is heard of Sommers's armor until the Tower inventory of 1660 lists an "Anticke Headpiece with Ramshornes, Coller, and spectacles upon it, one Jacke, and one sword, all said to be William Sommers' arms."[86] The "Anticke Headpiece with Ramshornes," or the horned helmet, is the most extraordinary part of this ensemble and still survives in the Royal Armories collection as item IV.22 (Figure 17). Yet its association with Will Sommers is entirely spurious.

Figure 17. The horned helmet. IV.22.

The horned helmet is in fact the only remaining piece of an exquisitely decorated parade armor sent to Henry VIII as a gift from the Emperor Maximilian in 1514.[87] The first reference to the helmet is in the 1547 inventory of Henry's possessions, where it is described as "A hedde pece with A Rammes horne silver parcell guilte," and is connected not with the rest of the Maximilian gift suit but with "A playne Tilte harnesse." For reasons unknown, the helmet had become detached from the rest of the Maximilian armor, with which it was reunited by 1561. In that year, an inventory addressed directly to Elizabeth I mentions the "Armour sent to your Majesties said ffather by Maxamilian the Emperor garnished with silver and Guilte with a Headpeice of fashion like a Rames head."[88] Because of its unique appearance, the horned helmet and its grotesque mask survived even as the rest of the harness was broken up and sold as scrap before 1660. Probably the last reference to the complete Maximilian harness is in an *Inventory of Goods Belonging to Charles I and Sold by Order of the Council of State 1649–1652* that mentions "Twenty six pieces of broken armour and buckles / Steel and silver gilt valued at £1 15s / Sold to Samle. Edwards the 27 Decr 1649 for £2 7s."[89]

At sometime, then, between 1561 and 1660 the provenance of the horned helmet was either forgotten or suppressed, with a new identity invented for it. Was the helmet's original identity simply lost in an age before curators and modern museum record keeping, or was it considered indecorous to associate Henry VIII with such a grotesque object, whose ram's horns would have suggested to many observers its wearer's status as a cuckold? Though we cannot answer these questions, we can appreciate why, of all the names that might have been associated with the helmet, Will Sommers's was chosen.[90] For, as I have been arguing, by the seventeenth century Sommers was integral to a popular view of Henry VIII as the good-humored, beloved ruler who could appreciate his own shortcomings and even laugh at himself. Artifacts associated with Sommers, like those associated with his royal master, were already finding their way into cabinets of curiosities and other collections by the late sixteenth century. Thus, Thomas Platter noted the belled cap of Henry VIII's jester in Walter Cope's *Wunderkammer* in 1599.[91]

When Ned Ward saw Henry VIII's codpiece in the Tower in 1698 he also saw "the armour of Will Sommers, the jester, to which they had added an ill-favoured face with horn upon his head and upon his nose a pair of spectacles; on which our jocular commentator was pleased thus merrily to descant. This figure, says he, represents that drolling gentleman Will Sommers who was jester to King Henry VIII." The "jocular commentator," or guide, also entertained Ward with a story about Sommers prompted by the helmet's horns and spectacles. According to this oft-told tale, Sommers's pretty wife was repeatedly unfaithful to him. Although everyone else realized Sommers was a cuckold, Sommers himself could not see his own cuckold's horns until a nobleman, after kissing Sommers's wife, gave him a pair of spectacles. The spectacles stood as a warning of the dangers faced by old men with young, attractive wives.[92]

The cultural attention given to Will Sommers helped foster an image of Henry as trickster and boon companion – an image that existed alongside and in tension with a competing view of the king as, at best, a deeply flawed and morally ambiguous figure and, at worst, England's most notorious tyrant and a national embarrassment. Indeed, the image of "bluff king Hal" seems to have been manufactured in part to offset this darker version of Henry that continued to circulate in the eighteenth century in the writings of Burnett, Lindsay, and, especially, Swift (see Paulson, chapter 6 in this volume).[93] Even the historical displays in the Tower armory could reinforce rather than mitigate such hostile views of Henry. Thus in the mid-eighteenth century, one Tower visitor contemplated the figure of "King Henry VIII. in his own proper armour":

In his right Hand he bears a Sword, but whether of Cruelty or Mercy, will hardly, I think, admit a Doubt. His Reign is mark'd with the Divorce and Murder of Wives, the Destruction of religious Houses and Monasteries, and by a Defiance of all Laws divine and human.[94]

In the face of such negative judgments, the disarming or domestication of Henry through posthumous myth-making continued across various cultural media and venues. At eighteenth-century masquerade balls, for example, Henry VIII costumes were frequently on show. Horace Walpole remarked of a masquerade he attended in 1742 that "the two finest and most charming masks, were their Graces of Richmond, like Harry the Eighth and Jane Seymour; excessively rich, and both so handsome!" Portraiture also helped disarm a threatening Henry: in Joshua Reynolds's mock-heroic portrait of *Master Crewe as Henry VIII* (1776), the Tudor wife-killer became a suitable historical persona for a child. In both the masquerade and the portrait, Henry's fearsome reputation is tamed by either carnivalesque impersonation or infantilization (see Figure 11).[95]

By the later eighteenth century, the Will Sommers exhibit in the Tower seems to have had more detractors than admirers. A visitor from Birmingham in 1784 considered it "a disparagement to the place," and wondered why the Lieutenant had not consigned both the figure and its accompanying story to the fire.[96] In 1829, Edward Wedlake Brayley labeled the figure of Sommers ("a block of wood, carved and painted to resemble life, surmounting a suit of armour") a "disgrace of decency," while at the end of the century, Harold Arthur Lee, Viscount Dillon (Curator of the Tower Armoury from 1895 to 1912 and a descendent of Elizabeth I's Champion Sir Henry Lee), blamed the visiting public for "lik[ing] stories to be told them about each object, and the inventive faculties of Tower warders and others have been fully exercised in pandering to this depraved taste."[97] The "depraved" stories surrounding the horned helmet worn by the figure of Will Sommers were not just of a sexual nature. Around the same time that Dillon was chastising the British Tower-going public and their guides, Sir William Fraser constructed a different narrative by claiming that "the real history, and meaning" of the helmet and its grinning face mask

had nothing to do with Will Sommers: nor any other jester. It was placed on wretched creatures, who proved the sincerity of their religious convictions by submitting to be burned at the stake: the object of its grotesqueness being to prevent the poor victim's contortions, exciting the compassion of the lookers-on. A similar mask, which I purchased at Lord Londesborough's sale, has a whistle added to the mouth: so that the screams of agony were made the source of merriment.[98]

While both stories about the horned helmet are equally fanciful, Fraser's story gestures, however indirectly and unwittingly, to a more sobering and realistic vision of Henrician England – an England characterized by religious violence rather than bawdy jests.

Before the advent of modern armor scholarship and curatorship in the late nineteenth century, the alleged provenance and identity of a piece of armor and the stories told about it often bore little relation to the historical record. When Viscount Dillon was appointed Curator of the Tower Armoury in 1895, "he was tasked with producing an up-to-date catalogue of the collection. As curator he was able to reduce historic inaccuracies that had built up over 25 or so years." Earlier in the century, "[curator] Samuel Meyrick had brought expert knowledge to the collection, but it had then fallen into the hands of the War Office storekeepers and unfortunately most his work was lost. Labels were misplaced, and suits wrongly mounted and erroneous traditions were established for public amusement."[99] Under these conditions, it was easy to see how the meanings attached to Henry's armors were not fixed but fluid, shaped by the larger narrative that a particular era wished to tell about this most multivalent of monarchs. The Victorians, for example, in reaction to their forebears' more relaxed morals, preferred a decorous version of the past which excluded "interactive" codpiece exhibits and ribald tales of cuckoldry.

HENRY'S SKIRT

Several scholars have recently stressed the ways in which early modern elites invested armor with the power to preserve the memory of a family's pedigree. As a "memorial system," armor was bequeathed from fathers to sons and was often displayed in the ancestral home or in the local church.[100] But what we have seen here is that in some ways the story of Henry VIII's armors is more about the loss than the preservation of memory, more about forgetting than remembering. One final example of this process comes between the late eighteenth and early nineteenth centuries, when a mannequin of Elizabeth I dismounting from her horse was displayed in the Tower. According to one report, the figure "was superbly dressed in the armour she had on ... to review her fleet at Tilbury" during the Armada crisis. Not until 1823, in light of recent advances in armor scholarship, was Elizabeth's so-called Armada armor exposed as nothing of the sort. A Tower guide book of that year asserted that "there is not the slightest evidence of Her Majesty having worn armour on this memorable occasion; and it further appears, that the fluted breast plate, and the *garde-de-reine* [a concave metal skirt], in which her figure is now environed, belonged to her father, and that they could not have been worn in a sitting posture."[101] The mannequin of Elizabeth was wearing parts of Henry VIII's Tonlet armor: the fluted breast plate and the rear section of the wide skirt-like base that gave the ensemble its distinctive "feminine" appearance (see Figure 14).[102] That the armor's provenance could be so "forgotten" was due in part to the absence of any individual marks of identity on its various parts. The Tonlet armor's etched decorations are dynastic rather than specifically Henrician in nature: the Tudor roses on the base as well as the Garter symbols on the left greave and collar were as appropriate for Elizabeth as for her father.[103] But this act of "forgetting" can also be seen as ideologically motivated and revealing of broader cultural fantasies about the national past. From the early seventeenth to the early nineteenth century, Elizabeth – the warrior queen with "the heart and stomach of a king" – could be effortlessly imagined wearing skirted armor, whereas Henry VIII – that icon of codpiece-clad English masculinity – could not. Indeed, the spectacle of Henry VIII in a skirt of steel is one that continues to unsettle present-day visitors to the Tower.[104]

ACKNOWLEDGEMENTS

This chapter has benefitted greatly from the assistance and suggestions of Bridget Clifford and Thom Richardson of the Royal Armouries Museum; members of The Ohio State University Renaissance Reading Group; and Susie Kneedler.

NOTES

1. Susan Doran (ed.), *Elizabeth: The Exhibition at the National Maritime Museum* (London: Chatto and Windus, 2003), 103, 106, 117.

2. Karen Hearn, *Marcus Gheeraerts II: Elizabethan Artist in Focus* (London: Tate Publishing, 2002), 34.

3. M. St. Clare Byrne (ed.), *The Letters of King Henry VIII: A Selection with a Few Other Documents* (London: Cassell, 1936), ix. On the literary aspects of Henry's private letters, see Seth Lerer, *Courtly Letters in the Age of Henry VIII: Literary Culture and the Arts of Deceit* (Cambridge: Cambridge University Press, 1997), ch.3. Also see Theo Stemmler, "The Songs and Love-Letters of Henry VIII: On the Flexibility of Literary Genres," in Uwe Baumann (ed.), *Henry VIII in History, Historiography, and Literature* (Frankfurt am Maim: Peter Lang, 1992) 97–111.

4. Simon Thurley, "The Early Stuarts and Hampton Court," *History Today* 53:11 (November 2003), 15–20; also see Simon Thurley, *Hampton Court: A Social and Architectural History* (New Haven: Yale University Press, 2003), 112–15, 290; *Calendar of State Papers Relating to English Affairs in the Archives of Venice*, vol. XV (1617–19) (London, 1909), 271.

5. Clare Williams (ed. and trans.), *Thomas Platter's Travels in England, 1599* (London: Jonathan Cape, 1937), 221; G. W. Groos (ed. and trans.), *The Diary of Baron Waldstein: A Traveller in Elizabethan England* (London: Thames and Hudson, 1981), 139; Horace Walpole (ed. and trans.), *Paul Hentzner's Travels in England during the Reign of Queen Elizabeth* (London, 1797), 54.

6. Williams (ed.), *Thomas Platter's Travels*, 160–1; Rathger quoted in Charles Ffoulkes, *Inventory and Survey of the Armouries of the Tower of London* (London: H. M. Stationery Office, 1916), 65.

7. Walpole (ed.), *Paul Hentzner's Travels*, 27.

8. Williams (ed.), *Thomas Platter's Travels*, 160.

9. Gottfried von Bülow (ed.), "Diary of the Journey of Philip Julius, Duke of Stettin-Pomerania, through England in the year 1602," *Transactions of the Royal Historical Society*, new series, 6 (1892), 15.

10. Arjun Appadurai (ed.), *The Social Life of Things: Commodities in Cultural Perspective* (Cambridge: Cambridge University Press, 1986).

11. Stephen Greenblatt, *Learning to Curse: Essays in Early Modern Culture* (New York: Routledge, 1990), 161–3; also see Stephen Greenblatt, *Shakespearean Negotiations: The Circulation of Social Energy in Renaissance England* (Berkeley: University of California Press, 1988), 112–13. Jonathan Gil Harris has challenged some of the underlying assumptions of a recent wave of early modern material cultural studies by insisting on the diachronic axis along which objects move and are reimagined. See his "The New New Historicism's *Wunderkammer* of Objects," *European Journal of English Studies* 4:2 (2000), 111–23; and "Shakespeare's Hair: Staging the Object of Material Culture," *Shakespeare Quarterly* 52:4 (2001), 479–91.

12. Albert Way, "Survey of the Tower Armoury in the Year 1660," *Archaeological Journal* 4 (1847), 341–54. On August 26, 1580, one Owen Hopton wrote to Cecil, Leicester, Hatton, and the rest of the Commissioners for the Office of the Armoury, stating that he had "made a survey of all the armour remaining in the Tower" and would "send an estimate of the charges for making rooms within the Great White Tower for hanging up all the armour" (*Calendar of State Papers Domestic: Edward VI, Mary and Elizabeth*, vol. I (1547–80), [ed.] Robert Lemon [London, 1856], 673).

13. *Acts of the Privy Council of England, 1542–1631*, ed. J. R. Dasent (London, 1890–1964), vol. X (1577–8), 441; see also Geoffrey Parnell, "The Early History of the Tower Armouries," *Royal Armouries Yearbook* 1 (1996), 45.

14. Quoted in Ffoulkes, *Inventory and Survey*, 65.

15. Peacham's comments are part of a commendatory poem to *Coryats Crudities* (London, 1611) (*RSTC* 5808) in praise of the shoes that have taken Coryat on his epic tour of Europe (sig. K4v).

16. David Starkey (ed.), *The Inventory of Henry VIII: the Transcript* (London: Harvey Miller Publishers, 1998).

17. *Calendar of the Manuscripts of the Most Honourable the Marquess of Salisbury* (London, 1883–1976), vol. XIV (Addenda), 181.

18. A tablet above Lee's funeral monument described him as owing "his Youthe to the Courte and Kinge Henry the eight, to whose service he was sworne at 14. Yeares olde" (E. K. Chambers, *Sir Henry Lee: An Elizabethan Portrait* [Oxford: Clarendon Press, 1936], 304).

19. Hall's dedication "To the most mightie, verteous and excellent prince Edward the sixt," in *The union of the two noble and illustre famelies of Lancastre [and] Yorke* (1548). *RSTC* 12721.

20. There was a statue of Henry VIII at Gresham's Royal Exchange. In the aftermath of the Great Fire (1666), John Evelyn noted "Sir Thomas Gresham's statue, though fallen from its niche in the Royal Exchange, remained entire, when all those of the Kings, since the Conquest, were broken to pieces" (William Bray [ed.], *Diary and Correspondence of John Evelyn* [London, 1850], vol. II, 14).

21. Peter Stallybrass, "Hauntings: The Materiality of Memory on the Renaissance Stage," in Valeria Finucci and Kevin Brownlee (eds.), *Generation and Degeneration: Tropes of Reproduction in Literature and History from Antiquity through Early Modern Europe* (Durham, NC: Duke University Press, 2001), 287–316, esp. 288–90.

22. John Speed, *The history of Great Britaine* (London, 1611; *RSTC* 23045), 784; Nigel Llewellyn, "The Royal Body: Monuments to the Dead, for the Living," in Lucy Gent and Nigel Llewellyn (eds.), *Renaissance Bodies: the Human Figure in English Culture c. 1540–1660* (London: Reaktion Books, 1990), 218–40.

23. Ian Eaves, "The Greenwich Armour and Locking-Gauntlet of Sir Henry Lee in the Collection of the Worshipful Company of Armourers and Brasiers," *Journal of the Arms and Armour Society* 16 (1998), 133–64.

24. *Calendar of the Manuscripts ... Salisbury*, vol. XIV (Addenda), 181; see also Chambers, *Sir Henry Lee*, 128.

25. Fine armor for royalty and social elites is different in kind from the mass-produced munitions armor of ordinary soldiers.

26. Karen Watts, "Henry VIII and the Founding of the Greenwich Armouries," in David Starkey (ed.), *Henry VIII: A European Court in England* (London: Collins Brown in association with the National Maritime Museum, Greenwich, 1991), 42–6; Thom Richardson, "The Greenwich Armouries," *The Court Historian* 11:2 (2006), 121.

27. See the essays in Starkey (ed.), *Henry VIII: A European Court in England*.

28. Marina Belozerskaya, *Rethinking the Renaissance: Burgundian Arts Across Europe* (Cambridge: Cambridge University Press, 2002), 1–6, 125–30. She includes fine armor-making among the "sumptuous arts" (5). On fine Italian armor, see Stuart W. Pyhrr and José-A. Godoy (eds.), *Heroic Armor of the Italian Renaissance: Filippo Negroli and his Contemporaries* (New York: Metropolitan Museum of Art, 1998).

29. Nina Taunton, *1590s Drama and Militarism: Portrayals of War in Marlowe, Chapman, and Shakespeare's* Henry V (Aldershot: Ashgate, 2001), 137–46; Allan H. Gilbert, "Spenserian Armor," *PMLA* 57 (1942), 981–87.

30. Thom Richardson, *The Armour and Arms of Henry VIII* (Leeds: Royal Armouries, 2002), 119–20; Eaves, "Greenwich Armour," 148–59.

31. On armor as gift, see Francis Henry Cripps-Day, *Fragmenta Armamentaria*, vol. I, ii, *An Introduction to the Study of Greenwich Armour* (Frome: Butler & Tanner, 1939), 38–50.
32. Quoted in ibid., I.ii.45.
33. Richardson, *Armour and Arms*, 23–4, and "Greenwich Armouries," 117–18; this gift armor is identified as the Genouilhac harness now in the Metropolitan Museum. See Helmut Nickel, "English Armour in the Metropolitan Museum," *The Connoisseur* (November 1969), 199–202.
34. James Gairdner (ed.), *Letters and Papers, Foreign and Domestic, Henry VIII*, vol. IX (August–December 1535) (London: Longman, Green, and Roberts, 1886), 58; Cripps-Day, *Fragmenta*, I.ii.45–8.
35. Cripps-Day, *Fragmenta*, I.ii.43–4; I.iv.18, 22.
36. Edward Hall, *The union of the two noble and illustre famelies* (1548), sig. AAAa iiii. Quoted in Cripps-Day, *Fragmenta*, I.iv.118n.
37. See Claude Blair and Stuart W. Pyhrr, "The Wilton 'Montmorency' Armor: An Italian Armor for Henry VIII," *Metropolitan Museum Journal* 38 (2003), 96–9. Herbert served Henry (as squire and armor bearer), as well as Edward and Philip and Mary.
38. Roger Bigelow Merriman (ed.), *Life and Letters of Thomas Cromwell*, 2 vols. (Oxford: Clarendon Press, 1902), 2, 177. Quoted in Cripps-Day, *Fragmenta*, I.ii.39–40.
39. *A Relation of a short survey of the western counties … in a seven weeks journey begun at Norwich and thence into the West.* Quoted in Cripps-Day, *Fragmenta*, I.iii.102–4; see also Blair and Pyhrr, "The Wilton 'Montmorency' Armor," 95.
40. *The Natural History of Wiltshire*, ed. John Britton (London, 1847), 86; Blair and Pyhrr, "The Wilton 'Montmorency' Armor," 136 n. 8.
41. Benedick makes the claim in *Much Ado*, 2.3.14–15. All references to Shakespeare's plays are to *The Norton Shakespeare*, ed. Stephen Greenblatt, Walter Cohen, Jean E. Howard, and Katharine Eisaman Maus (New York: W. W. Norton, 1997).
42. John Stow, *A Summarie of the Chronicles of England* (London, 1590; *RSTC* 23325.2), 728–9; Cripps-Day, *Fragmenta*, II, ii.
43. *The Manuscripts of the Earl of Dartmouth*, vol. III (London: Historical Manuscripts Commission, 1896), 3–4; Cripps-Day, *Fragmenta*, I.iv.90.
44. Cripps-Day, *Fragmenta*, I.ii.117–19, I.iv.6–7, 66, Richardson; "Greenwich Armouries," 122.
45. Cripps-Day, *Fragmenta*, I.iv.74ff.
46. Ibid., I.iv.11–12, 79; Richardson, *Armour and Arms*, 12–16.
47. Claude Blair, *European Armour, circa 1066–circa 1700* (London: Batsford, 1958), 116.
48. Richardson, *Armour and Arms*, 20–2; Claude Blair, "King Henry VIII's Tonlet Armour," *The Burlington House Fair*, 19–29 October 1983 (London: British Antique Dealers' Association, 1983), 16–20.
49. Starkey (ed.), *Inventory of Henry VIII*, 162, item 8405; the armor was referred to in 1611 and 1629 inventories as "an olde fashioned Armor called a Trundlett parcell guilte and graven." Blair, "Tonlet Armour," 18.

50. Cripps-Day, *Fragmenta*, I.iv.74, 80; Richardson, *Armour and Arms*, 18–19.
51. Cripps-Day, *Fragmenta*, I.iv.5, 81, 84.
52. Way, "Survey of the Tower Armoury," 341–54; Alan Borg, "The Museum: The History of the Armouries as a Showplace," in John Charlton (ed.), *The Tower of London: Its Buildings and Institutions* (London, Her Majesty's Stationery Office, 1977), 69–73.
53. Maurice Exwood and H. L. Lehmann (ed. and trans.), *The Journal of William Schellinks' Travels in England 1661–1663*, Camden Society, 5th series, I (London: Royal Historical Society, 1993), 48–50.
54. Borg, "History of the Armouries as a Showplace," 69. Another part of this project relating specifically to Henry VIII was Charles II's commission for a painted copy of Holbein's famous Whitehall mural (see Hoak and String, chapters 3 and 7 in this volume).
55. Alan Borg, "Two Studies in the History of the Tower Armouries," *Archaeologia*, 2nd series, 105 (1975), 332–52.
56. Ibid., 328–9.
57. Ibid., 319.
58. Blair, "Tonlet Armour," 16.
59. Borg, "Two Studies," 331.
60. W. H. Quarrell and Margaret Mare (ed. and trans.), *London in 1710 from the Travels of Zacharias Conrad Von Uffenbach* (London: Faber and Faber 1934), 41.
61. W. S. Lewis (ed.), *The Yale Edition of Horace Walpole's Correspondence* (New Haven: Yale University Press, 1937–1983), vol. XVII, 233–4.
62. Quarrell and Mare (eds.), *Travels of Zacharias Conrad Von Uffenbach*, 41. An Irish visitor to the Tower in 1752 described a somewhat more decorous variation on this ritual: "At the door is placed King Henry the Eighth a-foot, with a pincushion on his sleeve, wherein the ladies commonly stick a pin, in return of which they are shown another, though somewhat of larger dimensions" (Henry Huth [ed.], *Narrative of the Journey of an Irish Gentleman through England in the Year 1752* [London, 1869], 115).
63. Richardson, *Armour and Arms*, 38, shows the velvet lining.
64. Exwood and Lehmann (ed. and trans.), *The Journal of William Schellinks' Travels*, 49.
65. *The London Spy Compleat* (London, 1703), vol. 1 of 2, 315. Ward also mentions the codpiece on the armor identified as John of Gaunt's, "which was almost as big as a Poop-Lanthorn, and better worth a lewd ladies admiration, than any piece of antiquity in the Tower" (314). The John of Gaunt armor was actually made in Germany *c.* 1540 (II.22).
66. Ffoulkes, *Inventory and Survey*, 70. Ffoulkes's note also refers to Ned Ward's narrative and to the codpiece or brayette (braguette).
67. *The country spy; or a ramble thro' London. Containing many curious remarks, diverting tales, and merry joaks* (London, 1730), 27–8.
68. Cripps-Day, *Fragmenta*, I.iv.94. Attached and unattached codpieces of Henry's were noted in the Tower toward the end of the eighteenth century (Francis Grose, *A treatise on ancient armour and weapons, illustrated by plates taken from*

the original armour in the Tower of London, and other arsenals [London, 1786], 22). Some of Henry's codpieces are still in the Tower as items III.727 and II.8J.

69. Richard D. Altick, *The Shows of London* (Cambridge, MA: Harvard University Press, 1978), 52.

70. www.earlystuartlibels.net/htdocs/king_and_favorite_section/L5.html#f2c.

71. Samuel Butler, *Posthumous works in prose and verse, written in the time of the civil wars and reign of K. Charles II. by Mr. Samuel Butler* (London, 1715), 23–4.

72. I am indebted in this section to Will Fisher's excellent discussion of Henry's Tower codpiece in *Materializing Gender in Early Modern English Literature and Culture* (Cambridge: Cambridge University Press, 2006), 70–4, quotation at 73.

73. Early modern texts contain many references to the custom of sticking pins into one's codpiece. To give one example, Anthony Copley's *Wits fittes and fancies* (1595) (*RSTC* 5738), describes how "Bishop Gardener seeing one of his men waite at the boord with a monstrous great Codpeece prick'd full of pinnes on the top, tooke a peece of bread, and crumbled it towards him" (174).

74. Ffoulkes, *Inventory and Survey*, 70. See also Lewis (ed.), *Walpole's Correspondence*, vol. XXXVIII, 379.

75. *Public discontent accounted for, from the conduct of our ministers in the cabinet, and of our generals in the field* (London, 1743), 35. A late seventeenth-century poem refers to a London tavern sign as "the Head of Old Jolly Gruff great Codpeic'd Harry" (Richard Ames, *The search after claret, or, A visitation of the vintners a poem in two canto's* [London, 1691], canto 50).

76. *God's judgments against whoring. Being an essay towards a general history of it, from the creation of the world to the reign of Augustulus … with observations thereon* (London, 1697), 30–1.

77. W. G. Sellar and R. J. Yeatman, *1066 and All That* (London: E. P. Dutton, 1931), 54. See also Mark Rankin, "Henry VIII and the Nostalgia for 'Merry' England," ch.5 of "Imagining Henry VIII: Cultural Memory and the Tudor King, 1535–1625" (unpublished Ph.D. dissertation, The Ohio State University, 2007); and Eckhard Auberlen, "King Henry VIII – Shakespeare's Break with the Bluff-King-Harry Tradition," *Anglia* 98 (1980), 319–47.

78. Other examples in the genre focusing on Henry's interactions with commoners include *The pleasant and delightful history of King Henry the VIII, and the Abbot of Reading. Declaring how the King dined with the Abbot of Reading, and how the King brought the Abbot to a good stomach, &c.* (London, 1680).

79. William Shakespeare, *King Lear*, 1.4.166. In his *ODNB* entry on Sommers, J. R. Mulryne argues that "the familiar account of him as witty adviser and corrector of royal excesses, appearing in plays such as *Misogonus* (first performed 1564–77?), in Thomas Nashe's *Summer's Last will and Testament* (1592), and in Samuel Rowley's *When You See Me, You Know Me* (1605), probably owes more to posthumous myth making than to fact." For a brief account of the cultural after-life of Sommers, see John Southworth, *Fools and Jesters at the English Court* (Stroud: Sutton, 2003), 101–2.

80. *A pleasant history*, sig. C1v–C2r.

81. Ibid., sig. B8r.

82. The immediately recognizable image of Henry VIII appeared, for example, in seventeenth-century editions of Foxe's *Actes and Monuments*, on the title page of Rowley's *When You See Me, You Know Me* (1613, 1621, 1632; the image does not appear in the first edition of 1605), and in John Taylor's *A Briefe Remembrance of all the English Monarchs* (edns. 1618, 1621, 1622). Even into the eighteenth century the dominant "visual conception of Henry still derived from the swaggering figure isolated from Holbein's mural. The memory of it was imprinted on artists' subconscious through the various painted copies", Xanthe Brooke and David Crombie, *Henry VIII Revealed: Holbein's Portrait and its Legacy* (London: Paul Holberton, 2004), 61.

83. In 1796 when the pamphlet was published for the last time, the reference to "the late Archer" would have meant little to most readers. The editor thus included a gloss explaining that "Archibald Armstrong, commonly called Archer, was the last person retained as King's Jester; and was discharged from that office by Charles I. for an impudent jest on Archbishop Laud" (34).

84. *A pleasant history*, sig. c8r.

85. Claude Blair, "The Emperor Maximilian's Gift of Armour to King Henry VIII and the Silvered and Engraved Armour at the Tower of London," *Archaeologia*, 2nd series, 99 (1965), 18 n. 4.

86. The *OED* defines a jack as "a coat of fence, a kind of sleeveless tunic or jacket, formerly worn by foot-soldiers and others, usually of leather quilted, and in later times often plated with iron; sometimes applied to a coat of mail. (See Meyrick in *Archæol*. XIX. 224.)."

87. The identity and meaning of the horned helmet has been the subject of lively disagreement between two luminaries of the modern study of armor in Britain: Alan Borg and Claude Blair. See Alan Borg, "The Ram's Horn Helmet," *Journal of the Arms and Armour Society* 8 (1974), 127–37, and – in response – Claude Blair, "Comments on Dr. Borg's 'Horned Helmet'," *Journal of the Arms and Armour Society* 8 (1974), 138–85. Borg makes the case against the horned helmet being part of Maximilian's Imperial gift armor, while Blair makes what I see as the more persuasive case in favor of this view.

88. Blair, "Comments," 180.

89. Starkey (ed.), *Inventory of Henry VIII*, 161, item 8388; Cripps-Day, *Fragmenta*, I.iv.21; Richardson, *Armour and Arms*, 8–10; Blair, "The Emperor Maximilian's Gift of Armour," 18. While the horned helmet may seem unusually ornate, its design appears unremarkable when set alongside the extraordinary embossed parade helmets created for various distinguished clients including Charles V and the dukes of Urbino by Filippo Negroli from the 1530s. See Pyhrr and Godoy (eds.), *Heroic Armor of the Italian Renaissance*.

90. On the iconography of horns, see Borg, "Ram's Horn Helmet," 133–4, and Blair, "Comments," 178–80. There is a record from the reign of Edward VI of Sommers being equipped with "a harniss of paper boordes," or cardboard armor, for his part in a mock combat – an event that John Southworth describes as an important act "in the court fool's repertoire" (*Fools and Jesters*, 98).

91. The continuing association of Henry and Sommers into the seventeenth century can be seen in a recently discovered portrait of Sommers, Henry, and his three

children. This copy of an original from the early 1550s was created sometime between 1650 and 1680. See http://news.bbc.co.uk/1/hi/england/northampton-shire/7421051.stm. On the presence of "Will. Sommers sewtte" in the theatrical wardrobe of the Lord Admiral's Men in 1598, see Anne Rosalind Jones and Peter Stallybrass, *Renaissance Clothing and the Materials of Memory* (Cambridge: Cambridge University Press, 2000), 196, 248. "Will Summers was dead, but he survived in the clothes that bore his presence and that could be made to walk again in the theatrical costume that was made to awaken him from the grave" (196).

92. Ward, *The London Spy*, 315–16.
93. See Jack Lynch, *The Age of Elizabeth in the Age of Johnson* (Cambridge: Cambridge University Press, 2003), 66–7, and Dirk F. Passmann and Heinz J. Vienken, "That 'Hellish Dog of a King': Jonathan Swift and Henry VIII," in Baumann (ed.), *Henry VIII in History*, 241–79.
94. David Henry, *An Historical Description of the Tower of London and its Curiosities* (London, 1753), 53.
95. Terry Castle, *Masquerade and Civilization: The Carnivalesque in Eighteenth-Century English Culture and Fiction* (Stanford: Stanford University Press, 1986), 68; Lewis (ed.), *Walpole's Correspondence*, vol. XVII, 338, vol. XXIII, 193; Christopher Lloyd and Simon Thurley, *Henry VIII: Images of a Tudor King* (Oxford: Phaidon Press, 1990), 104–5.
96. W. Hutton, *A Journey from Birmingham to London* (Birmingham, 1785), 208.
97. Edward Wedlake Brayley, *Londinia, Or, Reminiscences of the British Metropolis: Including Characteristic Sketches, Antiquarian, Topographical, Descriptive, and Literary*, vol. I (London: Hurst, Chance, and co., 1829), 238; Harold A. Dillon, "Notes on Armour in the Tower," *The Antiquary: A Magazine Devoted to the Study of the Past* 29 (January–June, 1894), 28.
98. Sir William Fraser, *Hic et Ubique* (London, 1893), 304–5.
99. www.royalarmouries.org/collections/history-of-the-collection/early-scholars/harold-arthur-lee-dillon.
100. Stallybrass, "Hauntings: The Materiality of Memory," 290; R. A. Foakes, "'Armed at point exactly': The Ghost in Hamlet," *Shakespeare Survey* 58 (2005), 34–47.
101. Quoted in M. R. Holmes, "A Carved Wooden Head of Elizabeth I," *Antiquaries Journal* 40 (1960), 37–8; Claude Blair can find no reference to the Tonlet armour between 1629 and 1823 when it is referred to on the figure of Elizabeth ("Tonlet Armour," 18).
102. The skirt or base of the Tonlet armor consists of a front and a rear section which are joined by a set of straps. The reference to "*garde-de-reine*" or "rump defense" suggests that the figure of Elizabeth may have worn only the rear section of the base (Sir James Mann, *Wallace Collection Catalogues: European Arms and Armour*, vol. I, *Armour* [London: 1962], xxxix).
103. The Silvered and Engraved armor is the only one of Henry's surviving suits that features symbols of individual ownership (see above).
104. Susan Frye, "The Myth of Elizabeth at Tilbury," *Sixteenth Century Journal* 23 (1992), 95–114.

CHAPTER 9

Henry VIII: his musical contribution and posthumous reputation

Matthew Spring

In the common imagination Henry VIII's musical reputation is most likely to be based on his supposed composition of "Greensleeves," and possibly also of "Pastime with Good Company." As a ballad tune "Greensleeves" was not known before the Elizabethan period,[1] though it is based on a popular Italian ground-bass pattern – a set chord progression known as the "romanesca" that was popular across Europe from the 1540s.[2] We can safely say that "Greensleeves" is misattributed. On the other hand, there is little reason to doubt that Henry did compose some or all of "Pastime," though it too has parallels with Italian ground schemes. In fact there are some thirty-three surviving pieces, including "Pastime," ascribed to Henry in the so-called Henry VIII manuscript (BL, MS Add. 31922), plus a doubtfully ascribed three-part Latin motet, "Quam pulchra es," in the Baldwin manuscript (BL, MS Royal 24 D ii). There is also good contemporary evidence for his reputation as a performer and a composer. This chapter will review not only his surviving music, but also the contemporary accounts of his musical activities. These accounts were widely known, and his musicality was well established as part of his character profile by the later sixteenth century.

In succeeding centuries Henry's musical reputation grew and expanded yet rested largely on literary accounts and anecdotal evidence, rather than surviving music. By the eighteenth century there was already controversy over the matter of Henry's musical abilities. Sir John Hawkins described Henry as "deeply skilled in the art of practical composition," yet others, such as Charles Burney, were disparaging of Henry's efforts. The discovery of the Henry VIII MS in 1865 changed the situation by increasing the number of Henry's attributions from a handful to over thirty. Yet opinion on Henry as a composer is still divided today, with Peter Holman describing him "a composer of sorts, though his achievements in that direction have been exaggerated,"[3] while David Fallows is prepared to consider him seriously as a composer whose best pieces "reflect the genius noticed by all those who encountered him."[4] Disagreement is likely to remain, as few are happy with the idea that a hereditary monarch could be talented, preferring to believe that the accounts of his brilliance were expected forms of flattery. Yet recent scholarship has established the role he played in reforming and developing the royal music, and creating a musical culture that enriched the nation for centuries.

The fact that Henry played a range of instruments is important. In doing so he departed from tradition and increased the acceptance and desirability of domestic music-making in the great houses of the nation. A few English Kings before Henry had played the harp, notably Henry IV and Henry V, and there are a few pieces in the Old Hall manuscript attributed to "Roi Henri."[5] Yet Henry VIII's involvement is of an altogether different magnitude. As John Stevens says in his introduction to the modern edition of the Henry VIII manuscript, "Henry was not only a trained but an enthusiastic musician."[6] The traditional view was that music should form part of a courtier's education. The *Liber Niger* of Edward IV and "Regulations for the Government of prince Edward" (1474) mention the practice of music as a desired accomplishment for a prince.[7] Yet here the implication is that these are private pursuits developed more for connoisseurship than public performance. Much of this thinking is carried forward in Baldassare Castiglione's manual on the behavior appropriate to a Renaissance courtier, *The Booke of the Courtyer* (translated by Sir Hoby and published in England in 1561), and in Sir Thomas Elyot's *The boke named the governour* (1531), a treatise written for and presented to Henry VIII. Castiglione had visited England himself in 1506 to receive the Garter on behalf of Duke Guidobaldo della Rovere of Urbino, the patron who had inspired the original book, and was an early facilitator of Anglo-Italian cultural exchange.[8] Henry broke with the tradition of passive courtly connoisseurship by taking an active part in composing music, playing privately within his palaces, and even performing within the court in a semi-public way such that foreign ambassadors heard him.

His reorganization and expansion of the musical activities and employment of musicians at the Tudor court, however, was more important and lasting than his actual composition or reputation as a musician. Henry's desire to create a cosmopolitan court on a par with his European rivals, and the money that accrued to the crown as a result of the Reformation gave Henry the impetus and means greatly to expand and reorganize the music of the English court. Henry built upon the foundations laid by Henry VII in his overhaul of government. Around 1495 Henry VII developed the Privy

Chamber as an exclusive and private sphere in which to live and transact business.[9] These innovations were not laid down in statute until the Eltham Ordinance of 1526 but were put in place during Henry VII's reign. Throughout the medieval period royal musicians had been members of the Presence Chamber and were organized into the chapel, the trumpeters, and the minstrels. Minstrels tended to play individually or in small groups of diverse types. With the establishment of the Privy Chamber, some musicians were granted more intimate access as Grooms of the Privy Chamber. These were the confidantes of the king and were there not only to play for him, but also to instruct and play music with him and his immediate family. Typically these musicians performed on quiet instruments like the lute and keyboard, the instruments that Henry himself played. The Fleming Philip van Wilder (c. 1500–53) was effectively in charge of the music in the Privy Chamber for much of Henry VIII's reign. In addition to the musicians themselves, he selected and used boy singers in private performances for the chamber.

Henry's Reformation of the Church of England set in train the succession of events and acts that would lead to the first Edwardian Act of Uniformity (1549), which inaugurated services in English and replaced Latin service manuals.[10] Despite the large-scale upheaval within the church, the suppression of monastic houses, the new cathedral foundations, and suppression of musical churches, church services during Henry's reign continued to be sung, or said, in Latin, apart from an English Litany introduced in 1544.[11] One consequence of the Act of Supremacy (1534) was to make the King's Chapel Royal the pre-eminent sacred music establishment of the country, and one that other choirs in colleges, cathedrals, and churches should model themselves on.[12] Among the leading composers within the chapel at different times in Henry's reign were Robert Fayrfax, William Cornish, and Thomas Tallis. As a royal peculiar, the Chapel was under the direct control of the sovereign and therefore avoided the disbanding or reorganization of many of the other church musical establishments.

Of equally lasting importance was Henry's recruitment of instrumentalists from the continent. In particular the group of foreign families that dominated the royal music until the eighteenth century were recruited by agents acting for Henry in Italy in the period around the Cleves wedding in 1540. These families brought over the newest instruments and playing styles. With their recruitment the amorphous group of minstrels separated to form a rump group of old-style minstrels, and new "whole" consorts of strings (viols and violins), wind (flutes, sackbuts, cornets), and lutes emerged. These groups played polyphonic music in ensembles using instruments of different sizes. By recruiting and patronizing these foreign musicians, many of whom were Jewish and of Spanish or Portuguese extraction, Henry set the course for music at the English court until late into the seventeenth century. He laid the foundation for the development of polyphonic consort music that developed over time into the orchestras of the eighteenth century and beyond.

HENRY'S PATRONAGE OF PLAYERS OF THE KEYBOARD AND LUTE

The first half of the sixteenth century saw the final stages in the transformation of the medieval English minstrel into the Renaissance musician. Typically a fifteenth-century minstrel was an all-round entertainer, proficient on a number of instruments, who wore the livery of his patron and spent much of his time traveling around to regional fairs and visiting other great houses.[13] With the importation of a number of prominent families of foreign musicians by Henry VIII, the function of minstrels gradually changed into that of household music teachers, performers, and composers, with a much improved status and access to family members. This process was slow, and, outside the royal household and that of a few select magnates, did not take place until Elizabeth's reign, but the change was set in motion by Henry himself.

One of the earliest families of foreign musicians to arrive were the three members of the Flemish van Wilder family, Matthew, Philip, and Peter, some of whom were present at court as early as 1515.[14] The van Wilders were primarily lutenists who also played viols, and may have been the first to introduce the viol to England. The most obviously successful of the three was Philip, who rose to a position of unusual distinction, becoming the highest-ranking musician of his time. He provides the best example of the heightened status of musicians in the more secular society of Reformation England. In the course of his career, he received several licenses to import "wyne and woad."[15] An entry for December 14, 1529 in a book of Privy Purse expenses mentions Philip as "phillip wylde of the pryvay Chambre."[16] In 1539 he was granted denization by the king, which allowed him to own land and be styled Gentleman of the Privy Chamber.[17] His first of several grants of land also occurred in 1539. These extraordinary favors made Philip a rich and influential man. He was put in charge of the nine "Synginge Men & Children" of the Privy Chamber, which was no doubt specially formed to perform the French chansons

that Philip himself composed.[18] Philip had been authorized to impress
children throughout the country for service among his singers. He bought
instruments for the Crown, and it is clear from Great Wardrobe inventories of 1542/3 and 1547 that he had care of the royal instrument collection.
The second of these inventories is entitled "Instruments at Westminster
in the charge of Philipp Van Wilder," and was compiled after Henry's
death in 1547.[19] In his own time he was evidently a composer of some
importance, and from what does survive we can be sure he was fully able
to compose music for the lute in the Italian polyphonic style. Philip
maintained his pre-eminent position during the reign of Edward VI,
dying a few months before the king. A poem bewailing his death
appeared in Tottel's *Songs and Sonnets* (1557).[20]

Henry was fascinated by keyboard players, and his palaces were full of
a variety of keyboard instrument types. Two foreign organists who were
employed by Henry in 1516 were Benedictus de Opicijs and the Venetian,
Dionisius Memo. Memo had been organist in St. Mark's, Venice, from
1507 to 1516, and both he and Opicijs were probably accepted into the
Privy Chamber.[21] After the death of Opicijs in 1524 and the departure of
Memo in about 1525, two Englishmen, Simon Burton and Thomas
Heywood, took their places. Heywood in particular remained within
the Privy Chamber throughout Henry's reign and, despite a period of
disgrace for denying the king's supremacy (1543–5), continued in royal
service in the reigns of Edward and Mary (see Happé, chapter 1 in this
volume).[22]

Several important Italian lutenists were present at the Tudor court in
the early years of Henry's reign, to complement the organists mentioned
above. The most important was John Peter de Brescia, who is mentioned
first in 1512 as receiving an annuity of £40 p.a., and was still serving the
Princess Mary in 1533.[23] This man appears with some frequency in
accounts between 1514 and 1518 as John Peter de Brescia, John Piero,
Zuan Piero, and Giovanni Pietro de Bustis (as he once signed himself).
He was a particular favorite of the king at this time and is referred to in one
letter as the King's "confidential attendant."[24]

The great Alberto de Ripa, one of the foremost lute virtuosi of the age,
visited England in 1529 in the train of Cardinal Campeggio. De Ripa
received a generous reward from Henry but did not stay in England.
Instead, he was employed by Henry's rival, Francis I of France, by the
summer of 1529, and was richly rewarded with money and lands, occupying
a position of prominence at court similar to that of Philip van Wilder in
England.[25] According to one account, Henry unsuccessfully tried to entice

the Neapolitan virtuoso Luys Dentice into his service with an offer of a
yearly salary of 1,000 crowns (£240).[26]

HENRY'S OWN MUSICIANSHIP

The instruments that Henry favored throughout his life were those he
himself played, the lute and keyboard. He could certainly also sing and
play wind instruments, but it was to players of the lute and keyboard that
he gave most prominence at his court. The best first-hand evidence we
have of Henry playing and practicing come from the accounts of three
Venetian ambassadors, Pasqualigo, Badoer, and Guistinian, on a diplomatic mission and sent by the Doge to England in 1515. In one account
Henry is said to "play almost on every instrument." The best-known
remark is that which Pasqualigo made in 1515 of Henry, who at the age
of 23 had been king since 1509:

> He speaks French, English and Latin, and a little Italian, plays well on the lute and
> harpsichord, sings from books at sight, draws the bow with greater strength than
> any man in England, and jousts marvellously.[27]

In a letter from Sagudino, secretary to the embassy, we hear that Henry, "is
an excellent musician [and] plays the virginals well." On May 1, 1515,
Sagudino is put into a state of some excitement after he had played in
front of the nobles and prelates on the virginals and organ, as he was told
that "the king would certainly wish to hear him, for he practised these
instruments day and night."[28]

Henry VII gave lutes to all his children: Prince Henry at the age of
seven (1498); and the princesses Margaret and Mary at seven (1501) and
twelve (1505), respectively, and they all received instruction.[29] Like his
father, Henry VIII also had all his children taught the lute, including his
bastard son Henry Fitzroy, duke of Richmond, his son by Elizabeth
Blount.[30] The man responsible for teaching Henry and most of the
other royal children the lute was a Frenchman named Giles Duwes.
Duwes is first mentioned in 1501 in a warrant issued on November 2 in
which he is described as "Luter unto oure dearest Sone the Duke of
Yorke" and given "16 yards of good chamblet to make a gown against
the solemization of the marriage of the Prince" [Arthur].[31] He appears in
accounts as a lutenist among the still minstrels (1501–35), and is often
referred as simply "Giles" or "Master Giles."[32] Yet Giles Duwes was no
mere minstrel, but very much was a man "of the privy chamber." He had
been brought into the royal household not as a musician at all, but as

French tutor to Henry VII's children. He then combined this role with teaching Prince Henry the lute, and later was given responsibility as royal librarian. Henry VIII continued to employ not only Giles but also his son, Arthur Duwes (1510–40), who was the probable lute tutor to the duke of Richmond.[33] Giles was the recipient of many royal favors, including several lucrative licenses to import tons of Toulouse woad and Gascon wine, "custom from the port of Bristowe," and the posts of "keeper of the place called 'le Prince Warderobe'" and "keper of our lyberary" at the "manor" of Richmond.[34] Quentin Poulet, who occupied the post of royal librarian before Giles, was, like Giles Duwes, a denizened Frenchman.[35] Duwes kept his foreign status at least until 1514, as a document of that year refers to him as an "alien."[36]

The importance of Giles Duwes in shaping the young Henry's mind and accomplishments has been largely overlooked. Duwes as both French tutor and lute teacher had constant access to the young Prince from at least as early as 1501 and throughout his teenage years. Along with John Skelton and the poet Bernard André, who were also Henry's boyhood tutors, Duwes must have done much to shape Henry's mind and formidable intellect. In the years after 1502 Henry was based at Greenwich, was kept under constant close supervision, and was not allowed to leave the Palace "unless it was by a private door into the park, and then only in the company of specially appointed persons."[37] Among those persons was Giles Duwes. He was a linguist, a lover of books, and a musician. If Henry's first attempts at composition date from the years 1502–9 before he became king, surely Giles must have been the man with the contacts and the knowledge to have supplied Henry with his musical exercises, and supervise his tuition in music theory and composition as well. It is no surprise then that all these early pieces were French, as it is the sort of material Giles would have known and had with him.

The only image of Henry as a musician made during his life is that of Henry playing a harp to his fool. It appears in "Henry VIII's Psalter" (BL, MS Royal 2 A XVI, f. 63v) and was written and illuminated by Jean Mallard, the king's "orator in the French tongue," between 1530 and 1540 (see Figure 3).[38] Henry is clearly old in the illumination, and the image must have been taken from life, as is that of Sommers, the royal fool. The marginalia in the king's own hand shows that it was Henry's personal copy. That Henry is clearly being portrayed as King David explains the harp, but the presence of the fool is due to the text from Psalm 53. Just to the right of Sommers's head are the words "Dixit inspiens in corde suo: non est Deus" – "the fool says in the his heart, 'There is no God.'" Henry owned and used this psalter and must have been happy not only with his portrayal as King David (see King, chapter 2 in this volume), but also as a king playing to his fool.

THE CLEVES WEDDING AND THE NEW FAMILIES OF JEWISH MUSICIANS

After the van Wilders, the next group of foreign musicians to be taken into royal service were two Germans, Hans Highorne and Hans Hassenet, specialist viol players who arrived in the 1520s. In 1540, as part of the preparations for the Cleves wedding, a new consort of violins was instituted, drawn from four interrelated families of Sephardic Jews recruited in Italy.[39] Although described in accounts as players of "Vialles," for the most part they played violins, instruments then thought especially appropriate for dance music. This consort was an addition to the existing consorts for flutes and sackbuts. Thus during Henry's reign a new larger "King's Music" took shape, in which specialist pre-formed consorts of like instruments performed for specific functions. The increased revenues available to the crown as a result of monastic seizures helped to make this possible. Musicians from abroad were more privileged than the old royal minstrels and normally commanded greater respect and higher salaries. Their instruments and music were, in the main, drawn from northern Italian cities, where, as with the lute, new Renaissance musical ideas, instrumental techniques, and designs had first become popular. Through the royal musicians, the instruments and their playing techniques were established in England and imparted to English musicians both professional and amateur.

The major expansion of the King's Music around 1539–40 was directed by Thomas Cromwell and executed by Edmond Harvel, the English resident in Venice. As mentioned above, the families that Henry collected from Italy, the Bassanos, Comys, and Lupos, played in consorts of like instruments, were of Jewish origin, and had come previously from Spain or Portugal.[40] Most had concealed their identity, assuming Christianized names taken from the towns in Italy where they had previously lived or been employed. Thus, the Bassanos were a wind-playing family of five brothers who took their name from the town that had been their home in Italy.[41] The main string players came from Milan and were centered around Ambrose of Milan, who later took the name Ambrose Lupo. Some of the string players had been Marranos, Portuguese Jews living secretly in Milan.

It may have been that they were being pursued from Portugal to Milan by the Inquisition, and as Milan had fallen to the Spanish empire in 1535, so they made their way to England, probably via Venice, where it was known Henry was recruiting foreign musicians. The Jews in Venice were in close touch with those in London and saw ties between the struggles of the English Reformation and Judaism, and England a refuge from papal and Lutheran oppression. Despite the official ban on Jews in England, it seems to have been an act of policy to establish them there. Certainly it was realized that as Jews they would be reliable servants and men who were enemies of the pope. They were also paid much better in England than in Venice. They could practice music freely in London but their religion only in secret. The Bassano family made a further contribution in establishing instrument making in the London Charterhouse.[42]

With the influx of some nineteen Jewish musicians Henry hugely expanded the royal musical establishment. Most of the new groups remained in the Presence Chamber, playing in the family-based consorts to which they belonged. A select few among the musicians had access to the Privy Chamber, and were not always listed among the musicians but among the Grooms. Thus the musicians of the royal household, which around 1500 typically consisted of nine trumpets, three sackbuts and a cornet player, and three string players,[43] had by the beginning of Edward VI's reign expanded to some eighteen trumpets, seven viol/violin players, four sackbuts (who also played recorders and other wind instruments), a group of six that included lutes, harp, rebec and two singers, plus ten more assorted old-style minstrels.[44] This represents a threefold increase from some fifteen to forty-five, almost all of which occurred during Henry VIII's reign. Certainly, succeeding monarchs did not always maintain these numbers, and there were changes to the organizational groups, yet the main elements of this establishment remained in essence the same until the later part of the next century, and formal aspects of it until the last century.

HENRY'S COMPOSITIONS AND HIS REPUTATION AS A PLAYER AND COMPOSER

The idea that Henry VIII was a lover of music and proficient as a player and composer was well established by the late sixteenth century. According to Edward Hall's chronicle (1548), it was in the summer of 1510 that Henry "did set .ii. goodly masses, every of them five partes, whiche were songs oftentimes in hys chapel, and afterwards in diverse other places."[45] Hall's chronicle gives detailed accounts of the elaborated masks or "disguisings" that were a feature of court life in the first decade of Henry's reign. Introduced no later than 1513, they started with a loud fanfare, a moveable pageant of some sort, and the descent of courtly maskers from the pageant down the hall to dance. Masks involved elaborate costumes, elaborate symbolism, theatrical stunts, and theatrical elements. They were always the occasions for musical entertainment, both incidental and as interludes between items. These events centered on Henry and Catherine, and would involve Henry dancing but not usually performing in public.[46] In reference to Henry's instrumental performance, Holinshed (1587) says of the first year of Henry's reign: "From thense the whole court removed to Windsor, for then beginning his progresse, and exercising himselfe dailie in shooting, singing, dansing, wrestling, casting of the barre, plaieng at the recorders, flutes, virginals, in setting of songs, and making of ballads."[47] Holinshed then goes on to repeat Hall's account on the composition and nature of the two masses.

Herbert of Cherbury's popular and much reprinted *The Life and Raigne of Henry VIII* (1649) lists among the king's virtues "an harmonious Soul, for he was a good Musician, having among other things, composed two Anthems, which were usually sung in his Chapels."[48] Herbert repeats Holinshed in saying that he was "a curious musitian; as two intire Masses compos'd by him, and often sung in his Chappell, did abundantly witnesse."[49] He continues, placing Henry's musical abilities alongside his martial accomplishments:

Therefore though some relate that he used singing, dancing, playing on the Recorder, Flute and Virginals, making Verses, and the like: yet his more serious entertainments were study of History and Schoole-Divinity, (in which he especially delighted,) Justs, Turneys, Barriers but with the Two-handed-Sword, and Battle-axe. These, againe, were set forth with costly Pageants and Devises; and those so frequently, that it tooke up not onely much time, but consumed a great part of the Treasure. Of which who desires to see more may peruse *Hall* and *Hollinshed*, who have many particularities worth the looking on, for him that hath so much leasure.[50]

Erasmus was one important commentator who met Henry several times and whose letters have been widely known to later historians. In one letter, he praises the skills of the young Henry, saying "there is no kind of music in which he is not more than moderately proficient."[51] Erasmus is the source for Henry Peacham in *The Compleat Gentleman* (1622). Before mentioning princes of his day who were musicians, Peacham singles out Henry for praise. "King Henry the eighth could not only sing his part sure, but of himself composed a services of four, five and six parts as Erasmus in a certain Epistle testifieth of his own Knowledge."[52] Lord Herbert makes the point that before becoming heir to the throne in 1502, Henry had been destined for the church. Hawkins goes further, pointing out that Henry, as a second son, had been intended for the church by his father, with a view to the Archbishopric of Canterbury, and that "music was therefore a necessary part of his education."[53]

Hall and Hollinshed remained the basis for Henry's musical reputation in the eighteenth century, which, if anything, grew, though without any real basis. Roger North in his "Memoirs of Music" (1728) is typical in his notes on Henry. "But as one may guess, Church Musick was at its perfection in the reigne of Henry VIII. He was a lover, and they say composed anthems. In some times royall familys were all fighters, and in others all scollars; for as he [himself] was learned, so he bred all his children to learning, and also to musick, as some of the historys shew."[54] Hawkins, in his *General History of the Science and Practice of Music* (1776), enlarges his reputation as a composer, saying Henry VIII "not only sang, but was possessed of a degree of skill in the art of composition equal to that of many of its ablest professors, as appears by many of his works now extant."[55] Hawkins is at pains to back up his view that Henry "was deeply skilled in the art of composition"[56] and prints the three-part Latin anthem "Quam pulchra es" in full as proof of his skill. This piece appears in a collection of sacred music in the hand of John Baldwin of the Windsor choir. It is dated 1581 and has the words "Henricus Octavus" at the beginning, and "Quod Rex Henricus Octavus" at the end of the cantus part. Hawkins points to other pieces by Henry, including the anthem normally ascribed to John Mundy, "O Lord the maker of all things," saying that Bishop Aldrich had taken great pains to establish that it was after all by Henry not Mundy. Hawkins further says that Erasmus and Bishop Burnet asserted that Henry had composed offices for the church, and that Henry's stature as a composer was such that he should have been included in Morley's catalogue of composers in his *A Plaine and Easie Introduction to Practicall Musicke* (1597), from which he is indeed absent.[57]

Burney, in his *General History of Music* (1789), is scathing on the merits of English music before the mid-eighteenth century.[58] He finds the music of the Henrician period deficient in counterpoint, and has even less to offer on Henry. He includes the usual quotations from Cherbury and Holinshed and says, "It is generally allowed that Henry could not only perform the Music of others, but was sufficiently skilled in Counterpoint to compose the pieces that go under his name." He points out that singing a part in "full pieces of the time" was necessary for both private gentlemen and princes. He then translates a long, quoted discussion of the musical expertise of the Emperor Charles V and Kings Charles IX and Henry III of France.[59] Burney points out that Henry's retreat from the Church of Rome did not go so far as a general Reformation of the church and that "at least with respect to ecclesiastical Music, no change was made other than that of applying English words." He is aware that the Henrician composer John Marbeck's reforming zeal nearly got him burnt for heresy. Burney is prepared to admit that Henry might have composed "Quam pulchra es," "as it is not too masterly, clear, or unembarrassed for the production of a Royal Dilettanti," but cannot allow that he composed the anthem that Dr. Boyce printed in his *Cathedral Music*.[60]

William Chappell's *Popular Music of Olden Times* (1859) builds a much more ambitious musical profile for Henry. William (1809–88) inherited Chappell's music publishing house in 1834 and typified the Victorian gentleman-scholar, able to pursue his abiding interest in old tunes with the time, and money, to track them down. At a time when there was a developing interest in native music across the British Isles, he was at pains to build the profile of English music in response to the better-established interest in the national music of Scotland and Ireland. He was able to benefit from the antiquarian and historical societies that were printing large numbers of texts both literary and historical. Thus, his account of Henry and his music is enriched by references from the court accounts of foreign ambassadors and embassies. The Venetian ambassador Piero Pasqualigo's profile of the king is most glowing. Chappell points out that Rawdon Brown, the editor of the *State Papers Venetian*, had remarked that "As Pasqualigo had been ambassador at the courts of Spain, Portugal, Hungary, France, and of the Emperor, he was enabled to form comparisons between the state of the science in those kingdoms and our own."[61] Chappell trumpets not only the skills of the king but of the nation as well. Erasmus is credited with saying that the English are "the most accomplished in the skill of music of any people," a remark that Chappell is keen to corroborate with evidence of "three-man" songs or "Freeman's Songs." *The Life of Peter Carew* is quoted for evidence that the king and Carew would sing "certain songs they call Freeman's Songs, as namely, 'By the banks as I lay' and 'As I walked the wode so wylde.'" Chappell takes literally the subtitle of Ravencroft's book *Dueteromelia*, that it includes "K.[ing] H.[enry's] mirth, or Freemens Songs"[62] and are "compositions of very great antiquity." He prints a number of them as examples of music of the Henrician period, including the two mentioned above that Henry himself reputedly sang with Carew and others around 1515.[63]

Crucially Chappell was not aware of the Henry VIII MS when he published *Popular Music of Olden Times*, but was able to announce it to scholars with an article published in 1865/7.[64] Now instead of a handful of attributions and a reputation built on unsubstantiated historical record there was a group of some thirty-three pieces across a range in various forms, both instrumental and vocal. Among the attributed composers, Henry is the best represented, followed by William Cornish, Master of the King's Chapel. As a record of music-making at the court of Henry and Catherine in the second decade of the sixteenth century it is unsurpassed. It relates to the revels and devising that were such a feature of the court, but also contains "foster" songs (songs in which the singer assumes the role of a rustic forester or hunter or keeper), songs of departure, the earliest collection of part music for instrumental forces alone, and a good number of pieces from continental sources, particularly French and Flemish. Much of the music is for professionals, but much also is short and simple enough for amateurs. Chappell noticed a scribble on the fly-leaves at the end of the book that referred to Benenden in Kent, the home of Sir Henry Guilford, Controller of Henry's Household, and prosaically suggested the book had been created for the king's own use. John Stevens,[65] who transcribed and edited the book for publication in the *Musica Britannica* series, suggested that it was most likely a presentation anthology made up from diverse sources for Guilford. As Master of the Revels, he, like Carew, was a participant in many of the court revels; indeed, in many cases Guilford was the court official ultimately responsible for them, and may have commissioned the book as a record and reminder of those days rather than as a book for everyday use.

The first edition of Grove (1879) has a relatively terse entry on Henry that says only that "being originally designed for the church, [he] was duly instructed in music (then an essential part of the acquirements of an ecclesiastic), and appears to have attained to some skill in composition."[66] The most recent edition, *New Grove* (2001), includes an article by David Greer that gives a mixed account of Henry the composer. On the one hand, the foreign pieces, mostly French, to which Henry may have added an inner part or parts, are shown to demonstrate limited technique. Greer points to the simpler English pieces like "Alac alac what shall I do" and "Grene growith the holy" and says, "Yet the English songs, robust or plaintive as the case may be, have a memorable beauty of their own."[67] "Of the 13 untexted pieces most are short though attractive and suit many instruments, or could even be sung. The long and successful version of 'Tander naken' uses an existing tenor part but is otherwise original and a testing piece suitable for wind or string instruments."[68]

David Fallows, in his essay on Henry VIII as a composer, is perhaps kindest of all to Henry. He makes the point that the five-part Latin masses may have been deliberately lost or suppressed in the very changed political circumstances that followed the Reformation, and that "Quam pulchra es" shows good technique and command of musical proportions. Pieces like "Pastime" and "Tander naken" that were formerly seen as indebted to continental settings are shown in fact to be original and, in the case of "Pastime," to have been the model for the foreign piece.[69] Fallows discusses the weak, added parts to the French songs like "Gentil prince de renom" and "Helas ma dame" and posits that they were early compositional exercises that the boy Henry might have set and that they were kept only because they were the king's work. The best of the English pieces "reflect the genius noticed by all those who encountered him," the more so if the words of the songs are also by him.[70] Quite a different stance on Henry the composer is taken by Peter Holman, who doubts Henry's composition of all of "Pastime" and takes the attributions in the Henry VIII MS less literally.[71] With "Tander naken" he suggests that "perhaps the king's name became attached to it because it was associated with him in some way, rather than because he had a hand in its composition."[72]

In conclusion, many authors, particularly those writing more recently, have found much to praise in Henry's work. Certainly pieces like "Pastime" and "Green growth the Holy" have entered the national psyche, and they have an energy and innocence that is enduring. In recent decades they have been much recorded by both early music artists and also by well-established folk musicians. A whole chain of shops selling derivative items that pastiche or imitate past genres has taken its name, "Pastimes," from Henry's song. Given the popular conception of Henry as a composer, it is understandable that he became associated with "Greensleeves." The words of the 1580 ballad published as "A New Northern Dittye of the lady Greensleeves" would fit the story of Henry's courtship of Anne Boleyn and her refusal to be seduced, casting the king off "discourteously." Yet the association of Henry with the song seems to have occurred during the twentieth century. Certainly it had taken root by the time of Flanders and Swann's 1960 review "At the Drop of a Hat," where the definitive pseudo-history monolog "Greensleeves" was included.

Henry remains England's most musical monarch. His personal interest in the art made a very significant contribution to the musical life of the country, one that lasted for centuries. The popular conception of Henry as a composer and musician may not be right in detail but in essence is correct. His musical reputation as a composer has varied in the five centuries since his reign began, and will continue to be a matter of controversy. Ironically, the man who I believe was responsible for developing Henry's lifelong interest in music was a Frenchman, yet the royal interest that he engendered made a lasting difference to English musical life for centuries afterwards.

NOTES

1. Claude M. Simpson, *The British Broadside Ballad and Its Music* (New Brunswick, NJ: Rutgers University Press, 1966), 269. Simpson gives 1580 as the first dated reference to the ballad in print.
2. For a history of "Greensleeves" as a ballad tune, fiddle tune, morris dance tune, basis for nursery rhymes, and many other forms over four centuries see John M. Ward, "And Who But Ladie Greensleeves," in John Caldwell, *et al.* (eds.), *The Well Enchanting Skill: Music, Poetry, and Drama in the Culture of the Renaissance* (Oxford: Clarendon Press, 1990), 181–212.
3. David Starkey (ed.), *Henry VIII: A European Court in England* (London: Collins & Brown in association with The National Maritime Musuem, Greenwich, 1991), 104.
4. David Fallows, "Henry VIII as a Composer," in C. A. Banks, *et al.* (eds.), *Sundry Sorts of Music Books: Essays on the British Library Collections* (London: The British Library, 1993), 27–39, quoting 35.
5. John Southworth, *The English Medieval Minstrel* (Woodbridge: Boydell Press, 1989), 114–16.
6. John Stevens (ed.), *Music at the Court of Henry VIII*, Musica Britannica, XVIII (London: Stainer and Bell, 1962, and later revised editions), xxi.
7. John Stevens, *Music and Poetry of the Early Tudor Court* (Cambridge: Cambridge University Press, 1961), 272–3.
8. Starkey (ed.), *Henry VIII: A European Court in England*, 11.
9. Andrew Ashbee, "Groomed for Service: Musicians in the Privy Chamber at the English Court, c.1495–1558," *Early Music* (May 1997), 185–97, quoting 186.
10. Peter le Huray, *Music and the Reformation in England, 1549–1660* (Oxford: Oxford University Press, 1967), 18.
11. Ibid., 4.
12. Ibid., 11
13. Southworth, *The English Medieval Minstrel*, 142–55.
14. Mary Remnant, *English Bowed Instruments from Anglo-Saxon to Tudor Times* (Oxford: Clarendon Press, 1986), 73, 94. Quoted from Revel Accounts for January 6 and 7, 1515 for the court at Greenwich.

15. Andrew Ashbee, *Records of English Court Music*, 9 vols. (Snodland, Kent: the author, 1986–96), VII, 69, 72, 73, 74.
16. Ibid., VII, 362.
17. Ibid., VII, 77, 82.
18. David Humphreys, "Philip van Wilder: A Study of His Work and Its Sources," *Soundings* 9 (1979–80), 13–36.
19. BL, MS Harleian 1419, fo. 200r. Printed in Raymond Russell, *The Harpsichord and Clavichord* (London: Faber and Faber, 1959), 155–60; Francis. W. Galpin, *Old English Instruments of Music*, 4th edn. (London: Methuen, 1965), 215–22; and Ashbee, *Records*, VII, 383–98.
20. Richard Tottel (ed.), *Songs and Sonnets* (1557), fos. 70v–71. *RSTC* 13861.
21. Ashbee, "Groomed for Service," 190.
22. Ibid., 193.
23. Ashbee, *Records*, VII, 39, 70.
24. Ashbee, "Groomed for Service," 189.
25. Lyle Nordstrom, "Albert de Rippe, Joueur de luth du Roy," *Early Music* 7 (1979), 378–85.
26. John Ward, "A Dowland Miscellany," *Journal of the Lute Society of America* 10 (1977), 17, 96.
27. Rawdon Brown (ed. and trans.), *Four Years at the Court of Henry VIII: Selection of Despatches written by the Venetian Ambassador, Sebastian Justinian* (London, 1854; reprinted New York: AMS Press, 1970), I, 86.
28. William Chappell, *Popular Music of Olden Times* (London, 1859; revised edition by H. E. Wooldridge, 1893; Dover reprint of the 1859 edition, 1965), 50–1.
29. Ashbee, *Records*, VII, 163, 171, 177. Also see Sydney Anglo, "The Court Festivals of Henry VII: A Study Based upon the Account Books of John Heron, Treasurer of the Chamber," *Bulletin of the John Rylands Library* 43 (1960–1), 33, 36, 40. For a summary of the lute-playing activities of the Tudor royal family see Ward, "A Dowland Miscellany," 112–14.
30. In May 1531, Henry paid 20s to "Arthur [Duwes] the lewter for a lewte for the duke of Richemond." See Ashbee, *Records*, VII, 367.
31. Ashbee, *Records*, VII, 16.
32. Ibid., VII, 178, 185, passim.
33. Ashbee, "Groomed for Service," 189. Richard Rastall, "The Minstrels of the English Royal Households, 25 Edward I–1 Henry VIII: An Inventory," *Royal Musical Association Research Chronicle* 4 (1964), 1–41. Also Ashbee, *Records*, VII, 16, passim, 194, passim.
34. Ashbee, *Records*, VII, 47, 62, 66, 30, 31, 64.
35. Starkey (ed.), *Henry VIII: A European Court in England*, 155.
36. Andrew Ashbee and David Lasocki, assisted by Peter Holman and Fiona Kisby, *A Biographical Dictionary of English Court Musicians 1485–1714*, 2 vols. (Aldershot: Ashgate, 1998), 2, 369.
37. Alison Weir, *Henry VIII: The King and His Court* (London: J. Cape, 2001), 7.
38. BL, Royal MS 2 A XVI, fo. 63v. For an image and commentary see: www.bl.uk/onlinegallery/sacredtexts/henrypsalter.html.

39. Peter Holman, "The English Royal Violin Consort in the Sixteenth Century," *Proceedings of the Royal Musical Association* 119 (1983), 39–59, and Peter Holman, *Four and Twenty Fiddlers: The Violin at the English Court, 1540–1690* (Oxford: Clarendon Press, 1993), 75, 78–100.

40. Roger Prior, "Jewish Musicians at the Tudor Court," *Musical Quarterly* 69 (1983), 253–65, at p. 253.

41. Ibid., 255.

42. Ibid., 264.

43. Ashbee, *Records*, VII, 169 (for April 30, 1500).

44. Ibid., VII, 293–4 (for April 30, 1547).

45. Stanley Sadie (ed.), *The New Grove Dictionary of Music and Musicians*, 2nd edn., 20 vols. (London: Macmillan, 2001), XI, 380; Charles Whibley (ed.), *Henry VIII* (London: T. C. and E. C. Jack, 1904), I, 19, taken from Hall, *Union* (1548).

46. Stevens, *Music and Poetry*, 246–9.

47. Raphael Holinshed, *The Third volume of Chronicles, beginning at duke William the Norman* (London, 1586), 806.

48. Lord Herbert of Cherbury, *The Life and Raigne of Henry VIII* (London, 1649), preface, "An Analytyicall Character or Dissection of Henry the Eighth" (n.p.)

49. Ibid., 2.

50. Ibid., 13.

51. *Opus epistolarum Des. Erasmus Roerdami*, ed. P. S. Allen (Oxford: Clarendon Press, 1906–58), VIII (1934), Ep. 2143; see also P. S. Allen, *Erasmus* (Oxford: Clarendon Press, 1934).

52. Henry Peacham, *The Compleat Gentleman* (London, 1622), 99. RSTC 19502.

53. Sir John Hawkins, *General History of the Science and Practice of Music*, 2 vols. (London, 1776; new edn. 1858), I, 367.

54. *Roger North on Music: Being a Selection of His Essays Written during the Years c. 1695–1728*, ed. John Wilson (London: Novello, 1959), 341.

55. Hawkins, *General History*, I, 384.

56. Ibid., I, 362.

57. Thomas Morley, *A Plaine and Easie Introduction to Practicall Musicke* (London, 1597), modern edn. Thomas Morley, *A Plaine and Easy Introduction to Practical Music*, ed. R. Alec Harman (London: Dent, 1952).

58. Charles Burney, *A General History of Music* (1789; reprinted in 2 vols., ed. Frank Mercer [London: G. T. Foulis, 1935]), I, 785, 794.

59. Ibid., I, 800–1.

60. Ibid., II, 13–15.

61. Chappell, *Popular Music*, 51.

62. Thomas Ravenscroft, *Deuteromelia or The Second part of Musicks melodie* (London, 1609). RSTC 20757. Ravescroft includes seven "Freemens Songs to 3. Voices," and seven "Freemans Songs to 4 Voices," most of which Chappell includes in his section of music from Henry's time.

63. Chappell, *Popular Music*, 52, 66, 92.

64. William Chappell, "Some Account of an Unpublished Collection of Songs and Ballads by Henry VIII and His Contemporaries," *Archaeologia* 41 (1865–7), 371–86.

65. Stevens (ed.), *Music at the Court of Henry VIII*, xxiii.

66. George Grove, *Dictionary of Music and Musicians*, 4 vols. (London, 1879), I, 729.

67. Sadie (ed.), *The New Grove Dictionary*, XI, 380.

68. Ibid. See also Fallows, "Henry VIII as a Composer," 27–39.

69. Fallows, "Henry VIII as a Composer," 28. The piece appears in a contrapuntal version as Richafort's "De mon triste despaisir," first published in 1529.

70. Fallows, "Henry VIII as a Composer," 35.

71. Starkey (ed.), *Henry VIII: A European Court in England*, 104.

72. Holman, *Four and Twenty Fiddlers*, 65.

CHAPTER 10

Henry VIII and popular culture

Tom Betteridge

A Man for All Seasons (1966) opens in a closed room, Cardinal Thomas Wolsey's study at Hampton Court. Wolsey is depicted sealing a letter which he then passes to Thomas Cromwell, who in turn gives it to a messenger. Cromwell takes the letter from Wolsey and leaves the cardinal's study. He passes through a small ante-chamber. For a moment the camera focuses on the heavy wooden door of the room, suggesting for an instant that it is a barrier to the viewer's gaze, before it opens to reveal a well-lit, populated corridor. The opening shots of *A Man for All Seasons* take the viewer on a journey from Wolsey's dark, almost silent, inner sanctum into the noisy public world of the cardinal's court. Having established a number of key tropes that will run throughout the film, in particular an emphasis on voyeuristic moments of visual denial and exposure, the film then depicts Wolsey's messenger running through the gatehouses at Hampton Court and embarking on a rowing boat. At this stage the viewer is unaware of the nature of the letter he is carrying or even its addressee. The film's opening credits roll over the scene of the messenger's boat trip. This again empha-sizes a key feature of the way *A Man for All Seasons* constructs its viewer's consumption of Tudor history. The audience is invited to experience the messenger's boat journey as a participant. The film clearly suggests a collapse between its narrative motivation and the process of the letter's delivery by inviting the viewer into the boat with the messenger. The audience, however, is still in the dark about the letter's content. The opening of *A Man for All Seasons* takes the viewer on a journey from the inner sanctum of Wolsey's power, through the grand public and architectural space of Hampton Court Palace and onto a boat on the Thames. This journey concludes only when the letter reaches its addressee, Thomas More, in his house at Chelsea.

The scene then shifts to an interior shot of the More family engaged in a range of everyday activities including sewing and philosophical debate. It is to this scene of domestic tranquility that the messenger's letter is delivered. The effect is to plunge the More household and the audience into history. When More (Paul Scofield) reads the letter, he tells his family, and the duke of Norfolk, who happens to be there, that it is from Wolsey and is on the king's business. Meg (Susannah York) replies, "The Queen's business," to which Alice More (Wendy Hiller) provides the gloss, "Anne Boleyn." Given that the film depicts Wolsey as still in power, it is of course problematic to have characters referring to Anne Boleyn as queen.[1] More's reading of Wolsey's letter satisfies the audience's desire, which the film has gone out of its way to provoke, to understand what it is watching. At the same time the impact of the letter is not lost on More, who has to leave the happy family home and go to Hampton Court, or on the family, which responds to his departure with considerable disquiet. This response embodies a conservative historiography. More, the focus of the film, the "man for all seasons," is portrayed in these opening scenes and throughout the film as not only a reluctant courtier but also as a reluctant historical figure.[2]

Consistently the film invites the audience to equate the More family as a site of ahistorical normality, despite the period settings and costumes. This aspect of the film's historical thinking is given a particular twist in the casting of Susannah York as More's favorite daughter, Meg, who is depicted as the heroine of the film rather than More's wife. The film's emphasis on Meg's status betrays an anxiety over the place and function of desire in traditional historiography. The problem that *A Man for All Seasons* sets for itself is how to create a serious historical narrative focusing on the effects of Henry VIII's desire for Anne Boleyn when a key indicator of historical seriousness in traditional historiography is chastity and the erasure of the body. Robert Bolt's original play-script for *A Man for All Seasons* includes an "everyman" character that provides a running commentary on the action. This figure reflects the influence of Bertolt Brecht on Bolt's writing and, in particular, his understanding of the shape of serious historical drama. In the film version of *A Man for All Seasons* there is not an explicit everyman figure. However, the film does retain a clear Brechtian tone with its use of individuals to embody larger historical forces. In these terms *A Man for All Seasons* can be seen as an example of Catholic – or Humanist – Realism, in that it erases the body, and in particular the male body, as an object of voyeuristic desire in order to protect and normalize a masculine historical gaze as straight. The anxiety that haunts the film is that of a feminine More or more accurately a More queered by the consuming gaze of the audience. In her seminal article, "Visual Pleasure and Narrative Cinema," Laura Mulvey comments that,

In a world ordered by sexual imbalance, pleasure in looking has been split between active/male and passive/female. The determining male gaze projects its fantasy on to the female figure which is styled accordingly. In their traditional exhibitionist role women are simultaneously looked at and displayed, with their appearance coded for strong visual and erotic impact so that they can be said to connote *to-be-looked-at-ness*.[3]

York's performance as Meg functions in *A Man for All Seasons* to protect Scofield's More twice over from the possibility of being tainted by *to-be-looked-at-ness*. York is presented to the, implicitly male, viewer as a proper object of his desiring gaze and simultaneously functions within representations of the More family as the location of heterosexual desire. *A Man for All Seasons* uses Meg to close down the worrying possibility that the audience's consumption of More might be sexualized and, within the frame of the film, the danger that More's relationship with his wife could be viewed as sexual.[4]

A Man for All Seasons is an exemplary popular telling of the key event of Henry VIII's reign, his divorce of Catherine of Aragon and marriage to Anne Boleyn. In this chapter I am going to focus on three popular narratives and, in particular, on the way they tell the story of the fall of Anne Boleyn: *The Six Wives of VIII* (1970), Philippa Gregory's novel *The Other Boleyn Girl* (2001), and the television series *The Tudors: Series 2* (2008).

Anne Boleyn's fall is a particularly instructive historical event to focus on in relation to popular representations of Henry VIII because academic historiography has struggled to explain it. Reading back over the heated exchanges between historians in the early 1990s, one is struck by the circularity of much of the argument.[5] While E. W. Ives advanced the claims for a factional explanation of Anne Boleyn's fall, George Bernard instead argued for Henry's close personal involvement in the queen's fate. Both historians are quick to pour scorn on Retha Warnicke's suggestion that it was the deformed nature of the miscarried child that Anne Boleyn bore in January 1536 that was the ultimate cause of her fall. Greg Walker has recently proposed a partial compromise between at least the positions adopted by Ives and Bernard, arguing that:

An inquiry, prompted by accusations that could not be safely ignored, unearthed seemingly compelling evidence of guilt on the part of the queen and her intimate circle; that investigation gathered a momentum of its own in an atmosphere of frenzied accusation and interrogation, driven by Henry's furious search for the "truth," to the point at which any suggestion that the queen might be innocent seemed *prima facie* evidence of the speaker's own guilt.[6]

Walker's verdict on the events of April and May 1536 is judicious and persuasive. From one perspective it solves the problem of explaining Anne Boleyn's fall. But at the same time its very even-handedness is problematic. In creating a narrative that is authoritative in terms of academic history Walker inevitably avoids engaging with those aspects of the story that have figured so strongly in popular accounts of Anne Boleyn's fall. Even Walker suggests there was something excessive and frenzied, a sense of a machine running out of control, about the investigation that led to the downfall of Henry's second wife. This is undoubtedly the case. How else does one explain Henry's behavior in the spring of 1536? Anne Boleyn was the woman for whom Henry had risked so much, whom he had waited to marry for so many years. Why on the basis of some fairly unsubstantial gossip was Henry prepared suddenly and violently to destroy her? The charges against Anne Boleyn were preposterous and unnecessarily lurid. It was not necessary to charge her with incest with her brother. Did Henry really believe this allegation? Ives has commented that, "All discussion of the fall of Anne Boleyn ends in the ultimate unresolvable paradox of Tudor history: Henry VIII's psychology."[7]

Popular representations of Henry have consistently returned to this paradox and deployed it in various ways to provide a solution to the historiographic problems caused by Anne Boleyn's fall.

HENRY VIII IN POPULAR HISTORY: MODERN AND POSTMODERN

The Six Wives of Henry VIII (1970) starred Keith Mitchell as Henry and Dorothy Tutin as Anne Boleyn. The first episode in the series, not surprisingly, dealt with Henry's marriage to Catherine of Aragon, played by Annette Crosby, and the divorce. Anne does not appear in this episode and Catherine is absent from episode two. This has the effect of giving the individual episodes a very clear focus and structure. It also, however, creates a number of moments of historical slippage. Mitchell's Henry noticeably ages and puts on weight during the course of the two first episodes of the series. *The Six Wives of Henry VIII* presents a traditional view of Henry as a domineering man. A consistent theme in the series is his inability to cope with female tears. Episode 2 opens with a number of intimate scenes portraying Henry and Anne's happy married state. This focus has the effect of ignoring their long courtship and the attendant issue of the relationship between Henry's desire for Anne and his attack upon the English Church. This is significant and displays the series' commitment to a traditional historiography. *The Six Wives of Henry VIII* responds to the initial successes of second-wave feminism in its emphasis on each of Henry's wives as serious historical characters in their own right. It also, however, shares the failures of Anglo-American political feminism. In particular, while placing Anne at the center of the episode it does so in such a way as to prevent the emergence into the audience's historical gaze of the historical reality of Henry's sexual, corporeal desire for Anne.

There is a persistent sense of shame (or barely suppressed puerile enjoyment) running through modern historical accounts of the Henrician Reformation. How does one address the fact that one of the major events of English history ultimately had its genesis in Henry's loins? G. W. Bernard, for example, in his recent magisterial account of the Henrician Reformation, *The King's Reformation: Henry VIII and the Remaking of the English Church*, opens with the comment,

> How Henry arrived at the momentous conviction that his marriage was against the law of God is the first conundrum that we must resolve. Was the king persuaded by others – by John Longland, bishop of Lincoln and one of his confessors, or by John Stokesley, then a theologian but later to be bishop of London, or by various "well learned" divines?[8]

This is certainly a key question, but it is perhaps important to first ask why, not how. There are a number of answers to this question, including Henry's desire for a male heir and the effect of his and Catherine's tragic series of infant deaths and miscarriages. But at a fundamental level the reason Henry decided his marriage to Catherine was not legitimate was undoubtedly because of his desire to marry Anne Boleyn. A key element of Bernard's account of the Henrician Reformation is the denial that Anne Boleyn, and Henry's desire for her, played a significant part in the Reformation's course or direction. The structure of *The Six Wives of Henry VIII* creates a similar argument, although it is of course advanced with far less historical care than in *The King's Reformation*. By focusing first on Catherine, and then Anne, the series tells the story of the opening stages of the Henrician Reformation as a process of retreat and defeat. The narrative force of the first episode moves away from the court, and indeed away from Henry himself, into non-courtly domestic spaces dominated by Catherine and her female attendants. This encourages the audience to sympathize with Catherine, while at the same time unavoidably creating the sense that real history, symbolized in Henry himself, is taking place elsewhere, off-shot.

Episode 2 of *The Six Wives of Henry VIII* opens with a number of short vignettes aimed at portraying the happiness of Henry's early marriage to Anne Boleyn. The narrative force of the episode is Henry's loss of patience in Anne's behavior, which the programme often depicts as unreasonable. *The Six Wives of Henry VIII* portrays Thomas Cromwell, one of the villains of the series, as a central figure in Anne's fall, while Anne is portrayed as a victim of court plotting, of Henry's growing attraction to Jane Seymour, and her own unreasonable behavior. The series explicitly rejects any possibility that the charges against Anne were anything other than a concoction of lies and slanders designed principally by Cromwell to provide Henry with the justification he needed to leave Anne and marry Jane. From the moment Anne is sent to the Tower the series clearly constructs her in sympathetic terms. In particular, the court scene is deployed to make explicit Cromwell's guilt and Anne's innocence. *The Six Wives of Henry VIII* portrays Henry as a weak but typical man who, when he finds himself unable to cope with female assertiveness, is prepared, and finds it necessary, to deploy violence and lies in order to defeat it.

Anne's fall in *The Six Wives of Henry VIII* takes place within a fully transparent courtly space. Giuliana Bruno has argued that there is a relationship between cinema's creation of space and modernism's spatial logic. Bruno writes:

Film creates space for viewing, perusing, and wandering about. As in all forms of journey, space is physically consumed as a vast commodity. In film, architectural space becomes framed for viewing and offers itself for consumption as travelled space – for further travelling.[9]

The Six Wives of Henry VIII creates a modernist space for the audience. Its Henrician court is remarkably unpopulated. In particular, there the viewer is constantly offered long, straight views of wood-paneled corridors within which the principle characters walk and talk. These corridors are a metaphor for a version of history in which all that is seen, that is offered to the viewer's gaze, makes sense, is meaningful. The corridors that fill the screen of *The Six Wives of Henry VIII* create a clean, open, straight history. Within this space Anne's fall inevitably has to be depicted as, on one side, largely political and, on the other, as a result of Henry's changeability. The focus on Henry provides a space in which the inexplicable, the desire-filled and disturbing aspects of Anne's fall, can be mediated, explained, and brushed away.

The recent television series *The Tudors* (series 2, 2008), on the other hand, articulates a postmodern account of Anne's fall. This is not, however, because it treats history as simply a commodity, although this is clearly the case. Writer Michael Hirst has said that *The Tudors* is 85 percent accurate. Indeed, in relation to Anne's fall, it is noticeable that much of the program's dialogue is taken directly from historical records. In particular, *The Tudors* emphasizes the exchange between Anne and Henry Norris when she is reported to have told him, "You look for dead man's shoes, for if ought came to the king but good, you would look to have me."[10] As Walker suggests, this comment, and the exchange of which it is a part, was at best very unwise and clearly "transgressed the boundaries of courtly etiquette and political safety."[11] *The Tudors* presents Anne as politically sophisticated but prone to taking dangerous risks, particularly when Henry's behavior forces her on the defensive.

Henry VIII is played in *The Tudors* by Jonathan Rhys Meyers. This is a very different Henry from the one traditionally represented in popular culture. While Keith Mitchell's Henry only looks comfortable once he starts to put on weight and resemble the Henry that stares out of Holbein's famous portrait (see frontispiece), Meyers' Henry is an attractive, slim young man. Interestingly the producers and Meyers have made the decision not to portray Henry as overweight. Morgan O'Sullivan, the executive producer, was reported in the *Sunday Times* as commenting that,

We still want him [Meyers] to be appealing ... We don't want to destroy his good looks. An exact portrayal of Henry is not a factor we think is important.[12]

The Tudors may not be seeking exactitude in its portrayal of Henry, but what is interesting is its traditional approach to the events preceding Anne's fall. As in *The Six Wives of Henry VIII*, Anne is portrayed in *The Tudors* as a victim of Henry's burgeoning desire for Jane Seymour, Cromwell's political machinations, and her own high spirits. In the end she falls because she cannot give Meyers' Henry the son he desires. In particular, the central performances by Meyers and Natalie Dormer are impressive in portraying the trauma caused by Anne's miscarriage in January 1536. Henry in *The Tudors* is a strong man, but also one capable of convincing himself of the rightness of his actions. He is depicted as coming to believe some of the most extreme stories about Anne, including that she had slept with more than a hundred men – a charge which, given the nature of the Henrician court, was clearly a fantasy. *The Tudors* depicts Henry as losing himself in a fantasy of female sexual promiscuity, while at the same time presenting the viewer with a traditional image of female decorum in the figure of Jane Seymour.

A crucial moment in the narrative of Anne's fall is provided in *The Tudors* by a court scene set in a great hall. The camera pans around the crowded space, focusing on various different groups of courtiers including Anne entertaining a collection of foreign ambassadors. This panoramic viewpoint is associated with the poet Thomas Wyatt, played by Jamie Thomas King, who looks over the court and worries that while he knows something is going on he cannot say what. The space of the court is portrayed at this moment as lacking a clear or distinct center. There are large red hangings obstructing Wyatt's, and the viewer's, vision, so that he only obtains partial glimpses of what is taking place. The floor space is depicted as a mix of discrete groupings, individuals, servants going about their business, and gaps or paths between these various groups. There is no clear discernable pattern, no central passageway, and no focal point. In this moment *The Tudors* creates for the viewer a conflict between Wyatt's panoramic position looking down on the court and the lack of coherence that he, and the viewer, experience.

Wyatt is portrayed as desiring, but unable, to know what is happening. The viewer, however, is given a privileged glimpse into the heart of the court when Henry's great friend, Charles Brandon, the duke of Suffolk (played by Henry Cavill), informs him of rumors that Anne Boleyn has been "intimate" with other men. *The Tudors* gives the viewer sight of something that is not part of the historical record – the moment when Henry is told about Anne's alleged adultery. This moment of historical revelation, however, takes place within, indeed at the heart of, an image of the Henrician court that is designed to negate just such knowledge. *The Tudors* is an exemplary piece of postmodern history. It desires authenticity, makes it a fetish, while at the same time denying its possibility. *The Tudors* is history as conspiracy. As there can be no over-reaching explanation of the past, Wyatt cannot see what is happening in the court, and he is left frustrated and stalled, desiring knowledge and not being given it.[13]

At its heart *The Tudors* expresses a desire to be the kind of history that *The Six Wives of Henry VIII* is, while, at the same time, announcing that this is no longer possible. It looks back, nostalgically, to a time when the space of history was clear and transparent, like the broad, clutter-free corridors of *The Six Wives of Henry VIII*, which are filled with strong, coherent historical figures, Henry VIII, Catherine of Aragon, Anne Boleyn, and lucid rational dialogue. The historiographic clarity of *The*

Six Wives of Henry VIII is the exact opposite of the opacity of *The Tudors*. In this sense, however, these represent two sides of the same basic flawed approach to history. Slavoj Žižek comments that

external hindrances that thwart our access to the object are there precisely to create the illusion that without them, the object would be directly accessible.[14]

The hangings and crowds, the confusion and noise that fill the screen in *The Tudors* create the illusion that without them it would be possible to approach to the truth of history, that Wyatt and the viewer would be able to see and hear what is going on. But the transparency of *The Six Wives of Henry VIII* is as flawed and partial as the opaqueness of *The Tudors*; neither can deliver the historical accuracy and truth that they both so desperately desire.

The Tudors deploys the voyeuristic logic of the opening of *A Man for All Seasons* but turns it on its head. Instead of the viewer being offered a privileged gaze into the heart of the Tudor polity, that gaze, like Wyatt's, is caught and frustrated – and in these terms *The Tudors* articulates a profoundly conservative model of history. Ultimately it is Henry who is at the center of *The Tudors* as history.[15] With all other possible sources of historical explanation ruled out as flawed and partial, all that is left is to focus on Henry and his desires.

PUTTING THE BODY AT THE CENTER
OF THE HISTORICAL GAZE

Philippa Gregory's *The Other Boleyn Girl* (2001) is a radical work of historical redirection. It is important to note, however, that from a traditional historical perspective *The Other Boleyn Girl* is problematic. In particular, Gregory's basic explanation of Anne's fall draws heavily, in terms of ethos if not detail, on the contentious work of Retha Warnicke. *The Other Boleyn Girl* places the body, male and female, at the center of the historical gaze. In the process, it subverts the modernist fantasy of complete transparency staged in *The Six Wives of Henry VIII*, and its mirror image, as articulated in *The Tudors*. *The Other Boleyn Girl* is told by Mary Boleyn in a first-person narrative. This creates a sense of intimacy but also radically redirects the reader's historical gaze. Seeing Henry, and his court, through the eyes of Mary forces the reader to engage with historical details that rarely appear in more traditional historiography. Mary's view is partial, feminine, and often concentrates on specifically female concerns. Its partiality is, however, a key element of its truthfulness as history. In *The Other Boleyn Girl* Gregory invites the reader to note those things that traditional history ignores. In these terms Gregory's work can be seen as a standard piece of feminist revisionism, albeit a particularly radical one. *The Six Wives of Henry VIII* is also heavily influenced by feminism. Its Anne is a witty, self-possessed woman. But *The Six Wives of Henry VIII* ultimately fails as a feminist work because it does not engage with history at a theoretical level. Its argument is that Anne should be treated like other male characters, while Gregory's, in *The Other Boleyn Girl*, is that what is necessary is the subversion of the historical gaze by bringing new, or rather old, objects into its sight.

The space of history as imagined in *The Other Boleyn Girl* is saturated with moments of voyeurism, but unlike *The Tudors*, or indeed Bolt's *A Man for All Seasons*, Gregory encourages readers to acknowledge the extent to which their desires are implicated in or caught up with the text's history. *The Tudors*, for entirely understandable albeit conservative reasons, cannot but position its viewers as classic voyeurs, inciting them to enjoy the gap between what can be seen and what cannot. For example, Anne and Henry almost have sex in the woods, but the detail, such as Anne's and Henry's sexually aroused bodies, is left for the viewer to imagine and enjoy. It is a mistake to think that voyeurism is based on exposing or showing all. On the contrary, the voyeur desperately does not want to see all. Traditionally a symbolically masculine role, the voyeur in practice desires constantly to re-enact the moment of failed revelation, when almost all is shown, almost all is revealed. For the exposure to be complete would be to endanger the voyeur's position as subject; indeed it would create the possibility of the voyeur becoming the feminine object of another subject's gaze.[16] The combination of cultural restrictions on what can be seen on publicly viewed television and its own commitment to a relatively conservative model of what counts as history means that *The Tudors* is caught within a voyeuristic logic of incitement and denial.

The first part of *The Other Boleyn Girl* is an account of Mary Boleyn's affair with Henry VIII. Gregory stresses the extent to which Henry's seduction of Mary was part of a game of court politics in which the important men in Mary's life, her husband, William Carey, and her brother, father, and uncle, use her as a tool to secure wealth and power. At the same time, *The Other Boleyn Girl* insists that ultimately Henry's desire for Mary was sexual. Significantly, the corporal and intimate aspects of this affair are as important as the affair's effect on the public world of the court. At the key moment, when Mary is about to go to

Henry for the first time, her brother, George, and sister, Anne, prepare her
to meet the king.

> "Go as you are," she [Anne] said. "With your hair down around your
> shoulders. You look like a virgin on your wedding day. I'm right, aren't I,
> George? That's what he wants."
> He nodded. "She's lovely like that. Loosen her bodice a bit."
> "She's supposed to be a lady."
> "Just a bit," he suggested. "A man likes a glimpse of what he's buying."
> …
> She stepped back and looked at me as critically as my father had looked at the
> mare he had sent to the stallion. "Anything else?"
> George shook his head.
> "She'd better wash," Anne suddenly decided. "Under her arms and her cunny
> at least."
> I would have appealed to George. But he was nodding, as intent as a farmer.
> "Yes, you should. He has a horror of anything rank."[17]

This exchange is exemplary of the way in which *The Other Boleyn Girl*
encourages the reader's historical gaze to go beyond the surface of courtly
love and to take notice of the reality of the sexed female body. Mary's need
to wash her vagina in particular is portrayed in this passage as arising
from Henry's masculine fear of the reality of female sexuality. This is also
behind Anne's suggestion that Mary should go to Henry looking like
a virgin, despite being a married woman. Henry, as represented in *The
Other Boleyn Girl*, is torn between his sexual desire for Mary and a horror
of the corporal reality of the human body.

Having recounted the affair between Mary and Henry, *The Other Boleyn
Girl* goes on to describe the king's much more famous relationship with
Mary's sister, Anne. A key issue in traditional historical accounts of this
relationship is the amount of time that elapses between Anne becoming
Henry's mistress and their marriage. There has been a rather unpleasant
wink-wink, nudge-nudge attitude to what Anne "did" to keep Henry
waiting, particularly concerning how she satisfied his sexual desires.
Interestingly this rather puerile approach to Anne and Henry's pre-marriage
sex-life tends not to consider such options as male masturbation. Instead
the focus tends to be on the "French tricks" that Anne allegedly used to
satisfy Henry. *The Other Boleyn Girl* rejects this rather coy and implicitly
misogynistic approach. For example, Gregory portrays Mary as giving
Anne advice on how to please Henry. The conversation opens with Anne
expressing disgust at Henry's insistence that she masturbates him before
Mary goes on to suggest other sexual acts that she could use to keep
Henry happy.

"There are other things you can do," I volunteered.

"Tell me."

"You can let him watch you."

"Let him watch me do what?"

"Let him watch you while you touch yourself. He loves that. It makes him almost weep with lust."

She looked intensely uncomfortable. "For shame."

I laughed shortly. "You let him watch you undress, one thing then another, very slowly. Last of all you lift your shift and put your figures in your cunny and open it up to show him."

She shook her head. "I couldn't do it …"

"And you can take him in your mouth." I hid my amusement at her shrinking.[18]

Traditional history has no place for oral sex. Or rather it places it off-sight, behind the arras, hidden in the euphemism of "French tricks."

The Other Boleyn Girl is a work of fiction. But the way it represents Henry and, in particular, his relationship with Anne is truthful in a very different way than either *The Six Wives of Henry VIII* or *The Tudors*. History is not the past. Roland Barthes comments that:

> In the historical discourse of our civilization, the process of signification is always aimed at "filling out" the meaning of History. The historian is not so much a collector of facts as a collector and relater of signifiers; that is to say, he organizes them with the purpose of establishing positive meaning and filling the vacuum of pure, meaningless series.[19]

Barthes argues that history is a process of creating positive meaning out of the marks, or notes, of the past. "Filling out" the meaning of history, or, more accurately, creating history by adding textual matter to past "facts" – matter that history as a discourse has to deny in order to claim to be authoritative – is, however, neither passive nor politically neutral.[20] This is illustrated with particular clarity in the case of Henry VIII and his relationship with Anne. We cannot know what happened in their bedroom, or rather our knowledge can only be intuitive or based on contemporary human behavior – as it is in *The Other Boleyn Girl*. This does not mean, however, that it is inherently less authoritative or truthful than other accounts of Henry and Anne's relationship.

Anne's fall is movingly told in *The Other Boleyn Girl*. Gregory depicts Anne as desperately trying to hang on to Henry. In *The Tudors* there is a sense that Henry is almost passive in the events that surrounded Anne's fall. Certainly by staging the moment when Suffolk tells Henry about the rumors of Anne's infidelities, that television series effectively creates a narrative in which it is Anne who is at least partly to blame for her own downfall. *The Tudors* is, however, like much traditional historiography, rather incoherent at this point since it acknowledges that Henry was also at this time becoming increasingly enamored of Jane Seymour. The causal link between Henry's new amorous relationship and the downfall of Anne appears as problematic for traditional history as the identical problem of the connection between Henry's desire for Anne and his rejection of Catherine. In both cases what has to be denied, or cannot be squarely faced, is the extent to which Henry's sexual desire caused – or rather *is* – history.

The Other Boleyn Girl's narrative strategy means that the reader is left on the outside, with Mary, not knowing the details of Anne's arrest or trial. This positioning creates a space between the reader's assumptions about the events of the spring of 1536 and what the text actually contains. Mary's summing up of the evidence against her sister is strangely moving. She tells the reader that the evidence against Anne, the story told about her,

> sometimes touched the truth and sometimes veered off into the wildest of fantasies which anyone who knew the court would have realised could not be true. But it always had that fascination of scandal, it was always erotic, filthy, dark. It was the stuff that people wished that queens might do, that a whore married to a king would be sure to do. It told us much, much more about the dreams of secretary Cromwell, a low man, than it did about Anne, George, or me.[21]

It is this combination of truth and fantasy that is history. But the fantasy has to remain hidden. *The Other Boleyn Girl* presents the reader with an image of Henry that is unique and disturbing. Gregory's Henry is a bully and a misogynist. He is a man prepared to sanction the judicial murder of a woman he claimed to love on the basis of rumor, fantasy, and lies.

CONCLUSION

There have been numerous popular representations of Henry VIII in the last twenty years that this chapter has not addressed, from Sid James' Henry as letch to Ray Winstone's Henry as gangster. But none have been as radical as Gregory's in *The Other Boleyn Girl* and her later work, *The Boleyn Inheritance*. It is in the latter that Gregory paints her most devastating portrait of Henry, when the reader is invited to view him through the eyes of Anne of Cleves:

> he has small, piggy eyes and a small spoiled mouth, in a great ball of a moon face swelling with fat. His teeth must be very bad, for his breath is very foul.[22]

Henry as a disgusting, smelly old man is no more truthful then Henry as a dashing, chivalrous prince, but at least it is not how Henry himself would have wanted to be remembered, and that, in itself, makes Gregory's Henry one to cherish and enjoy.

NOTES

1. It is always possible when discussing popular versions of history to play "spot the mistake or inaccuracy." This is, however, largely a pointless and often a rather self-regarding exercise. Eric Josef Carlson, in a judicious article, has recently persuasively argued that popular versions of historical events, and in particular films, can be extremely useful in the teaching of Tudor history, if one focuses on films as embodying different ways of thinking historically. See Eric Josef Carlson, "Teaching Elizabeth Tudor with Movies: Film, Historical Thinking and the Classroom," *Sixteenth Century Journal* 38 (2007), 419–28.
2. For a sophisticated reading of the historiographic issues raised by *A Man for All Seasons*, see Peter Marshall, "Saints and Cinemas: *A Man for All Seasons*," in Susan Doran and Thomas S. Freeman (eds.), *Tudors and Stuarts on Film: Historical Perspectives* (London: Palgrave, 2008), 46–59.
3. Laura Mulvey, "Visual Pleasure and Narrative Cinema," in *The Sexual Subject: A Screen Reader in Sexuality* (London: Routledge, 1992), 22–34, quoting 27.
4. It is important to note that, despite some of the hagiography, there is no real historical evidence that More and his second wife, Alice, did not lead a normal married live. The fact that they did not have children does not prove that they did not express their love for each other physically.
5. See Retha Warnicke, "Anne Boleyn Revisited," *Historical Journal* 34 (1991), 953–4; E. W. Ives, "The Fall of Anne Boleyn Reconsidered," *English Historical Review* 107 (1992), 651–64; G. W. Bernard, "The Fall of Anne Boleyn: A Rejoinder," *English Historical Review* 107 (1992), 665–74; and Retha Warnicke, "The Fall of Anne Boleyn Revisited," *English Historical Review* 108 (1993), 653–65.
6. Greg Walker, "Rethinking the Fall of Anne Boleyn," *Historical Journal* 45 (2002), 1–29.
7. Ives, "The Fall of Anne Boleyn Reconsidered," 664.
8. G. W. Bernard, *The King's Reformation: Henry VIII and the Remaking of the English Church* (New Haven: Yale University Press, 2005), 1.
9. Giuliana Bruno, "Site-seeing: Architecture and Moving Image," *Wide Angle* 19 (1997), 9–24, quoting 17.
10. Quoted in Walker, "Rethinking the Fall of Anne Boleyn," 21.
11. Ibid., 22.
12. *Sunday Times*, August 31, 2008.
13. On postmodernism and authenticity, see Timothy Bewes, *Cynicism and Postmodernity* (London: Verso, 1997).

14. Slavoj Žižek, *The Metastases of Enjoyment: Six Essays on Women and Causality* (London: Verso, 1994), 94.

15. Thomas S. Freeman comments that the more *The Tudors* "subverts the traditional Henry, the more strongly it re-establishes it." Thomas S. Freeman, "A Tyrant for All Seasons," in Doran and Freeman (eds.), *Tudors and Stuarts on Film*, 30–45, quoting 45.

16. For the sexualized nature of curiosity within Western cinema, see Laura Mulvey, "Pandora: Topographies of the Mask and Curiosity," in Beatriz Colomina and Jennifer Bloomer (eds.), *Sexuality and Space* (Princeton: Princeton Architectural Press, 1996), 52–71.

17. Philippa Gregory, *The Other Boleyn Girl* (London: HarperCollins, 2008), 56.

18. Ibid., 255.

19. Roland Barthes, "The Discourse of History," trans. Stephen Bann, *Comparative Criticism* 3 (1981), 3–20, quoting 16.

20. Michel de Certeau argues that: Historiography (that is, "history" and "writing") bears within its own name the paradox – almost an oxymoron – of a relation established between two antinomic terms, between the real and discourse. Its task is one of connecting them and, at the point where this link cannot be imagined, of working *as if* the two were being joined. Michel de Certeau, *The Writing of History*, trans. Tom Conley (New York: Columbia University Press, 1988), xxvii.

21. Gregory, *The Other Boleyn Girl*, 522–3.

22. Philippa Gregory, *The Boleyn Inheritance* (London: HarperCollins, 2007), 87–8.

PART IV

Henry VIII through history

"Conveyance of history": narrative, chronicle, history, and the Elizabethan memory of the Henrician golden age

Andrew Fleck

> He gave you all the duties of a man,
> Trimmed up your praises with a princely tongue,
> Spoke your deservings like a chronicle
>
> *1 Henry IV*[1]

All Is True, Shakespeare's dramatic treatment of Henry VIII's break from the church that had once named him "Defender of the Faith," opens with Buckingham encountering Thomas Howard, the duke of Norfolk. Buckingham asks him to describe the opulent displays he witnessed at the Field of Cloth of Gold, when Henry and Francis I solemnized the Treaty of London (1518), and Norfolk – protesting his ability to capture the spectacle, "the view of earthly glory" – reluctantly agrees.[2] Unable to encompass fully the convergence of these two brilliant suns, Howard concedes that he must describe each indirectly, "As presence did present them: him in eye, / Still him in praise" (1.1.30–1). Norfolk confronts the historian's difficulty of comprehensively narrating two compelling, competing centers of attention with a single voice: diffuse simultaneity ultimately gives way to selective sequentiality. He concludes that describing "the tract of everything / Would by a good discourser lose some life / Which action's self was tongue to" (1.1.40–2). Having failed adequately to "translate" the experiential field of the Field of Cloth of Gold historiographically, Norfolk resorts to a shift of genre: Henry's and Francis's actions before Guines and Ardres were such that the "former fabulous story / Being now seen possible enough, got credit / That Bevis was believed" (1.1.36–8).[3] Evoking medieval romance to anchor his rhapsody about the ineffable wonders of this meeting, Norfolk ceases. For the audience at the Globe, the duke's *tour de force* initiates a dizzying and disorienting gambit in a play concerned with sifting the veracity of competing representations. Norfolk, in a theatrical gesture, parrots phrases from Holinshed's *Chronicles* as he struggles to find words to give shape to events. He traverses from theater, to historiography, to romance, all the while blurring the boundaries of genre in a futile attempt to describe a spectacle that – from his perspective – was a nearly unnarrateable current event that had happened all around him, but which would otherwise be accessible to the Jacobean audience only through the mediation of the narrative operations of history.

The duke of Norfolk, and behind him Shakespeare and his collaborator Fletcher, did not confront the challenge of representing Henry VIII alone. The Tudor fruit of the Lancastrian and Yorkist union, the frivolous and serious humanist King of England, the Defender of the Faith and the impetus for England's break with Rome, the jaunty cavalier and rotund king overwhelmed subsequent generations of Englishmen who sought discursively to contain him. Celebrated or reviled by those he left in his wake, King Henry came to stand for many things in the reigns of his children. The successes of his first decade or so – his capture of Tournai and Thérouanne, his throwing his weight behind alliances that changed the balance of power in Europe, his public exchange with Luther, his triumph at the Field of Cloth of Gold – entered into legend, in part through the agency of historians like Edward Hall, Richard Grafton, and John Stow, whose chronicles transformed them into discrete narrative events. Some, like Hall, celebrated the "triumphant reigne of Kyng Henry the VIII," while others simply recorded events without praise.[4] Recalled years later, such moments carried the glorious veneer of English national history. But as Henry VIII's royal bloodline reached its barren conclusion, as his ageing and childless daughter tried to preserve her father's legacy, England stood at a kind of crossroads.[5] The course of the dramatic changes initiated under Henry VIII could be reversed again, as had happened when his elder daughter took the throne, or that course could be confirmed with another generation of reformed princes at England's helm.

In that uncertain decade, Thomas Nashe and Thomas Deloney appropriated the history of Henry's early reign, chronicled in Holinshed and others, to dress their nostalgic fictions in the guise of a glorious national past. Holinshed, to be sure, as well as Stow, Grafton, Cooper, and the chronicles they had themselves ransacked, provided Nashe and Deloney with the material for the nostalgic vision of Henry VIII that frames *The Unfortunate Traveller* and *Jack of Newbury* (alias the *Pleasant History of John Winchcomb*).[6] Written during the 1590s, these two early experiments in prose fiction playfully appropriate the markers and tropes of the period's increasingly sophisticated and occasionally partisan historiography.[7] Their nostalgic gestures to people and events of the recent past take on valences as significant as those in the contested mid-Tudor historiographical texts they imitate. Written as English subjects contemplated the uncertain future to come after the death of Henry's last descendent, these texts look longingly backward to the time before Henry's decision to break with Rome, erasing half a century of persecution and death. Nashe and Deloney imagine Jack Wilton and Jack of Newbury, their everyman heroes, rubbing shoulders with famous historical figures, from Cardinal Wolsey and Queen Catherine to Thomas More and Henry Howard, the poet earl of Surrey.[8] Standing at the heart of each tale, the avuncular figure of the gallant young Henry VIII laughs and jokes with these lowborn heroes. Their protagonists enjoy fabulous adventures, framed by historically significant events celebrated in the chronicles of the young king's reign. These proto-novels romanticize the first decade of the reign as a Henrician golden age, a nationalist fantasy of a socially cohesive England led by a man with the common touch.

Despite these authors' framing of their tales with historical events and the colossal monarch who fought the Reformation before he advanced it, the lively fictions they construct trouble the limits of truth and fact. Deloney purports to offer a "pleasant history," both a fictional story and a factual history.[9] Nashe, who explicitly evokes the tomes he mines for the material he transforms into his "conueyance of historie," approaches his material with less reverence.[10] In offering this "conveyance" – both the delivery and the underhanded evacuation – of history, Nashe explodes the authority of the texts he uses.

These tales' nostalgic representations of Henry VIII limn story and history in complex ways. They present a yearning for an England not yet marred by the violent upheaval occurring beyond the nation's shores, creating a nostalgic but ambivalent fantasy of Henry's reign at the anxious transitional moment of the Tudor line's extinction. And yet – despite tepid criticism of the old church's corruption – neither *The Unfortunate Traveller* nor *Jack of Newbury* celebrates the early years of the king's reign for polemical purposes. A Tudor chronicler like Thomas Cooper must carefully address the seismic historical disruption through which he lived; written at the outset of Elizabeth's reign, the dedication of his continuation of Lanquet's chronicle carefully hedges recent history. Since he "must of necessitee speake of alteracion in religion, and mencion those that haue bene mainteyners of contrarie doctrines," he will do so "without reprochefull woordes" and leave "indifferent to the reader to iudge of things as he shall thynke good."[11] But Nashe and Deloney – who locate their narratives in the celebrated moments of Henry VIII's reign – can gesture to the authorizing modes of historiography without fretting that such gestures might endanger them, in part because they create an alternative space of authority within their texts that ultimately displaces that outsized monarch who anchors their tales.

THOMAS DELONEY AND THE USES OF HISTORY

The first sentence of Deloney's *Jack of Newbury* announces its setting in the intermediate past. This "pleasant history" will recount a kind of biography or *Bildungsroman* of an English patriot, born only a few decades before Deloney's readers. The first, long sentence of Deloney's story quickly establishes a date – "In the daies of King Henery the eight … in the beginning of his reigne" – and a locale – "in Newberie, a towne in Barkshire." These details create an atmosphere of harmony, optimism, and community – one characterized by "that most noble and victorious Prince" – and delineate the type of man who will be the subject of the narrative – a "wel-beloved," substantial "Weauer," known for his "merry disposition," "honest conuersation," and generosity.[12] Although the narrative immediately takes on some elements of its predecessors in jestbooks, Deloney frequently returns to historical events to frame his narrative.[13] His story's comic arc fuses generic folk tales to historical figures, to produce a new hybrid of fact and fiction. In essence a popular tale of an apprentice's meteoric rise to wealth – a forerunner of Horatio Alger, Jack marries his prosperous master's widow, inherits manufacturing capital when she dies unexpectedly, and then marries a docile beauty from the shop – the fantastic story narrates Jack's patriotic adventures in the service of Henry VIII.[14]

Genuine history intrudes into Deloney's legendary story at several key junctures early in the tale. The characteristic circumlocutions of Tudor chronicles intervene into the early scene of domestic bliss and private industry. Winchcomb's in-laws depart, and "[n]ot long after this, it chaunced while our Noble King was making warre in France" that Scotland invaded (30).[15] Required to furnish armed men, Jack outfits twenty-five times his quota. He arrives at the head of a company, to the amazement of his social betters as well as with some sparks of jealousy from others who consider him "more prodigall then prudent" (30). However, his display impresses Henry's first queen. Jack humbly addresses her, offering to "spend our blouds, but also to lose our liues in defence of our King and Countrey" (31). News then arrives from "the valianet Earle of Surrey, with tydings to her Grace, that now shee might dismisse her

Army, for that it had pleased God to grant the noble Earle victorie ouer the Scots: whome hee had by his wisedome and valiancie vanquist in fight, and slayne their King in battel" (32). The narrative goes on to describe the queen's joyful return to London and the rewards she grants to the noblemen who came to her aid, as well as her gratitude to low-born Winchcomb, "about whose necke she put a rich chaine of gold" (33). For several paragraphs, Deloney's hero disappears from the tale and these historical events come to the fore.

In fact, Deloney probably had chronicle materials in front of him as he created this legendary episode. He brackets the scene with material that closely echoes the mid-century Tudor histories. Events from outside the humble weaver's experience thrust themselves into Deloney's narrative and carry with them the judgment of the chroniclers. In "falsly breaking his oath," James IV sets in motion events that eventually touch the life of Deloney's hero, who must outfit soldiers to join the "great power to goe against the faithlesse king of Scots" (30). This vilification of Henry VIII's sister's husband echoes every mid-century chronicle's evaluation. In his necessarily terse judgment in his *Summary of English Chronicles*, for instance, Stow would lament that "the king of Scots, notwithstandinge that he was sworne on the Sacramente to kepe peace, inuaded this lande with the mighty army, but by the good dilige[n]ce of the Quene, and the policie and manhode of the Erle of Surrey the kinges lieuetenaunt, he was him selfe slayne."[16] In the space between James IV's "mighty army" and the "but" that introduces Queen Catherine and Thomas Howard's management of the crisis, Deloney invents the sentimental episode of his hero's selfless contribution to the national cause. Once the danger passes, Deloney again returns to the material typical of chronicle treatments of Henry VIII at this early moment in his reign. This invasion close to home, "when our King was in France," had occurred as England's absent king led an army abroad. The victory prompts Deloney to indulge in a bit of historical archaeology, as he links the humbling of James IV's boasts to the origin of a popular ballad, "which to this day is not forgotten of many," called "King Jamie had made a vowe" (33).[17] This modulation from the national cause to the individual cause and back creates the canvas for Deloney's fiction. Will Kemp may have scoffed at Deloney's celebration of Winchcomb and other lowborn heroes "omitted by Stow, Hollinshead, Grafto[n], Hal, froysart & the rest of those wel deseruing writers," but the attempt to imagine the men absent from those chronicles energizes Deloney, in whose history high and low meet on equal footing.[18]

When Jack finally does meet Henry VIII, Deloney introduces the monarch as a man of the people with the common touch, receptive to the concerns of his subjects. Again mixing an ambiguous folkloric setting, verifiable details, and legendary events, Deloney imagines one of Henry's progresses through Berkshire stumbling into the simple life of the thriving weaver. "About the tenth year of the kings reigne," the episode begins, "his Grace made his progresse into Barkshire, against which time Iacke of Newberie cloathed 30. tall fellowes" and headed out to a meadow along the king's path (32). Regal history-maker and quondam apprentice meet at the crossroads of a comma. The allegorical show that follows, in which Winchcomb as "Prince of Ants" professes to evade the social barriers between king and subject to warn him directly of the dangerous "idle Butterflyes" that surround him, could come straight out of Hall's or Holinshed's *Chronicle*, those compendia of Henry VIII's taste for entertainments and progresses.[19]

This sort of incident peppers the great Tudor chronicles. A disoriented Henry, in the midst of hostile French territory without a guide, for instance, chances to meet "with a vitayler commyng from the campe which was theyr guyde and brought them thither" in Hall.[20] Such anecdotes in the chronicles carry a structural analogy to the incidents that propel Deloney's narrative. For instance, Hall includes the story of the "Cooper of Calais," a miniature narrative of only about a hundred words, in the midst of his account of the French adventure that took Henry out of England at the time of Flodden. Hall offers a sensible evaluation of this humorous, folkloric anecdote, about a foolish English subject duped by a French soldier: "Thus thorowe foly was the poore Cowper deceaued" (544). As is typical in Holinshed, a brief anecdote becomes an occasion for elaborate commentary that dwarfs the episode itself: "Where of it is wisedome for a man to hold fast in his possession and to supply his want of strength by subtiltie," it begins, and adds proverbial folk wisdom over several additional lines.[21] It is the sort of anecdote that Annabel Patterson identifies as a hallmark of Holinshed's *Chronicles*, the sort of story that points to a "'system' under stress, [when] something in the 'official' account is up for grabs."[22] Such anecdotes, closely aligned with comic folk tales, are precisely the kind of material that Deloney and Nashe exploit for their popular chronicles. In shuttling between his humble protagonist's story and the larger events beyond Jack's ken, Deloney mirrors the heteroglossia of a text like Holinshed's with its primary historiographical narrative punctuated with intrusive anecdotes, though Deloney inverts the emphasis to tell the story of the lowborn and relegates historical intrusions to the place of anecdotes.

Jack's satiric skit earns his monarch's applause and initiates a convivial meeting of public and private authority. The jovial monarch claps the budding industrialist on the back and heartily declares, "I haue often heard of thee, and this morning I mean to visite thy house" (37).[23] The famous, fictional deeds of Deloney's hero have come to the ears of England's ebullient monarch, the more typical subject of histories.[24] Henry and his train pause in their progress to feast and be entertained in the private, domestic kingdom of Henry's prosperous cloth merchant. Only the offended Wolsey complains of Deloney's unpretentious hero, sneering that the weaver will "vndoo himselfe onely to become famous by receiuing of your Maiestie: like Herostratus the Shoomaker that burned the Temple of Diana, onely to get himself a name" (39). Navigating the boundaries of history and legend on the ship of fame, the text self-reflexively points to the ambiguous place of its own textual space. Indeed, this weaver does become famous for hosting Henry VIII, in part because Deloney records it in this particular scene. Nevertheless, Winchcomb's prosperous workshop impresses Henry VIII as an efficient microcosm of the national macrocosm, attesting to his own competing authority (58).

In negotiating chronicle history Deloney confronts the fact that the course of true history never did run smooth. As a result of the confessional gyrations that Henry set in motion, the possibility of being on the wrong side of history increased for everyone. The person who writes the story – whether recording the great deeds of kings and nations or the fictive deeds of patriotic weavers – has the benefit of hindsight and may attempt to give coherence to disparate events retroactively. The Tudor chronicles, unlike the writers of annals who recorded happenings successively, tried to give shape to the history that brought about their present situation.[25] Thus Hall, writing decades after the event, can anticipate that Henry VIII's marriage to his brother's widow was "doubtefull at the beginnyng"; he can even encode part of the retrospective justification for its subsequent dissolution, that Henry VIII was "young, and not vnderstandyng the lawe of God," and warn the reader that this "detestable" decision was "plain contrary to Goddes lawe, as you shall here, after. xx. yeres" (507). Hall and other chroniclers import the awareness of subsequent history into the opening pages of Henry's history. It becomes "plain" that the marriage was flawed only in hindsight.

Deloney, however, grounds his own narrative firmly in the past, with only passing acknowledgement of the intervening decades' shifts. Catherine, for instance, appears in the tale without reference to the fate awaiting her. Jack's adversary conveniently remains the detested Wolsey, bent on punishing Winchcomb for his earlier impertinence. When Winchcomb petitions Henry VIII to remove restrictions on trade, the king agrees and expects his cardinal to act.[26] Wolsey spitefully takes no action, frustrating Jack, who makes a comment that recalls Wolsey's own humble origins. The remark infuriates the cardinal, who imprisons Winchcomb until Somerset persuades him to complete the king's orders. Reluctantly, Wolsey sends "for the Clothiers before him to White-hall, his new built house by Westminster," releases them, and grants their suit (60). The incident creates a number of anachronisms and ironic moments that look proleptically ahead in the chronicles to Deloney's present. Referring to Wolsey's palace by the name it would take on after his disgrace only initiates the complexities of this episode. Most significantly, the irate cardinal tars the weaver with the brush of religious heterodoxy. To get the better of the weaver he perceives as an upstart, Wolsey draws on the domain of his own special authority to slander him. He asserts that the reminder of his low birth could only come from "an heretique: and I dare warrant you, were this Iack of Newbery well examined, hee would be found to bee infected with Luthers spirit" (59). Such a charge might have intimidated a lowly weaver in the decade of Wolsey's greatest authority. Moreover, given that Henry VIII had "late written a most learned booke" contesting Luther's claims, "in respect whereof the Popes holinesse hath entituled his Maiesty, Defender of the Faith," the cardinal intends his claim that Winchcomb carried Lutheran sympathies to be a damning one.

But history has a habit of making irony. Deloney's readers knew that Henry's domestic bliss with Catherine and his place as one of Rome's faithful sons in the contest against heresy and Reformation did not last. Deloney himself acknowledges that a time has passed and become the present, when Jack's philanthropy inspires Henry's entourage to employ as pages some of the orphans working in Winchcomb's factory. These boys, the narrator proleptically announces, "came to be men of great account and authority in the land, whose posterities remain to this day worshipfull and famous" (49).[27] The tale's anachronisms and inconsistencies destabilize the nostalgia for a more harmonious, golden age by recalling that that time has passed and is in the past. In other words, as much as this narrative effaces the corrosive effects of Henry's most famous action – his marriage to Elizabeth's mother and the break with Rome – by allowing its protagonist to return again and again to a timeless vision of a convivial and happily married young King Henry, the effects of the intervening decades (including the Reformation legacy) reassert themselves subtly from the margins and recall the uncertainty of the readers' present. The genuine experience of the past cannot be recovered; nostalgia compensates for that loss by appealing to narrative.[28] For Deloney's novel, then, history and historiography operate on different levels, both propelling the narrative and working against it. Although Deloney does not attempt the disorienting narrative gymnastics Nashe undertakes, his narrative does play on this awareness that a setting in the uncontested past conveniently avoids a contentious present.

THOMAS NASHE AND UNSTABLE HISTORY

Following Wolsey's death, as *All Is True* draws to a close, the disgraced Catherine and her usher trade conflicting evaluations of the disgraced cardinal. Griffith mitigates the harsh verdict of Henry's former queen, prompting Catherine to hope that "such an honest chronicler as Griffith" may recall her virtues to posterity (4.2.72).[29] The difficulty of finding an honest chronicler provides the occasion for mirth in Thomas Nashe's *The Unfortunate Traveller.* Nashe knew Deloney as "the Balletting Silke-weauer."[30] If Nashe had known Deloney's recourse to chronicles for his prose fiction, he might have mocked him in that mode as well.

Deloney's conservative gestures to the chronicles' techniques for encompassing England's irrepressible king within the "pleasant history" pale next to Nashe's exuberant appropriation of chronicle material for *The Unfortunate Traveller.* Nashe's prefaces alert readers to his mercurial approach to the polysemy of language.[31] They also foreground his playful approach to his novel's shadow genre, the chronicle, and the recurrent interest in staging and destabilizing history in the tale. The second edition's "Induction to the Dapper Monsieur Pages of the Court" in particular brings this unstable language and a destabilized history together. As Jonathan Crewe recalls, the *OED* credits Nashe with coining the use of the word "page" to mean a sheet of paper.[32] The praise of the collection of pages in the printer's bookstall or the reader's hands is one of Nashe's favorite jokes in the text, one that he pushes to extremes, piling on instances in antanaclasis that ultimately leaves meaning impossible to determine. In the Induction, where the page Jack Wilton, who only exists on the book's page, addresses the other imagined pages through the page in the reader's hand, the novel's hero demands fealty. The "pages of the court" must now take their oath on the pages of *The Unfortunate Traveller,* "this chronicle of the King of pages" (209). In a similarly disorienting maneuver, the dedication of the first edition

of the "phantasticall Treatise" to Southampton, in which Nashe playfully
mocks his "conueyance of historie" – both the presentation of history
and its misappropriation – further destabilizes its relationship to the
historical canvas on which he depicts his fictional pseudo-monarch
(201). From the outset, Nashe launches his narrative as an alternative
history of the early part of the century, with a different king at its center.

As with Deloney's *Jack of Newbury*, Nashe's *Unfortunate Traveller* also
begins with specificity that imparts the veneer of history to his tale.[33]
Nashe sets his novel early in the reign of Elizabeth's father, "About
that time that the terror of the world and feauer quartane of the French,
Henrie the eight (the onely true subiect of Chronicles) aduanced his
standard against the two hundred and fifty towers of Turney and
Turwin" (209). Henry's invasion of France in 1513 had drawn him out of
England and left the nation vulnerable to James IV's advances at Flodden,
the anchor of Deloney's fiction. These two incidents, the sort of material
out of which historiographers traditionally create chronicle histories,
posed a narrative challenge to sequence and simultaneity. Within days
of each other, Henry VIII had his first military victory – the capitulation of
Thérouanne – and his second, when 500 miles away he triumphed at
Flodden Field. Of course he could not command that victory in person.
Instead his deputy, Thomas Howard, the earl of Surrey who would
become duke of Norfolk, defeated the Scots king. News of that victory
reached Henry in France, just before his victory over the French forces in
Tournai. With Henry's triumphs, Tudor chroniclers butted against the
challenge of celebrating simultaneous victories of the king's authority in
geographically distant arenas. Edward Hall overcame the difficulty of
representing simultaneity by reverting to the conventions of epic and its
many "meanwhiles."[34] Focusing on Henry's person in France, Hall inter-
rupts his narration to backtrack and describe the treachery of James IV.
Leaving the first narrative at a kind of cliffhanger – "Thus was the citee of
Tornay beseged on all partes, & euer in hope of reskue valiantly defended
her selfe" – Hall shifts his focus to events near the Tweed: "Nowe must I
leue the kynge at the siege of Turnay, and diuerte to thinges done in
England in his absence, and declare how the kynge of Scottes inuaded the
realme of Englande, and how he was defended and fought with al, and in
conclusion slayn the .vii. daye of this moneth of September" (555). Following
this long digression, Hall returns again to his main narrative: "Nowe lett vs
returne too the kynge of Englande lyenge before Tournaye" (564).

In Holinshed's *Chronicles*, the narrative structure of history takes on a
different principle of coherence. For Hall, events are much more strictly tied

to the calendar and its relentless forward movement, a remnant of the older historiographical tradition of the annals. As a result, that shifting perspective that bears an analogy to the epic "meanwhile" becomes more frenetic in the simultaneous narration of the retribution wreaked on James IV and Henry's business in France. Holinshed, however, approaches his history as discrete episodes, narrating them to their conclusion. His *Chronicles* narrates all of Henry's campaign in France and then treats the nefarious Scots' invasion. This produces anticipations in which the historian plucks his reader by the elbow and tells him what will come to pass in a few pages. Thus, on the eve of Thérouanne's capitulation, Holinshed rearranges separate moments of Hall's narration and asks the reader to defer his questions and expectations. From "thus was the citie of Tornaie besieged on all parts," Holinshed's *Chronicles* proceeds immediately to the handling of the siege, where Henry "received letters from the earle of Surrie with the Scotch kings gantlet, whereby he was certified of the slaughter of the said king, and how all things had beene handled after the battell of Flodden, *whereof heereafter yee shall find further mention*" (588, my emphasis). The description of that battle must wait, however, because Holinshed remains focused on this narrative arc. "But now to our purpose of the siege of Tournai," he continues (588). To be sure, the battle fought at Flodden will be described, but the readers' expectations must await fulfillment. Only after the triumph following Tournai's capitulation does Holinshed's *Chronicles* return to that suspended story line: "But now I must returne to speake of the dooings in the North parts, betweene the Englishmen and Scots. Whilest the king was occupied in his warres against France in the summer (as before is mentioned) yee have heard how the king of Scots sent his letter unto the king, as then lieing at the siege before Terwine," the chronicler goes on, recapitulating the narrative thread that had been in abeyance while Henry pursued his dual victories in France (591). These narrative techniques, which Hayden White identifies more generally as sharing an underlying resemblance to literary plot in the urge to connect and shape the relationship between events, travel a parallel trajectory to the narratives of authors like Deloney and Nashe.[35]

As with Deloney, when Nashe locates his fictional plot within the frame of real events, he selects some of the same historiographical elements as the chronicles that he pillages and pillories. As Nashe's long opening sentence celebrates Henry VIII, it adds a self-congratulatory comment found in most sixteenth-century chronicles, that as the king "aduanced his standard," he "had the Emperour and all the nobilitie of Flanders,

Holand, & Brabant as mercenarie attendants on his ful-sayld fortune" (209). The Holy Roman Emperor's service in Henry VIII's army is a hallmark of the period's chronicles of this event; in enumerating the forces under Henry's command at the outset of the siege, for instance, Richard Grafton remarks that Maximilian served for wages in King Henry's army and that, "the Emperour as the kinges Souldiour ware a Crosse of saint George with a Rose," the symbol of Henry's national and imperial ambitions.[36] Similar remarks are to be found in the other Tudor chroniclers, across the range of religious loyalties. Wolsey's apologist George Cavendish, for instance, proudly includes this moment in English history when the Holy Roman Emperor took "of the kyng his graces wages … The wche ys a rare thyng seldome seen, hard, or red that an Emprour to take wages and to fight vnder a kynges banner."[37] On the more staunchly Protestant side, *An Epitome of Cronicles* (sometimes called *Cooper's Chronicle*, and referred to in *The Unfortunate Traveller* by the name of its originator, Lanquet) succinctly includes the same incident of Henry VIII, who, "hauing in wages under his banner the emperour Maximilian … conquered Terwine."[38] Nashe's choice of this event as the initial setting for Jack Wilton's adventures thus carries with it not simply the facts of history but also the indisputably patriotic stirrings associated with Henry VIII's first foreign campaign.

As Nashe's long first sentence continues, his narrative dynamism recreates in miniature the destabilizing movements of the historiography that Annabel Patterson elsewhere identifies with a more provisional notion of truth in late Tudor chronicles. Nashe also fuses the fictional commoner's story to the panorama of Henry VIII's triumph with a simple comma: as Henry VIII pursuded "his ful-sayld fortune, I, Iacke Wilton, (a Gentleman at least,) was a certain kind of an appendix or page belonging or appertaining in or vnto the confines of the English court" (209). Unlike Deloney's treatment of the affair at Flodden, however – when the Scots king manifested his "trayterous practise: which was when our King was in France, at Turney, and Turwin" (33) – Nashe's story ultimately undoes the gestures towards the authority of chronicles. Deloney may brashly interpolate a legendary story into historical events, but Nashe undermines the very ground on which he stands narrating. The dexterity of the hero's self-presentation finally bends under the weight of the final phrase of the novel's first sentence. Wilton was at the court, "where what my credit was a number of my creditors that I cosned can testify" (209). From the gestures of truth that should establish the reliability of this historical narrative, Nashe now removes any pretense of certainty.[39]

History and story combine in unstable alloy from the first sentence. The disorienting rhetorical gymnastics of the opening episodes of the novel serve to displace notions of authority in the text.[40]

In fact, Nashe's hero appropriates and challenges Henry's authority throughout the novel. Jack plays the role of trickster, testing the truth of his assertion that "the prince could but command men spend their bloud in his seruice, I could make them spend al the mony they had for my pleasure" (210).[41] He dupes a cider merchant into signing away all of his wealth.[42] He immediately sets out to humiliate an overbearing captain, tricking him into a foolish display of bravado. Burlesquing the epic heroism of "Vlysses, Nestor, and Diomed" (220), Jack's gull sneaks into the French camp and pretends to betray his English king. With the disguised French king observing skeptically, he promises a common French soldier who stands as a decoy of king, "let but the King of France follow his counsel, he would drive [Henry VIII] from Turwin wals yet ere three daies to an end" (223). As the captain's lies fall apart, however, the real French King steps forward and orders him to be whipped for his foolishness. In such incidents, Nashe grafts entirely fictional episodes – conventional jests – into a historical setting. Where anecdotes, as Annabel Patterson has argued, appear in chronicles like Holinshed's to complicate the historiographical trajectories of history of state, so these preliminary jests function ambiguously in Nashe's historical novel. On the one hand, they are clearly fictional, if conventional, episodes, but like the anecdotes that appear throughout the period's chronicles, they challenge the verifiable history of kings and monuments with oral tradition and folklore. More significantly, these opening pranks establish a ludic space that challenges conventional authority. When the English captain appears before the man he takes to be the French king, he addresses a lowly soldier with the same deference as he would the real Louis XII, behind the curtain. And momentarily, that lowly French soldier occupies the space of King of France. Such competing centers of royal authority, like Nashe's displacement of the authority of chronicles, proliferate in the novel so that Wilton not infrequently occupies a competing space, as a king of pages, lord of misrule, or prince of drunkards. When Henry VIII returns from victory in Thérouanne to reside in Hampton Court, Wilton tags along where his authority determines who may come among the pages as "authenticall" (228).

When his hero returns to the continent, Nashe transforms chronicle material to give his tale its own authority, an authority that underwrites the emergence of his narrative from the flat conventions of jestbooks and into a more provisional generic mode, somewhere between the

picaresque and the travel narrative.[43] After describing the aftermath of
two historical battles – one at Marignano recounted in Nashe's source,
Cooper's Chronicle, on the page facing the account of Henry VIII's victory
at Tournai and Thérouanne, the other a conflated account of Anabaptist
losses drawn from Sleidanus' *Famovse Cronicle of oure time* – Nashe's
protagonist returns to his own story with his meeting of the famous
Henrician poet Henry Howard, the earl of Surrey, grandson of the
Surrey who led Henry's forces at Flodden.[44] They have a series of
adventures, meeting Sir Thomas More, Cornelius Agrippa, Sir John
Russell, and several other historical personages along the way. Nashe's
hero and his master play a shifting game of identity, sometimes dressed
as themselves, sometimes dressed as each other, and more than once
being charged with counterfeiting coinage, a displacement for their
counterfeit authority.[45] Surrey's quest leads him to Florence, the birth-
place of his beloved "Geraldine." Nashe here weaves together the inter-
mingled threads of the literary and the historiographical, enshrining the
tradition – derived from Richard Stanyhurst's *Description of Ireland*
for Holinshed – that Surrey pined for a beautiful young Florentine lady.
In his discussion of the Fitzgeralds, Stanyhurst anchors his treatment
with literary evidence. The family, he notes, "is verie properlie toucht in
a sonnet of Surreies, made vpon the earle of Kidares sister, now countess
of Lincolne."[46] He goes on to quote in its entirety Surrey's poem, "From
Tuscane came my ladies worthie race." Of course, Surrey's poem itself
refers to the mythical genealogy of the family, so that by the time Nashe
uses the story, it has crossed from legendary history to the literary and
back several times. Surrey eventually passes out of the narrative's history
and back into chronicle history, as Wilton, accompanied by his wealthy
paramour who "inuested me in the state of a monarch" (267), pursues his
wanderlust in Rome.

Wilton's adventures in Rome both contest history and make room for
the playful narrator's emergence as a fictional rival to the typical subject
of history. Wilton has little reverence for Rome's antiquity. He lists the
monuments – the theaters, tombs, and other antiquities – typically contained in travelers' catalogues, even as he mocks their dubious origins
(280–1).[47] Although he has little patience for Romans' predilection to
memorialize themselves in marble, he admits, "to the shame of vs protestants," that "if good workes may merite heauen, [the Romans] do them,
we talke of them" (285). Their public foundations would put the
destructive tendencies of Protestants to shame. John Stow might have
been pleased.[48] Of course, Nashe is no papist. He excoriates Wolsey,

whose fall "Chronicles largely report, though not applie," and wishes that the example of corruption in the established church might bring about some reforms, since otherwise "some parcel of their punishment yet vnpaid I doe not doubt but wil be required of their posteritie" (238). At the same time he criticizes those who would continue to roil a church that he casts as otherwise settled.[49] Thus his scathing treatment of the Münster affair serves as a warning of "what it is to be Anabaptists, to be Puritans, to be villaines" (241). England has made its choice, and should be given leave, "if wee haue more cloth than they, to make our garment some what larger" (238). Ultimately, Nashe's momentary destruction of history's stability permits his narrative to triumph as he becomes "a historiographer of my owne misfortunes" (281). Later, when the lusty Countess Juliana enslaves him, he ends a digression in this way: "In a leafe or two before was I lockt vp: here in this page the foresayd good wife Countesse comes to me" (314). Nashe's narrating page has become both the subject and the object of his history.

The superficially penitent Wilton eventually makes his way home. Fleeing from the wickedness and cruelty of Italy, "[he] arriued at the king of Englands camp twixt Ardes and Guines in France, where he with great triumphs met and entertained the Emperor and the French King and feasted many days" (327–8). We are back to the Field of Cloth of Gold and the scene with which Shakespeare began his play. Wilton, despite an anachronic narrative, has returned to the displaced court of Henry VIII in a moment of triumph.[50] This opulent scene and Wilton's craving for Henry's approval might signal the recuperation of historiographical and Henrician authority. Nashe's temporary displacement of Henry VIII – nominally the "onely true subiect of Chronicles" – in favor of his "chronicle of the King of pages," both indulges nostalgia for Henry, even as it marginalizes Henry. As with Deloney's complex negotiation of the past, Nashe appropriates and evokes a supposed golden age that exists only in narrative, but unlike the selective memory of Deloney, Nashe restores some of the violent and destructive consequences of Henry's later years. Completing the ambit of his journey in the midst of another of Henry's glorious triumphs, Wilton at first gestures back to the authority of the king. But Wilton's submission is conditional and fleeting. If readers approve of his narrative, he will produce an equally pleasing sequel. If they do not, "I will sweare vpon an English chronicle neuer to be out-landish Chronicler more while I liue" (328). But what sort of oath is this to be, from a fictional narrator without credibility, whose every previous gesture towards chronicle has been met with efforts to destabilize its truth? After all, to quote Nashe's dedication, the pages the readers hold in their hands are merely a "conveyance of history" – simultaneously an expression of and a theft of history.

NOTES

1. William Shakespeare, *King Henry IV, Part One*, ed. David Scott Kastan (London: Thomson Learning, 2002), 5.2.55–7.
2. William Shakespeare, *King Henry VIII (All Is True)*, ed. Gordon McMullan (London: Arden Shakespeare, 2000), 1.1.14. Susan Stewart treats the difference in between discursive and experiential understanding at the heart of nostalgia. *On Longing: Narratives of the Miniature, the Gigantic, the Souvenir, the Collection* (Baltimore: Johns Hopkins University Press, 1984), 26. On the visceral experience of truth in the play, see Anston Bosman, "Seeing Tears: Truth and Sense in *All is True*," *Shakespeare Quarterly* 50 (1999), 459–76, at p. 470.
3. Michael de Certeau discusses historiography's "operation," its translation of undifferentiated experience into history in *The Writing of History*, trans. Tom Conley (New York: Columbia University Press, 1988), 71. On the importance of genre to the narratives of historical emplotment, see Hayden White, particularly *Figural Realism: Studies in the Mimesis Effect* (Baltimore: Johns Hopkins University Press, 1999), 29.
4. This is Hall's title for Henry VIII's reign in *The Vnion of the two noble and illustrate families*, sig. AAa 1r. Stow remained subdued about the reign. Patrick Collinson attributes Stow's lack of enthusiasm to conservative religious views combined with nostalgic antiquarianism that regretted the passing of older ways. "John Stow and Nostalgic Antiquarianism," in J. F. Merritt (ed.), *Imagining Early Modern London: Perception and Portrayals of the City from Stow to Strype, 1598–1720* (Cambridge: Cambridge University Press, 2001), 37.
5. Katherine Eggert argues that the imaginative nostalgia for Elizabeth's male ancestors in the 1590s represented a cynical anticipation of the male rule that would follow her death. "Nostalgia and the Not Yet Late Queen: Refusing Female Rule in *Henry V*," *English Literary History* 61 (1994), 523–50, at p. 527.
6. D. R. Woolf treats the Tudor transformation of the chronicle into "parasite genres," including the history play, but he does not comment on the historically informed, if chaotic narratives of Nashe and Deloney. *Reading History in Early Modern England* (Cambridge: Cambridge University Press, 2000), 26.
7. Phyllis Rackin argues that historiography generally – and especially in the case of the evolving historiographical values of Tudor chronicles – starts from an anachronistic nostalgia, a desire to recover the past for the purposes of the present. *Stages of History: Shakespeare's English Chronicles* (Ithaca: Cornell University Press, 1990), 94.
8. Georg Lukacs delineates the bounds of the historical novel and finds its earliest realization in Sir Walter Scott, excluding earlier novels for reflecting their own consciousness, rather than a sharply differentiated historical awareness. *The Historical Novel*, trans. Hannah Mitchell and Stanley Mitchell (Lincoln:

University of Nebraska Press, 1983), 20. The protagonists of both Deloney and Nashe may interact with historical figures in something resembling the historical novel, but they traverse the past and their authors' present without acknowledging the difference. Michael McKeon observes that both Nashe and Deloney use their historical settings to their advantage. *The Origins of the English Novel, 1600–1740* (Baltimore: Johns Hopkins University Press, 1987), 97, 226.

9. Blair Worden explores the close early modern relationship between history and story in "Historians and Poets," *Huntington Library Quarterly* 68 (2005), 71–93, at p. 81. See also Judith H. Anderson's discussion of the period's poets' striving after moral as opposed to experiential truth in their treatment of history. *Biographical Truth: The Representations of Historical Persons in Tudor-Stuart Writing* (New Haven: Yale University Press, 1984), 125. Lorna Hutson recalls that "plot" – whether historical or fictional – stood at the center of early modern humanist reading practices. "Fortunate Travelers: Reading for Plot in Sixteenth-Century England," *Representations* 41 (1993), 83–103, at p. 85.

10. Ronald B. McKerrow with F. P. Wilson (eds.), *The Works of Thomas Nashe*, 5 vols. (Oxford: Blackwell, 1958), II, 201. Further references are to this volume.

11. *Coopers Chronicle* (London, 1560), sig. a3r–[a3v]. *RSTC* 15218.

12. Merritt E. Lawlis (ed.), *The Novels of Thomas Deloney* (Bloomington: Indiana University Press, 1961), 5. Further references are to this edition.

13. Alexandra Halasz reads Deloney's difficulties in digesting this material as a signal of his efforts to display mastery in weaving together the elements for his story. *The Marketplace of Print: Pamphlets and the Public Sphere in Early Modern England* (Cambridge: Cambridge University Press, 1997), 133.

14. Eugene P. Wright summarizes the traditional biographical details Deloney knew in celebrating his fellow weaver. *Thomas Deloney* (Boston: Twayne, 1981), 60. Leonard Muztazza makes a compelling case for reading Winchcomb's rise as dependent on clever activity rather than simple good fortune. "Thomas Deloney's *Jacke of Newbury*: A Horatio Alger Story for the Sixteenth Century," *Journal of Popular Culture* 23 (1989), 165–77, at p. 167. Mihoko Suzuki argues that Winchcomb's desire for domestic mastery deflects his own lack of authority in the political realm. *Subordinate Subjects: Gender, the Political Nation, and Literary Form in England, 1588–1688* (Aldershot: Ashgate, 2003), 39.

15. Theo Stemmler makes the important point that Deloney's gestures toward history may signal an attempt to create a past for an emergent mercantile class. "The Rise of a New Literary Genre: Thomas Deloney's Bourgeois Novel *Jack of Newbury*," in Elmar Lehman and Bernd Lenz (eds.), *Telling Stories: Studies in Honour of Ulrich Broich* (Amsterdam: John Benjamins, 1992), 53. For a famous instance of the formulation, see Cooper's treatment of Elizabeth's succeeding her sister: "Not longe after, she came from Hatfield in Hartfordesheyre." *Cooper's Chronicle*, 377v.

16. John Stow, *The Summarie of English Chronicles* (London, 1566), T4v (*RSTC* 23319.5). Richard Grafton offers nearly the same evaluation in *Graftons Abridgement of the Chronicles of Englande* (London, 1570), 129r (*RSTC* 12151). Stow offers a marginally more elaborate version of James IV's failure at Flodden

in *The chronicles of England, from Brute vnto this present yeare* (London, 1580), 901 (*RSTC* 23333). John Carpenter points out that Deloney made extensive use of Stow in his ballads. "Placing Thomas Deloney," *JNT: Journal of Narrative Theory* 36 (2006), 125–62, at p. 132.

17. Deloney made his reputation as a ballad writer before turning to prose fiction. Carpenter argues that his embrace of ballads as a popular form carries into his subsequent fashioning of himself in his fiction. "Placing Thomas Deloney," 140.

18. *Kemps nine daies vvonder* (London, 1600), sig. D3v (*RSTC* 14923).

19. Neil Samman traces the significance of the conventions of progresses generally, and Henry VIII's several progresses through Berkshire more specifically (including one in 1516), in "The Progresses of Henry VIII, 1509–1529," in Diarmaid MacCulloch (ed.), *Reign of Henry VIII: Politics, Policy and Piety* (New York: St Martin's Press, 1995), 72.

20. For Edward Hall, I quote from the reprint of the *Chronicle*, ed. Henry Ellis (London, 1809); reprinted as *Hall's Chronicle; Containing the History of England* (New York: AMS, 1965), 554.

21. *Holinshed's Chronicles of England, Scotland, and Ireland* (London, 1587; reprinted, New York: AMS Press, 1965), 581.

22. Annabel Patterson, *Reading Holinshed's "Chronicles"* (Chicago: University of Chicago Press, 1994), 42. F. J. Levy dismisses such anecdotes as merely "random information." *Tudor Historical Thought* (San Marino: Huntington Library, 1967), 167.

23. Roger A. Ladd argues that this skit embodies the historical distancing Deloney undertakes in his critique of Elizabethan policy. "Deloney and the London Weavers' Company," *Sixteenth Century Journal* 32 (2001), 981–1001, at p. 987. Suzuki notices the skit's criticism of Henry's absence at the moment of the Flodden, but it much more clearly bypasses the king's intermediaries to point directly to Wolsey's corruption. *Subordinate Subjects*, 44. Constance Jordan reads Winchcomb's success as validating the protean, ludic space in Deloney's narrative. "The 'Art of Clothing': Role-Playing in Deloney's Fiction," *English Literary Renaissance* 11 (1981), 183–93, at p. 187.

24. Craig Dionne, attuned to the mercantile heroism of Deloney's heroes, points to dissembling and disguise as a counterpart to the humanist ideal of transforming the self to take advantage of mutable contexts. "Playing the 'Cony': Anonymity in Underworld Literature," *Genre* 30 (1997), 29–50, at p. 45.

25. On the relationship between annal, chronicle, and history, and these forms' complex relationship to the narrative urge for order and judgments, see Hayden White, *The Content of the Form: Narrative Discourse and Historical Representation* (Baltimore: Johns Hopkins University Press, 1987), 24.

26. Joan Pong Linton reads this episode as commenting on Elizabeth's failures to support the faltering cloth trades, a failure that would strike close to home for Deloney. *The Romance of the New World: Gender and the Literary Formations of English Colonialism* (Cambridge: Cambridge University Press, 1998), 74. Ladd shows that Deloney falsifies the historical Wolsey's actions

so that his fictional Wolsey embodies the resistance Deloney and other weavers encountered in the mid-1590s. "Deloney and the London Weavers' Company," 986.

27. Halasz points to the possibility of seeing this scene as a vast fantasy of upward mobility. *Marketplace of Print*, 132.

28. Stewart argues that nostalgia feigns an interest authenticity, but that the appearance of authenticity is one "which, ironically, [nostalgia] can achieve only through narrative." *On Longing*, 23.

29. Annabel Patterson argues that *All Is True* intentionally juxtaposes competing narratives of history as part of the "urbane skepticism" of playwrights, aware that historiography could not be objective. "'All Is True': Negotiating the Past in *Henry VIII*," in R. B. Parker and S. P. Zitner (eds.), *Elizabethan Theater: Essays in Honor of S. Schoenbaum* (Newark: University of Delaware Press, 1996), 160.

30. "Have With You to Saffron-Walden," in *The Works of Thomas Nashe*, ed. McKerrow and Wilson, vol. III, 84.

31. Halasz reads Nashe as exploiting the possibilities of print. *Marketplace of Print*, 96.

32. Jonathan V. Crewe, *Unredeemed Rhetoric: Thomas Nashe and the Scandal of Authorship* (Baltimore: Johns Hopkins University Press, 1982), 69. Crewe offers the best handle on the pyrotechnics of Nashe's style. See also Mihoko Suzuki, who argues that Nashe's ludic text destabilizes the political authority of its literary version of Henry VIII. "'Signorie ouer the Pages': The Crisis of Authority in Nashe's *The Unfortunate Traveller*," *Studies in Philology* 81 (1984), 348–71, at p. 357.

33. Robert Mayer sees both Nashe and Deloney as marking the obviously fictional quality of their narratives. *History and the Early English Novel: Matters of Fact from Bacon to Defoe* (Cambridge: Cambridge University Press, 1997), 148.

34. Erich Auerbach treats the narrative difficulty of simultaneity in *Mimesis: The Representation of Reality in Western Literature* (Princeton: Princeton University Press, 1968), 13.

35. White treats the interpretation involved in any attempt to arrange events in story in *Figural Realism*, 29.

36. *A Chronicle at Large* (London, 1569), 984 (*RSTC* 12147).

37. *The Life and Death of Cardinal Wolsey*, ed. Richard S. Sylvester (Oxford: Oxford University Press, 1959), 14.

38. Robert Crowley, *An Epitome of Cronicles* (London, 1559), fo. 273v (*RSTC* 15217.5). Barrett L. Beer untangles the relationship between Cooper's printings of Lanquet's work and Robert Crowley's more strident treatment of Mary's bloody reign in "Robert Crowley and Cooper's Chronicle: The Unauthorized Edition of 1559," *Notes and Queries* 55 (2008), 148–52, at p. 149.

39. Georgia Brown reads Nashe as inhabiting a world without fixed notions of truth. *Redefining Elizabethan Literature* (Cambridge: Cambridge University Press, 2004), 87. Arthur Kinney, however, sees the *Unfortunate Traveller* as lamenting the passing of humanist ideals. *Humanist Poetics: Thought, Rhetoric,*

and Fiction in Sixteenth Century England (Amherst: University of Massachusetts Press, 1986), 332.

40. Margaret Ferguson, "Nashe's *The Unfortunate Traveller*: The 'Newes of the Maker' Game," *English Literary Renaissance* 11 (1981), 165–82, at p. 168.

41. Joan Pong Linton reads Wilton as a "trickster" figure who cannot be interpolated into the merged system of "sovereignty and governmentality." "Counterfeiting Sovereignty, Mocking Mastery: Trickster Poetics and the Critique of Romance in Nashe's *Unfortunate Traveller*," in Naomi Conn Liebler (ed.), *Early Modern Prose Fiction: The Cultural Politics of Reading* (New York: Routledge, 2007), 130–47, at p. 139.

42. Brown reads Nashe's jests as exploding the prodigal son tradition to which the text also gestures. *Redefining Elizabethan Literature*, 71.

43. Andrew M. Kirk, "'Travail' to 'Strange Nations': Recalling the Errant in *The Unfortunate Traveller*," *Journal of English and Germanic Philology* 97 (1998), 523–44, at p. 525.

44. Johannes Sleidanus, *A Famovse Cronicle of our time, called Sleidanes Commentaries*, trans. John Dawes (London, 1560), fo. 127r (*RSTC* 19848). By the 1590s, a writer could have turned to numerous chronicles, so many that, as Woolf points out, the saturated market had made it impossible for new chronicles to appear. *Reading History*, 41. In the notes of his edition, McKerrow observes Nashe's use of Sleidanus. *Works*, vol. IV, 268.

45. Jonathan Crewe argues that Nashe's Surrey represents an Elizabethan desire for an unrepresentable originality, of a piece with the *Unfortunate Traveller*'s representation of Henry VIII. *Trials of Authorship: Anterior Forms and Poetic Reconstruction from Wyatt to Shakespeare* (Berkeley: University of California Press, 1990), 48. For Steve Mentz, this section allows Nashe to critique Sidney's recourse to chivalric romance. *Romance for Sale in Early Modern England: The Rise of Prose Fiction* (Aldershot: Ashgate, 2006), 191.

46. *Second volume of Chronicles: Conteining the description, conquest, inhabitation, and troublesome estate of Ireland* (London, [1587]), 33 (*RSTC* 13569). Patterson argues that the sonnet might be construed as a criticism of Henry VIII. *Reading Holinshed's "Chronicles"*, 49.

47. Julian Yates sees *The Unfortunate Traveller* as exploiting a paradox: the traveler experiences the exotic, but is single and mortal; the traveler's printed tale may outlive him, but it stands at a remove from authenticity. *Error, Misuse, Failure: Object Lessons from the English Renaissance* (Minneapolis: University of Minnesota Press, 2003), 125.

48. On Stow's grief at the loss of charity and of communal institutions after the Reformation, see Eamon Duffy, "'Bare ruined choirs': Remembering Catholicism in Shakespeare's England," in Richard Dutton, *et al.* (eds.), *Theatre and Religion: Lancastrian Shakespeare* (New York: Palgrave, 2003), 40–57, at p. 42.

49. Katherine Wilson offers a confused reading of this scene in *Fictions of Authorship in Late Elizabethan Narratives: Euphues in Arcadia* (Oxford: Oxford University Press, 2006), 169. Jennifer L. Andersen finds that Nashe

objected primarily to nonconformity. "Anti-Puritanism, Anti-Popery, and Gallows Rhetoric in Thomas Nashe's *The Unfortunate Traveller*," *Sixteenth Century Journal* 35 (2004), 43–63, at p. 45.

50. Anthony Ossa-Richardson argues that Nashe's ludic interests require him to reject chronology. "Ovid and the 'Free Play with Signs' in Thomas Nashe's *The Unfortunate Traveller*," *Modern Language Review* 101 (2006), 945–56, at p. 947.

CHAPTER 12

Henry VIII and the modern historians: the making of a twentieth-century reputation

Peter Marshall

The reputation of Henry VIII sailed into the twentieth century with a stout Victorian wind at its back. J. A. Froude's view of Henry as a hero-king, savior of the nation from obscurantism and founder of its modern imperial destiny, was posthumously distilled from his monumental history of sixteenth-century England into a three-volume account of the reign in 1908.[1] Some Catholic historians continued to grind their axes – Francis (later Cardinal) Gasquet had, for example, revealing sub-entries in the index of his 1889 *Henry VIII and the English Monasteries*: Henry VIII: "despotic power of," "avarice of," "perfidy of."[2] But, as the nineteenth century drew to a close, the leading voices of the English historical establishment were generally admiring of the accomplishments and achievements of the second Tudor monarch. In a pair of lectures delivered in Oxford in the 1880s, the Regius Professor of Modern History, William Stubbs, dissociated himself from "those critics who incline to a very disparaging estimate of Henry VIII." Stubbs had a high opinion of Henry's mental abilities, and thought him morally no worse than Francis I, Philip II, or Henry IV. Stubbs's Henry was admittedly a rather unlikeable figure, "self-confident, self-willed; unscrupulous in act, violent and crafty," but he was no capricious tyrant; rather "a man of purpose" and iron determination. Moreover, he was no puppet of parties or follower of the lead of great ministers. Stubbs was "inclined to regard Henry himself as the main originator of the greatest and most critical changes of his reign."[3]

Such an interpretation received weighty confirmation in the greatest monument of late Victorian historical scholarship, the *Dictionary of National Biography*. The author of the entry on Henry (published in 1891) was James Gairdner, an editor of the project which for a generation had been slowly transforming the prospects for studying Henry's reign, the calendar of *Letters and papers … of the reign of Henry VIII*. According to Gairdner, Henry's position among English monarchs was unique, owing to "the extraordinary degree of personal weight that he was able to throw into the government of the realm." Gairdner admired Henry's "consummate statesmanship," as well as his undoubted literary, theological, and diplomatic feats.[4]

A debt to Gairdner was warmly acknowledged by the author of Henry's first twentieth-century biography, and one that was to hold the field for over sixty-five years. The author in question was Albert Frederick Pollard, who at the time of the book's publication in 1902 was about to move to a chair of constitutional history at University College, London.[5] Pollard's was the first study of Henry to make full use of *Letters and papers*, and it combined a sharply drawn portrait of the king himself with a political and diplomatic history of the reign. Pollard's Henry was nothing less than "the most remarkable man who ever sat on the English throne." There was, Pollard considered, "nothing commonplace about him; his good and his bad qualities alike were exceptional. It is easy, by suppressing the one or the other, to paint him a hero or a villain." On balance, Pollard opted firmly for hero, seeing Henry as the king who satisfied "the popular demand for a firm and masterful hand" after the misrule of the fifteenth century, and as the far-sighted statesman who "laid the foundations of England's naval power," setting it on the path to empire.[6]

Pollard's reign of Henry VIII was also, to borrow a modern footballing cliché, a game of two halves. The real successes all followed the fall of Wolsey, and if Henry had died in around 1529, he would probably have been remembered as someone "who might have been thought capable of much, had he not failed to achieve anything." As Pollard elaborated in a later biography of the cardinal-minister, Wolsey was an outdated absolutist who would have set England on the path to a doomed *ancien régime*. Henry – "the greatest parliamentarian who ever sat on the English throne" – saved the nation from this fate, and his actions enabled the domestic institutions of the English church and state to develop in a positive and modern direction.[7]

The instrument of this realignment was, of course, the break with Rome. Pollard was firmly of the opinion that the divorce from Catherine of Aragon was solely the occasion and not the cause of the English Reformation. That Reformation he regarded not primarily as a doctrinal or religious movement, but as the culmination of an age-old struggle between the forces of church and state. Rising nationalism, and an endemic anticlericalism on the part of the English laity, ensured that an independent church was bound to be subordinated to and incorporated into the structures of the state. Henry's genius was to control and direct this manifest destiny to suit his own purposes. His "cold and calculated cunning" in effecting this was at the same time "a monument of farsighted statecraft." Aligning himself with the prejudices and interests of the lay middle classes, Henry, despite some despotic traits, became the constitutional monarch par excellence: no monarch was ever "a more zealous champion of parliamentary privileges, a more scrupulous observer of parliamentary forms, or a more original pioneer of constitutional doctrine." Indeed, in his cooperation with parliament, Henry "acted more as the leader of both Houses than as a King." His policies were successful because they coincided with "the national will," and the king "led his people in the way they wanted to go."[8]

Because Henry's rule "embodied an inevitable moment of politics," moral judgments about his actions were, Pollard thought, largely irrelevant. He was, of course, too much the late Victorian to eschew moralizing entirely. Commenting on the king's dressing in yellow in 1536 to celebrate the death of Catherine of Aragon, Pollard sniffed that "every inch a King, Henry VIII never attained to the stature of a gentleman." Pollard was no blinkered apologist for his subject. He recognized the "imperious egotism," an occupational hazard of monarchs, that was a consistent driving force of Henry's character, and he conceded a tendency towards despotism and "vindictive suspicion" in the latter part of his life. Yet Pollard was ultimately reluctant to endorse a generalization of the reign as exhibiting "a continuous development of Henry's intellect and deterioration of his character." The king's famous speech to parliament on unity and charity of December 1545 revealed "ethical ideas and aims." His life was as free from "vice" (by which Pollard meant sexual adventures) at the end of the reign as at the beginning, and "in seriousness of purpose and steadfastness of aim it was immeasurably superior."[9]

As a Russian political exile may have been thinking at the time Pollard was writing, you can't make an omelette without breaking eggs. Under Henry, "the nation purchased political salvation at the price of moral debasement; the individual was sacrificed on the altar of the State." But Pollard inclined to the view that the price was tolerable, and might have been much higher, since, whether Henry was king or no, the storm of the Reformation would still have burst over England. "It is probable that Henry's personal influence and personal action averted greater evils than they provoked ... Every drop of blood shed under Henry VIII might have been a river under a feebler king." In thus exonerating Henry, the biography culminated in a succession of lyrical cadences: "surrounded by faint hearts and fearful minds, Henry VIII neither faltered nor failed."[10]

Meanwhile, in parallel with Pollard's biography, Gairdner had attempted a second broad assessment of the monarch. This appeared in an essay for another textual temple of professional historical scholarship, the sixteenth-century volume of the Cambridge Modern History. Though the treatment of Wolsey was noticeably more sympathetic, several of the judgments resonated with those of Pollard. Henry's reign, Gairdner opined, "has left deeper marks on succeeding ages than any other reign in English history." Henry was "a monarch of consummate ability," whose "skilful use" of European complications increased English influence abroad, and who began the laudable process of seeking to unify the British Isles. But, at the same time, Gairdner allowed himself a freer editorial voice than he had done in the *DNB*, and a censorious tone that was distinctly sharper than that of Pollard. Where the latter saw a real partnership with parliament, Gairdner detected only the semblance of constitutional forms and credited Henry with the establishment of an English despotism. The king's character was marked by "wilfulness and obstinacy," and his course was "misdirected by passion and selfishness." Henry's policies towards the church, the monasteries, and the coinage "lowered the moral tone of the whole community. Men lost faith in their religion … Covetousness and fraud reigned in the highest places."[11] Here, in the divergences between Pollard, the Whiggish progressive, and Gairdner, the pessimistic Anglo-Catholic, Henry arguably serves as a signifier for some of the ideological and cultural fissures in English intellectual circles at the turn of the twentieth century. But both scholars concurred in their recognition of Henry's abilities, his commanding control of events, and, above all, his potential for "greatness."

There was further convergence in the assumption that an understanding of Henry's character and personality could illuminate the politics and events of the reign. Pollard and Gairdner shared with their predecessors an essentially Victorian notion of character as an amalgam of conscious intentions, ambitions, and exercises of the will. But the early twentieth century was midwife to a revolution in the understanding of human motivation. Though Pollard and Gairdner freely used terms like "egotism" without reference to the theories of Sigmund Freud, it was only a matter of time before someone approached the historical evidence around Henry's personality, not so much as a script to be read, but as a code to be cracked.

Such an undertaking was attempted shortly after the end of the First World War by John Carl Flügel, a distinguished if rather unorthodox academic psychologist and practicing psychoanalyst. Flügel lectured in psychology at University College, London, from 1920 until his death in 1955, and in 1919 he co-founded the British Psycho-Analytical Society.[12] Taking up a challenge thrown down many years earlier by Froude – that Henry's serial matrimonial misadventures must be due to some potentially discoverable common cause – Flügel sought to identify and trace "the operation of certain unconscious motives throughout the whole of Henry's sexual life." In approved Freudian fashion, the roots of these were to be sought in childhood, and though Flügel conceded that "our know-ledge of his early life is very slender," he nonetheless found sufficient evidence on which to ground a general theory of character and motivation. In short, Flügel argued that Henry exhibited throughout his life all the hallmarks of a powerful Oedipus complex. The natural envy felt by a son towards a father's powers and privileges were, thought Flügel, distinctly liable to be intensified when the father was a king, and they were accen-tuated further in Henry's case by the attested goodness and beauty of his mother, Elizabeth of York, and the coldness towards her of Henry VII. Flügel further concluded that the repressed hostility and incestuous desires that Henry felt towards his parents were transferred onto his brother and sister-in-law, a process perhaps stemming from the time in 1501 when the ten-year-old Henry had had to lead to the altar and hand to his elder brother the young bride, Catherine of Aragon. Henry's own subsequent marriage to Catherine combined a conscious performance of filial piety with an unconscious realization of feelings of aggression and jealousy towards his deceased father and brother. Thereafter, the impulses formed by Henry's relationship with his father constituted an unstable compound of "the egoistic and the venerative." For a time, Henry deferred to a number of father-substitutes – Wolsey, the pope – until the egotistical side of his character finally triumphed. The rupture with the papacy patently repre-sented "a displacement of the desire to overthrow the rule of the father and usurp his authority."

Meanwhile, the breakdown of Henry's marriage to Catherine was driven on by superstitious fears similarly intertwined with the king's Oedipal tendencies, principally the perception of sterility as a punishment for incest. Throughout his relationships with women, thought Flügel, Henry exhibited another characteristic of the Oedipus complex noted by Freud – the need for some obstacle to be present as a condition of erotic attraction, since a failure to develop beyond the infantile fixation on the parents required "an impediment of the kind that existed in the original incestuous love." Strong characteristics of Henry's psycho-sexual life were the simultaneous desire for, and hatred of, a sexual rival, as well as an attraction towards (and at the same time a horror of) incestuous relationships. Even Jane Seymour, Flügel noted, was a distant relative, and Henry made a habit of meeting with her in her brother's rooms. The charges against Anne Boleyn, including that of adultery with her own brother, represented a hate-filled projection on to her of Henry's own incestuous desires. Unconsciously, Henry was drawn to women (such as Catherine Howard) who were either unfaithful or had already had sex with other men, as only the sexually experienced could fill the role of a mother substitute. The chaste widowhood of Catherine Parr allowed for a more stable sublimation of these desires, her attractiveness enhanced by the fact that she had earlier been wooed by Sir Thomas Seymour, Henry's brother-in-law.

Flügel's lengthy analysis of Henry's personal drives was by no means lacking in insight, though parts of it clearly verged on the silly, such as the significance he drew from the fact that Henry's known or suspected mistresses – Elizabeth Blount, Mary Boleyn, and Margaret Shelton – bore the same Christian names as his mother and sisters. As befitted the trained psychoanalyst, Flügel eschewed moralizing or condemnation, and there were in fact professional reasons why he was reluctant to portray Henry in terms of monstrous pathology. Though he hoped that he had helped to elucidate historical problems, he felt that the principal value of studies of this sort was their role in confirming the findings of psychoanalysis performed on living subjects. There was a reliable objectivity in the analysis of historical personages. Having by definition no knowledge of Freudian theories or opportunity to act up to them, such case-studies could supply "a most necessary and desirable test of the validity of the psycho-analytic method itself." Though no historian, Flügel did allow himself a more than sneaking regard for Henry's political abilities: "few men have been able to reconcile, as he did, an intense egotism and an enormous lust for power with an undistorted vision of forces and events; and in the unique degree to which he achieved this combination is probably to be sought the secret of his political success."[13]

An intense interest in Henry's temperament and personality was an unsurprising characteristic of the spate of populist books about the king appearing in the interwar years, such as the journalist Francis Hackett's study of 1930 (whose author, in Flügelian fashion, billed himself as a "psycho-historian"), Frederick Chamberlin's 1931 *The Private Character of Henry VIII* (a remarkably friendly assessment of the king), or a short biography of 1934 by the Australian novelist Helen Simpson, best known as the author of *Saraband for Dead Lovers*.[14] But a strong emphasis on the personal as the key to the political was also evident in the most significant scholarly publication about Henry to appear in the 1930s, the extensive selection of the king's letters edited by Muriel St. Clare Byrne and published in that climactic year of British royal drama, 1936. Byrne – a prolific dramatist, as well as social historian, and close friend of Dorothy M. Sayers – explained that her principles of selection were designed not to illustrate the whole reign, but to concentrate on "the more or less coherent interest that can be found in following the development of Henry's personality as a monarch." It was a personality she clearly found fascinating, and by no means unappealing. While recognizing a streak of cruelty and ruthlessness, and a "degeneration of the finer qualities of his mind" in Henry's later years, Byrne was convinced that the letters revealed the real Henry, "not the popular Bluebeard … nor yet the bullying tyrant who muddled through, somehow, because he had the luck to secure clever ministers; but the king who has been described by his finest biographer as 'the most remarkable man who ever sat on the English throne.'" In fact, Byrne's assessment of Henry's abilities might aptly be described as "Pollard-plus": "about the fixity of his aims, the strength of his will, and his capacity for concentration and hard work there can be no dispute. It is possible to dispute his wisdom, impossible to deny the power of mind." Throughout the letters, Byrne found evidence of "energy and control," "dignity and balance," of a master intellect, who "never suffered from the divided mind, or the conflict of heart and head," waiting to thrust an inexorable conclusion on his correspondents after the patient intricacies of subordinate and co-ordinate clauses. In times of crisis, such as the Pilgrimage of Grace, what emerged was "Henry's real practical ability, his methods of statesmanship, and his capacity for handling a state of emergency." In this account, Henry comes across, not just as for Pollard the embodiment of the national will, but almost as a Nietzschean superman.[15]

   Yet a lengthy review article of St. Clare Byrne's volume, appearing in the *Quarterly Review* in July 1937, suggested that the majestic, Pollardian Henry did not command universal assent in academic circles in the interwar years. The author of "The Personality of Henry the Eighth" was Sir Charles Oman, Chichele Professor of Modern History at Oxford, and a renowned military historian and historical popularizer.[16] Tactfully ignoring St. Clare Byrne's intrusive editorial commentaries, Oman began by applauding her volume for leaving the reader free to assess Henry's character. While conceding that the letters offered evidence of the breadth of the king's intellectual interests, and of his extraordinary self-confidence,

Oman complained that many historians "have been so overwhelmed by the discovery of the colossal capacity of the man that they have tended to accept him at his own valuation, and have failed to recognise that his whole life-work was a failure." Henry had, in fact, few constructive achievements to boast of, and many of those were swept away after his death. The king was a tactless and incompetent diplomat, as well as a cynical and ruthless autocrat. He condoned crimes such as a projected murder of Cardinal Beaton, and he cut a bloody swathe through his own extended family. His breach with Rome was certainly "an epoch-making achievement," but unlike the Reformation of Gustavus Vasa in Sweden, it left a land "hideous with wrecked shrines, stakes and gibbets, and utterly bankrupt," while at the same time acquiring "a degrading and sinister aspect" from its association with the divorce. No one could read John Leland's "melancholy pilgrimage among devastated abbeys and decaying castles" without becoming aware of "the general wreckage of the realm" during the second half of Henry's reign.

In his own area of particular expertise, military history, Oman's observations were especially damning. Henry failed to address the hopelessly outdated organization and weaponry of English armies, and his horrendously expensive military campaigns achieved next to nothing. Noting the extravagant trappings and accoutrements which accompanied Henry on his first expedition to France, Oman cuttingly remarked that "with the tastes of Xerxes he wished to emulate the campaigns of Alexander, but never got a hundred miles from Calais." Oman was even reluctant to credit Henry with the usual plaudits for his sponsorship of the navy. Ships like the *Mary Rose* were poorly designed, and in the 1540s the French dominated the Channel. Where Pollard had detected genuinely ethical principles in Henry's last speech to parliament, Oman heard only an extreme complacency and a repulsive "autolatry." The tone of moral outrage which Pollard and even Gairdner had consciously eschewed was with Oman a marked one. Henry's treatment of servants like Wolsey or Cromwell was "incompatible with any generosity of character, or sense of obligation." Moreover, Oman had no time for the conventional tragic character arc of Henry's reign, a progression "from a self-assertive and not ungenerous youth, through stages of growing egotism to an old age of ruthless megalomania." Rather, "cold-blooded, deliberate cruelty marked not only his advancing years but his whole reign," from the 1509 executions of Richard Empson and Edmund Dudley onwards. Oman even wondered if Mendelian principles – the reappearance generations later of ancient ancestral traits – could be applied to Henry's case. He was descended on his father's side from Bernabo Visconti of Milan, and on his mother's from Peter the Cruel of Castile. Both fourteenth-century rulers "were in the first rank of political murderers."[17]

The middle years of the twentieth century, of course, were well acquainted with political murderers. In the case of Oman, it is tempting to wonder whether exposure to the crimes of Nazi Germany and Stalinist Russia was prompting a reappraisal of the moral culpability of Henry as an exemplar of an earlier form of authoritarianism. Some such thoughts may have been in the air. In 1940, the publisher and critic Milton Waldman produced a triple study of Henry, Elizabeth I, and Oliver Cromwell, provocatively titled *Some English Dictators*.[18] But in fact, relatively few writers at this time seem to have thought comparisons between Henry VIII, Hitler, and Stalin to have been particularly instructive ones. When the editor of the *New Statesman*, Kingsley Martin, suggested, by analogy with the Russian leader, that though Henry VIII might have done terrible things, he had nonetheless served the cause of progress, he was firmly slapped down by a more politically acute journalist, George Orwell. "Henry VIII has not a very close resemblance to Stalin," Orwell remarked in his 1945 essay on "Catastrophic Gradualism."[19] The statement of A. L. Rowse, that Henry was "the nearest the English have ever had to an Ivan the Terrible or a Stalin" was more symptomatic of that historian's proclivity for provocation and controversy than indicative of any deep groundswell of historical opinion.[20] In fact, the most eminent British historian of the immediate post-war years, A. J. P. Taylor, in a radio broadcast of 1949, compared Henry VIII not to Stalin, but to the Yugoslav Communist leader Tito, whom Taylor admired for breaking away from the Soviet monolith, just as the orthodox Catholic Henry had broken from Rome.[21] It is possible, as the American historian Lacey Baldwin Smith suggested in a review article of 1960, that exposure to the industrialized horrors of modern tyranny had encouraged a sense of proportion about the sixteenth-century past: "somehow the description 'despotic' no longer seems to be an adequate or even just characterization of Tudor government and methods." Unlike modern tyrants, "Henry VIII was a 'constitutional monarch,' limited and ruling by divine, natural and common law."[22]

Although the quatercentenary of Henry's death in 1947 was the occasion of no new biography or major public exhibition, there was little sign of a lull of interest in Henry in the years after the Second World War. Assessments flew in from an eclectic range of directions. A popular biography (1949) by the amateur historian, poet, naturalized American, and Catholic convert Theodore Maynard[23] was followed in 1952 by an intriguing study from an eminent British surgeon, Sir Arthur MacNalty. This sought to dispel forever the myth that Henry suffered from syphilis. Rather, his painful leg was caused by a varicose ulcer, the pain from which was the key to the king's "Jekyll and Hyde" personality, and the "sombre contrast" between the first half of the reign and the second.[24] MacNalty was seconded by the historical novelist Philip Lindsay, whose biography of the king, *The Secret of Henry the Eighth*, struck a noticeably understanding and forgiving note (the secret was Henry's long-term sexual impotence).[25]

Perhaps the soundest scholarly treatment in these years, however, was the balanced, but rather conventional picture drawn by the ecclesiastical historian and Anglican priest Henry Maynard Smith in his *Henry VIII and the Reformation* of 1948. Maynard Smith was no admirer of Henry as an individual, or as a principled statesman. Like most renaissance princes, he "thought only of his own interests and of what was expedient." In his dealings with others, whether foreign princes or subjects like Robert Aske, Henry was a dissimulator. He was capable of protecting friends – Cranmer, Catherine Parr, or George Blagge – where the security of the state was not at issue, but he would ruthlessly sacrifice his closest servants when his own interests were involved. He was also, "like many cruel men," a sentimentalist, easily moved to laughter or tears. Unlike Charles Oman, Maynard Smith was happy to endorse the gradual moral decline theory of Henry's career, pointing to "the slow corruption of his nature due to his long enjoyment of unrestricted power." Henry had begun his reign with a zest for life, a desire for pleasure and an insatiable craving for applause. "He ended his life as a gloomy tyrant, no longer capable of pleasure, who found his one satisfaction in seeing the men about him grovel at his feet."

But at the same time, Maynard Smith was more than willing to recognize Henry's achievements: "without perhaps intending to do so, he founded a secularised state and may be called the Maker of Modern England." Over the course of his reign, England's power and prestige overseas was enhanced, along with the foundations of naval power and the improvement of trade; at home, the remnants of feudalism were stamped out, and law and order was established in Wales; the privy council began to serve as the executive of the state; and parliament became "a real legislative assembly." Little of this was planned. Henry was no far-sighted statesman, working from a blueprint to achieve autocracy in England. He was, rather, a brilliant pragmatist or opportunist who retro-spectively appealed to general principles, or to authority and tradition, in order to justify the obtaining of immediate objectives. This was true

also of his religious policy, though here Maynard Smith recognized that
Henry was no shameless hypocrite, but a genuinely religious man with
an intelligent grasp of his faith. Maynard Smith's Anglo-Catholicism
made him an instinctive anti-Erastian, but it was to Henry's credit that
"he never intended that Parliament should have any voice in determining
the doctrine, discipline or ritual of the Church. His supremacy was
personal and pertained to himself alone."

Maynard Smith had little doubt that tyranny was the appropriate
designation for the pattern of kingship exercised by Henry, the man
who "proclaimed himself God's Vicar, so that disagreement with him,
apart from disobedience, was an unforgivable sin." In medieval England,
individuals and institutions possessed rights, the recognition of which is
the condition of freedom. But in Henry's kingdom no rights could be
asserted against the crown. Maynard Smith's attitude towards Henry, like
that of many preceding writers, in fact encased a striking paradox: the
price of the king's real and remarkable achievements was the discredit that
they reflected upon him, and his was a life lived in tragic mode. "Henry
was always an egoist, but he was not always a detestable egoist. Had he, for
instance, died in 1525 he would have been a favourite hero for writers of
romance, and grave historians would have speculated on the splendid
things he might have done."[26]

Broadly speaking, this interpretation of Henry – as an ignoble egoma-
niac, but a highly effective ruler and modernizer – was the orthodox
template for the historiography of the 1950s, reflected in standard text-
books like J. D. Mackie's *The Earlier Tudors* for the Oxford History of
England series, and S. T. Bindoff's *Tudor England* for the Pelican History
of England. Mackie's Henry was "brutal, crafty, selfish, and ungenerous,"
but also "a great king." He was respected, even popular, with his subjects,
and that popularity was not unmerited: "he gave to them, or let them
have, the things which were most desired by most of those who were
politically conscious; and he kept the development of England in line
with some of the most vigorous, though not the noblest forces of his
day."[27] Bindoff wrote of Henry's "extreme effectiveness"; he was a political master-craftsman, who knew how to make the most of tools like
Wolsey and Cromwell. Nor was he "even in his later degeneracy, the
human monster which one legend has made of him."[28] That these judgments sound distinctly Pollardian is no accident. It is remarkable
that as the 1960s dawned, no serious scholarly biography of Henry had
been published since Pollard's in 1902. Most assessments of Henry in
the interim had been variants on a theme. While Charles H. Williams's

thesis of a system of early Tudor despotism had not been universally accepted, through the first half of the twentieth century the designations "tyrant" and "despot" were regularly used in connection with Henry.[29] Attitudes to the king himself, as a man, father, husband, and master, ranged from mildly indulgent disapproval to full-blown moral outrage. But all agreed that Henry was the driving force of the extraordinary events of his reign.

Yet a revolution was brewing in Tudor studies in the 1950s. Its architect was the Cambridge scholar, and pre-eminent Tudor political historian of the middle half of the twentieth century, Geoffrey Elton, whose doctoral thesis, revised in 1953 as *The Tudor Revolution in Government*, argued that Thomas Cromwell was the originator of a fundamental restructuring of English government in the 1530s.[30] In a celebrated article of 1954, Elton posed the question "King or Minister?: The Man behind the Henrician Reformation," and came down firmly on the side of the minister.[31] A few years later, in 1962, Elton took the occasion provided by a Historical Association pamphlet to consider directly the personal and political qualities of Henry VIII, subtitling the work "an essay in revision." This essay was a thoroughgoing critique of the picture painted by Pollard, in particular his interpretation of a king who, after he had matured as a statesman and thrown off the tutelage of Wolsey, personally devised, dominated, and directed the policy of state. Like Oman before him, Elton simply did not buy the concept of the early Henry as an innocent youth, who only gradually picked up political skills along with a talent for ruthlessness. Pollard, Elton thought, "glides easily over the executions of Empson and Dudley." Like all men, Henry changed with age, but "he did so within clearly defined limits of character, intellect and purpose." There was no slow evolution from playboy to statesman, as Henry "had never really been the first and was never really to be the second." In Elton's opinion, Pollard also failed to appreciate the marked contrast between the effectiveness and direction of policy initiatives in the 1530s, and their ineffectual drift into pointless foreign engagements in the following decade. It followed either that "Henry VIII was not the unfailing political genius of Pollard's imagining," or that policy in the second half of the reign was not so exclusively dominated by one man.

In fact, Elton believed both these suggestions to be true, the common factor being the removal of the guiding hand (and head) of Thomas Cromwell in 1540. Elton's Henry was profoundly influenced and manipulated by those around him, not least in the matter of Cromwell's fall.

"A man who marries six wives is not a man who perfectly controls his own fate." This did not mean that Henry was not a powerful personal monarch, who "always remained the last and ultimately decisive factor in government." But although shrewd and forceful, Henry was also a shallow and unoriginal opportunist, leaving the detailed formulation of secular or religious policy to subordinates, and picking between the options they generated. Elton doubted if Henry was really the architect of anything, "least of all the English Reformation." The only business in which Henry from first to last consistently took the lead was the harrying of political opponents, an area where his personal participation resulted in "real viciousness." Nonetheless, Elton's assessment of the king's achievements was by no means entirely negative. Pursuit of his selfish desires did not necessarily do damage to the realm, and he was a monarch who knew how to take advice and delegate power. "Better men without these gifts have certainly done much greater harm; Henry VIII, neither a good nor a wise man, employed them to make himself into a great king."[32]

Elton's pamphlet consciously threw down a gauntlet to would-be biographers, emphasizing the challenge posed to them by "a man of such evident powers, equipped with such mixed qualities and presiding over such catastrophic events."[33] The mid-1960s, in fact, witnessed a renewed spurt of Henry VIII biography: no fewer than four studies appeared in rapid succession between 1962 and 1964, though none of these really answered the Eltonian clarion call. Three of them, by the local historian John Joseph Bagley, the popular writer Beatrice Saunders, and the novelist Nancy Brysson Morrison, were lightweight affairs; the fourth, by John Bowles, a solid but conventional biography in fairly Pollardian mold.[34] Further "life and times"-type studies appeared just after the end of the decade from the pens of Neville Williams and Robert Lacey.[35]

In the meantime, however, the first original academic biography of Henry in two-thirds of a century had materialized, making its appearance in a year of political and cultural turmoil on university campuses, 1968. Its author was J. J. – "Jack" – Scarisbrick, appropriately enough a former student of Elton's, and freshly appointed to a chair of history at the recently founded University of Warwick. Scarisbrick's book was avowedly "neither a 'private life' of Henry VIII nor a comprehensive study of his life and times," but something in-between. It was in fact the best sort of political biography, making full use of the manuscript sources in the Public Record Office, where Pollard had largely confined himself to the calendars of documents in *Letters and papers*. Scarisbrick's assessment of Henrician rule was considerably closer to Elton's than to Pollard's.

He rejected the latter's perception that Wolsey's foreign policy served his own papal ambitions, and he accepted that Thomas Cromwell was "a genius, perhaps the most accomplished servant any English monarch has enjoyed, a royal minister who cut a deeper mark on the history of England than have many of her monarchs."[36] Nonetheless, Scarisbrick was not prepared to follow Elton's lead in regarding Cromwell as the brains behind the break with Rome, seeing the minister merely as "the executant of the king's designs" in the creation of the royal supremacy.[37] In that sense, his Henry was a more traditional one than Elton's, the undisputed colossus of the political arena.

But Scarisbrick dramatically broke ranks with the majority of previous scholarly interpreters, including the revisionist Elton, in concluding that Henry VIII was not only a bad man but an egregiously bad king as well. Henry directed the divorce campaign, but he also mishandled it, losing an opportunity to exploit a weakness in the original bull of dispensation.[38] The judgments in Scarisbrick's concluding chapter, "Henry the King," were damning ones, both on a personal level – "it is difficult to think of any truly generous or selfless action performed by him" – and on a political one: "rarely, if ever, have the unawareness and irresponsibility of a king proved more costly of material benefit to his people." Henry's foreign policy, with its pattern of military adventures in France, produced nothing of material value and only fleeting prestige; meanwhile, the opportunities presented by the discovery of the New World were ignored. Another opportunity – to bestow the confiscated wealth of English monasticism on social and educational reform – was similarly squandered, while the artistic and cultural heritage the monasteries represented was obliterated in a campaign of destruction unparalleled since the Danish invasions. As well as beautiful buildings, Henry struck down "incomparable men and women" – Catherine of Aragon, Thomas More, Robert Aske, John Fisher, Cromwell – and the king who promised to lead England out of papal bondage ended up imposing unprecedented levels of taxation on the English Church. Was all this a necessary price to be paid for dynastic security? Scarisbrick thought not. The king's efforts to solve his dynastic problem were for ten years "dangerously unsuccessful," and they were not particularly happy thereafter. What he *had* achieved was bitter religious division, "sending fissures down English society to its lowest strata and setting neighbour against neighbour, father against son, in a disunity from which that society has not yet fully recovered."[39] The model of Henry and his reign constructed by Pollard is here turned inside out, and its essential hollowness exposed.

Scarisbrick's acerbic view of Henry and his achievements was arguably what one might expect from a Catholic scholar of a fairly conservative hue. But an equally negative portrayal was soon forthcoming from another quarter, academic biographies of the king proving to be like buses, with two coming along in quick succession after a long period of waiting. The American historian Lacey Baldwin Smith, who had earlier offered some pungent assessments of Henry's character in a biography of Catherine Howard, produced in 1971 a life of Henry which the publishers billed as "an enthralling study of the monarch behind the mask."[40] Smith discarded the conventional chronological framework of a biography in favor of a sequence of thematically focused essays on aspects of the king's character and their impact on court and national politics. The Henry who emerges is, from first to last, self-pitying, shallow, humorless, emotionally unstable, superstitious, hypocritical, and irresponsible. Although possessed of a quick mind, he was "devoid of speculative thinking," substituting habits of compilation and cataloguing for real thought. His principal talent was for manipulation and control of those around him, something in which he took an "intensely personal pleasure." Smith detected a pattern of "perversity and mental sadism" in Henry's dealings with his leading servants, and like Scarisbrick, he suspected that J. C. Flügel may have been right about the king's Oedipus complex.[41]

Smith's was to be the last full scholarly life of Henry published in the twentieth century.[42] After Scarisbrick and Smith, there perhaps seemed nowhere for a biographer to go, other than towards full-scale personal rehabilitation, and that was a direction Tudor historians were on the whole markedly unwilling to take. From the late 1970s, the scholarship on the early Tudor period concerned itself principally with debates about the structures of government and the mechanisms of Henrician politics, though in these questions the role and personality of the king naturally remained important. The controversy kicked up by Elton's "revolution in government" thesis had, by the 1980s, more or less resolved itself into an emergent consensus that Henrician government remained in fundamental ways unbureaucratic, and that the court was a crucial focus of both political and administrative activity.[43] This, of course, served to highlight further questions of the king's personal responsibility for the formulation of policy. An undergraduate essay title the present writer was required to attempt in the mid-1980s – "Was Henry VIII the puppet or the puppet-master of politics in his reign?" – represents a more or less reasonable summary of an academic debate that rumbled through the last two decades of the twentieth century, as historians argued over whether "faction" was a structural condition of Henrician politics, and, if so, whether Henry was able to use the factions to pursue his own agenda (as L. B. Smith had suggested), or was maneuvered by them into policy positions he might not otherwise have chosen.[44]

This late twentieth-century scholarship attained to levels of evidential and methodological sophistication unknown in the era of Gairdner and Pollard, though as far as the assessment of Henry VIII was concerned, much of it represented variations on an old theme. Another early twentieth-century problem – whether Henry's exercise of personal monarchy exemplifies coherence and continuity across the reign or inconsistency and contrasts – also continued to be explored. Interestingly, here historians were now beginning to find connections and continuities in the one area where virtually all earlier scholarship had assumed a 180-degree turn: the king's religious attitudes. Two leading interpreters, George Bernard and Diarmaid MacCulloch, though they disagree about how coherent Henry's religious policies were after the break with Rome, both find traces of the later reformer in the young Henry: in an incipient anticlericalism, for example, and in a critical outlook on shrines and popular religion.[45]

In another respect, the interpretative wheel has come full circle over the course of the twentieth century. Pollard's reluctance to sit in moral judgment on the king's actions, and to weigh dispassionately the constructive and destructive effects of his policies, finds a strong echo in the work of David Starkey, the historian who has emerged at the end of the century as the new doyen of early Tudor political history. In the introduction to the 1991 catalogue of an exhibition commemorating the five-hundredth anniversary of Henry's birth, Starkey presented Henry as the monarch who "built and accumulated more than any other English king," but also "demolished, destroyed and dispersed more." There was no obvious way for us to decide, Starkey argued, whether the glories of the royal library cancelled out the dispersal of monastic ones, or whether the building of fifty-five royal palaces compensated for the dissolution of several hundred religious houses.[46] After half a lifetime's work on the Henrician court and politics, Starkey in 2008 finally published a study of Henry himself, one of a clutch of scholarly lives of the king to appear in the first decade of the new century, thereby ending a more than thirty-year dearth of academic Henry biography.[47] Yet here too there are Pollardian echoes. For Starkey decided initially to tackle only the first part of Henry's life, insisting that "there are *two* Henrys ... the one old, the other young," and asserting a greater contrast between them than some post-Pollard interpretations were prepared to allow.[48]

All historical reputations fluctuate, a function of the changing political and cultural contexts in which history is read and of the need for scholarship to sustain itself by emphasizing the inadequacy of what has been written before. Although few have questioned the fact that Henry's was a reign of more than usual historical significance, there is also little doubt that the claims of the second Tudor to statesmanship or "greatness" took a significant battering over the course of the twentieth century, the century in which England lost the empire that Henry (arguably) set her on course to obtain, and in which the Protestant religion for which he acted as unwitting godfather effectively ceased to be a key source of national identity. Perceptions of the king's effectiveness as a political operator dipped in the mid-twentieth century, and (in some quarters at least) have risen again. But there has been little or no corresponding positive reassessment of Henry's character and qualities.[49] The theme is, of course, scarcely separable from the analysis of politics. In a personal monarchy, the personality of the monarch is a fundamental determinant of political events.

Yet it is striking how in modern times, despite the emergence of scientific psychology, the objectivity to which practicing historians are professionally committed, and the supposed moral relativism characterizing developed Western societies, questions of Henry's moral culpability – framed in terms of character defect – have rarely been ducked or evaded by either popular or academic authors. It is possibly true that over much of the last century the tone of popular historical writing has been slightly more forgiving towards Henry than that of academic scholarship, though this is a question on which one hesitates to generalize. In the introduction to her 1963 pop-biography of the king, Beatrice Saunders candidly admitted that "I have searched in vain, in my efforts to be fair to Henry, for any redeeming feature in his character."[50] More recently, on the front cover of a book entitled *Monsters: History's Most Evil Men and Women*, the Holbein bust-portrait of Henry appears, flanked by images of Hitler, Stalin, and Lucrezia Borgia.[51] Admiration for Henry the man, even in the hands of a Froude or a Pollard, was never unqualified, and the qualifications have tended to grow rather than diminish. The nineteenth century's most memorable epitome of Henry was that of Charles Dickens in his *Child's History*: "a disgrace to human nature, and a blot of blood and grease upon the History of England."[52] The twentieth century could not quite match that, though some of its judgments have been scarcely less pejorative. What the scholarship of the twenty-first century will make of him – once it has recovered from the excitement of the five-hundredth anniversary of his accession – remains to be seen. But it seems unlikely that attempts to fathom and comprehend Henry VIII's psychological make-up and personality facets will cease any time soon. For the enduring fascination of Henry for both popular and academic biographers stems from the fact that his "tyranny" was not so much the expression of a system of governance as the tone governing a web of personal relationships. He remains an unrivalled case-study in the effect of untrammeled power on the development of a personality, and of a personality on power.

NOTES

1. J. A. Froude, *The Reign of Henry VIII*, 3 vols. (London: J. M. Dent, 1908).
2. F. A. Gasquet, *Henry VIII and the English Monasteries*, 2 vols. (London: John Hodges, 1889), II, 585–6.
3. William Stubbs, *Seventeen Lectures on the Study of Medieval and Modern History and Kindred Subjects* (Oxford: Clarendon Press, 1886), 241–91, quotations at 244, 291, 261, 244.
4. Available in the *DNB* archive at E. W. Ives's entry on Henry VIII in the *ODNB* (online).
5. Patrick Collinson, "Pollard, Albert Frederick (1869–1948)," *ODNB* (online).
6. A. F. Pollard, *Henry VIII* (London: Longmans, [1902] 1905), v, 26, 100–1, 343.
7. Ibid., 196; A. F. Pollard, *Wolsey* (London: Longmans, 1929), 366–70.
8. Pollard, *Henry VIII*, 187–91, 206–22, 344–9, quotations at 207, 211, 222, 344–5.
9. Ibid., quotations at 351–2, 268, 195, 67, 259, 343.
10. Ibid., 352–3.
11. J. Gairdner, "Henry VIII," in A. W. Ward, *et al.* (eds.), *The Reformation*, Cambridge Modern History, II (Cambridge: Cambridge University Press, [1903] 1934), quotations at 462, 473, 470.
12. Graham Richards, "Flügel, John Carl (1884–1955)," *ODNB* (online).
13. J. C. Flügel, "On the Character and Married life of Henry VIII," *International Journal of Psychoanalysis* 1 (1920), 24–55, quotations at 54, 25, 32, 38, 41, 55, 39–40.
14. Francis Hackett, *Henry the Eighth* (London: Cape, 1930); Frederick Chamberlin, *The Private Character of Henry VIII* (London: John Lane, 1931); Helen Simpson, *Henry VIII* (London: P. Davies, 1934).
15. Muriel St. Clare Byrne (ed.), *The Letters of King Henry VIII: A Selection with a few other Documents* (London: Cassell, 1936), quotations at ix, xvi, xiii, 135, iv, x.
16. See Paddy Griffith, "Oman, Sir Charles William Chadwick (1860–1946)," *ODNB* (online).
17. C. W. C. Oman, "The Personality of Henry VIII," *Quarterly Review* 269 (July, 1937), 88–104, quotations at 89, 92, 101, 92, 104, 98, 97, 99–100.
18. Milton Waldman, *Some English Dictators* (London: Blackie, 1940).

19. George Orwell, "Catastrophic Gradualism," in S. Orwell and I. Angus (eds.), *The Collected Essays, Journalism and Letters of George Orwell: An Age like This: 1920–1940* (London: Secker & Warburg, 1968), 16–17.

20. A. L. Rowse, *Ralegh and the Throckmortons* (London: Macmillan, 1962), 266.

21. C. J. Wrigley, *A. J. P. Taylor: Radical Historian of Europe* (London: I. B. Tauris, 2006), 229.

22. L. B. Smith, "The 'taste for Tudors' since 1940," *Studies in the Renaissance* 7 (1960), 167–83, at 168.

23. T. Maynard, *Henry the Eighth* (Milwaukee: Bruce Pub. Co., 1949). See T. W. Hendriks, "Theodore Maynard: A Historian of American Catholicism – 1890–1956," *Modern Age* 45:1 (1 January 2003), 37–48.

24. A. S. MacNalty, *Henry VIII: A Difficult Patient* (London: Christopher Johnson, 1952), 182–3.

25. Philip Lindsay, *The Secret of Henry the Eighth* (London: Meridian Books, 1953).

26. H. Maynard Smith, *Henry VIII and the Reformation* (London: Macmillan, 1948), quotations at 228, 230, 231, 226, 232, 236, 228–9.

27. J. D. Mackie, *The Earlier Tudors 1485–1558* (Oxford: Clarendon Press, 1952), 442–3.

28. S. T. Bindoff, *Tudor England* (Harmondsworth: Penguin Books, 1950), 96.

29. C. H. Williams, *The Making of the Tudor Despotism* (London: Nelson, 1928).

30. G. R. Elton, *The Tudor Revolution in Government: Administrative Changes in the Reign of Henry VIII* (Cambridge: Cambridge University Press, 1953).

31. G. R. Elton, "King or Minister?: The Man behind the Henrician Reformation," *History* 39 (1954), 216–32.

32. G. R. Elton, *Henry VIII: An Essay in Revision* (London: Routledge & Kegan Paul, 1962), quotations at 8–9, 10, 13, 8, 11, 27, 15, 26.

33. Ibid., 28.

34. J. J. Bagley, *Henry VIII and His Times* (London: Batsford, 1962); B. Saunders, *Henry the Eighth* (London: Alvin Redman, 1963); N. B. Morrison, *The Private Life of Henry VIII* (London: Hale, 1964); J. Bowles, *Henry VIII: A Biography* (London: Allen and Unwin, 1964).

35. N. Williams, *Henry VIII and His Court* (London: Weidenfeld and Nicolson, 1971); R. Lacey, *The Life and Times of Henry VIII* (London: Weidenfeld and Nicolson, 1972).

36. J. J. Scarisbrick, *Henry VIII* (London: Methuen, 1968), ix, 46–50, 383.

37. Ibid., 304. See here Elton's criticisms on this point in an otherwise laudatory review essay: "The King of Hearts," in Elton, *Studies in Tudor and Stuart Politics and Government: Papers and Reviews 1946–1972* (Cambridge: Cambridge University Press, 2003), 100–8.

38. Scarisbrick, *Henry VIII*, 196–7.

39. Ibid., 498–526, quotations at 507, 526, 509, 508.

40. L. B. Smith, *A Tudor Tragedy: The Life and Times of Catherine Howard* (London: Jonathan Cape, 1961); L. B. Smith, *Henry VIII: The Mask of Royalty* (St Albans: Panther Books, [1971] 1973), rear cover.

41. Smith, *A Tudor Tragedy*, 23–4, 28, 31, 71, 104. Cf. Scarisbrick, *Henry VIII*, 17.

42. Two substantial popular biographies were published in the 1980s. Carolly Erickson's *Great Harry* (London: J. M. Dent, 1980) follows a conventional character arc from an attractive "young Harry" to the "inhuman tyrant" of the 1540s (14); Jasper Ridley, *Henry VIII* (London: Constable, 1984) is unsympathetic to the king.

43. See C. Coleman and D. Starkey (eds.), *Revolution Reassessed: Revisions in the History of Tudor Government and Administration* (Oxford: Clarendon Press, 1986).

44. For the "factional" view, see E. W. Ives, *Faction in Tudor England*, 2nd edn. (London: Historical Association, 1986); E. W. Ives, "Henry VIII: The Political Perspective," in Diarmaid MacCulloch (ed.), *The Reign of Henry VIII: Politics, Policy and Piety* (New York: St Martin's Press, 1995), 13–34; D. R. Starkey, "From Feud to Faction," *History Today* 32 (November 1982), 16–22; and D. R. Starkey, *The Reign of Henry VIII: Personalities and Politics* (London: George Philip, 1985). Contrast G. W. Bernard, "Politics and Government in Tudor England," *Historical Journal* 31 (1988), 159–67; P. Gwyn, *The King's Cardinal: The Rise and Fall of Thomas Wolsey* (London: Barrie and Jenkins, 1990); and Greg Walker, *Persuasive Fictions: Faction, Faith, and Political Culture in the Reign of Henry VIII* (Aldershot: Scolar Press, 1996).

45. MacCulloch, "Henry VIII and the Reform of the Church," in MacCulloch (ed.), *The Reign of Henry VIII*, 165–6; G. W. Bernard, "The Piety of Henry VIII," in N. S. Amos, A. Pettegree, and H. van Nierop (eds.), *The Education of a Christian Society: Humanism and Reform in Britain and the Netherlands* (Aldershot: Ashgate, 1999), 62–88.

46. David Starkey, "The Legacy of Henry VIII," in David Starkey (ed.), *Henry VIII: A European Court in England* (London: Collins Brown in association with the National Maritime Museum, 1991), 8–13, quotation at 8.

47. The others are M. A. R. Graves, *Henry VIII: A Study in Kingship* (Harlow: Pearson, 2003); D. Loades, *Henry VIII: Court, Church and Conflict* (London: The National Archives, 2007); Eric Ives, *Henry VIII* (Oxford: Oxford University Press, 2007), based on Ives's entry on Henry for *ODNB*; L. Wooding, *Henry VIII* (London: Routledge, 2009). The latter, a balanced and persuasive survey, emphasizes Henry's control of policy and ability to transcend faction, as does G. W. Bernard, *The King's Reformation: Henry VIII and the Remaking of the English Church* (New Haven: Yale University Press, 2005).

48. David Starkey, *Henry: Virtuous Prince* (London: Harper Press, 2008), 3.

49. Note here, in a short book, the twenty-two separate index entries for "weaknesses and the dark side of his character" in Graves, *Henry VIII*.

50. Saunders, *Henry the Eighth*, 10.

51. S. Sebag Montefiore, *Monsters: History's Most Evil Men and Women* (London: Quercus Publishing, 2008).

52. Charles Dickens, *The Works*, ed. A. Lang, 34 vols. (London: Chapman and Hall, 1897–9), vol. XXX, 306.

Select bibliography

PRIMARY SOURCES

Acts of the Privy Council of England, 1542–1631, ed. J. R. Dasent, *et al.* 46 vols. (London, 1890–).

Adams, Barry B. (ed.). *John Bale's "King Johan"* (San Marino: Huntington Library, 1969).

Ashbee, Andrew. *Records of English Court Music.* 9 vols. (Snodland, Kent: the author, 1986–96).

Axton, Richard (ed.). *Three Rastell Plays* (Cambridge: D. S. Brewer, 1979).

Axton, Richard and Peter Happé (eds.). *The Plays of John Heywood* (Cambridge: D. S. Brewer, 1991).

Bale, John. *An expostulation or complaynte agaynste the blasphemyes of a franticke papyst of Hamshyre* (London, 1552).

  Complete Plays of John Bale, ed. Peter Happé. 2 vols. (Cambridge: D. S. Brewer, 1985–6).

  Illustrium maioris Britanniae scriptorium ... summarium (Ipswich [i.e., Wesel], 1548).

  King Johan by John Bale, ed. J. H. Pafford and W. W. Greg. Malone Society Reprint (Oxford: Oxford University Press, 1931).

Bang, W. (ed.). *Bales Kynge John.* Materialien zur Kunde des älteren Englischen Dramas 25 (Louvain: Uystpruyst, 1909).

Banks, John. *Vertue Betray'd: or, Anna Bullen, a Tragedy*, ed. Diane Dreher, Augustan Reprints (Los Angeles: William Andrews Clark Memorial Library, 1891).

Beholde here (gentle reader) a brief abstract of the genealogie of all the kynges of England (London, 1560?).

Birche, William. *A songe betwene the Quenes maiestie and Englande* (London, 1564).

Bond, Donald F. (ed.). *The Tatler.* 3 vols. (Oxford: Clarendon Press, 1987).

Bray, Gerald (ed.). *Documents of the English Reformation* (Minneapolis: Fortress Press, 1994).

Brown, Rawdon (ed. and trans.). *Four Years at the Court of Henry VIII: Selection of Despatches written by the Venetian ambassador, Sebastian Justinian.* 2 vols. (London: Smith, Elder, and Co., 1854; reprinted, New York: AMS Press, 1970).

Bullough, Geoffrey (ed.). *Narrative and Dramatic Sources of Shakespeare.* 8 vols. (Cambridge: Cambridge University Press, 1957–75).

Burnet, Gilbert. *The History of the Reformation of the Church of England*, 2 vols. (London: Henry G. Bohn, 1857).

Butler, Samuel. *Posthumous works in prose and verse, written in the time of the civil wars and reign of K. Charles II. by Mr. Samuel Butler* (London, 1715).

Calendar of the Manuscripts of the Most Honourable the Marquess of Salisbury, ed. Richard Arthur Roberts, *et al.* 24 vols. (London, 1883–1976).

Calendar of State Papers, Domestic Series, of the Reigns of Edward VI, Mary, and Elizabeth, 1547–[1625], ed. Robert Lemon, *et al.* 12 vols. (London: 1856–72).

Calendar of State Papers and Manuscripts, relating to English affairs, existing in the archives and collections of Venice, and in other libraries of Northern Italy, ed. Rawdon Brown, *et al.* 38 vols. in 40 (London, 1864–1947; reprinted, Nendeln, Liechtenstein: Kraus Reprint, 1970–).

Carley, James P. (ed.). *The Libraries of King Henry VIII* (London: The British Library in association with the British Academy, 2000).

Catalogue of the Harleian Manuscripts, in The British Museum, with Indexes of Persons, Places, and Matters, vol. III (London, 1808).

Cavendish, George. *The Life and Death of Cardinal Wolsey*, ed. Richard S. Sylvester (Oxford: Oxford University Press, 1959).

Chaloner, Thomas. *Thomas Chaloner's In Laudem Henrici Octavi*, ed. and trans. John B. Gabel and Carl C. Schlam (Lawrence, KS: Coronado Press, 1979).

Chappell, William. *Popular Music of Olden Times* (London, 1859; revised edition by H. E. Wooldridge, 1893; Dover reprint of the 1859 edition, 1965).

The country spy; or a ramble thro' London. Containing many curious remarks, diverting tales, and merry joaks (London, 1730).

Deloney, Thomas. *The Novels of Thomas Deloney*, ed. Merritt E. Lawlis (Bloomington: Indiana University Press, 1961).

Elton, G. R. (ed.). *The Tudor Constitution: Documents and Commentary*, 2nd edn. (Cambridge: Cambridge University Press, 1982).

Evelyn, John. *Diary and Correspondence of John Evelyn*, ed. William Bray. 4 vols. (London, 1850).

Exwood, Maurice, and H. L. Lehmann (ed. and trans.). *The Journal of William Schellinks' Travels in England 1661–1663*, Camden Society, 5th series, I (London: Royal Historical Society, 1993).

Fielding, Henry. *Contributions to The Champion and Related Writings*, ed. W. B. Coley (Oxford: Clarendon Press, 2003).

Henry Fielding Miscellanies, ed. Bertrand A. Goldgar, vol. II (Oxford: Clarendon Press, 1993).

Forrest, William. *The History of Grisild the Second*, ed. W. D. Macray (London: Roxburghe Club, 1875).

Fortescue, Sir John. *The Governance of England: otherwise called The Difference between an Absolute and a Limited Monarchy*, ed. Charles Plummer (Oxford: Oxford University Press, 1885; reprint, London: Humphrey Milford, 1926).

Foxe, John. *Actes and monuments of these latter and perillous dayes, touching matters of the church* (London, 1563).

Actes and monuments of matters most speciall in the church (London, 1583).

Froude, J. A. (ed.). *The Pilgrim: A Dialogue on the Life and Actions of King Henry the Eighth* (London, 1861).

Ganz, Paul. *The Paintings of Hans Holbein: First Complete Edition* (London: Phaidon Press, 1956).

Gardiner, Stephen. *The Letters of Stephen Gardiner*, ed. James Arthur Muller (Cambridge: Cambridge University Press, 1933).

    Obedience in Church and State: Three Political Tracts, ed. P. Janelle (Cambridge: Cambridge University Press, 1930).

The Great Chronicle of London, ed. A. H. Thomas and I. D. Thornley (London: George W. Jones, 1938).

Greg, W. W. (ed.). *A New Enterlude of Godly Queene Hester*. Materialien zur Kunde des älteren Englischen Dramas 5 (Louvain: Uystpruyst, 1904).

Groos, G. W. (ed. and trans.). *The Diary of Baron Waldstein: A Traveller in Elizabethan England* (London: Thames and Hudson, 1981).

Hall, Edward. *Chronicle*, ed. Henry Ellis (London, 1809). Reprinted New York: AMS Press, 1965.

    Henry VIII, ed. Charles Whibley. 2 vols. (London: T. C. and E. C. Jack, 1904).

    Performance and Spectacle in Hall's Chronicle, ed. Janet Dillon (London: Society for Theatre Research, 2002).

    The union of the two noble and illustre famelies of Lancastre [and] Yorke (London, 1548).

Hayward, Maria (ed. and transcr.). *The 1542 Inventory of Whitehall: The Palace and Its Keeper*. 2 vols. (London: Illuminata Publishers, 2004).

Henry VIII, King of England. *The Letters of King Henry VIII: A Selection with a Few Other Documents*, ed. M. St. Clare Byrne (London: Cassell, 1936).

Herbert, Edward, Baron Herbert of Cherbury. *The Life and Raigne of Henry VIII* (1649).

Hogarth, William. *The Analysis of Beauty* (1753), ed. Ronald Paulson (New Haven: Yale University Press, 1997).

Holbein and the Court of Henry VIII. The Queen's Gallery exhibition catalogue (London: Buckingham Palace, 1978).

Holinshed, Raphael. *The Third volume of Chronicles, beginning at duke William the Norman* (London, 1586).

Hooper, John. *The later writings of Bishop Hooper*, ed. Charles Nevinson (Cambridge: Parker Society, 1852).

Howard, Henry, earl of Surrey. *Poems*, ed. Emrys Jones (Oxford: Clarendon Press, 1964).

Hume, David. *The History of England from the Invasion of Julius Caesar to the Abdication of James the Second, 1688*. 6 vols. (Boston, 1853).

Hume, Martin A. Sharp (ed. and trans.). *Chronicle of King Henry VIII of England. Being a Contemporary Record of some of the Principal Events of the Reigns of Henry VIII. and Edward VI. Written in Spanish* (London: George Bell and Sons, 1889).

James I, King of England. *Basilicon Doron* (Edinburgh: Robert Waldegrave, 1599).

    King James VI and I: Political Writings, ed. Johann P. Sommerville (Cambridge: Cambridge University Press, 1994).

Knighton, C. S., and D. M. Loades (eds.). *The Anthony Roll of Henry VIII's Navy. Pepys Library 2991 and British Library Additional MS 22047 with related documents* (Aldershot: Ashgate Publishing Company for the Navy Records Society, 2000).

Latimer, Hugh. *Select Sermons of Hugh Latimer*, ed. Allan G. Chester (Charlottesville: University Press of Virginia for the Folger Shakespeare Library, 1968).

    Sermons by Hugh Latimer, ed. George Elwes Corrie (Cambridge: Parker Society, 1844).

Letters and Papers, Foreign and Domestic, of the Reign of Henry VIII, 1509–1547, ed. James Gairdner, *et al.* (London, 1862–1910, 1920).

Lord, George de Forest (ed.). *Poems on Affairs of State*. 7 vols. (New Haven: Yale University Press, 1963–1975).

Mayer, Thomas F. (ed.). *The Correspondence of Reginald Pole*. 4 vols. (Aldershot: Ashgate, 2002–2008).

Merriman, Roger Bigelow (ed.). *Life and Letters of Thomas Cromwell*. 2 vols. (Oxford: Clarendon Press, 1902).

Nashe, Thomas. *The Works of Thomas Nashe*, ed. Ronald B. McKerrow with F. P. Wilson. 5 vols. (Oxford: Blackwell, 1958). Originally published 1904–10.

Nichols, John Gough (ed.). *Literary Remains of King Edward the Sixth*. 2 vols. (London: Roxburghe Club, 1857).

Opie, Iona, and Peter Opie (eds.). *The Oxford Dictionary of Nursery Rhymes* (Oxford: Clarendon Press, 1952).

The Passage of our Most Drad Sovereign Lady Queen Elizabeth through the City of London to Westminster the Day before her Coronation (London, 1558).

The pleasant and delightful history of King Henry the VIII, and the Abbot of Reading. Declaring how the King dined with the Abbot of Reading, and how the King brought the Abbot to a good stomach, &c. (London, 1680).

Quarrell, W. H. and Margaret Mare (ed. and trans.). *London in 1710 from the Travels of Zacharias Conrad Von Uffenbach* (London: Faber and Faber, 1934).

Ridley, Nicholas. *The Works of Nicholas Ridley, DD*, ed. Henry Christmas (Cambridge: Parker Society, 1853).

Rowley, Samuel. *When You See Me, You Know Me* (London, 1605). Subsequent editions 1613, 1621, and 1632.

Shakespeare, William. *Henry VIII*, ed. Gordon McMullan, *The Arden Shakespeare* (London: Thomson Learning, 2000).

Sidney, Sir Philip. *The Defence of Poesy*, in Gavin Alexander (ed.), *Sidney's "The Defence of Poesy" and Selected Renaissance Literary Criticism* (London: Penguin, 2004).

Skelton, John. *Magnificence*, ed. Paula Neuss (Manchester: Manchester University Press, 1980).

Speed, John. *The history of Great Britaine* (London, 1611).

Spenser, Edmund. *The Faerie Queene*, 2nd edn., ed. A. C. Hamilton (Harlow: Pearson Education, 2007).

The Yale Edition of the Shorter Poems of Edmund Spenser, ed. William Oram, *et al.* (New Haven and London: Yale University Press, 1989).

Starkey, David (ed.). *The Inventory of Henry VIII: The Transcript* (London: Harvey Miller Publishers, 1998).

The Statutes of the Realm. 12 vols. (London: Record Commission, 1810–28).

Stevens, John (ed.). *Music at the Court of Henry VIII*, Musica Britannica, XVIII (London: Stainer and Bell, 1962).

Stow, John. *A Summarie of the Chronicles of England* (London, 1590).

Swift, Jonathan. *Directions to Servants and Miscellaneous Pieces 1733–1742*, ed. Herbert Davis (Oxford: Blackwell, 1959).

Miscellaneous and Autobiographical Pieces, Fragments and Marginalia, ed. Herbert Davis (Oxford: Blackwell, 1962).

A Proposal for Correcting the English Tongue, Polite Conversation, etc., ed. Herbert Davis and Louis Landa (Oxford: Blackwell, 1964).

Taylor, John. *A Briefe Remembrance of all the English Monarchs* (London, 1618). Subsequent editions 1621, 1622.

Tottel, Richard (ed.). *Songs and Sonnets, written by Henry Howard Late Earl of Surrey, and Other* (London, 1557).

Tunstall, Cuthbert. *Certaine godly and deuout prayers*, tr. Thomas Paynell (London, 1558).

Turner, William. *The huntyng of the romyshe vuolfe* (Emden, 1555).

The rescuynge of the Romishe fox other vvyse called the examination of the hunter … The seconde course of the hunter at the romishe fox (Bonn, 1545).

Van Lennep, W., *et al.* (eds.). *The London Stage 1660–1800: A Calendar of Plays, Entertainments and Afterpieces, together with Casts, Box-Receipts and Contemporary Comment*, 5 vols. in 11 (Carbondale, IL: Southern Illinois University Press, 1960–8).

Vergil, Polydore. *The Anglica Historia of Polydore Vergil*, ed. and trans. Dennis Hay (London: Camden Society, 3rd series, vol. LXXIV, 1950).

Von Bülow, Gottfried (ed.). "Diary of the Journey of Philip Julius, Duke of Stettin-Pomerania, through England in the year 1602," *Transactions of the Royal Historical Society*, new series, 6 (1892), 1–67.

Walpole, Horace. *Horace Walpole's Miscellaneous Correspondence*, ed. W. S. Lewis and John Riely, 3 vols. (New Haven: Yale University Press, 1980).

Memoirs of King George II, ed. John Brooke (New Haven: Yale University Press, 1985).

The Yale Edition of Horace Walpole's Correspondence, ed. W. S. Lewis, *et al.* 48 vols. in 49 (New Haven: Yale University Press, 1937–83).

Walpole, Horace (ed. and trans.). *Paul Hentzner's Travels in England during the Reign of Queen Elizabeth* (London, 1797).

Williams, Clare (ed. and trans.). *Thomas Platter's Travels in England, 1599* (London: Jonathan Cape, 1937).

Wyatt, Sir Thomas. *The Complete Poems*, ed. R. A. Rebholz (New Haven: Yale University Press, 1981).

SECONDARY SOURCES

Anderson, Judith H. *Biographical Truth: The Representations of Historical Persons in Tudor-Stuart Writing* (New Haven: Yale University Press, 1984).

Anglo, Sydney. *The Great Tournament Roll of Westminster* (Oxford: Clarendon Press, 1968).

Images of Tudor Kingship (London: Seaby, 1992).

Spectacle, Pageantry and Early Tudor Policy, 2nd edn. (Oxford: Clarendon Press, 1997).

Ashbee, Andrew. "Groomed for Service: Musicians in the Privy Chamber at the English Court, c.1495–1558," *Early Music* (May 1997), 185–97.

Ashbee, Andrew and David Lasocki, assisted by Peter Holman and Fiona Kisby. *A Biographical Dictionary of English Court Musicians 1485–1714.* 2 vols. (Aldershot: Ashgate, 1998).

Auberlen, Eckhard. "King Henry VIII – Shakespeare's Break with the Bluff-King-Harry Tradition," *Anglia* 98 (1980), 319–47.

Auerbach, Erich. *Mimesis: The Representation of Reality in Western Literature* (Princeton: Princeton University Press, 1968).

Barthes, Roland. "The Discourse of History," trans. Stephen Bann, *Comparative Criticism* 3 (1981), 3–20.

Baumann, Uwe (ed.). *Henry VIII in History, Historiography and Literature* (Frankfurt am Main: Peter Lang, 1992).

Bernard, G. W. "The Fall of Anne Boleyn: A Rejoinder," *English Historical Review*, 107 (1992), 665–74.

The King's Reformation: Henry VIII and the Remaking of the English Church (New Haven: Yale University Press, 2005).

"Politics and Government in Tudor England," *Historical Journal* 31 (1988), 159–67.

Power and Politics in Tudor England (Aldershot: Ashgate, 2000).

"The Tyranny of Henry VIII," in G. W. Bernard and S. J. Gunn (eds.), *Authority and Consent in Tudor England: Essays Presented to C. S. L. Davies* (Aldershot: Ashgate, 2002), 113–29.

Bevington, David. *Tudor Drama and Politics: A Critical Approach to Topical Meaning* (Cambridge, MA: Harvard University Press, 1968).

Blair, Claude. "The Emperor Maximilian's Gift of Armour to King Henry VIII and the Silvered and Engraved Armour at the Tower of London," *Archaeologia*, 2nd series, 99 (1965), 1–52.

"King Henry VIII's Tonlet Armour," in *The Burlington House Fair*, 19–29 October 1983 (London: British Antique Dealers' Association, 1983).

Blair, Claude, and Stuart W. Pyhrr. "The Wilton 'Montmorency' Armor: An Italian Armor for Henry VIII," *Metropolitan Museum Journal* 38 (2003), 96–9.

Borg, Alan. "The Ram's Horn Helmet," *Journal of the Arms and Armour Society* 8 (1974), 127–37.

Brooke, Xanthe, and David Crombie. *Henry VIII Revealed: Holbein's Portrait and Its Legacy*, exhibition catalogue (Liverpool: Walker Art Gallery, 2003; London: Paul Holberton, 2004).

Campbell, Thomas P. *Henry VIII and the Art of Majesty: Tapestries at the Tudor Court* (New Haven and London: Yale University Press, 2007).

Carley, James P. *The Books of King Henry VIII and His Wives* (London: The British Library, 2004).

De Certeau, Michel. *The Writing of History*, trans. Tom Conley (New York: Columbia University Press, 1988).

Dillon, Janette. "John Rastell's Stage," *Medieval English Theatre* 18 (1996), 15–45.

Doran, Susan and Thomas S. Freeman (eds.). *Tudors and Stuarts on Film: Historical Perspectives* (London: Palgrave, 2008).

Doran, Susan and Glenn Richardson (eds.). *Tudor England and Its Neighbors* (Basingstoke: Palgrave Macmillan, 2005).

Elton, G. R. *Henry VIII: An Essay in Revision* (London: Routledge & Kegan Paul, 1962.

"The King of Hearts," in G. R. Elton, *Studies in Tudor and Stuart Politics and Government: Papers and Reviews 1946–1972* (Cambridge: Cambridge University Press, 2003), 100–8.

"King or Minister?: The Man behind the Henrician Reformation," *History* 39 (1954), 216–32.

Policy and Police: The Enforcement of the Reformation in the Age of Thomas Cromwell (Cambridge: Cambridge University Press, 1972).

The Tudor Revolution in Government: Administrative Changes in the Reign of Henry VIII (Cambridge: Cambridge University Press, 1953).

Fallows, David. "Henry VIII as a Composer," in C. A. Banks, *et al.* (eds.), *Sundry Sorts of Music Books: Essays on the British Library Collections* (London: The British Library, 1993), 27–39.

Fisher, Will. *Materializing Gender in Early Modern English Literature and Culture* (Cambridge: Cambridge University Press, 2006).

Flügel, J. C. "On the Character and Married Life of Henry VIII," *International Journal of Psychoanalysis* 1 (1920), 24–55.

Foister, Susan. *Holbein and England* (New Haven and London: Yale University Press, 2004).

"Holbein's Paintings on Canvas: The Greenwich Festivities of 1527," in Mark Roskell and John Oliver Hand (eds.), *Hans Holbein: Paintings, Prints, and Reception* (Washington, DC: National Gallery of Art, 2001), 109–24.

Fox, Alistair. *Politics and Literature in the Reigns of Henry VII and Henry VIII* (Oxford: Basil Blackwell, 1989).

Freeman, Thomas S. "A Tyrant for All Seasons," in Susan Doran and Thomas S. Freeman (eds.), *Tudors and Stuarts on Film: Historical Perspectives* (London: Palgrave, 2008), 30–45.

Froude, J. A. *The Reign of Henry VIII*. 3 vols. (London: J. M. Dent, 1908).

Frye, Susan. "The Myth of Elizabeth at Tilbury," *Sixteenth Century Journal* 23 (1992), 95–114.

Gasquet, F. A. *Henry VIII and the English Monasteries.* 2 vols. (London: John Hodges, 1889).

Greenblatt, Stephen. *Renaissance Self-Fashioning: From More to Shakespeare* (Chicago: University of Chicago Press, 1980).

Gregory, Philippa, *The Boleyn Inheritance* (London: HarperCollins, 2007).
The Other Boleyn Girl (London: HarperCollins, 2008). First published 2001.

Grose, Francis. *A treatise on ancient armour and weapons, illustrated by plates taken from the original armour in the Tower of London, and other arsenals* (London, 1786).

Grove, George. *Dictionary of Music and Musicians.* 4 vols. (London, 1879).

Gunn, S. J. "The Accession of Henry VIII," *Historical Research* 64 (1991), 279–88.
"The French Wars of Henry VIII," in J. Black (ed.), *The Origins of War in Early Modern Europe* (Edinburgh: John Donald Publishers Ltd, 1987), 28–47.

Guy, John. "Thomas Wolsey, Thomas Cromwell and the Reform of Henrician Government," in Diarmaid MacCulloch (ed.), *The Reign of Henry VIII: Politics, Policy and Piety* (New York: St. Martin's Press, 1995), 35–57.

Happé, Peter. "Dramatic Images of Kingship in Heywood and Bale," *Studies in English Literature* 39 (1999), 239–53.
"'Rejoice ye in us with joy most joyfully': John Heywood's Plays and the Court," *Cahiers Élisabéthaines* 72 (2007), 1–8.
"Sedition in *King Johan*: Bale's Development of a Vice," *Medieval English Theatre* 3 (1981), 3–6.

Happé, Peter and Wim Hüsken (eds.). *Interludes and Early Modern Society: Studies in Gender, Power and Theatricality* (Amsterdam: Rodopi, 2007).

Hayward, Maria. *Dress at the Court of Henry VIII* (Leeds: Maney Publishing, 2007).

Hearn, Karen (ed.). *Dynasties: Painting in Tudor and Jacobean England, 1530–1630,* exhibition catalogue (London: Tate Gallery, 1995).

Herman, Peter C. (ed). *Rethinking the Henrician Era: Essays on Early Tudor Texts and Contexts* (Urbana: University of Illinois Press, 1994).

Highley, Christopher. "'A Pestilent and Seditious Book': Nicholas Sander's *Schismatis Anglicani* and Catholic Histories of the Reformation," *Huntington Library Quarterly* 68 (2005), 151–71.

Hoak, D. E. "The Coronations of Edward VI, Mary I, and Elizabeth I, and the Transformation of the Tudor Monarchy," in C. S. Knighton and Richard Mortimer (eds.), *Westminster Abbey Reformed: 1540–1640* (Aldershot: Ashgate, 2003), 114–51.
Review of D. MacCulloch (ed.), *The Reign of Henry VIII: Politics, Policy and Piety* (New York: St. Martin's Press, 1995), in *Albion,* 28 (1996), 686–7.
"The Secret History of the Tudor Court: The King's Coffers and the King's Purse, 1542–1553," *Journal of British Studies* 26 (1987), 208–31.

Ives, E. W. *Faction in Tudor England,* 2nd edn. (London: Historical Association, 1986).
"The Fall of Anne Boleyn Reconsidered," *English Historical Review,* 107 (1992), 651–64.
Henry VIII (Oxford: Oxford University Press, 2007).
"Henry VIII: The Political Perspective," in Diarmaid MacCulloch (ed.), *The Reign of Henry VIII: Politics, Policy and Piety* (New York: St. Martin's Press, 1995), 13–34.

"Henry VIII's Will – A Forensic Conundrum," *Historical Journal* 35 (1992), 779–804.

"Stress, Faction and Ideology in Early-Tudor England," *Historical Journal* 34 (1991), 193–202.

King, John N. "Henry VIII as David: The King's Image and Reformation Politics," in Peter C. Herman (ed.), *Rethinking the Henrician Era: Essays on Early Tudor Texts and Contexts* (Urbana: University of Illinois Press, 1993), 78–97.

Tudor Royal Iconography: Literature and Art in an Age of Religious Crisis (Princeton: Princeton University Press, 1989).

Koebner, Richard. "'The Imperial Crown of this Realm': Henry VIII, Constantine the Great, and Polydore Vergil," *Bulletin of the Institute of Historical Research* 26 (1953), 29–52.

Latré, Guido. "The 1535 Coverdale Bible and Its Antwerp Origins," in Orlaith O'Sullivan and Ellen N. Herron (eds.), *The Bible as Book: The Reformation* (London: The British Library and Oak Knoll Press, 2000), 89–102.

Lerer, Seth. *Courtly Letters in the Age of Henry VIII: Literary Culture and the Arts of Deceit* (Cambridge: Cambridge University Press, 1997).

Levy, F. J. *Tudor Historical Thought* (San Marino: Huntington Library, 1967).

Llewellyn, Nigel. "The Royal Body: Monuments to the Dead, for the Living," in Lucy Gent and Nigel Llewellyn (eds.), *Renaissance Bodies: The Human Figure in English Culture, c. 1540–1660* (London: Reaktion Books, 1990), 218–82.

Lloyd, Christopher, and Simon Thurley (eds.). *Henry VIII: Images of a Tudor King* (Oxford: Phaidon Press, 1990).

Loach, Jennifer. "The Function of Ceremonial in the Reign of Henry VIII," *Past and Present* 142 (1994), 43–68.

Loades, David. *Henry VIII: Court, Church and Conflict* (London: The National Archives, 2007).

Lukacs, Georg. *The Historical Novel,* trans. Hannah Mitchell and Stanley Mitchell (Lincoln: University of Nebraska Press, 1983).

Lüttenberg, T., "The Cod-piece – A Renaissance Fashion between Sign and Artefact," *The Medieval History Journal* 8:1 (2005), 49–81.

MacCulloch, Diarmaid. "Henry VIII and the Reform of the Church," in MacCulloch (ed.), *Reign of Henry VIII: Politics, Policy and Piety* (New York: St. Martin's Press, 1995), 159–80.

Thomas Cranmer: A Life (New Haven and London: Yale University Press, 1996).

MacCulloch, Diarmaid (ed.). *The Reign of Henry VIII: Politics, Policy and Piety* (New York: St. Martin's Press, 1995).

Marshall, Peter. "Is the Pope Catholic? Henry VIII and the Semantics of Schism," in Ethan Shagan (ed.), *Catholics and the "Protestant Nation": Religious Politics and Identity in Early Modern England* (Manchester: Manchester University Press, 2005), 22–48.

Religious Identities in Henry VIII's England (Aldershot: Ashgate, 2006).

McDiarmid, John F. (ed.). *The Monarchical Republic of Early Modern England: Essays in Response to Patrick Collinson* (Aldershot: Ashgate, 2007).

McKeon, Michael. *The Origins of the English Novel, 1600–1740* (Baltimore: Johns Hopkins University Press, 1987).

Millar, Oliver. *The Tudor, Stuart and Early Georgian Pictures in the Collection of Her Majesty the Queen* (London: Phaidon, 1963).

Neal, Derek. "Masculine Identity in Late Medieval English Society and Culture," in Nancy F. Partner (ed.), *Writing Medieval History* (London: Hodder Arnold, 2005), 171–88.

North, John. *The Ambassador's Secret: Holbein and the World of the Renaissance* (London and New York: Hambledon and London, 2002).

Oman, C. W. C. "The Personality of Henry VIII," *Quarterly Review* 269 (July, 1937), 88–104.

Passmann, Dirk F., and Heinz J. Vienken. "That 'Hellish Dog of a King': Jonathan Swift and Henry VIII," in Uwe Baumann (ed.), *Henry VIII in History, Historiography, and Literature* (New York: Peter Lang, 1992), 241–79.

Patterson, Annabel. "'All Is True': Negotiating the Past in Henry VIII," in R. B. Parker and S. P. Zitner (eds.), *Elizabethan Theater: Essays in Honor of S. Schoenbaum* (Newark: University of Delaware Press, 1996), 147–66.

Paulson, Ronald. *Emblem and Expression: Meaning in English Art of the Eighteenth Century* (London: Thames and Hudson; Cambridge, MA: Harvard University Press, 1975).

  Hogarth: The Making of the Modern Moral Subject (New Brunswick, NJ: Rutgers University Press, 1991).

  Hogarth's Graphic Works (New Haven: Yale University Press, 1965, 1979; London: The Print Room, 1989).

Persels, J. C. "Bragueta Humanistica, or Humanism's Codpiece," *Sixteenth Century Journal* 28 (1997), 79–99.

Pollard, A. F. *Henry VIII* (London: Longmans, [1902] 1905).

  Wolsey (London: Longmans, 1929).

Prescott, Anne Lake. "Evil Tongues at the Court of Saul: The Renaissance David as a Slandered Courtier," *Journal of Medieval and Renaissance Studies* 21 (1991), 163–86.

Rackin, Phyllis. *Stages of History: Shakespeare's English Chronicles* (Ithaca: Cornell University Press, 1990).

Rankin, Mark. "Imagining Henry VIII: Cultural Memory and the Tudor King, 1535–1625," unpublished Ph.D. dissertation (The Ohio State University, 2007).

Rex, Richard. "The Crisis of Obedience: God's Word and Henry's Reformation," *Historical Journal* 39 (1996), 863–94.

Richardson, Glenn. "Eternal Peace, Occasional War: Anglo-French Relations under Henry VIII," in Doran and Richardson (eds.), *Tudor England and Its Neighbors* (Basingstoke: Palgrave Macmillan, 2005), 44–69.

  Renaissance Monarchy: The Reigns of Henry VIII, Francis I, and Charles V (London: Arnold, 2002).

Richardson, Thom. *The Armour and Arms of Henry VIII* (Leeds: Royal Armouries, 2002).

Rowlands, John. *The Paintings of Hans Holbein the Younger* (Boston: David R. Godine, 1985).

Ryrie, Alec. "Divine Kingship and Royal Theology in Henry VIII's Reformation," *Reformation* 7 (2002), 49–77.

The Gospel and Henry VIII: Evangelicals in the Early English Reformation (Cambridge: Cambridge University Press, 2003).

Sadie, Stanley (ed.). *The New Grove Dictionary of Music and Musicians*, 2nd edn. 20 vols. (London: Macmillan, 2001).

Salter, F. M. "Skelton's Speculum Principis," *Speculum* 9 (1934), 25–37.

Samman, Neil. "The Progresses of Henry VIII, 1509–1529," in Diarmaid MacCulloch (ed.), *The Reign of Henry VIII: Politics, Policy and Piety* (New York: St. Martin's Press, 1995), 59–73.

Scarisbrick, J. J. *Henry VIII* (London: Methuen, 1968).

Shagan, Ethan. *Popular Politics and the English Reformation* (Cambridge: Cambridge University Press, 2002).

Sillars, Stuart. *Painting Shakespeare: The Artist as Critic, 1720–1820* (Cambridge: Cambridge University Press, 2006).

Simpson, Claude M. *The British Broadside Ballad and Its Music* (New Brunswick, NJ: Rutgers University Press, 1966).

Smith, L. B. "The 'taste for Tudors' since 1940," *Studies in the Renaissance* 7 (1960), 167–83.

Starkey, David. "From Feud to Faction," *History Today* 32 (November 1982), 16–22.

Henry: Virtuous Prince (London: Harper Press, 2008).

"*The Legacy of Henry VIII*," in David Starkey (ed.), *Henry VIII: A European Court in England* (London: Collins & Brown, 1991), 8–13.

The Reign of Henry VIII: Personalities and Politics (London: George Philip, 1985).

Six Wives: The Queens of Henry VIII (London: Chatto and Windus, 2003).

Starkey, David (ed.). *Henry VIII: A European Court in England* (London: Collins & Brown in association with the National Maritime Museum, Greenwich, 1991).

Stemmler, Theo. "The Songs and Love-Letters of Henry VIII: On the Flexibility of Literary Genres," in Uwe Baumann (ed.), *Henry VIII in History, Historiography, and Literature* (New York: Peter Lang, 1992), 97–111.

Stevens, John. *Music and Poetry of the Early Tudor Court* (Cambridge: Cambridge University Press, 1961).

String, Tatiana C. *Art and Communication in the Reign of Henry VIII* (Aldershot: Ashgate, 2008).

"Henry VIII's Illuminated 'Great Bible'," *Journal of the Warburg and Courtauld Institutes* 59 (1996), 315–24.

Strong, Roy. *Coronation: A History of Kingship and the British Monarchy* (London: HarperCollins, 2005).

Holbein and Henry VIII (London: Routledge & Kegan Paul, 1967).

Tudor and Jacobean Portraits. 2 vols. (London: Her Majesty's Stationery Office, 1969).

The Tudor and Stuart Monarchy: Pageantry, Painting, Iconography, vol. I, *Tudor* (Woodbridge: The Boydell Press, 1995).

Thurley, Simon. "The Early Stuarts and Hampton Court," *History Today* 53:11 (November 2003), 15–20.

Hampton Court: A Social and Architectural History (New Haven: Yale University Press, 2003).

"Henry VIII: The Tudor Dynasty and the Church," in Lloyd and Thurley (eds.), *Henry VIII: Images of a Tudor King* (Oxford: Phaidon Press, 1990), 9–40.

Whitehall Palace: An Architectural History of the Royal Apartments, 1240–1698 (New Haven and London: Yale University Press, 1999).

Trapp, J. B. and Hubertus S. Herbrüggen. *"The King's Good Servant": Sir Thomas More, 1477/8–1535* (London: National Portrait Gallery, 1977).

Tudor-Craig, Pamela. "Henry VIII and King David," in Daniel Williams (ed.), *Early Tudor England: Proceedings of the 1987 Harlaxton Symposium* (Woodbridge: Boydell Press, 1989), 183–205.

Vicary, G. Q. "Visual Art as Social Data: The Renaissance Codpiece," *Cultural Anthropology* 4:1 (1989), 3–25.

Walker, Greg. *Persuasive Fictions: Faction, Faith, and Political Culture in the Reign of Henry VIII* (Aldershot: Scolar Press, 1996).

Plays of Persuasion: Drama and Politics at the Court of Henry VIII (Cambridge: Cambridge University Press, 1991).

"Rethinking the Fall of Anne Boleyn," *Historical Journal* 45 (2002), 1–29.

Writing under Tyranny: English Literature and the Henrician Reformation (Oxford: Oxford University Press, 2005).

Warner, J. Christopher. *Henry VIII's Divorce: Literature and the Politics of the Printing Press* (Cambridge: D. S. Brewer, 1998).

Warnicke, Retha. "Anne Boleyn Revisited," *Historical Journal* 34 (1991), 953–4.

"The Fall of Anne Boleyn Revisited," *English Historical Review* 108 (1993), 653–65.

Watts, Karen. "Henry VIII and the Founding of the Greenwich Armouries," in David Starkey (ed.), *Henry VIII: A European Court in England* (London: Collins & Brown, 1991), 42–6.

White, Hayden. *The Content of the Form: Narrative Discourse and Historical Representation* (Baltimore: Johns Hopkins University Press, 1987).

Whitehead, S. M. *Men and Masculinities* (Cambridge: Cambridge University Press, 2002).

Woolf, D. R. *Reading History in Early Modern England* (Cambridge: Cambridge University Press, 2000).

Index